The Evolution of the International Monetary System

The Evolution of the International Monetary System:

How Can Efficiency and Stability Be Attained?

Proceedings of the Fourth International Conference Sponsored by the Institute for Monetary and Economic Studies of the Bank of Japan

edited by **Yoshio Suzuki, Junichi Miyake,** *and* **Mitsuaki Okabe**

UNIVERSITY OF TOKYO PRESS

© University of Tokyo Press, 1990

All rights reserved. No part of this book may be reproduced in any form by any electronic or mechanical means (including photocopying, recording, or information storage and retrieval) without permission in writing from the publisher.

Printed in Japan

ISBN 4-13-047046-9
ISBN 0-86008-457-4

Contents

Editors' Introduction vii
Opening Remarks
    Satoshi Sumita, Governor, Bank of Japan xiii

Summaries of the Conference
1. The Evolution of the International Monetary System: Summing Up
    Andrew D. Crockett 3
2. The Evolution of the International Monetary System: Where Next?
    Ralph Bryant 15

Keynote Speeches
3. Efficiency and Stability in World Finance
    Allan H. Meltzer 41
4. Factor Mobility and the International Monetary System
    Stanley Fischer 59

Lessons from the History of the International Monetary System
5. International Monetary Instability Between the Wars: Structural Flaws or Misguided Policies?
    Barry Eichengreen 71
6. Evaluation of the Bretton-Woods Regime and the Floating Exchange Rate System
    Yoichi Shinkai 117
Comments
    Teh Kok Peng 151
    Jan Michielsen 157
    William E. Norton 163
    Richard Marston 169

Theoretical and Empirical Issues Concerning International Currencies and the International Monetary System

7. The International Use of Currencies
   Stanley W. Black 175
8. Financial Integration and International Monetary Arrangements
   Alexander K. Swoboda 195
   Comments
   Michael Prell 223
   Masahiro Kawai.................................... 229
   John Murray 235

Towards a Better International Monetary System

9. The EMS Experience
   Francesco Giavazzi 249
10. What Future for the International Monetary System?
    Richard N. Cooper 277
    Comments
    Philippe Lagayette 301
    Leonhard Gleske 305
    Koichi Hamada 311
    Jacob A. Frenkel.................................. 315

Program of the Conference 321
Participants 325
Index 331

Editors' Introduction

This book is a record of the proceedings of the Fourth International Conference sponsored and organized by the Institute for Monetary and Economic Studies of the Bank of Japan and held in Tokyo on May 30–June 1, 1989. The topic was "The Evolution of the International Monetary System: How Can Efficiency and Stability Be Attained?"

The aim of the conference, as the opening address makes clear, was to discover the future courses of international currencies and to explore the possibility of a better international monetary system against the background of significant economic and technological changes. One such change is the globalization or worldwide integration of financial markets, which has resulted in the increased substitutability of some national currencies in international financial transactions, and another is the metamorphosis of the United States into a debtor nation, thus occasioning growing concern over the stability of U.S. dollar exchange rates. To arrive at a better understanding of the wide range of issues involved in the international monetary system, the conference sought to make its investigations as comprehensive as possible by focusing on historical, theoretical, and institutional aspects.

The conference consisted of five sessions. The first commenced with opening remarks by Governor Satoshi Sumita of the Bank of Japan and was followed by two keynote speeches by Professor Allan H. Meltzer and Dr. Stanley Fischer, both Honorary Advisers of the Institute. The second session discussed "Lessons from the History of the International Monetary System," and the third dealt with "Theoretical and Empirical Issues Concerning International Currencies and the International Monetary System." Bringing together the preceding historical and theoretical arguments, the fourth session, "Toward a Better International Monetary System," focused on normative aspects and dealt with proposals for reform. The final session was devoted to

viii *INTRODUCTION*

summary presentations and general discussion of issues that had emerged as the most important in the preceding sessions.

In the first four sessions, the papers presented were all to the point and of high academic quality. The subsequent discussions, among senior staff members and specialists from central banks and international organizations and world-renowned scholars in international finance, were, in the organizers' view, also of a very high standard. All these discussions are well summarized in two papers by Dr. Andrew Crockett and Dr. Ralph Bryant, which are the lead papers of this volume. In many respects complementary, these papers provide a well-balanced overview of the entire conference, and thus we strongly recommend them. We would like to take the liberty here, though, of giving our view of the key conclusions reached by the conference.

I. The Experience Between the Two World Wars

(1) Three different exchange rate systems were observed during the interwar period: pure floating, fixed, and managed floating systems. Of these, the fixed exchange rate system (the gold exchange standard from 1927 to 1931) exhibited relative advantages in many respects over the other two, namely the achievement of relatively stable exchange rates and the subsequent reduction of uncertainty in the domestic economy. In contrast, the floating exchange rate systems proved superior in insulating domestic economies against disruptive factors from overseas.

(2) The collapse of the fixed exchange rate system was attributable to (a) the behavior of central banks that put the maintenance of stable domestic economies before stable exchange rates, (b) an insufficient display of leadership by the United States as the successor to Great Britain, (c) the failure of the international coordination of macroeconomic policies, and (d) the absence of a system providing a stable supply of international liquidity. An important lesson drawn from this experience was that for a fixed or stable exchange rate system to be viable, policy coordination among the leading nations is essential.

II. Assessment of the Two Systems in the Post-World War II Years: The Bretton Woods System and the Subsequent Floating Exchange Rate System

(1) The Bretton Woods system, a fixed exchange rate system with the U.S. dollar as the key currency, collapsed because (a) the growth

in cross-border capital flows made maintenance of fixed exchange rates increasingly difficult, and (b) the United States gradually abandoned its role as the key currency nation, which required the policy of pursuing stable prices domestically and responding passively to the international balance of payments.

(2) Participants gave a mixed assessment of the performance of the floating exchange rate system that followed. On the one hand, the float was criticized for generating large current account imbalances among major nations and for permitting disturbances to domestic economic structures, or hysteresis, arising from the misalignment of exchange rates. On the other hand, the system was credited with enabling the world economy to adjust to such shocks as the oil crises and with insulating domestic economies from overseas inflation. However, on one point, at least, the participants reached a broad consensus: exchange rate fluctuations themselves did contribute, in many respects, to the stabilizing of national economies, although the degree of exchange rate fluctuation remained a debatable issue.

(3) The "managed" float or system of international policy coordination that has been in place among major industrialized nations since the Plaza Agreement of September 1985 received a generally favorable assessment. Most participants attributed the recent stabilization of the world economy to this system, although some voiced criticism, saying that the system has degenerated into a means of covering up or justifying the behavior of the world's preeminent hegemonic nation, the United States.

III. *The Trend of International Currencies and the Role of the Yen*

(1) In every aspect of the international use of currencies, i.e., for the settlement of trade, capital transactions, and official reserve holdings, the role of the yen and the Deutsche mark has continually increased while that of the U.S. dollar has declined—a phenomenon symptomatic of the trend toward a world of multiple international currencies. However, since the law of inertia has been at work in the international use of currencies, the decline of the dollar has been a very slow process, despite the shift of the United States to debtor-nation status.

(2) If the Japanese authorities continue to maintain or improve the qualitative aspects required of any national currency which is to become an international currency, that is, the maintenance of stable domestic

prices, avoidance of exchange control, and improvement of the domestic short-term money market, the yen can be expected to play a greater role as an international currency. On the other hand, concerning the possibility of the yen leading the way toward the formation of an EMS-type currency bloc in Southeast Asia, the prevailing view among participants was skeptical, at least in regard to the near future, because economic and political integration in the region still remains far weaker than in the EC, although trade expansion within the region has been sizable in recent years.

IV. The Recent Trend toward the Multipolarization of the World's Financial Centers, and Its Implications

(1) Tokyo broadly satisfies the conditions required of an international financial center that include, among others, the existence of appropriate political, social, and economic infrastructure to secure free transactions and physical and human resources to support the banking industry. This has led to its growing importance in recent years in world finance; thus the current international financial scene is now characterized by a move toward a "multipolar world" with several major centers, especially London, New York, and Tokyo.

(2) Discussion of whether this trend toward a multipolar world would lead to the emergence of closed economic blocs aroused divided views, and the issue remained unreconciled.

V. Assessment of the Experience of the European Monetary System

(1) The EMS, which has been in existence for more than ten years since its inception, can be regarded as a *de facto* expanded Deutsche mark currency zone in that all other currencies have been pegged essentially to the mark while West Germany has conducted its own monetary policy independently. This situation has been viable because both West Germany and all other EMS nations have been able to take advantage of being members. (a) For all other member nations, it has facilitated the control of inflation by allowing them, in their domestic policies, to exploit the credibility of the West German Bundesbank, which enjoys a strong image as the guardian of stable prices. (b) For West Germany, it has stabilized the terms of trade, thus avoiding the loss of competitive edge over other EMS members and allowing its

trade to expand within the region, even when the Deutsche mark appreciated against the U.S. dollar.

(2) The success of the EMS in featuring more stable exchange rates and in imposing discipline on domestic policies of member nations stem largely from uniquely European circumstances. As such, it cannot necessarily serve as an effective model for monetary reform for the rest of the world or for the world as a whole.

VI. Prospects for an International Monetary System

(1) Given the increased worldwide integration of financial markets, the policies of individual nations now tend to have a greater influence on the world economy and finance than before. In this context, a consensus has emerged that any future international monetary system must be able to cope effectively with such an environment.

(2) Although various proposals for reform of the international monetary system have been put forward recently, none could command majority support in the conference. (a) Professor James Tobin's "Exchange Transaction Tax" scheme was met with skepticism by an overwhelming majority that especially questioned its implementability in an effective form. (b) The "Target Exchange Rate Zone" introduced by a group led by Dr. John Williamson received many negative reactions, including criticism about technical difficulties in, among other things, computing an "equilibrium exchange rate" in a world of high capital mobility. (c) The "Common World Currency" concept suggested by Professor Richard Cooper as an idealistic system for the 21st century drew many dubious comments, although it did have some supporters. The critics focused on, among other things, the absence of an effective adjustment mechanism in the event divergences in economic performance are seen among nations and also the lack of political incentives for the realization of the scheme.

(3) A consensus seemed to emerge that the question of an international monetary system is basically a policy issue inseparably linked to a broader spectrum of other issues, such as how to secure effective domestic policies and how to ensure a consistency of policies among the leading nations. This has led to a common awareness that, as a realistic scenario, the current tripolar financial center system should be the starting point and that the improvement of that system is important at present. To this end, it was widely agreed, on the one hand, that further effort is required for policy coordination among the regions represented by these three centers, especially with respect to

fiscal policies, and, on the other, that each nation must pursue policies to stabilize its own economy.

Finally, with respect to planning and organizing the conference, we would like to acknowledge the invaluable advice we received from many individuals, including Professor Allan H. Meltzer and Dr. Stanley Fischer, the present Honorary Advisers of the Institute, and also Professors James Tobin and Milton Friedman, former Honorary Advisers. Our thanks are also extended to all conference participants, who willingly shared their expertise through active discussion. We would also like to express our appreciation to the staff of the Bank of Japan, notably those in the Institute, for their devoted efforts to make the conference a success. Because of the extensive cooperation we received, the conference did succeed, we believe, in clarifying many issues concerning international currency and the international monetary system, and we hope the publication of this book will make the conference results a common asset for those interested in this important topic in today's world economy.

September 1989   YOSHIO SUZUKI
Tokyo   JUNICHI MIYAKE
                                                                         MITSUAKI OKABE

Opening Remarks

I would like to extend my hearty welcome to all of you to the Fourth International Conference sponsored by the Bank of Japan's Institute for Monetary and Economic Studies.

As you may already know, our Institute was established in 1982 to commemorate the centenary of the Bank of Japan. It aims to explore and propose theoretical and operational frameworks for efficient monetary policies through active interchange with academic and other research organizations both in Japan and abroad. As a means to achieve this objective, the Institute has organized international conferences on three occasions over the past seven years, each one meeting with great success.

Similarly, in attendance at this Fourth International Conference are many distinguished economists from academia, international organizations, and central banks throughout the world. We take it as a great honor not only for the Institute but for the Bank of Japan as well. And in this regard, we owe special thanks to the Honorary Advisors to the Institute, Professor Allan Meltzer and Dr. Stanley Fischer. We are very grateful for their valuable advice through the preparatory stage of this conference and for their kind acceptance of our request for keynote speeches despite their heavy workloads.

This conference has been convened today under the theme, "The Evolution of The International Monetary System: How Can Efficiency and Stability Be Attained?" It is a subject with wide international dimensions reflecting our keen awareness of the two major developments in the world economy today—the globalization of finance and the large trade imbalances among the leading nations.

First, as we witness the worldwide integration or globalization of finance, its future implications must be examined closely. In recent years, the technology for computerized data processing has experienced dramatic progress and increasing sophistication. This trend has stimulated various forms of financial innovations in the markets of many nations. At the same time, this development has accelerated the move toward an integrated world market, as is already demonstrated by the rapid growth in the flow of capital across national borders. The implications that this trend has for the international role of currencies and the future of the international monetary system require our urgent attention.

Second, large trade imbalances still persist among the advanced economies, and, as a result, the United States has become a debtor nation. We must carefully examine the impact that this trend has on the key role played by the U.S. dollar as an international currency and on the international monetary system as a whole. Contrary to initial expectations, the floating exchange rate system introduced in 1973 failed to prevent major imbalances in the current accounts of the leading industrial nations. This situation has led to the United States becoming the largest debtor nation in the world. Thus we hear warnings that confidence in the U.S. dollar as the most important international currency is being measurably eroded. In this context, search for an efficient and stable international monetary system is indispensable as a basic condition for sustained growth in the world economy. This is not a subject for purely intellectual curiosity. Rather, it is an issue for the entire world, with potentially serious practical consequences.

Here it should be emphasized that issues regarding the international monetary system are complexly intertwined with each national economy as well as with the world economy as a whole. Therefore, we can expect to correctly understand these issues and design viable policy alternatives only through multifaceted and comprehensive approaches.

As a first step in this direction, we must gain a clear understanding of the development of the international monetary system and draw as many lessons as possible from its history.

Let us take, for example, the years between the two world wars. During this period, the central currency of the international monetary system shifted from the British pound to the U.S. dollar. What were the factors behind this transformation? During the transition, the international monetary system experienced serious turbulence as a matter of course. What was the link between these disruptions and the disastrous depression in the world economy that led to the emergence of closed economic blocs during the 1930s? Before we can make a meaningful reexamination of the current international monetary system, we must first address ourselves to these questions.

We will also be able to draw useful lessons from experiences gained more recently. This means making an extensive study of the relative advantages and disadvantages of the IMF-Bretton Woods system utilized during the post-war period and of the floating exchange rate system that took over after the collapse of Bretton Woods in 1973. What were the factors that undermined the IMF-Bretton Woods regime, which operated on an adjustable peg centered around the U.S. dollar? Under the floating exchange rate system, the leading industrial nations have been suffering from aggravating imbalances in their current accounts. What are the causes of this problem? A serious review of this history will open a treasure trove of invaluable lessons for the future.

Second, as we consider what an ideal international currency should be and the requirements for a new international monetary system against the backdrop of the accelerating globalization of finance, our work must be based, above all, on solid economic theories and analyses. As is widely recognized, currencies serve as a unit of account, as a medium of exchange, and as a store of value. What, then, are the conditions necessary for a national currency to become an international currency, whereby it performs these three functions on an international scale? For example, of what importance is the stability of the currency's value, both internally and externally, or the degree of development of the nation's domestic financial markets, or the nation's share in world trade? And how will these characteristics be affected by the ongoing globalization of finance? In sum, what currencies will emerge as new international currencies? These questions have an important bearing on the future of the world economy.

The world today has three major centers for international financial transactions—New York, London, and Tokyo. What type of arrangement will be most efficient and stable under this multicentered system for international financial transactions? This, too, is an issue requiring our serious investigation. Should we maintain certain constraints over capital flows between these centers to protect the independence of each nation's financial policy? Or should we instead opt for coordination of each nation's macroeconomic policy, and allow cross-border capital flows without any restrictions? As a third alternative, should we leave all adjustment functions to exchange rate fluctuations, and forsake any controls? In this area, we again face many questions that are quite challenging from the viewpoint of economic theory.

Third, we wish to welcome active discussion on policy options regarding an optimal international monetary system, as well as on various alternatives for reform, based on the historical and theoretical approaches I have just mentioned. For example, how should we assess the advantages, disadvantages, and feasibility of such concrete proposals as the institution of a reference range and target zone, which are proposed as reforms of the floating exchange rate system? Or, what useful hints can we draw from the past experience of EMS, the quasi-fixed exchange rate system in Europe, and the EC's new movement toward currency unification?

The various questions I have enumerated are basic issues of international economics. Now I wish to offer you some of our own views.

First of all, our understanding is that free capital flows and market transactions are very natural as the globalization of world financial markets progresses. Therefore, we are doing our best to liberalize and internationalize the Tokyo market as its international importance steadily rises.

We feel it is important to remove obstacles, if any exist, to the international use of the yen. At the same time, however, we would like to leave the question of to what extent the yen is to be used as an international currency to the actual needs of the market.

Concerning foreign exchange rates, our own approach is a pragmatic one, through which we seek the stabilization of foreign exchange markets on the basis of policy coordination among the nations concerned, including cooperative market intervention.

These are some of our views. It is not easy, of course, to find a unified answer to any of these issues. I am fully aware that just as the economic structures of our nations differ, there is a broad spectrum of diverse views on these questions among the participants at this conference.

It is our sincere hope that this conference will become a forum for the free exchange of opinions on these issues. Bringing together experts in policy formulation and in academic research from around the world, this conference, I believe, will contribute to our mutual understanding and will promote closer collaboration in the years to come.

I wish to close my remarks by earnestly hoping that the three-day conference now beginning will lay a new milestone on the way toward a more effective international monetary system and a healthier world economy.

SATOSHI SUMITA
Governor, Bank of Japan

Summaries of the Conference

1

The Evolution of the International Monetary System: Summing Up

Andrew D. Crockett

I. Introduction

The evolution of the international monetary system is a favorite conference theme. A differentiating characteristic of this conference, apart from its unique combination of distinguished academics and central bankers from G-10 countries and East Asian nations, is the juxtaposition of the concepts of efficiency and stability in the title. I suspect that in choosing this title, the organizers of the conference were reflecting a concern that the objectives of efficiency and stability might sometimes come into conflict.

The background material circulated for the conference reveals dissatisfaction with the way the international monetary system has operated in the period since the collapse of the Bretton Woods system in 1973. It also points to sources of concern in more recent developments. Participants were invited to consider, in particular, the implications of large trade imbalances among the major industrialized economies and the emergence of the United States as a major international debtor. Not mentioned explicitly in the conference material, but also probably a source of concern, was the high degree of volatility, and the periodic misalignment, of exchange rates. In addition, our attention was drawn to the phenomenon of rapid technological change in the financial sector. Such change is leading to even greater capital mobility and the growing globalization of financial markets. These trends may enhance efficiency, but do they constitute a threat to systemic stability?

In assessing the implications of a changing world environment for the international monetary system, the conference was organized around three main themes, each covered in one of the sessions of the meeting. The first session took a historical perspective, asking what lessons could be drawn from relevant historical experience. The second session examined the forces affecting the development and evolution of international currencies and financial centers. And the third session turned its attention to the future and how the world monetary system might best evolve from now on. This summary is likewise organized in three main sections—though it has to be acknowledged that many strands of the discussion overlapped these broad topic headings.

II. Historical Perspective

In the papers and discussion devoted to the lessons of historical experience, two periods on which attention was focused were the interwar years, in which regimes of free floating, fixed exchange rates and managed floating followed one another in quick succession; and the postwar period, in which the Bretton Woods adjustable peg system gave way after 1973 to a flexible rate system that has since been operated with varying degrees of management and policy coordination.

Eichengreen's paper on the interwar experience throws light on two issues: *first*, the relative merits of fixed and flexible exchange rates; and *second*, within a system of flexible rates, the relative merits of free floating versus managed floating. Starting with the second, and narrower issue, managed floating appears at first sight to have some advantages over free floating; nominal and real exchange rate variabilities were less in the managed floating period of the early 1930s than under free floating in the early 1920s. Closer examination, however, shows these advantages to be more questionable. In terms of the *predictability* of changes in real exchange rates, which is perhaps more relevant for assessing the degree of uncertainty the exchange rate system introduces into the trading system, there is little to choose between the two regimes. Going beyond this evidence, the open discussion that followed Eichengreen's presentation suggested other possible drawbacks to managed floating; for example, if manipulation of rates leads to competitive international policies that spill over into trade restrictions, as happened in the 1930s, the case for active management of a flexible system would be even more open to question.

The other comparison highlighted in Eichengreen's paper was that between the fixed rate period of the late 1920s and the flexible exchange rate regimes that both preceded and succeeded it. The conclusions to be drawn from this comparison are not clear-cut. On the one hand, the operating characteristics of the fixed exchange rate regime, in terms of the stability and predictability of real and nominal exchange rates, were clearly superior to those of floating rates. On the other hand, as was recognized in the discussion, there are at least two reasons why operating characteristics may be an inadequate standard for judging the performance of an exchange rate regime. In the first place, they do not tell us whether a regime will be resilient in the face of external disturbances: we do not know whether the regime will be sustainable. In the second place, as Meltzer and others pointed out, they do not tell us whether or not the uncertainty that is suppressed in the exchange rate area will simply reappear elsewhere, with potentially more serious welfare implications.

In the case of the fixed exchange rate system of the 1920s, we do know that it collapsed after barely five years and that its collapse was associated with the onset of the Great Depression. As Fischer noted, however, this experience permits two very different conclusions. The first would be that the specific weaknesses that led to the breakdown of the fixed rate system need to be avoided, so that its superior operating characteristics can be enjoyed. The second is that an alternative regime has to be sought, that will be more resilient in the face of the disturbances it is bound to encounter.

There was little disagreement in the conference with Eichengreen's conclusion, that a lack of policy coordination among major countries was perhaps the most important single reason for the failure of the fixed rate system of the 1920s to withstand the shocks to which it was subjected. Michielsen suggested this was another way of saying the system suffered from lack of leadership, since cooperation will emerge only if one country will act in a leadership role. And Wijnholds noted that lack of policy cooperation is closely associated with another reason that is sometimes advanced for the collapse of the system in the 1930s, namely, the failure of the major countries to play by the gold exchange standard "rules of the game."

The experience of the postwar period provides another source of historical perspective on the operation of exchange rate regimes. The collapse of the Bretton Woods system shows clearly that in a world of free capital movements, the desire of countries to have independent monetary policies is incompatible with a fixed exchange rate system. Again the question arises: should the operation of a fixed rate system be strengthened, so as to enjoy its presumed advantages while dealing with this internal inconsistency; or should it be accepted that the subordination of domestic objectives required to make a fixed exchange rate system work satisfactorily is simply not compatible with the other pressures (political as well as economic) that governments face?

The conclusions that can be drawn from the post World War II experience are rather clear in this regard. Shinkai's paper concludes that no fixed exchange rate system could have been expected to survive the disturbances to which the world economy has been subject in the past 20 years or so. This conclusion was shared by other speakers. Moreover, it is not clear that we should even want to return to fixed rates. As Meltzer pointed out, performance under flexible rates has not been all that bad. True, there have been exchange rate swings, but as he said, it is not a legitimate criticism of a fluctuating rate system to say that rates fluctuate. The variability of output, consumption, and prices have actually been lower in several countries under a flexible exchange rate regime than under fixed exchange rates. Moreover—a point made by Fischer and others—there is no satisfactory analytical basis for choosing a specific pattern of exchange rate parities to which to return. All in all, most speakers seemed content to continue to live with the present managed floating regime among the major currencies.

Agreement that fixed rates are impractical in current circumstances leads naturally to a consideration of what other means are available to achieve better macroeconomic performance and more stable exchange rates. Shinkai's paper is rather skeptical about the scope for fruitful policy coordination (almost to the point, as Teh observed, of being cynical). A first reason for scepticism lies in the shortcomings of forecasting techniques as an adequate basis for judgmental coordination. The emphasis on the deficiencies of forecasts echoed those made by Meltzer and Fischer in their keynote addresses. Interestingly, this skepticism was not challenged by anyone in the subsequent discussion.

A second obstacle to effective coordination, according to Shinkai, lies in what might be called the "rogue elephant" theory of U.S. economic policy behavior (this is the summarist's term, not Shinkai's). If the United States is disposed to set its own political and economic priorities and then to demand acquiescence from its trading partners, cooperation will be a one-sided affair. Shinkai sees a pattern here, running from the unwillingness of the United States to devalue in 1971, to the insistence on a "Reaganomic" policy mix in the early 1980s, to a failure to play a proper role in the policy shifts agreed to be desirable in the Plaza and Louvre meetings.

The subsequent discussion revealed a certain amount of sympathy with Shinkai's scepticism. Marston underlined the conclusion of a study by Frankel and Rockett, which shows that coordinated policy making on the basis of a "wrong" model will normally reduce welfare; and Papadia suggested that coordination often involved quite high political costs for relatively small economic benefits. Nevertheless, most speakers (including Teh and Michielsen) seemed to feel that Shinkai had overstated his case. In the first place, as Cooper pointed out, the Frankel/Rockett result is not beyond challenge. The recent paper by Ghosh and Masson shows that if policy makers take proper account of model uncertainty, the scope for fruitful coordination is enhanced. A similar point was made by Teh, who noted that policy makers can learn from experience, thus improving the prospects of gains from coordination.

There was also disagreement with Shinkai's contention that U.S. obstinacy was an obstacle to policy coordination. Most U.S. policy makers believed (with good reason, as Dealtry confirmed) that the scope for dollar devaluation in 1971 was circumscribed by the way in which the IMF rules worked. And Prell said that Shinkai was incorrect to characterize the U.S. proposal for a commodity price indicator as simply a cynical attempt to make other countries adapt to the unwillingness of the United States to change its own fiscal policy.

Given these views, it is not surprising that several speakers offered a somewhat more sanguine view of the past achievements and future possibilities of policy cooperation. It was noted that recent years had produced a growing consensus concerning the way in which domestic policies affected exchange rates and the adjustment process; and that as a result there had been a tendency for fiscal divergence to be arrested, and even partially reversed. This had contributed to a more sustainable pattern of exchange rates and the beginnings of balance of payments adjustment. Moreover, Frenkel said that the joint response to the stock market crash of 1987 should be viewed as a success for cooperation.

All this is not to deny, of course, that the remaining imbalances in the world economy are large and troublesome. Moreover, if coordination is diverted from a concern with fundamentals to an exclusive preoccupation with exchange rates—which are largely a *symptom* of underlying disequilibria—tensions in the system could quickly come to the fore again. Still, provided these mistakes can be avoided, cooperation and a willingness to use economic indicators to signal the emergence of problems can play a constructive role.

III. *International Currencies and the International Monetary System*

The papers presented on international currencies (those by Stanley Black and Alexander Swoboda) were concerned with the dynamics by which currencies and financial centers evolve and acquire an international role. This is a subject of particular interest in the context of the conference, taking place as it did in Tokyo at a time when Japan's role in the world economy is both growing and changing. Does Japan's growing economic weight portend an equivalent role for the yen as an international currency and for Tokyo as an international financial center? And would such a development, in the direction of a more multi-polar system, be a source of stability or instability?

Black's paper starts with the straightforward, but nevertheless very important, proposition that the roles currencies play emerge in response to market forces. Money, as we know, serves the functions of means of payment, store of value, and unit of account. The more a currency is used in trade and financial transactions, the greater the demand to hold it as a vehicle currency is likely to be. And the more stable a currency is, the greater its attractiveness as a store of value and a predictable yardstick for borrowing and lending transactions.

These considerations make it easy to understand the growing international role of the yen, revealed clearly in the statistical tables in Black's paper. (Although, as Patrick and others pointed out, it may be that the bare statistics tend to overstate the yen's use in transactions that are truly international, as opposed to domestic transactions taking place "offshore.")

There was some doubt as to whether Black's analysis applied fully in the case of the yen. Suzuki and Prell questioned the importance of the vehicle function in explaining the increasing use of the yen. They said that one consequence of technological advances was to diminish the need for vehicle currencies by making direct transactions more practical and economical. Masunaga and Kawai also noted new financial techniques that undermined the significance of the specific currencies that were used in transactions. However, Suzuki and others agreed that currency areas were likely to emerge, and that the hard currency would predominate in each area. Following this line of reasoning, several speakers felt that the yen would be the key currency for Asia, although it was pointed out by several, including Kawai, that the structure of trade in Asia would prevent this happening in a straightforward manner.

Swoboda's paper, in parallel fashion, identified some of the preconditions for an international financial center. He noted in particular the need for a social, economic, and political system that provides the necessary stability and freedom for transactions to take place. Also important are the availability of human skills and a satisfactory legal framework. Less obviously, Swoboda cites the need for an international center to have domestic currency that is an international reserve asset, and the existence of a current account surplus. In this connection, it may be noted that there are good examples of financial centers having prominence at the same time their domestic currencies play a secondary international role—London and Zurich, for example.

Even if there can be quibbles about certain aspects of Black's and Swoboda's papers, there was little dissent from the proposition that the world was moving toward a more multi-currency, multi-polar world, in which the preeminence of the U.S. dollar and New York would continue to be eroded. Should this be viewed as a source of concern, from the standpoint of global economic stability? Black notes that the literature produces no clear conclusion on this issue, and he himself is too circumspect to take sides. Swoboda, by contrast, is rather clear that a multicurrency system creates the danger of currency blocs, which in turn will lead to protectionism and "dis-integration" of the world economy. This view foreshadowed the one that Cooper was to present in the subsequent session of the conference. Swoboda considers in his paper various ways in which a flexible exchange rate relationship among currency blocs might be managed, but finds them all wanting. His conclusion is that attention should therefore be focused on working toward a common currency arrangement of the kind suggested (though in a much longer time-frame) by Cooper.

Swoboda's analysis provoked considerable disagreement, both about the reasons for rejecting flexible arrangements, and about the presumed benefits of a common currency. Both Prell and Murray, as opening discussants, felt that justice had not been done to the significant successes of the present system. Although it was true that flaws remained and needed to be addressed, it could not, in their view, be concluded that the system was unsatisfactory by comparison with any realistic alternative or, for that matter, incapable of being strengthened. Suzuki also questioned the inevitability of the slide into protectionism foreseen by Swoboda.

If there was disagreement with Swoboda's characterization of the current system, there were also doubts about the practicability and desirability of the common currency approach. Robert Black suggested it was simply unrealistic politically to think on these lines for the foreseeable future. On economic grounds, Murray, echoing points made earlier by Fischer and Norton, put in a plea for retaining the exchange rate as an adjustment mechanism, at least for economies like Canada's. Murray noted that important structural differences among economies remained, and perfect economic integration was far from being achieved. Under these circumstances, economic disturbances would affect different economies in different ways, and exchange rate flexibility could provide a useful degree of freedom in dealing with them.

This position seemed to command a wide measure of support, though Frenkel cautioned that in a highly interdependent world one should not overestimate the room for maneuver that could be gained through exchange rate flexibility.

Since most speakers were more optimistic than Swoboda about the possibilities for making the present exchange rate regime work satisfactorily, it is not surprising that attention shifted to the mechanisms and content of policy coordination. Interestingly, no one spoke up (at least in the discussion on Swoboda's paper) for the Williamson/Miller target zone scheme, or for McKinnon's proposal for a joint monetary policy for the three major countries. Perhaps there was agreement with Swoboda that both proposals are too mechanistic to work satisfactorily, and also with the two keynote speakers that our knowledge of exchange rate determination is too sketchy to provide much confidence that officials can do any better than the market in identifying an appropriate and sustainable pattern of exchange rates and in specifying how to react to disturbances.

Such observations provoked an outbreak of "humbleness" among conference participants about the professional limitations of economists. (As someone noted, such lapses are a periodic conference phenomenon, but they do not usually endure for long, nor do they have any lasting adverse effect on economists' opinion of themselves.) On this occasion, humility did not preclude a willingness to consider strengthened coordination, and even the application of rules to the process. It was stressed, however, that rules need not be rigid. Meltzer set the tone here with his suggestion in his keynote address for contingent and adaptable rules governing monetary policy. Others would probably want to be less prescriptive than that, but could nevertheless favor some *ex ante* guidance in the coordination process. Frenkel pointed out that rules can be designed in such a way as to incorporate new information as it becomes available. And Lagayette argued that the contrast between rule-based and pragmatic (or discretionary) coordination was overplayed; the important thing was to preserve credibility in the consistency with which policy authorities responded to changing circumstances.

IV. Towards a Better International Monetary System

The last conference session, prior to the summing up, had the ambitious title "Towards a Better International Monetary System." It was based on papers by Cooper and Giavazzi. Giavazzi's paper on the European Monetary System could perhaps be considered historical in nature. However, it is very relevant in the context of a forward look at the future of the international monetary system. For it is in Europe that the most interesting recent developments in monetary arrangements have been occurring, and it is appropriate to focus attention there. Moreover, the prospective development of the EMS can be viewed as a common currency on a regional scale.

Giavazzi's analysis should serve to dampen the enthusiasm of those who see the recent history of the EMS (and the future mapped out in the Delors Report) as heralding a smooth and rapid acceptance of the common currency idea. This is not because the EMS has been unsuccessful. Indeed, there was agreement at the conference with the view, put most forcefully by Lagayette, that it has been remarkably successful. Still, it was accepted that merely fixing an exchange rate in the context of the EMS could not produce the advantages that many members of the exchange rate mechanism were now enjoying. Credibility had to be earned over time, Giavazzi pointed out. Current members of the ERM seemed to have served an apprenticeship, of varying length, before markets gave them full credit for their policy. Moreover, in some circumstances, belonging to the ERM could be destabilizing; Murray pointed to sterling's experience of shadowing the Deutsche mark in this connection.

In considering the wider lessons that EMS experience offered for the international monetary system, Giavazzi recommended caution. Both he and Gleske said that the performance of the EMS had to be seen against the background of the development of the European Community at large. There were political and institutional reasons for member countries' aversion to exchange rate volatility, which would not necessarily be replicated in other contexts. Moreover, in the early history of the Exchange Rate Mechanism, the Bundesbank had played (and was still playing) a unique role. The Deutsche mark offered a stability anchor that other countries, endeavoring to bring inflation under control, had found of considerable value.

There was broad agreement that the European experience was sufficiently unique that general lessons could not be drawn for the international monetary system at large. Furthermore, the EMS was now entering a testing time, with the removal of exchange controls, the completion of the single market, and the moves proposed in the Delors Report toward economic and monetary union. Gleske cautioned that many questions surrounded the issue of the structure of decision making in the proposed monetary union. So there was considerable agreement with Hamada's suggestion that the best lesson for the rest of the world to draw from Europe was "wait and see."

Cooper's paper was more explicitly forward-looking, reviewing as it did a number of proposals that are currently on the table for strengthening the functioning of the international monetary system. Discussion focused for the most part on the pros and cons of the common currency proposal—following on, therefore, from the observations that had been made earlier on Swoboda's paper. The other reform suggestions described by Cooper were touched on only superficially. The transaction tax idea, associated chiefly with the name of Tobin, got particularly short shrift, with critical comments (in ascending order of intensity) from Hamada, Frenkel, Meltzer, and Darby. The Williamson/Miller target zone proposal and the McKinnon coordinated monetary policy proposal received a somewhat more sympathetic airing than in the previous day's discussion on Swoboda's paper. Nevertheless, the fact that fallible economic models had to be used to both set and subsequently change exchange rates was widely regarded as a fatal drawback to both schemes. Hamada and others again noted that there was no satisfactory theoretical basis for establishing par values or exchange rate bands.

Given this view, it might seem strange that the common currency proposal, which involves permanent and rigid fixing of exchange rates, should attract so much attention. Part of the answer lies in Cooper deliberately labeling his proposal as one for the far distant future. This enabled the conference to deal with the question of its steady-state characteristics and to largely ignore the tricky question of "how do you get there from here?" It also allowed speakers to duck the difficult issue of the political accountability for a common monetary policy in a world of separate and sovereign political authorities.

Cooper put up a spirited defense for the proposition that adjustment would not necessarily be more difficult if governments formally abjured use of the exchange rate. He pointed out that structural differences *between* the three major blocs at the "core" of the international economy (the U.S., Japan, and Europe) were not significantly greater than the difference *within* the blocs. When, say, Texas was affected by shifts in the oil price, nobody considered changing the value of the Dallas dollar against the Boston dollar (although, being different Federal Reserve districts, they had, technically at least, different currencies and could, in principle, change their relative values).

Cooper also took issue with the point made by Fischer in his keynote address that exchange rate flexibility represented, in effect, a "degree of freedom" in the adjustment process that it would be undesirable to forgo. This was only true, he pointed out, if retention of exchange rate flexibility was costless. If the ability to move rates created uncertainties, it could impose costs that could hamper economic efficiency more generally. Cooper pointed to the effects of exchange rate volatility on the volume and allocational efficiency of investment, as well as to the possibility of encouraging protectionist pressures.

While Cooper won a measure of support from conference participants, the majority were unpersuaded that exchange rate fixing would be desirable, at least until economic integration had proceeded much further than at present. A number of speakers pointed out that factor mobility, which was one of the vehicles by which adjustment to real economic disturbances took place, was still much more limited between political entities than it was within them. And fiscal transfers, whether through tax progressivity and social security provisions or through explicit regional policy, could be used to ease the adjustment process domestically, but they were not available internationally. These considerations, coupled with the view that structural economic differences were probably still quite important among the three major regions in the world economy, led the majority of conference participants to regard a common currency as an idea to be considered only in a very long-term time frame. (This was, it should be said, the context in which Cooper had originally advanced the idea.)

2

The Evolution of the International Monetary System: Where Next?

Ralph C. Bryant

Even though the subject of the evolution of the international monetary system is an old chestnut, this Fourth International Conference sponsored by the Bank of Japan has been characterized by thoughtful and provocative discussion.[1] I cannot do justice to the variety of views that have been expressed. But my task has at least been made easier by Andrew Crockett's overview remarks. Because Crockett organizes his summary according to the chronological order of the conference sessions, I have been freed to follow a different approach.

I will begin by summarizing some salient features of the world economy and world polity as they exist today. I will then ask how comfortable or uncomfortable conference participants, and the policy community more generally, seem to be with this state of affairs. Then I will sketch a composite vision of how the world policy community might take incremental steps toward better performance of the world economy and an improved international monetary system. My aspiration is to identify something like a center of gravity for the variety of views expressed at the conference, although I will also liberally mix in some of my own personal views.[2]

---

[1] This overview of the papers and discussion in this volume was prepared while I was a Visiting Scholar at the Bank's Institute for Monetary and Economic Studies. I am grateful to Junichi Miyake, Mitsuaki Okabe, Akira Kuroda, Hideo Futamura, and all the other members of the Institute staff who helped to organize a stimulating and congenial conference and who extended their gracious hospitality to me during my visit.

[2] My assigned task was to summarize our current understanding of existing knowledge and issues. This task does *not* include saying something original; indeed, oriignality for its own sake would detract from my assignment. It is difficult enough to state sound conclusions! To be sound *and* original requires the assistance of angels—which, unfortunately, has been denied to me.

I. A Perspective on the World Economy and Polity Today

The Extent of Economic Integration

When the conference organizers identified issues for our discussion, they highlighted the increasing internationalization of world markets. Virtually everyone at the conference has alluded to these forces. But just how far have economic integration and cross-border economic interdependence actually progressed?

Participants spoke most often about integration among national *financial* markets, in effect about the cross-border mobility of financial capital. It is helpful here to use the analogy of national financial systems resembling "reservoirs."[3] When the current-period consumption of spending units falls short of their income, the resulting savings flow into the national reservoir. Businesses and other economic agents whose current-period spending exceeds their income draw funds out of the reservoir as they borrow to finance their excess spending. The existence of the reservoir permits the saving and investment decisions of individual agents to be taken independently. To a rough first approximation, one can think of the level of the fluid in each nation's reservoir as flat: whenever circumstances change, no matter where in the reservoir the funds are put in or dipped out, the fluid in the reservoir finds a single uniform level fairly rapidly.

Individual nations' reservoirs were relatively isolated at the beginning of the postwar period. But, progressively, most of the "separation fences" (various government regulations and controls) around each nation's reservoir have been dismantled. Even more important than the lowering of the separation fences, the various national reservoirs have been progressively better connected by enhanced communications technology, lowered transport costs, and greater international awareness of investment opportunities. As was keenly recognized by the participants at this conference, national financial markets in recent years have thus been joined together much more closely than in the 1950s and 1960s.

Nonetheless, nations' financial markets are not yet completely integrated. Nor are assets denominated in different currencies perfect substitutes. It has become analytically fashionable to assume that financial integration is complete; theoretical papers typically assume this complete integration as a matter of course.[4] But that assumption

---

[3] See, for example, the discussion in Bryant (1987a), chaps. 3–5.

[4] For example, see Swoboda's paper for this conference and the papers by Fukuda

is too polar. The actual situation in financial markets is best characterized as "intermediate interdependence." In particular, the conceptual paradigm of a unified world capital market, implying a nearly uniform level throughout a single world reservoir, is not appropriate for analyzing most aspects of international financial intermediation. To be sure, that paradigm is less misleading than the opposite extreme of completely segmented national markets. But both extreme analytical representations are too far from reality. If one thinks of a spectrum, running from completely separated national reservoirs at one end to a fully unified world reservoir at the other, my view is that the major nations and currencies are perhaps some three-fourths of the way—but probably not further than that—toward the single world reservoir.

Now consider the mobility across national borders of *physical* capital, of *labor*, and of other factors of production. Integration of the markets for these factors, too, is stronger now than several decades ago. Yet, as several contributors to the conference rightly emphasized, these other factors are much less mobile across borders than financial capital.[5]

The situation for *product* markets is similar to that for labor and physical capital. The world economy exhibits considerably more integration than several decades ago, but we are still quite far from completely integrated markets for goods and services.[6]

Most of the important problems discussed at the conference stem from—or are powerfully influenced by—the basic fact that the cross-border integration of goods markets, labor markets, and the markets for physical capital is very much less advanced than the cross-border integration of financial markets.

In particular, I want to emphasize an important implication for government policies: national macroeconomic policy actions in today's highly but not completely integrated world economy have relatively weaker effects at home and relatively stronger effects abroad than those experienced in past decades. Yet a significant degree of autonomy

---

and Hamada, by Niehans, and by Sachs presented at the Bank of Japan's Third International Conference two years ago (Suzuki and Okabe, 1987).

[5] At the Third International Conference two years ago, participants engaged in considerable discussion about the distinction between mobility of *financial* capital and the much smaller degree of mobility of *physical* capital, a distinction emphasized in Niehans' paper for the conference (Suzuki and Okabe, 1987, chap. 8).

[6] Stanley Fischer's keynote paper for the conference contains a thoughtful summary of the varying degrees of integration now existing in the markets for goods, financial capital, and factors such as physical capital and labor—what I have termed "intermediate" and "imperfect" integration—and some of the issues thereby raised for the conference.

still remains for national policies. Therefore, the effects of a government's policy actions still have differentially more powerful effects within the economy where they originate. Unlike in a perfectly integrated world economy, one nation's policy actions are not immediately and fully diffused throughout the world. The point also applies to nonpolicy shocks originating in any part of the world; it typically takes time for the effects of the shock to diffuse, and the effects abroad are seldom if ever as large as those in the country where it originates.

Richard Cooper referred in his spoken remarks to adjustment between the Hamburg and Stuttgart regions within Germany, and to the issue of why within the United States adjustment is not facilitated by separate regional currencies (a "Dallas dollar" and a "Boston dollar"). Cooper is right in calling our attention to issues of intra-regional adjustment and in asking us to apply the same analytical principles to them that we apply to international adjustment. And in a hypothetical world in which each different region within a nation had its own currency, adjustment between regions would be easier. But my own view, somewhat in contradiction to Cooper's, is that at present the adjustment within regions of a country—for example, between Hamburg and Stuttgart, and between Dallas and Boston—is considerably more effective than that between nations. Of course adjustment problems between regions of the same country are sometimes difficult. But Cooper overstates his case by asserting that (apart from policy disturbances) there is virtually as much adjustment across national borders as there is between regions within a nation.[7]

Moreover, the political processes for dealing with intra-regional adjustment are altogether different from those that can be brought to bear on adjustment between nations. Within a nation, there typically exists a national (supra-regional) political authority with significant powers to force compromises on a nationwide scale. For example, even within the federal structure of the United States, the federal government's authority is dominant for many issues of interstate adjustment. No comparable political processes and institutions exist for dealing with adjustment between nations. This political point seems decisive to me.

The Political Structure of the World

The preceding observation brings me naturally to another basic fact

---

[7] Several participants at the conference, including Professors Hamada and Black, commented in a similar vein on this point.

about today's world: the processes of *political* integration have lagged far behind increasing economic interdependence. If anything, the world in recent decades has been characterized by more, not less, political pluralism. There has been in the world as a whole an increase in the number of governmental decision-making units and a greater diffusion of power among them. Hence the familiar, key dilemma: the world has been experiencing a growing "mismatch" between its economic and political structures. The effective domains of economic markets coincide less and less well with national governmental jurisdictions.

Though lagging far behind the world economy, the world polity has not been static. Perhaps the most striking changes are the large strides toward political integration within Europe, emphasized in the paper by Francesco Giavazzi and discussed in the fourth session of the conference. Even in Europe, the political evolution has not kept pace with economic integration. But the development of EEC-wide political institutions and a "European civil-service bureaucracy" in Brussels are nonetheless notable developments.

Measurements of political and economic phenomena can be made in a variety of units. For example, there is the definition, inspired by Homer's epics of the Greeks' war against Troy, of a "millihelen." A millihelen is the amount of female beauty required to launch a single ship. I once proposed the "Gaullicycle" as an analogous measure of political integration in Europe. A Gaullicycle is the amount of evolution in European-wide political institutions required to make Charles DeGaulle turn one full revolution in his grave.

There can be little doubt that there have been many Gaullicycles of political progress in Europe in the past two decades. President DeGaulle was already rolling in his grave at the initiation of the EMS in 1979. Just imagine the response if DeGaulle were to be briefed on the conclusions of the April 1989 report of the Delors Committee on European monetary unification and asked about the appropriateness of studying a European central bank! And consider his likely reactions if he could have heard the comments made at this conference by Philippe Lagayette of the Banque de France, Leonhard Gleske of the Deutsche Bundesbank, J.A.H. de Beaufort Wijnholds of De Nederlandsche Bank, and Jan Michielson of the Banque Nationale de Belgique!

It is also germane here to recall the many changes taking place within the Soviet Union, Eastern Europe, and mainland China. If perestroika and domestic economic reforms should continue in socialist countries, economic and political integration *within* the Eastern bloc would presumably increase further. (There, too, for the foreseeable future the political reforms would probably lag well behind the economic changes.) Moreover, if economic interdependence among the socialist countries should increase, then it is a plausible conjecture that integration *between the East and the West* would also gradually become greater (though, again, with political evolution lagging the economic changes).

Distribution of Political Power in Today's World

How is political power distributed in today's world? Within the Western bloc, is the United States still a hegemon? Can the United States largely "call the plays" in international discussions and do pretty much what it pleases at home without the constraints of international forces?

Professor Shinkai's paper for the conference can be read as answering this question in the affirmative. He asks whether the United States has been a "benevolent despot," and he then diplomatically observes that benevolence has been more conspicuous by its absence than presence, at least in the area of macroeconomic policies. But Professor Shinkai does appear to regard the United States as still a despot or a hegemon.

Professor Shinkai is right, it seems to me, in having doubts about the benevolence of the United States. U.S. policies have been neither as sensible in terms of basic U.S. interests nor as internationally responsible as they could, and ought, to have been. But I believe that Professor Shinkai is wrong about the despotism. The weight of the United States in political decisions among the Western countries is of course still the largest for any individual nation—in military matters, but even in political and economic ones. Yet I believe that the political situation in the large bloc of capitalist nations is no longer well described by the term hegemony. Most fundamentally, we have a political situation in which one or a few nations no longer effectively dominate international decision making.

Most conference participants seemed to share the view that the political structure of the world has become progressively more *multipolar* and *pluralistic*. For example, if I understood him correctly, this is the view taken by Governor Sumita in his opening speech. It is the view taken by Yoshio Suzuki in recent speeches and in his recent book. Suzuki labels the international monetary arrangements we have today as, de facto, a "trilateral currency system" with some coordination of national economic policies and some cooperative intervention to

[8] The three "currencies" may be thought of as a North American dollar area;

stabilize exchange rates.[8] Swoboda in his conference paper explicitly labels the world today as multi-polar. A large majority of academics in the fields of international relations and politics, I believe, share this judgment about the waning of hegemony.

If we acknowledge recent trends exhibited by the socialist countries and extrapolate those trends into the future, it becomes still clearer that the political world is multi-polar, and if anything likely to become still more so.

Intergovernmental Cooperation in a Multi-polar World

With a multi-polar world politically and the process of international economic integration racing ahead of the evolution of international political institutions, cooperation between nations unfortunately tends to get even more difficult than it used to be. Cooperating "after hegemony" introduces some new problems and exacerbates others.[9]

For better or for worse, a hegemon no longer designs the main features of international arrangements in the old dominant way. More nations typically have to be involved in any given cooperative effort. Yet decision making in large groups is considerably more difficult than in small groups, for well-known reasons.

The greater diffusion of political and economic power creates stronger incentives for each individual nation to ignore the consequences of its own actions for other nations. You know the argument well: each nation sees itself as "small and open"; it regards itself as buffeted by the rest of the world, but too insignificant in the world as a whole to worry about the effects of its actions on others.

On this very point, I was amused during the second session of the conference at how the four discussants of the Eichengreen and Shinkai papers began their remarks. Teh Kok Peng observed that Singapore was a "small country" and the issues of policy coordination and the evolution of the international monetary system were not urgent for Singapore. Jan Michielson began by emphasizing that Belgium was small, and that his country was a "policy taker," not a "policy maker." Then William Norton opened his remarks by saying that Australia was a small country exporting primary commodities. I was holding my breath when Richard Marston from the United States started to speak!

Indeed, I am sorry to report that I have heard even some Americans

---

a "European/ECU" area with Germany as the center nation; and a "yen area" with Japan at the center. See Suzuki (1989).

[9] See, for example, the discussion in Keohane (1984).

resort to this line of reasoning. In effect, they have argued that "the United States is no longer a dominant force in the world economy. And in any case, we don't know much about how one economy influences other economies. Therefore the appropriate stance for the United States is merely to get its own policies set appropriately; it should not pay so much attention to the international consequences of U.S. policies."

Note also that Alexander Swoboda's paper for the conference is written largely from the theoretical perspective of a small open economy—too much so for my taste.

I ask a bit plaintively: is there *any* country left that is "large"? And in a multi-polar world, where almost every nation perceives itself as "small," may it not be possible for each country inadvertently to become something of a "free rider" in the world economy? A possible outcome in this type of multi-polar world is that international collective goods and the overall global climate of policies can suffer even more than they otherwise might have under hegemony. At any rate, there is an uncomfortably high probability that nations may not act collectively to foster their mutual interests.

In principle, of course, the way to counteract this inherent bias against cooperative responses to global problems is for individual national governments to recognize the systemic interdependence of their actions and to nurture international processes and institutions that catalyze the requisite cooperation.

The International Monetary System

The international monetary system we have today is, in essence, a reflection of the basic features of the world economy and polity I have just summarized. I also believe that the breakdown of the Bretton Woods system at the beginning of the 1970s can be traced fundamentally to the gradual evolution of these economic and political trends during the postwar period.

The conference papers by Fischer, Shinkai, Swoboda, and Cooper—as well as many comments made at the conference itself—describe various features of the current system. I will therefore not repeat those descriptions and not say anything more to characterize the existing international monetary system, but instead turn directly to a discussion of the future.

II. Should We Just "Live With" the Current Arrangements?

How comfortable are the governments of major nations with the set of international monetary arrangements that we now have? Is it feasible or desirable, or both, just to "live with" the current arrangements for the indefinite future?

Some participants in the conference did seem to be content—or at least not too unhappy—and would advise governments to accept existing arrangements more or less as they are. For example, Professor Shinkai, in the conclusion to his paper, asserted that we effectively have no other choice (even though we might be discontented here or there with some detail of present arrangements). Yoshio Suzuki, Michael Prell, and Michael Dealtry spoke in support of current arrangements. Stanley Fischer appeared to take this view, too, even while expressing some sympathetic yearning for a better set of arrangements. Koichi Hamada, reminding the conference of the Tokugawa Ieyasu's "wait and see" motto, suggested that nations outside Europe might patiently observe the evolution of the European Monetary System before trying to reach conclusions about reform of the wider world monetary system.

A great many other participants in the conference, however, seemed to harbor reservations. They expressed some serious discomfort with the present international monetary regime.

In keeping with my application of alternative measuring units, I propose a new "Fukai Index." Japanese weather stations broadcast a "fukaishisu" as a sort of weather misery index, somewhat analogous to Arthur Okun's misery index combining the current values of the unemployment rate and inflation rate. My Fukai index is a measure of dissatisfaction with current international monetary arrangements. Its base is an index of 1978 = 100, the average dissatisfaction in the official policy community with the arrangements in existence in 1978 at the time of adoption of the Second Amendment to the IMF Articles of Agreement. The typical value of this index for academic economists ranges between 150 and 500. In the official community, the Fukai index has fallen as low as a value of 13 in the early 1980s in the U.S. Treasury under Donald Regan and Beryl Sprinkel. I judge the value of the Fukai index at this conference, where central bankers have a sizable weight, as around 130—significantly higher than in the late 1970s, but not yet at distress levels.

In passing, I want to stress an important analytical point. When we register our discomfort with international monetary arrangements on the Fukai index, we need to be self-conscious about how much of our discomfort stems from international monetary arrangements *in themselves*. In other words, do we believe that these arrangements have *independent* adverse causal influences that are separable from the other basic policy and nonpolicy forces that shape macroeconomic outcomes? My own view, which is also the view taken by a majority of the participants at the Third Bank of Japan International Conference, held in 1987, is that international monetary arrangements are a significant—but nonetheless only secondary—influence on world macroeconomic performance. If this judgment is right, we should not allow ourselves to get too excited, *one way or the other*, about the international monetary system. The even more fundamental issues have to do with the politics and economics of how governments choose domestic policies and with the efficiency and stability of the behavior of private economic agents.

If my reading of the average Fukai index for this conference is correct, a majority of the participants have doubts not only about the desirability of current international monetary arrangements, but also about their *sustainability*. Most of us, to be sure, doubt that much can change in the immediate future. But over the medium and long runs, pressures may well build that will push things in one direction or another from the existing status quo. I tend to share this view about sustainability.

To overdramatize a bit, let me suggest *either* that governments will find a way to go forward with one form or another of "enhanced multilateral cooperation," *or*, alternatively, that governments may find themselves retreating toward "dis-integration" of the world economy. In principle, such dis-integration could occur in a deliberate and controlled way. But things could go badly, in which case the dis-integration could be disruptive and noncooperative.

I will not elaborate here on this broad choice of slipping backward or trying to step forward. Let me just assert my own view.[10] Disorderly dis-integration, with high levels of conflict among nations and the reimposition of all sort of controls and restrictions at borders, would be terrible. Efforts to attain "cooperative dis-integration" have some attractions in principle, but I surmise they would prove infeasible or excessively costly in practice.

Note, by the way, that the essence of proposals like Tobin's transac-

---

[10] My views are given in more detail in Bryant (1987a, 1987b).

tion tax is to achieve some measure of cooperative dis-integration. By and large, conference participants had few kind words to say about such proposals. Those who were critical, or very critical, included Swoboda, Hamada, Frenkel, and Darby. I do take note, however, of the exception registered by Moon Soo Kang that countries such as Korea may want to give consideration to such tax measures. Similarly, I am reminded of Mr. Kang Nam Lee's observation that the problems of Korea and other countries in the Asian region do not invariably make them sympathetic to the trends of internationalization and financial-market integration.

Richard Cooper stated the case most forcefully that the policy community cannot indefinitely rest with today's status quo. I would not put the point so strongly, but I do believe that the status quo may be subject to progressively stronger pressures. If the world as a whole is not going to slip backwards, or engage in an orderly retreat from interdependence, the remaining direction of movement has to be forward—with incremental improvements in arrangements and policies brought about by enhanced cooperation.

III. A Composite Vision for the Medium-Run Future

Several alternative visions of the future monetary system were spelled out for us at the conference. I am not an enthusiast for any of the classes of reform that were described. Nor did I detect general enthusiasm from most of the conference participants. Hence I am emboldened to sketch a somewhat different vision of the way forward. My "composite vision" takes into account the range of views at the conference and tries to identify a center of gravity among them. At the same time, I make no effort to suppress my own prejudices.

The time horizon I have in mind is about ten years—in other words, between now and end of this century. This is an *incrementalist* time frame. I am mainly concerned with the next steps forward and the medium run, though of course, as we all do, I want the short- and medium-run steps to lead to a long-run situation that will be appropriate.

My vision is conditioned by judgments of what is desirable, but it is also influenced by the constraints of what seems politically feasible. For example, it is much less far-reaching than Cooper's long-run vision of a world common currency, and considerably less far-reaching than McKinnon's proposals for close harmonization of monetary policies among the major countries. It does *not* place primary emphasis on the exchange rate regime, in contrast with most proposals for target zones for exchange rates.

My composite vision is nonetheless fairly ambitious. My optimistic premise is that national governments can reasonably aspire to better macroeconomic performance, to heightened international cooperation, and to strengthened international institutions.

My vision entails "enhanced intergovernmental cooperation" under five headings:
1. Cooperative improvements in analytical knowledge.
2. Improved international cooperation about national economic policies.
3. Enhanced cooperation about the exchange rate regime.
4. Renewal of cooperative management of the reserve asset characteristics of the international monetary regime.
5. Gradual strengthening of international institutions.

I take up each of these dimensions in turn.

Cooperative Improvements in Analytical Knowledge

Improving analytical knowledge about how national economies and the world economy function is a logical prerequisite—a necessary, but of course not sufficient, condition—for implementing virtually all types of possible reform of the international monetary system. What is needed is a better knowledge (particularly empirical knowledge useful to policymakers) *and* a wider understanding of that knowledge, both within the policy community and among the informed public concerned with economic policy. A convergence of views among policymakers about what cooperative actions are feasible and desirable cannot take place without a convergence of analytical views about what the consequences of these actions will be.

A great deal was said at this conference about how inadequate our "knowledge base" is. Among others, Meltzer, Shinkai, Fischer, Marston, and Prell all emphasized how little economists know.

We can measure expressions of opinion on this matter on the International Economists' Humble Index. This index ranges from values of -10 to $+10$. The norm value is zero. Overweening confidence and a high degree of arrogance are represented at $+10$. Eating humble pie is measured at -10. I would rate the attack of humbleness that infected this conference at a value somewhere between -4 and -6: in other words, definitely excessive. Jacob Frenkel identified the attack as an "overshooting" of humility; that verdict seems entirely correct to me.[11]

Without doubt, the understanding of policymakers and economists of macroeconomic interactions among the major countries, of exchange rate determination, and of almost any aspect of open economy macroeconomics is inadequate. But we do have a moderate amount of useful theoretical knowledge. And for some important cross-border interactions, we even have identified broad ranges within which plausible empirical estimates fall. We know *something*, in other words, and in every circumstance I can imagine I would rather use the limited knowledge we do have rather than trusting someone who generates his views by sucking his thumb. Moreover, there are plausible grounds for moderate optimism that we can improve our stock of theoretical and empirical knowledge through further systematic research.[12]

Consider the example, referred to several times during the conference, of savings-investment imbalances and current account positions. Can we make precise statements about how a nation's saving preferences and investment opportunities will translate into national excess savings or excess investment? Hence can we make accurate forecasts of "warranted" current account imbalances? Of course we cannot. But we need not be carried away by humbleness. We can say something in empirical terms about these phenomena within very broad ranges. And there are occasional times and circumstances when one can be quite confident in making qualitative statements. In my view, for example, we can confidently condemn the saving-investment and current balance situation of the United States today as inappropriate and due in significant part to an excessive budget deficit and an insufficient national savings rate.

It is surely in the interest of national governments to give stronger support to research seeking to improve the knowledge base of how the world economy functions. It makes especially good sense for governments to encourage the international economic organizations to strengthen their research programs. I could give a variety of examples of the type of research that could have a payoff for national

---

[11] On the final day of the conference, at first I thought the participants might be recovering from the attack. But then just before lunch, Professors Meltzer and Cooper showed renewed symptoms. Andrew Crockett might even have been subtly influenced, though with a very mild dose, in his summary comments at the final session.

[12] For overviews of some of the recent empirical research, see, for example, Bryant and others (1988); Bryant, Holtham, and Hooper (1988); Helliwell (1988); Bryant (1989); Bryant, Helliwell, and Hooper (1989); and Helliwell, Cockerline, and Lafrance (1989).

policymaking and for international cooperation, but for the sake of brevity will identify just two. Research is needed that evaluates alternative proposed policy "rules" under a wide range of analytical circumstances, including the techniques of stochastic simulation. And research is needed on alternative methods for calculating internationally consistent "equilibrium" paths for exchange rates, current account imbalances, and hence savings-investment imbalances under a variety of alternative policy assumptions. (On this second topic, note that it is not sufficient merely to focus on paths for "equilibrium exchange rates"; rather analysts need to calculate paths for an entire range of macroeconomic variables in an internally consistent manner within countries and across countries.)

Improved International Cooperation about National Economic Policies

Several of us participating in the conference felt it helpful to make a distinction between "cooperation" and "coordination." "Cooperation" is a general term best used to refer to the entire spectrum of collaborative activities among national governments. "Coordination" is the most ambitious form of cooperation, characterized by mutually discussed and designed adjustments of policy actions. In a clear-cut case of coordination, explicit bargaining occurs and governments agree to behave differently than they would have behaved without the agreement.[13]

In my composite vision of the future, it will not be feasible during the next few years to engage in ambitious efforts to cooperate. Rather, governments should aspire to improve the extent of information exchange, consultation, and other more limited types of cooperation. This type of cooperation should not be considered unimportant. On the contrary, it is a precondition for more ambitious forms of cooperation—including coordination proper.

As analytical knowledge and techniques improve, and as awareness of those advances in knowledge influence policymakers' views, it may gradually become more feasible to implement analytically ambitious forms of "coordination." That cooperation/coordination would extend across the entire range of economic policy actions, domestic and not merely external. There is no reason on analytic grounds to exclude any policy area; so, for example, policies in the monetary and fiscal and trade areas would *all* be candidates.

[13] For further discussion of the distinction, see Bryant (1987b) and Horne and Masson (1988).

Part of what I envisage is a gradual intensification of "multilateral surveillance," through the Group of Seven, the IMF, the OECD, and possibly other forums as well. The evolution might have the following elements. Each national government participating in the surveillance process would submit projections of the baseline economic outlook (either with own-country policies unchanged, or incorporating policy changes that have already been decided on). Each projection would preferably be derived from some analytical framework ("model") that tries to be internally consistent. An individual government would concentrate most on projecting the key macroeconomic variables pertaining to its own economy. But each government would also be free to submit projections for other economies if it chose to do so. The international institution, or institutions, that provide the secretariat for the monitoring of the process would also provide its own baseline projections of the outlook for each major country or region.[14]

Which variables would be focused on in these projections? In principle, a variety would be projected and evaluated, not merely a small handful. Equally important, the actual instruments and the ultimate target variables of national policies would both feature prominently in the projections. In no sense would the exercise focus only on intermediate, "indicator" variables.

Then, in addition to the baseline projections, the exercise would typically consider "what if" simulations. Such simulations would examine what the consequences might be if this or that policy instrument were to be changed. Similarly, the questions would be asked: What if such and such a nonpolicy shock were to occur? Changes resulting from these hypothetical policy and nonpolicy alterations would be measured relative to the baseline outlook. Such what-if scenarios would be prepared, at a minimum, by the international secretariat. Ideally, national governments would also be interested in preparing their own "what if" simulations for changes in their own policy instruments especially, but even for changes in other governments' policy instruments and for various nonpolicy shocks. (Differences in preferred models would lead to differences in the answers to the what-if questions.)

At periodic meetings of policymakers or their deputies, the discussions would examine both the baseline-outlook projections and the what-if scenarios. No less important, the discussions would involve frank exchanges of information on what individual governments' goals

---

[14] The IMF World Economic Outlook and the OECD Economic Outlook exercises can be viewed as nascent prototypes of such surveillance.

were. Efforts would be made to classify differences in baseline projections and what-if scenarios according to whether they were due to differences in goals, differences in preferred models, or differences in assumptions about nonpolicy shocks.

The international secretariat would play, and would be acknowledged as playing, a key analytical role. In particular, the secretariat would catalyze a systematic comparison of the previous meetings' *ex ante* projections with new information about how the ex post outcome was turning out. And the secretariat would try to use judiciously chosen what-if scenarios to catalyze mutually supportive changes in policies.

On days when I am feeling optimistic, I even think that the past few years of G-7 discussions have been hesitantly groping in the direction I have described. To be sure, on my pessimistic days, I fear that actual G-7 discussions have focused primarily on "exchange-rate cooperation." The Louvre accord of February 1987, if one can accept the account of it by Funabashi (1988), suggests an example of poorly conceived cooperation that emphasized exchange-rate stability without sufficient attention to domestic-policy fundamentals.

My vision of the evolution of enhanced cooperation about economic policies, eventually even coordination, is not a congenial one for some of the conference participants. The issue of "coordination of policies" perhaps caused more controversy at the conference than any other. Yet the issue does not deserve to be quite as controversial as the different rhetorics make it seem. We should not let views about "coordination" be a litmus test for more general views. The genuine differences among people about "rules" and "discretion" are also less striking than would at first appear.

For example, let me cite several points—all made during the conference at one time or another—on which there is essential agreement. First, governments would make a serious error if they regarded coordination as a *substitute* for sound domestic policies; Teh Kok Peng and Jacob Frenkel, two of those expressing some support for coordination, both emphasized this point in their comments. Second, as a variety of participants observed, if cooperation or coordination should entail stabilization of exchange rates *and only that*, coordination could be a bad idea. Third, if a government views coordination as a way of getting foreign nations to take actions so that it can avoid needed adjustment of its own domestic policies, that posture too could lower world (and even own-country) welfare. Fourth, it is possible that attempted coordination of economic policies could be mistaken and could lead to welfare losses; in particular, if policymakers use models of how the world economy functions that are in fact seriously incorrect, they are likely to get into hot water and do damage to welfare.[15] Fifth, however, as several conference participants, dubious of the benefits of coordination in practice, had no difficulty acknowledging, there is a strong case in principle that welfare for all countries *could* be enhanced by coordination. Finally, policymakers must adopt *some* analytical posture about how the world economy functions. It is of course true all existing analytical models are highly uncertain. Yet policymakers lack the option of ignoring all models; they cannot set all their policy instruments at "zero" values, so to speak, and just decide to have no policy at all; if a policymaker chooses to ignore all explicit models, he merely decides to use an implicit one. Cross-border spillovers will exist, and may sometimes be large, even if the policymakers decide to ignore these effects when they make decisions.

By stressing points of agreement, I do not wish to go so far as to argue that the differences in views about policy cooperation and co-ordination are minor. But I would argue that there is substantial scope for a convergence of views, especially as the knowledge base and the extent of analytical understanding improve.

We need some units of measurement here too. When speaking of cartons or boxes in the Japanese language, one uses the counter "-hako." Accordingly, I offer the definition of a "Meltzer-hako": a Meltzer-hako is the number of cartons of refereed journal articles on macroeconomic models sufficient to nudge Allan Meltzer one step closer to sympathetic contemplation of forward-looking forecasts as part of governmental policymaking. I conjecture that a Meltzer-hako is a finite number, possibly measured even with a single digit.

The Japanese-language counter for drops, or small doses, is "-teki." For symmetry, we need the unit of measurement "Fischer-teki": a "Fischer-teki" is the minimum number of doses of sound, credible judgment required of policymakers before Stanley Fischer can agree to accept Jacob Frenkel's flexible and discretionary version of policy coordination. A "Fischer-teki" is possibly also a fairly small number in practice.

On this point I conclude, perhaps too optimistically, that over the medium-run future there is some hope of seeing a convergence of views about policy cooperation and coordination, even from those most inclined to be suspicious of it.

---

[15] Jeffrey Frankel and other authors have stressed this point in recent widely cited papers; see, for example, Frankel and Rockett (1988). As observed at the conference, however, others paper concerned with model uncertainty—for example, Ghosh and Masson (1988a, 1988b) and Holtham and Hughes Hallett (1987)—reach less pessimistic conclusions than those stressed by Frankel.

Enhanced Cooperation about the Exchange-Rate Regime

The third dimension in my composite vision is the exchange-rate regime. Given improvements in analytical knowledge (including procedures for calculating internationally consistent paths for "equilibrium" exchange rates based on best-available analytical models) and given improved incorporation of that knowledge in overall macroeconomic policymaking, I can envisage policymakers in the major countries moving, gradually and very cautiously, toward official indications of reference ranges for exchange rates. This evolution would not happen in isolation, but as part and parcel of improved coordination of all macroeconomic policies.

We have been observing this evolution already happening within Europe during the past two decades. If worldwide progress were made along the two dimensions already considered (improvements in analytical knowledge; gradual enhancement of cooperation about domestic economic policies), it does not take wild imagination to envisage an analogous evolution of exchange regime arrangements among the "trilateral currency areas" of Europe, the dollar, and the yen.

I believe such an evolution could be, eventually, both feasible and desirable because I believe the exchange rate regime can have significant independent influences on macroeconomic outcomes. In other words, I do not myself believe that the international monetary system is merely a mirror, reflecting what originates elsewhere. More generally, I do not believe that monetary and financial systems—both domestically and in their international aspects—act merely as channels for more basic forces rather than themselves sometimes playing an influential role. Possibilities of "excess variability" and "misalignments" in exchange rates (and asset prices, more generally) are, legitimately, a source of policy concern. In large part, those possibilities justify the judgment that the exchange-rate regime can have significant independent influences.

Nevertheless, to repeat, influences on macroeconomic outcomes from the exchange-rate regime itself are probably less important than other causal factors. Problems and turbulence in the world economy originate *primarily* from nonpolicy shocks (for example, supply shocks, such as innovations in technology, resource discoveries, political upheavals, and OPEC cartels) and from the policy actions of national governments (which frequently work at cross-purposes). The soundest position on this matter, in my view, is somewhere intermediate between the positions espoused at the conference by Cooper and Meltzer.

No conceivable exchange rate regime could insulate one nation's economy from turbulence originating elsewhere in the world economy. And no conceivable regime could be "optimal" in all circumstances—appropriate "for all seasons"—when disturbances originate in the home economy.[16]

The implication of this conclusion is that the choice of exchange-rate regime and more broadly the choice of international monetary system, is less salient an issue than (for example) how to adjust domestic policies appropriately and how to minimize inconsistencies among them across countries.

Reserve-Asset Characteristics of the International Monetary Regime

My crystal ball for the medium-run future does not differ significantly from that of Stanley Black or Alexander Swoboda about the evolution of national currencies in international uses. My prediction, too, is that there will be a continued evolution toward multipolar uses of currencies, and no dominant trend toward any will develop.

On another aspect of the use of currencies, however, my views do differ somewhat from those of the majority of participants. The Black and Meltzer papers for the conference scarcely mention either the SDR or gold. It is easy for me to agree with the omission of gold from the discussion. Gold as a reserve asset has a highly uncertain value, and the flow of new gold production is uncertain and plagued with political difficulties; justifiably, no central bank wishes to bring gold back to the center stage of the international monetary system. But questions about the SDR—or, more generally, an "outside" reserve asset for the world as a whole—are another matter.

It is my view that, if not now, then eventually, the world financial system is likely to need an outside reserve asset that is not the reserve liability of any individual nation. Within particular national financial systems, we now take it for granted that it is the exclusive responsibility of a central bank to supply high-powered money, namely, national money that is an "outside" asset for all private financial institutions. The basic rationale for this within-nation outside money stems in part from the responsibilities of the central bank as the ultimate lender of last resort. Another part of the rationale stems from a desire for the (within-nation) collective management of money. (I doubt that any of the conference participants, for example, are proponents of the Hayek view that a competition among privately issued monies within

[16] The Fukuda-Hamada (1987) paper for the Third Bank of Japan International conference is a thoughtful demonstration of these points in terms of a theoretical model.

the national economy would have benefits exceeding the potential costs.)

As we look ahead to the medium and long run, I believe that we should be thinking of an analogous set of arguments at the global level. Just as we believe that an unfettered competition among private monies within nations might produce financial instability and create uncertainty about ultimate lender-of-last-resort responsbilities, I believe we should be focusing attention on the disadvantages as well as the advantages of the "multiple reserve currency system" at the world level. It is certainly conceivable that a shifting of reserve assets by central banks and governments among assets denominated in different national currencies could exacerbate the inevitable volatility in exchange markets stemming from shifts of assets by private investors. Moreover, a multipolar currency world without an outside reserve asset might eventually engender concerns about inadequate provision on a global scale of lender-of-last-resort assistance to illiquid financial institutions. To be sure, a shifting of assets among national currencies—whether by private investors or by governments—can have a constructive disciplining effect on reserve-center nations, causing them to hesitate in pursuing irresponsible economic policies. But in any case we ought to be self-consciously raising questions about both the pros and the cons of the existing multiple reserve currency system. It is peculiar, to say the least, to spend a great deal of time analyzing a world common currency for private uses (as we have done at this conference) without also analyzing the issue of a world outside reserve asset.

In my own vision of the longer-run future, I envisage a gradual evolution toward increasing use and importance of a world "outside" reserve asset and hence toward cooperative understandings about reserve-asset characteristics of the monetary system. This evolution, though it would come very slowly, would entail an eventual diminution in the relative importance of all *reserve*-currency uses of national currencies (the dollar, DM, yen, and others).[17]

I want to provoke reflection on this subject by raising one further question. Imagine a set of circumstances in which the U.S. dollar becomes very weak in exchange markets and stays depressed for an extended period of time. (I wish it were harder to imagine such a thing than it is!) Is it not likely that the idea of a "substitution account"

---

[17] Although the issue of the SDR and international liquidity was neglected in the early sessions of the conference, Messrs. Frenkel, Lind, Wijnholds, and Masunaga all brought up the issue on the final day, arguing that it nedeed analytical and policy attention.

would then once again emerge for discussion? And is it not possible in such circumstances that some of those who now regard the SDR as a despicable reserve asset could find themselves re-evaluating their views?

Strengthening of International Institutions

I turn finally to the fifth of my dimensions of enhanced cooperation. The fundamental general rationale for international institutions is to catalyze intergovernmental cooperation and to facilitate the supply of collective goods at the international level. There are strong grounds for presuming that with the increasing interdependence of the world economy, externalities and collective-goods problems with international dimensions have become more numerous and conspicuous over time.

Thus my composite vision of the medium run implies deliberate efforts to strengthen international institutions and to be more self-conscious about their prospective functions and responsibilities.

Surprisingly little was said at the conference on this subject. To provoke discussion, let me raise just three of the important and difficult questions that governments will gradually have to face more directly.

First, what should be the relative responsibilities of the International Monetary Fund and the Organization for Economic Cooperation and Development? In particular, what evolution of the OECD's functions in the area of macroeconomic surveillance should governments try to encourage?

Second, should cooperation about national monetary policies be channeled primarily through the Bank for International Settlements? Or over time, should monetary policies be discussed more intensively in forums such as the G-7 and the IMF? This question is self-evidently a highly sensitive matter politically, being inseparable from the issues within countries of the appropriate degree of central-bank independence and—eventually—the issues at the world level of to what degree monetary policies should be insulated from the political process.

Third, which additional nations, if any, should become members of limited-membership organizations such as the BIS and the OECD? For example, will nations such as Korea, Brazil, and Mexico—and, still further in the future, India, Indonesia, and Nigeria—become members? Alternatively, does the policy community in the existing member nations envisage a limited membership persisting indefinitely? If so, will some functions now evolving at the BIS and the OECD (for example, intergovernmental cooperation in bank supervision and regulation through the BIS) have to be transferred to universal-membership organizations such as the IMF?

A complete "vision" of enhanced intergovernmental cooperation will eventually have to confront issues of this type. No doubt it is not urgent to have a clear prospectus about these issues now. But it will gradually become more important to do so.

IV. International Cooperation in Perspective

As a concluding perspective, I want to add something that I believe falls squarely into the center of gravity of views represented at the conference. Suppose we ask: What is the essence of international cooperation? And why can one realistically aspire to see more of it?

A few participants—for example, Professors Shinkai and Kawai—implied that international cooperation can entail a nation having to give up some of its national interests, perhaps surrendering some of its sovereignty. Jacob Frenkel argued against that perspective, and I too want to challenge it.

International cooperation, in my view, is only a self-interested mutual adjustment of the behavior of national governments. Cooperation does not entail a sacrificing of national interests. It does not entail a surrendering of effective national sovereignty. It is not a synonym for altruism or international harmony. And it certainly does not imply that national governments have the same goals, or goals that are compatible. (Plainly, governments have very different goals, often incompatible, and will have for decades into the future.) The essence of cooperation is merely that the various governments take into account the interactions among their economies and polities, and as a result mutually adjust their policies *so that each nation can act intelligently to better achieve its own, selfish objectives.*

Seen in this light, enhanced international cooperation does not seem so unattainable. And that is why we do not have to be hopelessly idealistic or optimisitic to aspire to achieve more of it in the remaining years of the 20th century.

The Bank of Japan's International Conferences can be seen as harbingers, in symbol and in practice, of the enhanced cross-border dialogue that needs to be nurtured. I thus close my remarks by praising the Bank of Japan for its leadership in promoting this cooperative dialogue and by thanking the Bank warmly for its example and its hospitality. Domo arigatoo gozaimashita!

References

Bryant, R.C. 1987a. *International Financial Intermediation*. Washington, D.C.: Brookings Institution.

———. 1987b. "Intergovernmental Coordination of Economic Policies: An Interim Stocktaking." In *International Monetary Cooperation: Essays in Honor of Henry C. Wallich*. Princeton Essays in International Finance No. 169, December 1987.

———. 1988. "Macroeconomic Interactions between the United States and Japan: An Interim Report on the Empirical Evidence." Brookings Discussion Paper in International Economics No. 67. Washington, D.C.: Brookings Institution, December 1988. Published version in *Tokyo Club Papers No. 2. 1988* (Tokyo: Tokyo Club Foundation for Global Studies, Nomura Research Institute, 1988).

———. 1989. Comment on Jeffrey A. Frankel, "A Modest Proposal for International Nominal Targeting (INT)." forthcoming in William Branson, Jacob Frenkel, and Morris Goldstein, eds., *International Policy Coordination and Exchange Rate Fluctuations*. Chicago: University of Chicago Press.

Bryant, R. C., Helliwell, J.F., and Hooper, P. 1989. "Domestic and Cross-Border Consequences of U.S. Macroeconomic Policies." In Bryant, R.C., Currie, D., Frenkel, J.A., Masson, P.R., Portes, R. eds., *Macroeconomic Policies in an Interdependent World*. International Monetary Fund with Brookings Institution and Centre for Economic Policy Research, 1989. Unabridged version available as Brookings Discussion Paper in International Economics No. 68, Washington, D.C.: Brookings, January 1989.

Bryant, R. C., Henderson, D.W., Holtham, G. Hooper, P. and Symansky, S.A., eds. 1988. *Empirical Macroeconomics for Interdependent Economies*. Washington, D.C.: Brookings.

Bryant, R.C., Holtham, G., and Hooper, P. 1988. *External Deficits and the Dollar: The Pit and the Pendulum*. Washington, D.C.: Brookings.

Frankel, J.A., and Rockett, K. 1988. "International Macroeconomic Policy Coordination When Policymakers Do Not Agree on the True Model." *American Economic Review*, Vol. 78 (June 1988).

Fukuda, S., and Hamada, K. 1987. "Toward the Implementation of Desirable Rules of Monetary Coordination and Intervention." In Yoshio Suzuki and Mitsuaki Okabe, eds. *Toward a World of Economic Stability: Optimal Monetary Framework and Policy*, Tokyo: University of Tokyo Press.

Funabashi, Y. 1988. *Managing the Dollar: From the Plaza to the Louvre*. Washington, D.C.: Institute for International Economics.

Ghosh, A.R., and Masson, P.R. 1988a. "International Policy Coordination in a World with Model Uncertainty." *IMF Staff Papers*, vol. 35.

———. 1988b. "Model Uncertainty, Learning, and the Gains from Coordination." Mimeographed (revised).

Helliwell, J.F. July 1988. "The Effects of Fiscal Policy on International Imbalances: Japan and the United States." In *Global and Domestic Policy Implications of Correcting External Imbalances*, Papers of the Fourth EPA International Symposium. (Tokyo: Economic Planning Agency). Also available as *NBER Working Paper* 2650.

———, Cockerline, J., and Lafrance, R. 1989. "Multicountry Modelling of Financial Markets." Paper presented at the Federal Reserve Board conference on Monetary Aggregates and Financial Sector Behavior for Interdependent Economies, May 1988. Forthcoming in Peter Hooper and others, eds., *Financial Sectors in Open Economies: Empirical Analysis and Policy Issues*, Washington, D.C.: Board of Governors of the Federal Reserve System.

Holtham, G., and Andrew, H.H. 1987. "International Policy Coordination and Model Uncertainty." In Bryant, R., and Portes R. (eds.), *Global Macroeconomics: Policy Conflict and Cooperation*, London: Macmillan, 1987.

Horne, J., and Masson, P.R. June 1988. "Scope and Limits of International Economic Cooperation and Policy Coordination." *IMF Staff Papers*, vol. 35.

Keohane, R.O. 1984. *After Hegemony: Cooperation and Discord in the World Political Economy*. Princeton, N.J.: Princeton University Press.

Suzuki, Y. 1989. *Japan's Economic Performance and International Role*. Tokyo: University of Tokyo Press.

———, and Mitsuaki Okabe, eds. 1987. *Toward a World of Economic Stability: Optimal Monetary Framework and Policy*, Tokyo: University of Tokyo Press.

Keynote Speeches

3

Efficiency and Stability in World Finance

Allan H. Meltzer

Ths years 1950 to 1980 appear in retrospect as a period of above-average growth for most of the world's market economies. More people in more countries experienced increases in their standards of living than at any time in recorded history. World trade expanded faster than world output, increasing the efficiency of the world economy. Improvements in technology that reduced costs of transport and communication played a role. Sufficient political stability to prevent a major war encouraged many countries to direct efforts toward growth and away from war and costly rivalries.

The institutional structure of international economic relations contributed also. Under the General Agreement on Tariffs and Trade (GATT), tariff barriers on manufactures were reduced to relatively low levels, although quotas and other nontariff barriers offset some of the reduction in tariff barriers, and the protection of agriculture probably increased. GATT permitted countries to adopt strategies of export-led growth. The financial system operated first under a system of fixed but adjustable exchange rates and later under a system of fluctuating exchange rates between major currencies. In both systems, the dollar served as the principal medium of exchange and unit of account for the world, or at least for the market economies. Capital movements, though restricted at times and places, rose from the low levels of the 1940s and 1950s to the relatively high rates of the 1970s and 1980s.

This set of arrangements is now in flux. We can do no more than speculate on whether the future lies in proposals to strengthen the rules of multilateral trade, as in the Uruguay round of GATT negotiations, or in bilateral arrangements with rising protection between groups of countries in Europe, North America, and Asia. Bilateral arrangements include the recent Canada-U.S. Free Trade Agreement and proposals to reduce barriers to trade and finance within the European Community while maintaining and perhaps increasing barriers against third parties. The increased use of bilateral agreements opens the possibility of trade diversion from third countries, protectionist policies against third countries, and a turn back toward the system of trading blocs, with barriers against nonmembers, more characteristic of the interwar period than of the postwar years. On the financial side, there are now important alternatives to the dollar as a medium of exchange and unit of account. The mark or possibly the ECU is emerging as a partial substitute for the dollar within Europe, and the yen serves increasingly as money for parts of Asia. Japan's role in relation to its neighbors is broader than in the past. Formerly, Japan mainly processed raw material imports into finished goods; recently, its relations with its Asian partners have developed more interdependence. It is not surprising that, with this development, more of the trade and lending between Japan and its Asian trading partners is now denominated in yen. A manufacturer of sub-assemblies or components in Korea or Taiwan who borrows in Tokyo and sells in Japan is likely to find the yen superior to the dollar as a unit of account and a medium of exchange.

The increased holding of non-dollar reserves is not a new event or necessarily a cause for concern. The Deutsche mark and the Japanese yen were the second and third currencies used as reserves a decade ago—before the real appreciation and subsequent depreciation of the dollar and before the United States began to borrow heavily abroad. If we exclude ECUs, the U.S. share of official holdings of foreign reserves in 1980 was 73%, the mark's share was 12%, and the yen's was about 3.5%. By the end of 1987, the dollar's share had fallen to 67%, whereas the shares of the mark and the yen had increased to 15% and 7% respectively.[1] In both years, the three currencies made up 90% of the countries' reserves, with changing composition of the total. These data suggest that movement toward a multi-currency world has been gradual, not precipitate.

Those with memories of the currency problems of the interwar period may find movement toward a multi-currency world disquieting. One reason is that the advantages are often neglected. A multi-currency world can serve to discipline country policies, lowering inflation and anticipations of differences in rates of inflation. A disadvantage is that,

---

[1] Data are from the International Monetary Fund, *Annual Report 1988*, Washington, Table 1.2, p. 68. Allowing for the holdings of ECU reduces the dollar's share to 57%, but it also reduces the shares of the other currencies.

with more rapid adjustment of asset markets than of output markets, shifts between currencies can generate or exacerbate real disturbances. Hence, a multi-currency world may be subject to greater short-term variability, greater risk, and therefore excess burden. Concerns of this kind, and concerns about potential efficiency losses from the development of bilateral trading blocs, arouse fears of a retreat from the institutional framework that contributed to the increased efficiency, widespread development, higher rates of growth, and increased economic stability experienced by many countries during the past 40 years. The conference treats a subset of this topic, the financial system. My subsequent discussion recognizes the link between finance and trade, but concentrates on money and finance.

I. The Interwar Years as Precedent

During the interwar years, the dollar replaced the pound as the world's major currency, and the relative importance of New York as a world financial center increased. At about the same time, or a little earlier, the United States became a net creditor, and Britain was no longer able to maintain its prewar position as the world's principal lender. Further, reparations and war debts called for transfers from debtors to creditors and the financing of payments imbalances.

It is much too easy to leap from the relative positions of Britain and the United States in the interwar period to the relative positions of Germany, Japan, and the U.S. at present. The analogy gains strength from the repetition of an unfortunate feature of the interwar experience —the principal creditor country or countries continued to run relatively large trade surpluses. Further strengthening the analogy is the similarity between the interwar transfer and debt problems and the transfer and debt problems arising from the current international debt of developing countries.

There are important differences, however. Britain ran merchandise trade deficits for several decades before 1920 while sustaining its position at the center of the world financial system. The United States began to have surpluses on merchandise trade in the 1880s, long before the dollar became a leading international money. The U.S. merchandise trade deficit and the Japanese trade surplus are relatively recent events, and it is far from clear whether they will continue for decades. Demographic factors affecting Japan and the United States are an important reason, but by no means the only reason, for expecting sizable changes in the saving and investment balances of the two countries and hence in their trade and current account balances in the decades ahead. Analogies are often misleading, so it may be useful to look more carefully at the conditions that would have to arise for the pattern to repeat with Germany and Japan replacing the United States in the 1990s as principal financial centers, much as New York supplanted London in the interwar period. Of particular interest at this conference is the role of the mark and the yen in the future development of the international monetary system; so I begin with the role of an international money.

II. International Monies

In a system of fixed exchange rates, there is an obvious role for an international money or monies. It should be apparent that in practice there is a role for an international money in a system of fluctuating exchange rates as well. Loans and contracts are denominated in some unit, and payments are typically made in that unit. Transactors hold balances in anticipation of payments, and central banks hold asset reserves. Holders and users of money are not indifferent about the choice of money. They do not randomly choose the money used to make payments, denominate contracts, or hold reserves. Ninety percent of measured international reserves are in three currencies, as noted above, and similar dominance would quite likely be found if we had measures of the other services of money. This section considers some of the factors leading to the choice of particular currencies as international money.

Standard transactions costs explain a small part of the observed concentration on a small number of monies.[2] The costs of acquiring information are more relevant. These costs are not distributed uniformly over all assets or even over all national monies. The marginal cost to the user of acquiring information depends on the choice of the asset to be used as money. The cost declines as the frequency with which the asset is used increases.

Frequency of use rises with the relative importance of trade. Together, the United States, Germany, and Japan had more than 30% of the world's exports and imports in 1987, so it is not surprising that the currencies of these countries are widely used and held as money.

[2] This section follows Brunner and Meltzer (1971).

Averaging export and import shares of world trade puts the United States first, Germany second, and Japan third, the same order as the use of the currencies of these countries in international reserves. See GATT (1988).

The relative decline in the role of the dollar as an international money, noted above, accompanied the decline in its share of world trade. The expansion of intercountry trade, for example, in the European Community or in East Asia, to which the United States is not a party, contributed to the development of alternatives to the dollar. As information spread about the properties of alternative currencies, they became more widely used as money.

The relative importance of trade is not the only reason for choosing a currency as money. Under fluctuating exchange rates, countries and individuals or firms can reduce risk by diversifying currency reserves. There are limits to a country's gain from diversification, however; each new currency used as money imposes a cost of acquiring information about its quality or properties. With fixed exchange rates within blocs such as the EMS, it is more efficient to hold a representative currency, say the Deutsche mark, than to hold currencies in proportion to bilateral trade shares.

Why choose the Deutsche mark? Why not the French franc or some other EMS currency? Information about the properties of each national money, such as its relative quality as protection against inflation or the risk of exchange controls, distinguishes different monies. Both the information and the cost of acquiring it differ by countries. Germany has an established reputation as a low inflation country and one that is not likely to impose exchange controls, but France or Italy do not. The quality of the mark is higher, so fewer resources must be allocated to monitoring German policies. Higher quality increases the relative demand for the Deutsche mark as an international money. If all the currencies in the EMS agree to fix exchange rates, there is no net gain from holding each, but there is an expected gain from holding marks under the system of fixed but adjustable exchange rates if the mark has higher quality and is more likely to appreciate relative to the other EMS currencies.

Under the Bretton Woods agreement, the dollar was linked to gold. The operation of the system and the economic climate of the period made large changes in the dollar's value improbable in the early years. When the link to gold was broken, the risks associated with holding dollars increased, so the return to diversification rose. Inflationary policies in the United States that lowered the quality of the dollar as an international money and contributed to the demise of the Bretton Woods system contributed to the perceived increase in the benefits of a diversified portfolio.

Although the United States has not been party to a currency agreement such as Bretton Woods or the EMS since 1973, many countries have kept fixed but adjustable exchange rates with the dollar. The costs of acquiring information about U.S. policies are lower than for Latin American countries, and the risks of inflation and instability are also lower, so the dollar is held as a reserve by countries in the area and used as a unit of account and a medium of exchange in transactions between and within countries.

A relatively large share of the final sales of East Asian countries go to the United States and are denominated in dollars. Many of the prices of their imported materials are quoted in dollars also. It remains efficient to use the dollar as a unit of account on a large share of the region's trade. Increased Japanese imports of final goods from the region, or relatively wide swings in the U.S. rate of inflation, would reduce the role of the dollar in the region's trade, payments, and reserves. The dollar's role as an international money would decline further.

The literature on seigniorage highlights the gain to a money issuer and the cost to a holder of a particular money. These costs and benefits are relevant, but they do not fully explain the choice of international monies. Countries like Panama or Hong Kong do not have central banks to issue domestic money and collect seigniorage. Some countries permit "dollarization" or, more generally, permit banks to offer foreign currency deposits, more often as a store of value than as a medium of exchange. A country's history of inflation does not explain all these decisions. The costs of acquiring information help to explain why a country would choose to forego the gain from seigniorage to reduce the costs of information and transactions. Panama is an example of a country that, by using the dollar as money, imported greater stability of domestic values than many of its neighbors were able to produce. The imposition by the U.S. of financial restrictions on Iran and later on Panama reduces the relative informational advantage of the dollar and increases uncertainty about relevant aspects of U.S. policy, thereby raising both the costs of acquiring information about U.S. policies and the costs of using the dollar as money.

Periods of anticipated rapid inflation or heightened instability in Argentina, Brazil, Bolivia, and elsewhere provide evidence on costs of information. Although the rate of inflation in the United States is higher than that in Germany or Japan, the dominant movement by money holders at this time is to the dollar, not to the currencies with lower inflation rates. People appear willing to pay the higher cost of holding dollars on the expectation that others will make the same choice. For centuries, gold has had a similar attribute in many parts of the world, even though its price changes with the prices of other metals.

These experiences suggest that non-uniform costs of acquiring information about money function as a barrier to entry by alternative monies. The barrier acts as an established brand name; it provides information about the quality of the product. The producer can, of course, exploit the barrier to entry, but repeated exploitation changes the quality of the product and induces the search for an alternative.

III. Debtors and Creditors

Published statistics show that the United States became a net international creditor at about the time of World War I and remained a creditor until 1985. After 1985, the reported net debt position increased each year. The published data are not entirely accurate, however. Direct investment is valued at historic cost, and most Latin American assets of U.S. banks are carried at face value. Gold is included in the net position, but it is currently valued at $42 an ounce. For these and other reasons, published statistics do not give a clear picture of the net debtor or creditor position of the United States. What is clear is that the U.S. is no longer the principal creditor nation and will be a net debtor, if even now it is not. My discussion of the reasons for holding and using an international money has not mentioned a country's net debtor position. Is this an oversight or an error?

A common error, I believe, confuses money and credit. Countries may continue to use the dollar as an international money and denominate securities and contracts in dollars even if the U.S. is a net borrower. A Japanese banker may lend dollars to a Korean producer to purchase oil. If oil or other commodities continue to be priced in dollars, someone must bear an exchange risk. These issues or problems arise continually in financial markets. Neither their occurrence nor their solution depends on whether the U.S. is a creditor or a debtor. Further, the fact that the United States is, or will be, a debtor is a statement about its balance sheet. It does not imply that the U.S. will not be a net lender in the future.

What matters much more than debtor-creditor position is the cost borne by transactors using a particular money. The role of the dollar as an international money would decline if transactors become convinced that costs would be lowered by pricing and denominating oil, loans, and many other transactions in non-dollar currencies. A country's political and economic stability—or instability—affects these costs. A country particularly subject to coups, insurrections, or revolutions would be unlikely to produce a relatively stable money, so costs of acquiring information would rise. A country with highly variable policies, variable rates of inflation, and economic instability would impose high costs of acquiring information. Relative instability lowers the quality of money, reduces confidence, and raises the cost of using a particular money as unit of account, medium of exchange, and international reserve currency.

Debtor status could influence the use of money if a country borrows in its own currency, then inflates. Concerns about future inflation could raise the cost of using the dollar in the future. Past experience in countries with high inflation, or even hyperinflation, suggests, however, that established money continues to be used at least internally. This suggests, again, that costs of shifting to a different unit of account or medium of exchange are high, although these costs are higher nationally than internationally. Available evidence on dollarization in Israel and some Latin American countries shows, however, that the presence of a currency with known properties speeds the adjustment to an alternative money within countries.

Growth in the use of alternatives to the dollar depends also on the policies of the countries (or private issuers) producing the alternative monies. If the new creditor countries follow mercantilist policies, such as lending internationally mainly to promote domestic expansion, tying foreign loans to domestic purchases, maintaining barriers to trade, and restricting competition, an international use of the new monies will be restricted.

I conclude that if variability is not substantially greater than that experienced in recent decades, the dollar will continue to serve as an international money. Other monies will be used and perhaps will continue to grow in importance relative to the dollar. This is more likely to happen if the role of the United States in trade and payments declines relative to other countries and the other countries follow liberal trade and exchange policies. The problem for the international economy, then, is to develop a system that reduces the risk of fluctuations in a multi-currency world toward the minimum arising from nature and trading arrangements. This raises the much-discussed issue of monetary coordination and various proposals for coordination.

IV. Coordination as Intervention

Policy coordination has many meanings. The most common use, I believe, refers to efforts to coordinate policymakers' actions. Country A is headed toward recession or has a current account deficit. Country B has inflation and a current account surplus. The countries agree on a mix of monetary and fiscal actions by each country that is intended to move both countries toward a position of growth with low inflation and with current accounts nearer to balance.

This type of coordination should not be called policy coordination. Coordination is at the level of actions, not policies, so the more appropriate term is intervention. The presumption is that policymakers or their advisers know the mix of actions that is consistent with equilibrium in both, or in some cases several, countries. Coordination of this kind attempts to adjust economies by using forecasts and judgment in much the same way, but on a larger scale, than the efforts to control inflation by managing Phillips curves in the 1970s. The earlier policies failed, I believe, mainly because they substituted what economists would like to believe they know for what they actually know. The latter does not include detailed knowledge of the nature of shocks and the size of structural parameters required to design optimal mixes of monetary and fiscal actions that reduce risks to a minimum. Nor is there evidence that it includes an ability to forecast output, prices, and current account balances with sufficient accuracy to reduce variability on average. Meltzer (1987) shows that average forecast errors are a large fraction of average changes in output and inflation. Although economists' forecasts are probably the best available, they cannot distinguish booms and recessions a quarter or a year ahead.

Consider the information required to coordinate the responses in two (or more) economies. The timing of responses to policy action differs across countries. Wage rates adjust to prices more rapidly in Japan than in the United States or Europe. Labor markets are commonly believed to be less flexible in the U.S. than in Japan, but more flexible than in Europe. Countries produce different product mixes. For these reasons, expansions and contractions can give rise to short-term changes in relative prices and output. These differences stimulate capital flows and changes in exchange rates. Efforts to offset these movements by playing against an evanescent international Phillips curve require more information and greater forecasting accuracy than economists can claim reliably. We have not produced evidence showing that there is a reliable Phillips curve or that we can reduce variability and uncertainty by coordinated actions to expand or contract. We cannot speak with confidence on the effects of coordinated actions on short-term exchange rates, since we have not developed a theory capable of predicting short-term movements in exchange rates.

Much the same can be said about proposals to coordinate changes in the demand for money or in aggregate demand so as to maintain aggregate world demand rising at a nearly constant rate, or to reduce fluctuations in world growth. A profession that cannot reach firm conclusions on whether unanticipated changes are shocks mainly to aggregate demand or to aggregate supply or whether shocks are mainly permanent or transitory, even after the fact, lacks sufficient information to reduce variability by coordinating responses to unanticipated changes. Even if these difficult econometric problems could be resolved for particular samples, what reason would there be to claim that the distribution of shocks would remain constant in subsequent samples? Nothing in economic theory implies that the distribution of shocks is fixed or invariant to the structure of institutions in the domestic and the world economy. On the contrary, differences in the initial responses to fixed and fluctuating exchange rates depend on such structural features of the economy as the prevailing type of labor contracts or the flexibility of labor and product markets. These structural features are not givens. They depend, *inter alia*, on the anticipations generated under a particular monetary or fiscal regime and on history or experience as it affects the credibility and reputation of the policymaker.

Comparisons of responses in Japan to monetary changes under fixed and fluctuating exchange rates illustrate the point.[3] From 1956 to 1973, under fixed exchange rates, there were relatively large fluctuations in money growth (M_2+CDs). After a few quarters, the growth of nominal and real GNP and the rate of inflation seem to replicate the pattern of fluctuations in money growth. After 1973, Japan had a fluctuating exchange rate. Beginning in 1975, the Bank of Japan announced projections for money growth and attempted to hold actual money growth close to the projections. Fluctuations in money growth are smaller in this period than under fixed exchange rates, and fluctuations in real and nominal growth are smaller also. The trend rates of growth in money and nominal GNP declined at about the same average rate, and the rate of inflation fell to 1% or less. Under fluctuating exchange rates, real GNP growth is less variable and, prior to the Plaza agreement, appears to be less responsive to previous changes in money growth. The regime of fluctuating exchange rates and preannounced monetary targets appears to have changed the short-term relation

---

[3] Data and comparisons are from Suzuki (1988). See also Meltzer (1985).

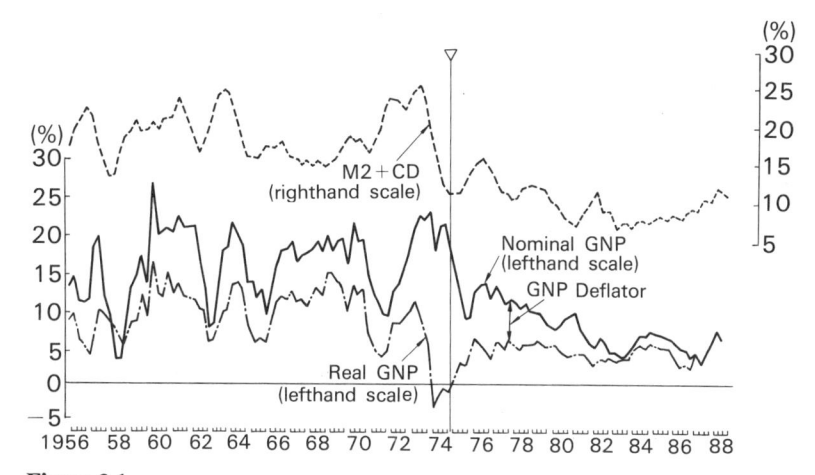

Figure 3.1
Money Stock and GNP (Nominal and Real) in Japan
Notes: 1. Growth rates of money stock and GNP are calculated not against the previous quarter, but against the same quarter in the previous year.
2. "$M_2 + CD$" data (before first quarter 1979, "M_2" data) are averages of end-of-month observations. For example, the first quarter is an average of the data at the end of January, February, and March.
Source: Suzuki (1988).

between money and real output by changing perceptions about policy, about the persistence of deviations from the trend rate of money growth, and about variability. The data hint that the short-term response of real GNP to money rose following the Plaza accord. Figure 3.1 shows some data that illustrate these differences.

This experience suggests that Japan was able to use monetary control in the fluctuating rate regime to reduce variability and uncertainty and also to reduce inflation. Similar results have been found for Germany.

Recent literature on credibility suggests an additional way in which information about policy affects the timing of responses to policy actions across countries and over time. Let credibility be defined as the difference between the policymaker's plans and the public's anticipation of these actions. The smaller the difference, the more information the public has about policy, and the greater the policymaker's credibility. The degree of credibility affects both the timing and the magnitude of some responses. A credible announcement that the policymaker intends to reduce inflation would be expected to generate a more rapid response of prices and a smaller, temporary effect on real output. Comparative Japanese experience under fluctuating and fixed rates, just considered, is one example. Swiss experience provides another. A bulge in domestic money, following exchange market intervention, had little lasting effect on Swiss prices in the late 1970s. A plausible explanation is that the Swiss National Bank had a reputation for a policy of non-inflationary money growth; so the bulge was expected to be a temporary or transitory change. Considerations of this kind suggest that the public's initial beliefs about the permanence of a policy shock depend on the past history of policy.

Proposals to coordinate actions using several indicators to guide policy actions have drawbacks similar to those just discussed. The relation of indicators to actions and of actions to outcomes is not something on which economists have developed useful knowledge. Once we shift from long-term consequences to short-term effects, we confront the problems of forecasting and estimates of lags that have until now not been resolved by our increasingly sophisticated econometric techniques.

Proposals for the use of indicators have an additional drawback. Movements of most economic variables are difficult to interpret unambiguously. It would be interesting to see the model or framework that would be used to interpret some of the proposed indicators so as to learn whether their use would provide information that could be used to increase or reduce variability. This is obviously a difficult problem, since the designation of a particular variable as an indicator would be likely to affect its covariance with other variables.

An alternative proposal calls for the use of target zones, or bands, within which nominal exchange rates are free to vary. At the band, countries are expected to intervene to keep the exchange rate from rising or falling further. Where real exchange rates are relatively constant, the target zone is a less-efficient means of reducing variability than a fixed exchange rate. Where real exchange rates change in response to differences in productivity, perceived risks, and other real factors, the target zone, like a fixed exchange rate, forces more of the adjustment to be made in labor and product markets. Where costs of production and prices change at different rates, real exchange rate adjustments are often a less costly means of adjusting prices and production costs than the adjustments in money wages and prices required by a target zone. It is not an answer to say that we can change the target band as required. We do not know the equilibrium real exchange rate. Economic theory does not tell precisely how to determine the market clearing prices for assets. Inevitably, there will be errors. Why should we expect variability to be minimized or reduced?

Some proposals for coordination or for target zones may be based on a vulgar error. The fact that real exchange rates vary more under fluctuating than under fixed exchange rates is not evidence of excessive variability or excess burden. Exchange rates are, at least in part, substitutes for adjustments in labor and product markets. Exchange rate adjustments are particularly useful when real shocks to productivity change equilibrium values of relative prices and wages. Evidence cited earlier suggests that output has been less variable in Germany and Japan (and has not been more variable in the U.S.) under fluctuating exchange rates than under Bretton Woods, despite the oil shocks of the 1970s and the recession of the early 1980s. Fluctuating rates may have reduced shocks from abroad, or provided the opportunity for more stable domestic policies, or increased the public's confidence that stabilizing policies would be followed in the future, or all of the above. Whatever the reason, or mix of reasons, future policy should not concentrate on the variability of exchange rates, but it should recognize the increased stability that some countries have achieved under fluctuating exchange rates.

V. Rule-Based Policy Coordination

Markets coordinate responses by adjusting prices. Fluctuating exchange rates coordinate real and nominal differences among countries. A valid case for international policy coordination cannot be based on policymakers' abilities to coordinate better than markets. The case for coordination depends on finding net benefits to society that can be achieved on favorable terms.

The case for monetary policy coordination arises from the opportunity to achieve jointly what individual country policy cannot achieve alone. There are two aspects. First, small countries generally cannot maintain domestic price stability acting alone. A large share of their consumption goods is imported, so they must depend on their trading partners to maintain price stability. As specialization and trade increase, imported goods have more weight in consumer and producer baskets in large countries. What is true of small countries becomes applicable to the large. Second, no country, large or small, acting alone, can maintain stability of both internal and external prices. Acting together, major countries can increase the stability of external prices and provide a public good for small countries. If central banks in these countries—the U.S., Germany, Japan—follow a common policy rule that aims for domestic price stability, their individual efforts will reduce variability of nominal and real exchange rates.[4] In time, anticipations of sustained price stability would also contribute to greater exchange rate stability. Further, a common monetary rule expands the choice set for small countries. Under the rule, a third country can increase domestic price stability by fixing its exchange rate to a basket of major currencies.

Information cost is a chief characteristic distinguishing types of coordination that are likely to be welfare-improving and that are more likely to raise than to lower variability and uncertainty. The exchange of information among governments about policies, plans, and interpretations is a low-cost form of coordination that is now well established. Such exchanges lower costs of acquiring information and reduce uncertainty. Coordination by policy rule, if the rule is easily monitored, lowers the cost of acquiring information relative to agreements that coordinate discretionary policy action. Rules that do not rely on forecasts depend less on uncertain future events, are less subject to manipulation, and are therefore less costly to monitor.

A common policy rule can achieve some of the benefits of policy coordination while avoiding some of the costs. If the rule is adaptive, it can adjust to changes in the economy without relying on forecasts of future values. In the past, I have proposed a rule that maintains price stability on average and reduces fluctuations of exchange rates. The rule is adaptive; current money growth rises with the moving average rate of growth of output and falls with the moving average rate of growth of monetary velocity. The rule adjusts to changes in the growth rate, changes in the demand for money, and intermediation. The rule can be adopted by each country separately, but all countries can gain if it is used more widely.

McCallum (1988) used simulation to study the operating characteristics of a similar rule for a single country, the United States. Hall (1988) studied the characteristics of the rule in the United States, Germany, Japan, and Canada. Their simulations suggest that an adaptive rule of this kind would have reduced variability for the United States and Canada, but not in Germany and Japan. The finding that Germany and Japan did not reduce variability under the rule suggests that the proposed rule may not be an improvement over the policy rules used in those countries in recent years. One reason is that the policies followed by Germany and Japan are similar to the

---

[4] Mussa (1986) shows that ex post real and nominal exchange rate movements are correlated.

proposed rule. However, the studies to date consider neither the additional reduction in variability that would arise from the use of a common rule by principal countries, nor the welfare gain to third countries from increased international stability.

In principle, fiscal policy can make adherence to a monetary rule impossible. Support for this proposition based on data for developed countries is weak. Countries as different as Canada, Italy, and the United States have run persistent budget deficits while reducing inflation. Further, the effects of fiscal policy on interest rates have been hard to detect empirically. One reason for this is that issues about the proper measurement of fiscal policy have not been resolved. Clearly, there are other explanations including near-Ricardian equivalence or closely integrated capital markets.

The failure to find strong evidence of aggregative effects of fiscal policy on interest rates and prices does not mean that fiscal actions are irrelevant. Tax and spending decisions may have large allocative effects. They may bias spending toward consumption or reduce the efficiency of resource use. These allocative effects may influence welfare, but they have little importance for the choice of an anti-inflation policy.

VI. Conclusion

This paper began by pointing to the above-average gains in living standards achieved in many countries under the postwar order. I argued that the institutional arrangements—including GATT and the role of the dollar as an international money—contributed to those gains. Although these arrangements were not without flaws, they helped to make the past 40 years a remarkable period in human history.

Growth has not been uniform, so countries' relative positions have changed. Shifting patterns of trade, fluctuating exchange rates, and the emergence of Japan and Germany as major trading countries increased the importance of the mark and the yen as international currencies. More stable prices in these countries than in the United States increased the benefits of diversification in reserve holding under fluctuating exchange rates. The development of trading areas in Europe, North America, and Asia, as economies developed and matured, also encouraged the use of alternative monies.

The development of trading areas may be the start of a retreat from the multilateral arrangements of the postwar era toward a system in which country blocs have a larger role. A return to the instabilities of the interwar period is not inevitable, however. Beneficial postwar multilateral arrangements that encouraged trade and, for parts of the period, maintained reasonable price stability can be sustained by concerted action. Countries that have benefited most from the open trading arrangements of the past 40 years are in a position to take the lead in maintaining and extending the scope of the multilateral system.

The leading countries can contribute to monetary stability and the growth of trade and living standards by strengthening trading rules, including rules for dispute settlement, and by agreeing on a common rule for monetary policy similar to the rules followed in Germany and Japan before the Plaza agreement. By following common rules, countries reduce uncertainty and costs of acquiring information, and increase economic welfare. Efforts to coordinate policies of the emerging blocs by using forecasts of GNP, target zones, or other ad hoc adjustments that require estimates or forecasts, are most unlikely to be successful. These efforts depend on information that economists and policymakers do not now have and are not likely to have reliably in the future. Further, prior agreement on policy rules reduces the conflicts that arise periodically between countries. The choice between rules and discretion for trade and finance will, I believe, make a critical difference to the growth and stability of the decades ahead, just as the rules of the 1940s contributed to the growth and stability of the past 40 years.

Bibliography

Brunner, K., and Meltzer, A.H. 1971. "The Uses of Money: Money in the Theory of an Exchange Economy." *American Economic Review* 61 (Dec.): 784–805.

GATT. 1988. *International Trade 87–88*, Vol. 2, Geneva.

Hall, T.E. 1988. "McCallum's Base Growth Rule: Results for the United States, West Germany, Japan and Canada." Working paper, U.S. Dept. of State (December).

McCallum, B. 1988. "Robustness Properties of a Rule for Monetary Policy." *Carnegie-Rochester Conference Series on Public Policy* 29: 173–203.

Meltzer, A.H. 1985. "Variability of Prices, Output and Money under Fixed and Fluctuating Exchange Rates: An Empirical Study of Monetary Regimes in Japan and the United States." *Bank of Japan Monetary and Economic Studies* 3 (Dec.): 1–46.

———. 1987. "Limits of Short-Run Stabilization Policy." *Economic Inquiry* 25 (Jan.): 1–14.

Mussa, M. 1986. "Nominal Exchange Rate Regimes and the Behavior of Real Exchange Rates: Evidence and Implications. *Carnegie-Rochester Conference Series on Public Policy* 25 (Autumn): 117–213.

Suzuki, Y. 1988. "Japanese Monetary Policy under the Floating Exchange Rate Regime." Working paper, Bank of Japan.

4

Factor Mobility and the International Monetary System

Stanley Fischer[1]

This Fourth International Conference sponsored by the Institute for Monetary and Economic Studies of the Bank of Japan is designed to stimulate thinking about the future of the international monetary system in the light of recent history. That history includes the Bretton Woods system, with its successes and ultimate failure, and the flexible rate system with its unexpectedly large exchange rate fluctuations and current account imbalances. In particular, we are asked to consider the implications for the future of the international monetary system of the increasing sophistication of domestic and international financial markets and the large scale of international capital flows. Here it is necessary to take into account not only the sizable net flows that mirror current account imbalances, but also the phenomenal scale of gross flows that are now routine in the major financial markets.

The best known of the proposals for reducing exchange rates and perhaps current account fluctuations are discussed in several of the papers to be presented at this conference.[2] These range from the target zone proposal of Williamson (1985) and Williamson and Miller (1987), which comes closest to describing the post-Plaza agreement relations among the major currencies, through an adjustable peg system, which exists within the European Monetary System and between some individual currencies and other major currencies, to Richard Cooper's proposal for a world money, which is described in his paper for this conference.

Certainly the most radical and intellectually most appealing is the proposal for a single world money. Of course, Cooper is not proposing or predicting that the world should or will move immediately to such

---

[1] The views expressed in this paper are entirely my own and do not represent those of the World Bank or its management. I am indebted to Barry Eichengreen and Cliff Papik.

[2] Particularly in the paper by Shinkai.

a system. But he does suggest it is the logical direction in which the world is heading—and at this hopeful time, when some long-lasting international conflicts have been settled, others are moving in surprising and beneficial directions, and there is far less diversity of views about appropriate national economic policies and the necessary role of markets than in over half a century, it is easy to be sympathetic to this view.

In this paper I discuss, first, the requirements for the successful use of an international money and, second, the difficulty of estimating equilibrium exchange rates at a time of major international capital flows. These two topics are linked by the role in each of them of factor mobility. I will argue that the absence of sufficient factor mobility makes the use of a world money remote, but that the existing degree of capital mobility makes the restoration of an adjustable peg unlikely and the maintenance of meaningful target zones very difficult. Accordingly we have to live for some time with the imperfections of the current system.

I. Factor Mobility and a World Money

In discussing the requirements for and desirability of a world money, I shall draw extensively on the recent "Report on Economic and Monetary Union in the European Community,"[3] the Delors Report. I shall examine four issues: the role of fiscal policy coordination; the role of goods and factor mobility; the adjustment mechanisms that would operate in a single currency world; and the desirability of a world money.

There is no difference in principle between the use of a single world money and a system in which nominal exchange rates among countries are irrevocably fixed. It may be, though, that the only way to attain irrevocably fixed exchange rates is to use a single money—though even here it has to be recognized that currency unions have in the past broken down and been replaced by several national currencies. For simplicity we shall assume that we are discussing a single fiat money that is the only money in existence. We shall further assume that there are no capital controls.

The Delors Report defines three necessary conditions for a monetary union: the assurance of total and irreversible currency convertibility;

[3] Report of the Committee for the Study of Economic and Monetary Union, April 12, 1989.

the complete liberalization of capital transactions and financial markets; and the irrevocable fixing of exchange rates. It regards the creation of a single currency as a desirable further step to cement the monetary union.

Among the conditions necessary for economic union, the Commission includes the completion of the single European market, in which "persons, goods, services and capital can move freely," and macroeconomic policy coordination, including binding rules for fiscal policies. The Report argues that economic union and monetary union are inextricably linked and would have to be implemented in parallel.

The key question about the use of a single money is whether the conditions described by the Commission as necessary for economic union—goods and factor mobility, and macroeconomic policy coordination—are also needed for the success of a monetary union. We discuss the issue in general, not in the specific context of the European Community.

Fiscal Policy Coordination

Consider first fiscal policy coordination. The seigniorage revenue collected by the central monetary agency would still be available for distribution among the member countries. However, the adoption of a single money eliminates the independent use of seigniorage as a policy instrument. This could have significant budgetary implications for countries which, whether because they grow more rapidly or inflate more rapidly, collect relatively large amounts of seigniorage revenue. With removal of the right of individual countries to print money to finance future budget deficits, the use of a single money would also to some extent limit the size of deficits that governments could finance by borrowing, and thereby limit divergences among aggregate fiscal policies.

The extent to which explicit fiscal policy coordination among countries would be necessary for the survival of a monetary union depends on the efficiency of markets and the rationality of governments. Suppose that one government wished to run relatively large deficits, thereby drawing disproportionately on the world's saving. It might want to do this because it has a different demographic profile than other countries, or because its citizens through the political process express a different rate of time preference than those in other countries. In principle the government would choose its deficit recognizing the intertemporal tradeoffs it faces—that a higher deficit today means a smaller deficit tomorrow[4]—and the financial markets would price that government's debt appropriately.

There might nonetheless be positive externalities from fiscal policy coordination, particularly among the larger countries. Fiscal policy coordination could help regions adjust to shocks, both those that hit the entire currency area and those that affect different regions differentially. Fiscal policy coordination can be seen as a useful complement to the other potential adjustment mechanism that we examine below, namely factor mobility and wage and price flexibility. Fiscal policy coordination is more necessary when the other adjustment mechanisms are less effective.

The use of a single money would not force or require full convergence of tax rates and government spending patterns among countries, which could continue to differ as they do in many federal states. The convergence that would be required here would depend in part on the mobility of factors; full mobility of capital would mean that capital tax rates would have to be very similar, but if any factor, such as labor, were not mobile, governments could impose different tax rates. Even if all factors were fully mobile, governments could compete by producing different tax and benefit packages for their residents, as envisaged by the Tiebout (1956) hypothesis.

Thus full fiscal policy coordination does not seem necessary for the adoption of a single money. Rather, the adoption of a single money would tend to produce some, though limited, fiscal coordination by limiting the independent use of seigniorage. Whether it forced convergence of tax rates and government spending patterns would depend on the extent of factor mobility.

Goods and Factor Mobility

The "Report on Economic and Monetary Union" describes goods and factor mobility as essential to economic union. To some extent this is true by definition. There remains, though, the interesting question of whether *both* goods and factor mobility are necessary to attain the benefits of an economic union. Goods mobility is indeed essential. The factor price equalization theorem implies that in some cases goods mobility alone suffices to produce factor price equalization and thus would appear to make factor mobility unnecessary.[5] But the conditions under which factor prices would be equalized through free trade

---

[4] Assuming that the real interest rate exceeds the economy's growth rate.
[5] Samuelson (1949).

in goods are unlikely to hold in practice. Would capital mobility plus goods mobility suffice? At the theoretical level, that depends on whether there are non-traded goods. Since there are, capital mobility plus goods mobility would not in general produce the same allocation of resources as would exist if all factors were fully mobile.

Labor is frequently immobile in practice even when it is legally free to move, for instance among regions in existing unified states. Regional problems, including persistent high unemployment in some regions, are more likely to persist in the absence of a mechanism that allows relative price adjustments. If nominal wages and prices are sticky, then a change in the exchange rate is one potential adjustment mechanism; but if it is real wages that are sticky, then exchange rate changes do not provide an additional adjustment mechanism. Where wages and prices are not sticky, adjustment can take place through differential changes in wages and the prices of non-traded goods. Such a mechanism does seem to operate in the United States, where regional price changes (particularly as reflected in housing prices) in effect allow quite significant real exchange rate changes to take place.

Thus labor mobility would be desirable in the creation of an economic union, but it is not essential, provided relative wages and other prices can adjust across regions. If labor is not mobile, and if regional nominal wages and prices are sticky, then the creation of a monetary union would exacerbate regional problems.

Large regional disparities would place a strain on the currency union. These could be overcome by budgetary transfers and other regional policies. Certainly, sizable regional disparities persist in existing federal states without local governments seeking to institute their own monies.

To summarize, the Commission on Economic and Monetary Union has set out conditions for economic union—namely, fiscal policy coordination and goods and factor mobility—that would be desirable in their own right, and that would certainly strengthen a monetary union. However, under certain circumstances full fiscal policy coordination and complete factor mobility would not be essential for the adoption by several countries of a single currency or its equivalent.

Under what conditions might countries that have not moved as far to economic union as envisaged by the Commission agree to use a single currency? Governments that see very little to be gained by retaining the right to produce inflation rates that differ persistently from others, and that believe that adjustment mechanisms other than changes in nominal exchange rates are available, might well want to use a single currency or move toward irrevocably fixed exchange rates. Since there is little to be gained by retaining the right to create independent inflation rates, the issue comes down to one of the existence of alternative adjustment mechanisms.

Adjustment Mechanisms

Coordination of fiscal policies, including agreement on budgetary policies to deal with regional problems, provides a source of adjustment. So do wage and price flexibility. Adoption of a single currency could help create local wage and price flexibility by increasing the credibility of the government's commitment not to accommodate inflationary pressures, along the lines suggested by Giavazzi in his paper for this conference. But it was true during the gold standard period that commercial policy was frequently used as an alternative (to the exchange rate) adjustment mechanism, and it was also true that the collapse of the gold exchange standard in 1931 led to the use of tariffs as an alternative (and counterproductive) adjustment mechanism.

Economists believe that it should be possible, through the strengthening of GATT and of individual governments' resolve, to limit the use of such trade interventions. However, recent experience gives reason to fear the strength of protectionism.

The Desirability of a Monetary Union

The Committee for the Study of Economic and Monetary Union was given the task of studying concrete steps to attain those goals, not asked to appraise their desirability. Would an extension of the area of use of a single currency be desirable? Closer economic integration that does not increase barriers to external trade would in general be beneficial. Such integration would be improved by the use of a single money. In the absence of such integration, the use of a single currency would remove an adjustment mechanism—exchange rate changes—that could be useful under some circumstances. This could lead to increased use of trade restrictions.

For that reason, and because wage and price flexibility may be slow in coming, early attempts to move toward the use of a single currency could be counterproductive and undesirable. By insisting on factor mobility and coordination of fiscal policies as necessary accompaniments to monetary union, the Delors Committee seeks to put in place alternative adjustment mechanisms. However, such mechanisms require close political coordination that is not at present attainable on a larger scale. Without such coordination, it would be premature to attempt to extend the area of currency union.

II. The Adjustable Peg and Other Alternatives

The adjustable peg system is one step short of currency union, since it allows the possibility of sometimes adjusting the exchange rate. A return to that system could be a step toward a world money, in the same way as the EMS is serving as an interim step on the path to a European money.

However attractive the adjustable peg system, whether as a step toward a world money or because it stabilizes both real and nominal exchange rates, it has to be recognized that we are in the current flexible rate system because the Bretton Woods adjustable peg system proved unworkable. Nothing that has happened since 1973, except the creation of the EMS, suggests that the major countries are willing to constrain their economic policies in a way that would make it possible to return to the adjustable peg system. Further, the increase in capital mobility since 1973 makes a return to the Bretton Woods system even more difficult.

It is common to suggest in light of the large current account imbalances during this decade that the flexible exchange rate system may encourage protectionism. A case can be made to this effect: namely, if exchange rates had been truly fixed during this period, the real appreciation of the dollar until 1985 would probably have been smaller than it was, therefore current account imbalances would have been smaller, and therefore protectionist pressures would have been less. However, it is highly doubtful that fixed exchange rates could have been maintained in the face of divergent fiscal policies in the early 1980s; it is the underlying divergences in fiscal policies and saving rates that lead to the large deficits that are proximately responsible for protectionism.

Target Zones

Exchange rates were allowed to fluctuate without official intervention for only a short period in the early part of this decade. Particularly since the 1985 Plaza agreement, shortly after the dollar had peaked, the world appears to have been operating with flexible target zones for exchange rates. From time to time the authorities appear able to keep exchange rates within the target zones, but occasionally, as in recent months, capital movements become so strong that rates may move outside their target zones.

There may be two arguments for target zones: first, capital movements may frequently be irrational, that is to say, not justified by the economic fundamentals; second, capital movements are more likely to be rational if the markets have information about the authorities' intentions. The authorities apparently do not subscribe to the latter argument, for they do not make the target ranges public.

The question of whether private capital movements are at any particular time irrational can be answered only if there is a good estimate of the equilibrium exchange rate. These estimates are based almost entirely on estimates of the exchange rates needed to achieve particular current account targets, typically close to balance, over some specified horizon.

The major difficulty with such estimates is that we know relatively little of the size of long-term capital flows that may be desired by market participants. International capital flows have been severely restricted in much of the world for over 50 years. U.S. residents have been free to purchase foreign assets during this period, but the residents of other countries have suffered or continue to suffer from restrictions on the foreign assets they can buy. Estimates of optimal international portfolios suggest that individuals should diversify internationally more than they have; this may be so especially for residents of small open economies and developing economies.

Given that U.S. residents have been subject to fewer capital controls than others, it is likely that there will continue to be some pressure for a net inflow of capital into the United States as part of a stock readjustment of portfolios as international capital markets become more open.[6] Such pressures are not independent of rates of return or the exchange rate, but their potential existence indicates the difficulty of estimating equilibrium exchange rates from the current account alone.

Of course, the intertemporal budget constraint limits the potential paths of the current account: the constraint is that the present value of a country's future primary external surpluses must be equal to the current value of its net external debt. One implication is that a country that is currently a net debtor has to look forward to running trade surpluses in future; another is that a debtor country that continues to receive net capital inflows has to look forward to having to increase its net transfers to foreigners in future years above the levels that would otherwise have been needed.

But this constraint places very few restrictions on justifiable sizes of current account deficits or net ownership of foreign assets. Net

---

[6] There will also be flows from the countries that have not had capital controls to those now opening up to foreign investment.

asset positions have been far larger in the past than they are currently: Britain in 1914 had external assets equal to about 125% of its GNP,[7] and about 15% of world GNP. Japan currently holds external assets worth about 15% of her GNP and less than 2% of world GNP. Canada's current net indebtedness as a share of GNP is about 40%, and there has not been any concern about its inability to service the debt. The plain fact is that although economists can easily agree that current account deficits on a significant scale cannot continue forever, we have little idea of how long they can continue.[8] Although concentration on the current account in estimating equilibrium exchange rates is ultimately justified, it is difficult to know what these rates should be at a particular moment of time.

The difficulty of knowing the equilibrium exchange rate at any given time, a difficulty that is heightened by the remarkable international mobility of capital, means that both an adjustable peg system and a meaningful target zone system are unlikely to become effective any time soon. Of course, a target zone system with sufficient flexibility is always possible, but the question then is whether the target zones are meaningful, both as constraints on national policies and as constraints on the ability of capital flows to move exchange rates significantly.

III. Concluding Comments

The conclusion is that exchange rates among the major economic blocs are likely to continue to be set as at present, by the markets, with periodic intervals of intense intervention by the authorities. If countries were willing to coordinate their fiscal policies much more closely, exchange rate movements could be reduced; and if there were fewer obstacles to the movements of goods and services—for instance, if the Uruguay Round attains its ambitious goals—exchange rate movements could be further attenuated. While the notion of a world money is intriguing, it is still, as Richard Cooper argues, a remote possibility. It will take increased political integration among the major blocs to bring a world money closer. In the meantime, we will be able to study the costs and benefits of closer monetary and economic integration by watching the progress of economic and monetary union in the European Community.

[7] See Platt (1986).
[8] This is an application of a law attributed to Herbert Stein of the American Enterprise Institute.

How then can efficiency and stability be attained? Efficiency in the sense of low transaction costs in the flow of international capital has increased remarkably in the last two decades. But low transaction costs do not necessarily produce an efficient allocation of resources. The efficiency of resource allocation can be improved by adopting policies that encourage the mobility of goods and factors and removing policy-related impediments to goods and factor mobility, and by providing a stable macroeconomic framework. Stability can be enhanced in the first instance by each country following sustainable and consistent macroeconomic policies and, in the second and less important instance, through the international coordination of policies. However, it has to be recognized that efficiency does not imply stability, but rather the ability to deal appropriately with inevitable economic shocks.

Bibliography

Cooper, Richard N. 1989. "What Future for the International Monetary System?" presented at this conference.

Giavazzi, Francisco. 1989. "The EMS Experience," presented at this conference.

Platt, Desmond C.M. 1986. *Britain's Investment Overseas on the Eve of the First World War*. New York: St. Martin's Press.

Samuelson, Paul A. 1949. "International Factor-Price Equalization Once Again." *Economic Journal* 58 (June): 181–97.

Shinkai, Yoichi. 1989. "Evaluation of the Bretton-Woods Regime and Floating Exchange Rate System," presented at this conference.

Tiebout, Charles M. 1956. "A Pure Theory of Local Expenditures." *Journal of Political Economy* 62 (5): 416–24.

Williamson, John. 1985. *The Exchange Rate System*. Washington, D.C.: Institute for International Economics.

───── and Miller, Marcus H. 1987. *Targets and Indicators: A Blueprint for the Coordination of Economic Policy*. Washington, D.C.: Institute for International Economics.

Lessons from the History of the International Monetary System

5

International Monetary Instability Between the Wars: Structural Flaws or Misguided Policies?

Barry Eichengreen*

I. Introduction

The interwar period provides a natural laboratory for the study of exchange rate systems. It divides into three distinct regimes: freely floating exchange rates from 1921 through 1926, fixed rates from 1927 through 1931, and managed floating rates for the remainder of the 1930s. The rapid succession of regimes provides a singular opportunity to assess the implications for asset and commodity markets of different exchange rate arrangements.

Not just the operation of the successive regimes but also the transitions between them are of interest. The collapse of the laboriously reconstructed fixed-rate system of the 1920s coincided with the spread of the Great Depression. An obvious question concerns the causal connection between the two events. Was the Depression responsible for the collapse of the exchange rate system, and if so through what channels was its destabilizing influence transmitted? Alternatively, should the operation of the international monetary system be held responsible, in part at least, for the severity of the Depression?

In this paper I reassess the history of the international monetary system between the wars. Like the history of the period, the discussion is best divided into several parts. As background for what follows, I start in Section II with an overview of international monetary relations in the 1920s and 1930s. Section III then provides evidence on the implications for the operation of asset and commodity markets of alternative exchange rate arrangements. In Section IV, I consider

---

* I thank Yeongseop Rhee and Carolyn Werley for advice and assistance and Jeffrey Frankel, Michael Bordo, and Bronwyn Hall for helpful comments. This paper is part of a larger research project, supported in part by grants from the German Marshall Fund, the National Science Foundation, and the Institute of Business and Economic Research of the University of California at Berkeley.

explanations for the collapse of the fixed exchange rate system of the period 1927–31. Was that collapse the result of flaws in the structure of the fixed-rate system or of misguided national economic policies? What was the role of the Great Depression in the system's disintegration? In Section V, I turn the question around and explore the role of the international monetary system in the Great Depression. Was the operation of the fixed-rate system, its collapse, or both, responsible for the severity of the macroeconomic crisis? This is followed by a brief conclusion and summary of implications.

II. An Overview of Interwar Experience

The classical gold standard provided the framework for international monetary relations in the decades preceding World War I. That system of fixed exchange rates collapsed abruptly with the outbreak of hostilities. The convertibility of currencies into gold was suspended.[1] Monetary and fiscal policies were detached from exchange rate targets and subsumed to the war effort. But wartime exchange rates neither exhibited the volatility they were to display subsequently nor diverged to the same extent as national price levels. Frequently exchange controls were adopted to minimize the fluctuation of nominal rates. Where markets were allowed to operate, currency prices were heavily influenced by government intervention, notably support operations conducted by the United States on behalf of Britain and France.

With the conclusion of hostilities, these support operations were terminated. Exchange controls were relaxed gradually. Exchange rates began to float freely and were subjected to competing pressures. International inflation differentials having greatly exceeded nominal exchange rate movements, currencies which had depreciated were still overvalued, while those which had not were undervalued. Given prevailing price levels, further exchange rate changes were required to restore long-run competitive balance. But there was no reason to assume that current prices would continue to prevail. National authorities were universally committed to restoring prices to prewar levels and returning exchange rates to prewar parities. So long as this com-

---

[1] While generally the case, this response by the belligerents was not universal. Great Britain, for example, nominally retained convertibility throughout the war, although moral suasion and bureaucratic impediments discuoraged residents who might have wished to exchange domestic currency for gold. Most of the neutrals, for whom the problem was gold inflows rather than outflows, also retained official convertibility, although they pursued various policies designed to discourage attempts to obtain domestic currency for gold.

mitment was credible, weak exchange rates would be bid up in anticipation of their eventual revaluation. If, however, the official commitment to strengthening weak exchange rates was not regarded as credible, this mechanism would not operate. So long as budgets remained in deficit and monetary expansion remained the rule, inflation rather than deflation would be in the offing. In this case, the logical expectation would be depreciation, not appreciation.

Between 1921 and 1926, exchange rates fluctuated in response to these pressures. A notable feature of this episode is that spot and forward rates were determined in the foreign exchange market subject to a minimum of government intervention. Governments, as a rule, did not intrude directly in the foreign exchange markets. Exceptions, such as France in 1923–24 and 1925–26 and Germany during its hyperinflation, were few. Thus, the early 1920s provide a relatively pure example of a freely floating exchange rate regime. This is not to deny that fiscal and monetary policies could be altered in response to movements in the exchange rate. The point is that governments rarely intervened in the foreign exchange market to damp its response to these changes in policy.

The behavior of exchange rates during this period remains controversial. The standard account (Nurkse, 1944) emphasizes the volatility of nominal exchange rates, attributing it to destabilizing speculation. The classic rebuttal (Friedman, 1953) challenges each element of the standard characterization.

In the middle years of the decade, fixed exchange rates were restored. Among the first countries to do so were those that had endured hyperinflation. In Austria, Germany, and Hungary, price-cost disparities were eliminated by the disappearance of nominal contracting and the adoption of currency reform. The task of balancing the budget was simplified by the inflation-induced erosion of the public debt. Opposition to tax increases and public expenditure cuts was overwhelmed by the trauma of uncontrolled inflation. Perhaps most important, a fixed exchange rate was seen as a necessary concomitant of successful stabilization. The exchange rate was pegged by Austria in 1923, Germany in 1924, and Hungary in 1925. Other countries that had experienced more moderate inflations soon followed: Belgium in 1925, France in 1926, and Italy in 1927 all returned to gold at somewhat devalued rates.[2] Adjustment was generally more protracted, if less

---

[2] In the case of France, this refers to de facto stabilization of the franc. Although the franc remained stable from December 1926, de jure stabilization followed only in June 1928.

dramatic, in countries attempting to reduce prices and costs in order to restore the prewar gold parity and the traditional dollar exchange rate. Of the industrial countries, Sweden was first to complete the process in 1924. Britain's stabilization in 1925 prompted similar actions by Australia, the Netherlands, Switzerland, South Africa, and others. Four countries followed in 1926. By the end of 1927, the transition to fixed exchange rates was largely complete.

The new fixed exchange rate regime was a gold exchange standard, a variant of the prewar system. Gold coin no longer circulated internally, but citizens were entitled to convert domestic currency in excess of certain minimum amounts into ingots of gold. Gold imports and exports were unrestricted. Central banks, with few exceptions, were authorized by national statute to hold a portion of their backing for liabilities in convertible foreign assets rather than gold. The principal reserve currency countries, the United States and Britain, continued to hold mainly gold, while other central banks held a portion of their international reserves in the form of claims on London and New York. The same practice had been followed before World War I, with two notable differences. First, it had been neither so widespread nor so formal. Few central banks had been permitted to hold their official cover in the form of foreign exchange, although their excess reserves often took the form of interest-bearing foreign assets. Second, the currency diversification of foreign exchange reserves had not been so pronounced. Before the war, sterling accounted for fully half of the foreign currency reserves of central banks.[3] Now, as a result of the war the dollar had emerged as a full-fledged competitor with sterling for the mantle of leading reserve currency. But neither sterling nor the dollar accounted alone for a majority of the foreign exchange holdings of central banks.

If France's de facto stabilization in December 1926 is taken to mark the advent of this system and Britain's devaluation in September 1931 to mark its demise, this new fixed-rate regime survived for less than five full years. Even before its demise, its operation was viewed as unsatisfactory. The adjustment mechanism seemed inadequate. Some countries, such as Britain, were saddled with persistently weak balances of payments and hemorrhaged reserves for much of the period. Others, such as France and the United States, were in persistent surplus. The adjustments in asset and commodity markets that were supposed to restore external balance did not seem to operate. The management of

---

[3] Estimates of the currency composition of reserves before 1913 are provided by Lindert (1969).

international liquidity seemed inadequate. The supply of reserves declined precipitously in 1931 as central banks scrambled to liquidate their foreign deposits, and the flow of new gold into their coffers was slow to respond to the rise in real gold prices.

Four explanations for the unsatisfactory operation and early collapse of the fixed exchange rate system can be distinguished. Nurkse (1944) emphasized the failure of central banks to play by the "rules of the game"—in other words, their tendency to disregard balance-of-payments targets and to adapt policy instead to domestic economic conditions. Kindleberger (1973) emphasized the failure of the leading participant, the United States, to accept its responsibility for stabilizing the system by acting as international lender of last resort. Clarke (1967) and Eichengreen (1985) emphasized the lack of international economic policy coordination among the United States, Britain, France, and Germany. Finally, Mlynarski (1929) emphasized intrinsic instabilities—structural flaws—in the reconstructed system.

The gold exchange standard did not even guarantee nominal exchange rate stability. The fixed rate system began to crumble in 1929, after barely three years of operation. Argentina and Uruguay suspended gold payments in December of that year. Canada introduced new monetary restrictions tantamount to devaluation. Brazil, Chile, Paraguay, Peru, Venezuela, Australia, and New Zealand, without officially suspending gold convertibility, permitted their currencies to slip below par.

In 1931, depreciation spread to the industrial center. Austria and Germany, having experienced a decline in long-term capital inflows from the United States and the United Kingdom and confronting domestic banking panics, suspended gold convertibility and imposed exchange controls. Much of Eastern Europe followed. In general, these countries maintained their official gold parities but were able to adopt more expansionary policies, given the insulation of exchange controls. Britain's balance of payments weakened for different reasons, namely, a decline in interest and dividends on investments overseas. The devaluation of sterling in 1931, following a run on the Bank of England's reserves, induced some two dozen other countries to follow suit. Many pegged their currencies to the pound and, as time passed, held an increasing proportion of their international reserves in the form of sterling deposits in London. The world of international finance thus was partitioned into three segments: one in which currencies were pegged to gold; a second in which they were pegged, sometimes loosely, to sterling; and a third in which exchange control dominated. A few countries belonged to no group: Canada, for example, split the difference between sterling and the dollar, while Japan depreciated relative to sterling.

The next round of devaluations occurred in 1933, when Franklin D. Roosevelt took the U.S. off gold. The dollar lost 41% of its value against the gold standard currencies in the following nine months. Cuba, Guatemala, Panama, and the Philippines quickly followed the United States off gold. Many of the South American countries allowed their currencies to depreciate further to maintain competitiveness in the U.S. market, creating an informal dollar area. This pseudo dollar area lacked the stability and definition of its sterling counterpart, however. With France, Belgium, Switzerland, the Netherlands, Czechoslovakia, and Poland still maintaining gold convertibility and the sterling area countries tightening their pegs, the world was fragmented into not two but three currency areas. The pressure on the remaining gold standard countries intensified as their number dwindled. Czechoslovakia devalued in 1934, Belgium in 1935, France in 1936. France's action having reduced the group of gold standard countries enjoying exchange rate stability vis-à-vis one another to a negligible residual, those that remained devalued in response.[4]

A notable aspect of this episode is the extent to which governments attempted to influence currency movements through foreign exchange market intervention. In contrast to the experience with freely floating rates in the first half of the 1920s, between 1932 and 1936 governments intervened continually to damp fluctuations. Exchange equalization funds were established for the purpose. Endowed typically with some of the capital gains accruing to the authorities with the revaluation of the national gold reserve, these funds were charged with damping temporary exchange rate fluctuations. Whether to sterilize their intervention was officially a matter for the central bank, not for the Treasury authorities who controlled the equalization fund. It is suggested, however, that these funds sometimes operated in concert with the central bank to artificially depress the exchange rate, with the goal of enhancing the international competitiveness of domestic producers.[5]

Accounts of this managed floating regime portray it as no more

---

[4] The negotiations surrounding the French devaluation, which led to the Tripartite Agreement signed by Britain, France, and the United States, are interesting in their own right and for their implications for the subsequent course of exchange rates. These matters, which are discussed in Eichengreen (1985), are beyond the scope of the present paper.

[5] Two studies that examine the British case in detail are Hall (1935) and Howson (1980). The operations of other equalization funds are analyzed by Nurkse (1944).

satisfactory than the eras of free floating and fixed rates that preceded it. The transition to managed floating is portrayed as especially damaging. Devaluations were "beggar thy neighbor." They exacerbated the Great Depression overseas, it is alleged, while doing nothing to promote economic recovery in the initiating country.[6] Following the transition to managed floating, other damaging consequences surfaced. Although the authorities may have succeeded in reducing exchange rate volatility, they failed to eliminate exchange rate unpredictability. The uncertainties that ensued discouraged investment and exports that could have hastened recovery from the Great Depression.

Thus, the literature conveys an overwhelmingly negative impression of all three exchange rate regimes. Beyond this negative assessment, it provides little information with which to gauge the comparative performance of the alternative systems. It is to this question that I now turn.

III. Implications for Asset and Commodity Markets

The exchange rate data analyzed in this section are drawn mainly from Einzig (1937). Einzig compiled forward market quotations from weekly circulars of the Anglo-Portuguese Colonial and Overseas Bank. The spot and forward market observations are for the close of business each week. The forward rates are for delivery in 90 days.

Einzig's data cover seven countries: the United States, Switzerland, France, the Netherlands, Belgium, Italy, and Germany. These are the countries to which the analysis will be limited when forward market data are employed. When spot rates only are utilized, the sample can be extended to other countries by using exchange rate quotations drawn from *The Economist* magazine and the *Monthly Statistical Bulletin* of the League of Nations. When nominal and real exchange rates are compared, both are computed as monthly averages, with data on nominal exchange rates and wholesale prices from the League of Nations.

The three periods I consider are January 1922 through August 1926 (free floating), January 1927 through August 1931 (fixed exchange rates), and January 1932 through August 1936 (managed floating). As always, the division into periods is arbitrary. Continuous quotations of forward rates first became available in January 1921, but for

---

[6] This is the assertion of Kindleberger (1973), which has gained considerable currency.

reasons having to do with the availability of other variables, it is convenient to start the analysis in January 1922.[7] I choose January 1927 to mark the start of the fixed exchange rate period, since the French franc was stabilized in December 1926. Because most of the other currencies considered were stabilized at earlier dates, the choice of January 1927 should highlight the distinguishing features of the fixed-rate period. I end the fixed-rate period with August 1931. Britain floated the pound in September 1931, with Sweden, Norway, and Denmark following at the end of September, Finland in October, and Japan in December. But policies designed to manage the fluctuation of these exchange rates were adopted only in 1932. For this reason (and for symmetry with January 1922 and January 1927), I choose January 1932 to mark the start of the period of managed floating. I end the analysis in August 1936, the month before France, the Netherlands, and Switzerland devalued and the international monetary system was again transformed. The two periods of transition between regimes (September-December 1926 and September-December 1931) are difficult to assign to a particular period. I therefore omit them entirely.

I follow Einzig in using the pound sterling as the reference currency. The choice of reference currency for the computation of bilateral rates makes little difference for most of the conclusions that follow.[8] It turns out to matter for rankings of exchange rate stability across countries within periods, but not for rankings of overall stability across periods. Obviously, countries that pegged to sterling appear to have enjoyed the greatest exchange rate stability when sterling is used as the reference currency, while countries that pegged to other currencies appear to have enjoyed the greatest stability when those other currencies are used. But the average volatility of exchange rates under free floating compared with managed floating is largely unaffected by the choice of bilateral rate.

Here, even more than in other similar analyses, conclusions are likely to be dictated by outliers. The extreme behavior of exchange rates, interest rates, and prices during the German hyperinflation has a profound influence on international averages for 1922–26 compared with 1927–31 or 1932–36, even when a large cross-section of countries is considered. Therefore, I recalculate many of the summary statistics omitting the German data.

---

[7] I also limit my analysis of the flexible-rate period to 1922–26 in order to maximize comparability across tables. This periodization makes little if any difference for the results, as I indicate below.

[8] For the 1930s, it is also possible to compute trade-weighted effective exchange rates. These behave in similar fashion. See Eichengreen (1989a).

Figures 5.1 and 5.2 show the weekly spot and forward rate data for the entire period. Visual inspection of Fig. 5.1 makes it clear that spot rates behaved very differently between 1927 and 1931 than either before or after, but it does not suggest clear hypotheses about the relative stability of spot rates under free and managed floating.[9] The French, Belgian, and Italian rates appear to have been more volatile in the early 1920s than in the early 1930s, but it is not clear that this generalization holds for the Netherlands, Switzerland, and the United States. Similarly, French, Belgian, and Italian forward discounts appear to the naked eye to have displayed more volatility under free floating in the 1920s than under managed floating in the 1930s, but the same is not clearly true of the Netherlands, Switzerland, or the United States.

Table 5.1 summarizes the variability of spot exchange rates under

Table 5.1 Standard Deviations of Spot Rates and Risk Premiums: Weekly Data (£ as reference currency)

	Period 1: 1922–26	Period 2: 1927–31	Period 3: 1932–36
Spot Rates: $\log S_t - \log S_{t-1}$			
Belgium	.03307	.000520	.01715
Germany	.34851	.000956	.01053
Netherlands	.00331	.000743	.00959
Italy[a]	.01917	.008140	.00984
U.S.[b]	.00532	.000637	.01426
France	.03572	.000794	.00912
Switzerland[c]	.00567	.000844	.01117
mean w/o Germany	.01704	.000195	.01221
mean w/Germany	.06440	.001802	.01199
Risk Premiums: $\log F_t - \log S_{t+1}$			
Belgium	.12582	.00173	.07588
Germany[d]	.59342	.00288	N/A
Netherlands	.01343	.00218	.03492
Italy[e]	.07558	.04820	.03722
U.S.[b]	.02347	.00246	.05832
France	.11250	.00278	.03553
Switzerland[c]	.02194	.00325	.03589
mean w/o Germany	.06212	.01010	.04913
mean w/Germany	.20817	.00907	N/A

Notes: [a] Missing 11/30/35–12/21/35 (5 obs)
[b] Missing 3/11/33 (2 obs)
[c] Missing 12/10/32 (2 obs)
[d] Missing 1923.09–1924.11
[e] Missing 11/30/35–8/31/36
Source: See text.

[9] The horizontal lines in Fig. 5.2 for Germany in the 1930s reflect missing data.

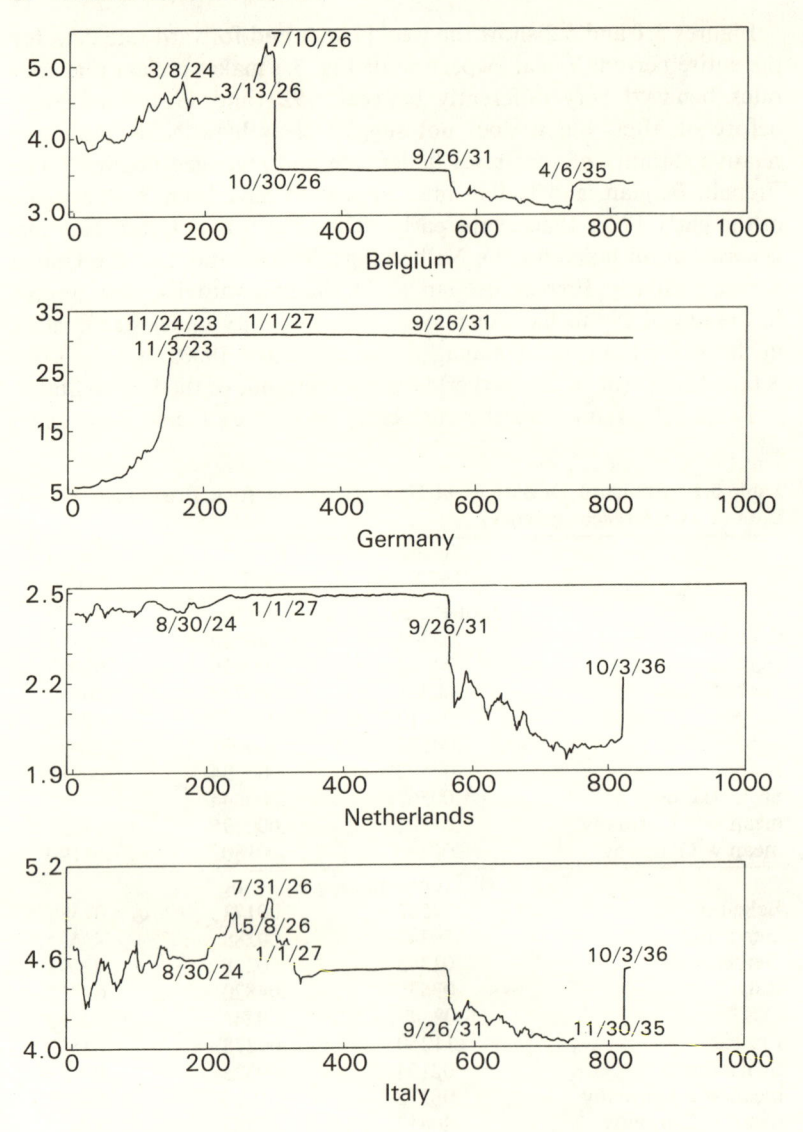

Figure 5.1
End-week Spot Rate

INSTABILITY BETWEEN THE WARS 81

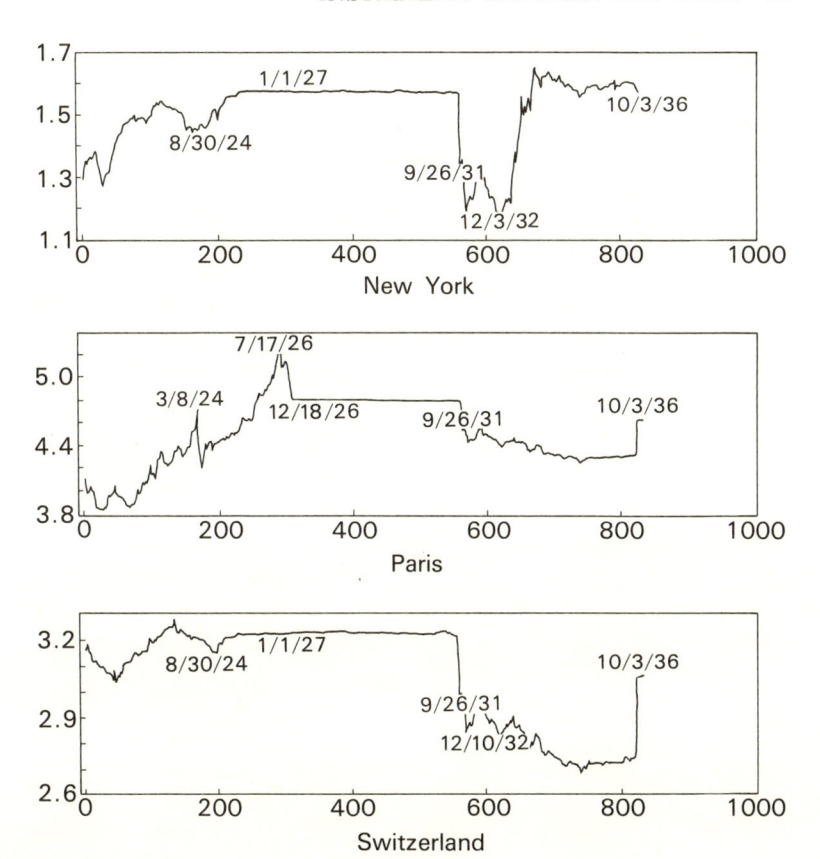

New York

Annotations: 1/1/27, 8/30/24, 9/26/31, 12/3/32, 10/3/36

Paris

Annotations: 7/17/26, 3/8/24, 12/18/26, 9/26/31, 10/3/36

Switzerland

Annotations: 1/1/27, 8/30/24, 9/26/31, 12/10/32, 10/3/36

82 BARRY EICHENGREEN

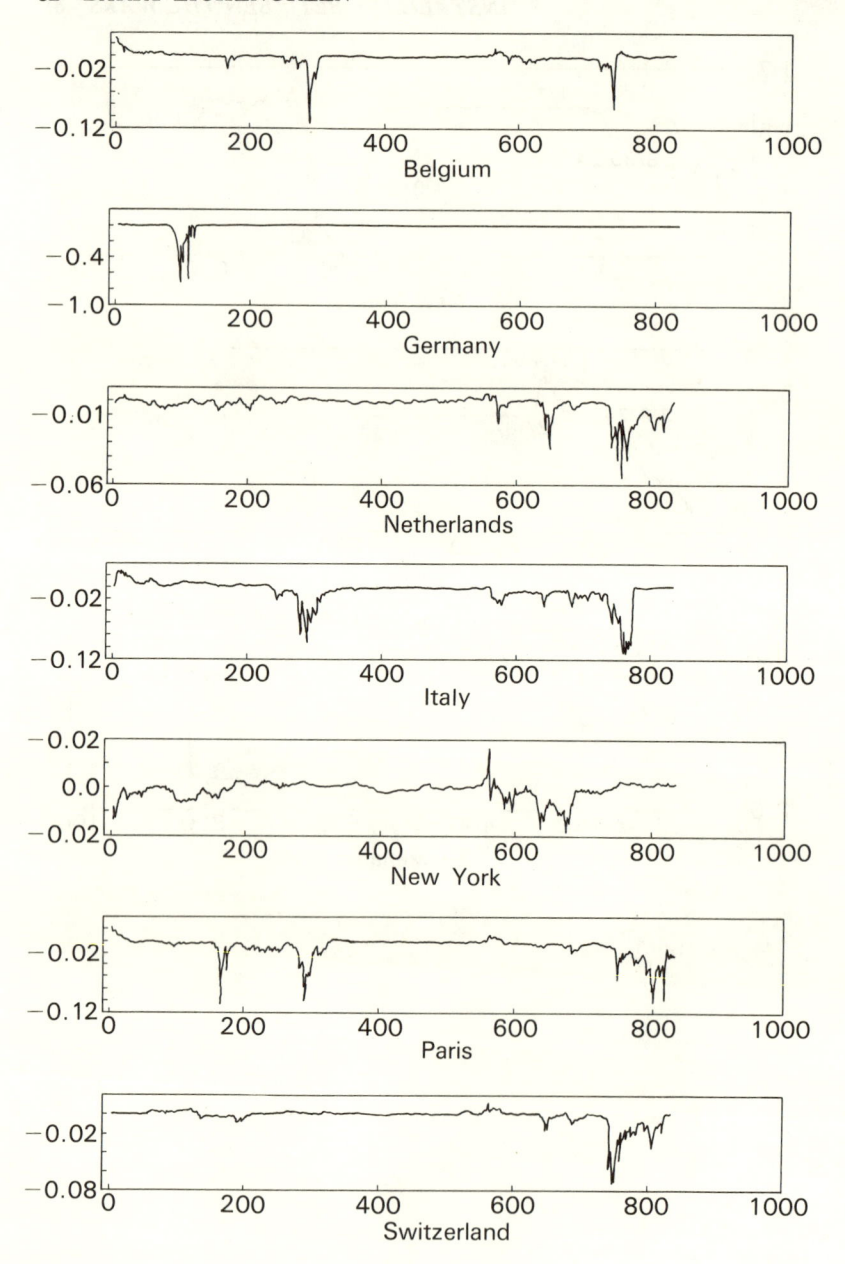

Figure 5.2
End-week Forward Rate

the three regimes. The exchange rate is defined as the foreign-currency price of the home currency. I measure variability using the standard deviation of the first difference in the log spot rate. By that measure, nominal exchange rate variability was greater during the period of freely floating exchange rates at the beginning of the 1920s than under managed floating in the 1930s. It was much greater in both periods of floating than under pegged rates from 1927 through 1931. Part of the contrast between 1922–26 and 1932–36 derives from the extreme behavior of exchange rates during the German hyperinflation. But even with Germany omitted, the standard deviations for 1922–26 are on average 40% larger than those for 1932–36. Intervention seems to have been associated with increased nominal exchange rate stability.

The *ex post* risk premium (the log forward rate minus the log spot rate at the time the forward contract matures) is shown in Figure 5.3. The bottom panel of Table 5.1 shows that on average the magnitude of the risk premium declined along with the variability of the spot rate with the shift from free to managed floating. But the extent of the decline is relatively small. The variability of the spot rate falls by 28% from the early 1920s to the early 1930s (Germany omitted), whereas the average risk premium falls by only 21%.[10]

The extreme variability of the risk premium is episodic. These episodes of large risk premiums tend to be associated with strong (overvalued?) exchange rates and coincide with depreciation abroad. Large risk premiums in the 1930s are evident in Fig. 5.3 for France, the Netherlands, and Switzerland. The panel for the Netherlands, for example, displays large spikes in the autumn of 1931 (following the devaluation of sterling), the summer of 1933 (following devaluation of the dollar), and the summer of 1935 (following devaluation of the belga).

The overall picture is one in which the reduction in nominal exchange rate variability achieved with the shift from free to managed floating was not accompanied by a comparable reduction in the exchange risk premium. An interpretation is that government policy succeeded in damping fluctuations in spot exchange rates on average, but was subject to periodic changes that were difficult to predict. That the

---

[10] When the sample is extended backward by a year and the periods 1921–26 and 1932–36 are compared, the average variability of the spot rate (Germany excluded) falls by 48%, while the average risk premium falls by 40%. A more sophisticated measure of the risk premium would subtract from the forward rate not the realized future spot rate, but a proxy for the expected future spot rate, perhaps constructed by projecting S_{t+1} on information available at time t. I plan to pursue this line of inquiry in future work.

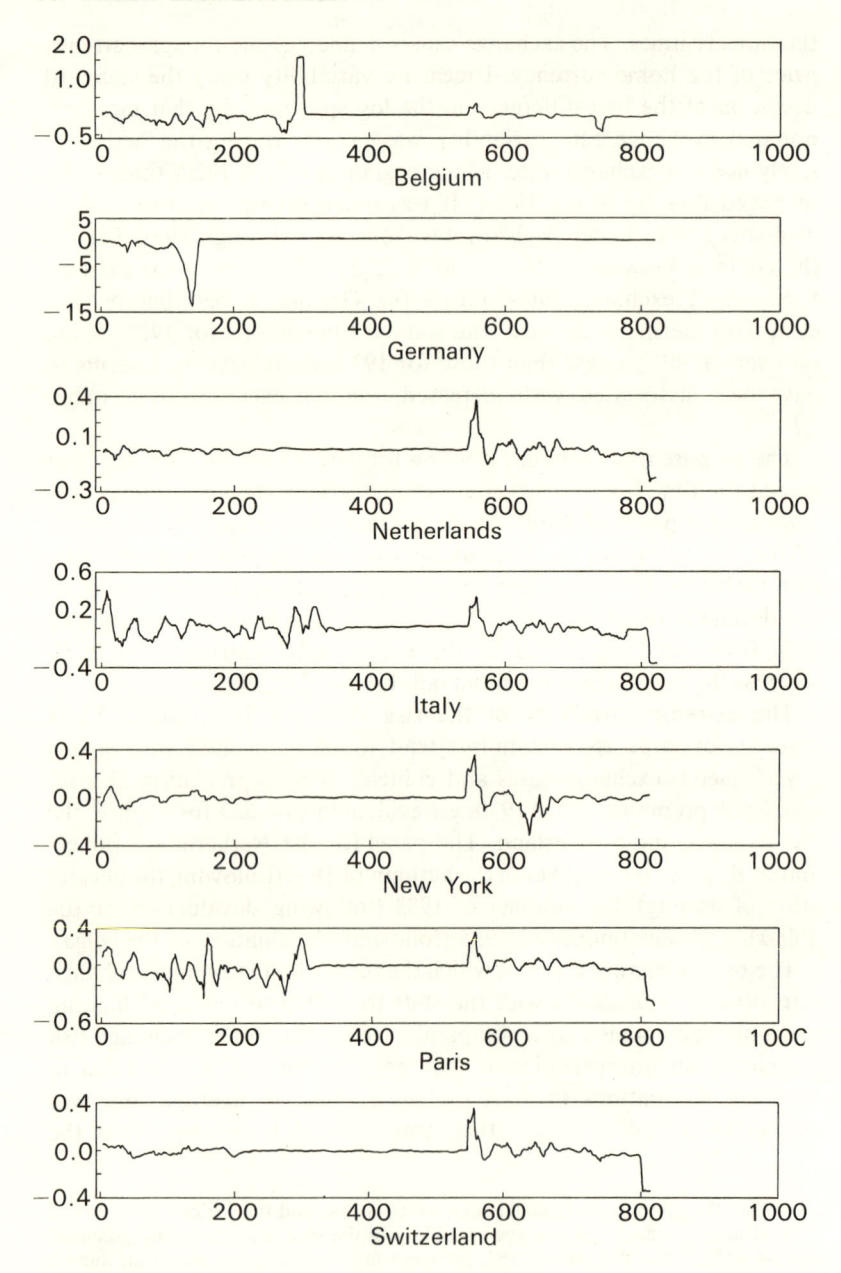

Figure 5.3
End-week Risk Premium

Table 5.2 Standard Deviations of Real Exchange Rates: Monthly Rates (mid-points) (£ as reference currency)

	Real Exchange Rate: $\log R_t - \log R_{t-1}$		
	Period 1 1922–26	Period 2 1927–31	Period 3 1932–36
Belgium	.0480	.0105	.0330
Germany[a]	.1380	.0077	.0212
Netherlands	.0148	.0109	.0231
Italy	.0371	.0156	.0204
U.S.	.0153	.0102	.0358
France	.0395	.0129	.0194
Switzerland	.0173	.0113	.0205
mean w/o Germany	.0292	.0121	.0254
mean w/Germany	.0584	.0114	.0248

Notes: [a] Missing 1923.09–1923.12 because of a break in the wholesale price index.
Source: See text.

decline in the variability of spot rates between the early 1920s and early 1930s was not accompanied, for most countries, by a commensurate decline in the variability of the risk premium suggests that the greater stability of spot rates in the 1930s did not imply a comparable reduction in uncertainty, nor did it necessarily indicate a significant improvement in welfare.

Table 5.2 summarizes the variability of the real exchange rate under the three regimes. Since wholesale price level data are not available for a wide sample of countries on a weekly basis, the real exchange rates in Table 5.2 are computed as monthly averages. The standard deviation of the first difference of the log real rate is on average 15% larger in the period of free floating than under managed floating.[11] The correlation between the standard deviation of the first differences of (log) nominal and real rates is extremely high in both the early 1920s and the early 1930s. For both periods, a regression of the standard deviation of real rates on the standard deviation of average monthly nominal rates (and on a constant term) yields t-statistics indicating statistical significance at better than the 99% per cent level.[12]

These questions can be considered from another perspective, subject

[11] The differential rises to 136% when Germany is included.
[12] This remains true for the early 1920s when the German outlier is excluded. A more demanding test of the significance of the association between real and nominal exchange rate variability is the rank sum statistic testing the hypothesis that real and nominal rates are drawn from distributions identical but for their medians. According to this statistic, the null hypothesis cannot be rejected for the early 1930s at the 95% level and for the early 1920s at the 90% level.

to assumptions about the information used to predict exchange rates. Table 5.3 summarizes the variability of the residuals from a standard exchange rate forecast. The log spot rate is regressed on a constant term and its own lagged value, and the standard deviation of the residuals from the forecasting equation is computed.[13] Monthly data are used (to facilitate comparisons with real exchange rates) and, since forward rate data are not utilized, the sample of countries can be expanded. Although the standard deviations of the exchange rate forecasts are larger under the managed float of the 1930s than the free float of the 1920s for 5 of the 11 countries, on average (excluding Germany) this measure of exchange rate unpredictability falls by about 15% when moving from the free to the managed float. Consistent with Table 5.1, this suggests that the reduction in exchange rate risk was smaller than the accompanying reduction in exchange rate variability.

Also interesting is the analogous measure of real exchange rate predictability in the second panel of Table 5.3. The standard deviation of the residuals from the real exchange rate forecast is larger under managed floating in 7 of 10 cases (Germany excluded). The unweighted average of this measure of the forecast error is nearly 10% larger under managed floating in the 1930s than under free floating in the 1920s (Germany again excluded). The exceptions are the high inflation countries of the 1920s: France, Belgium, and Italy. It would appear that there is a positive association between nominal and real exchange rate unpredictability when nominal rate variability and unpredictability reach high levels; otherwise, other factors may dominate. There is some evidence of a positive relationship between the predictability of nominal exchange rates and the predictability of real exchange rates in both periods of floating.[14] That relationship is slightly stronger under free than under managed floating: the correlation coefficient for the real and nominal exchange rate forecast errors is 0.89 under free

---

[13] This is more general than previous analyses, such as Rogoff (1985a) and Artis (1987), which construct the forecast on the assumption that the exchange rate follows a random walk with no drift. The regression coefficients underlying the forecasts are reported in the appendix tables. In most cases it is impossible to reject the random walk hypothesis, however. In Eichengreen (1989a), I also estimate forecasting equations by using a more general ARMA model and compute the same summary statistics. In future work, I plan to estimate forecasting equations that include also other information, such as lagged money and lagged prices.

[14] In Eichengreen (1988a), I documented the strong positive correlation between the variability of real and nominal exchange rates within both periods. The present result for the correlation between the variability of real and nominal exchange rate forecast errors within both periods is suggestive of stronger welfare implications.

Table 5.3 Exchange Rate Predictability (Standard deviations of residuals from exchange rate forecasts)

	Period 1: 1922–26	Period 2: 1927–31	Period 3: 1932–36
	Nominal Exchange Rate Predictability (in logs)		
Denmark	.03264	.00513	.03070
Finland	.02621	.00168	.02985
Norway	.03252	.00311	.02808
Sweden	.01061	.00178	.02995
Switzerland	.00993	.00156	.01729
U.S.	.01050	.00168	.02781
France	.06329	.00088	.01689
Netherlands	.00626	.00119	.01694
Belgium	.06998	.00093	.04190
Italy[e]	.03654	.01361	.01953
Germany[a]	.35805	.00128	.01953
Germany[b]	.01459		
Average excluding Germany	.02984	.00279	.02589
	Real Exchange Rate Predictability (in logs)		
Denmark	.02090	.02055	.02956
Finland	.01819	.01193	.03091
Norway	.02938	.01226	.03238
Sweden	.01384	.00930	.03039
Switzerland	.01553	.01084	.01863
U.S.	.01333	.01019	.02633
France	.03661	.01323	.01614
Netherlands	.01456	.01078	.02203
Belgium	.03589	.01007	.02685
Italy[e]	.03655	.01361	.01953
Germany[c]	.01836	.00755	.01953
Germany[d]	.01760		
Average excluding Germany	.02348	.01128	.02526

Notes: [a] 1922.01–1923.07 and 1923.12–1926.08
[b] 1922.01–1922.05 and 1924.01–1926.08
[c] 1922.01–1923.07 and 1924.01–1926.08
[d] 1924.02–1926.08
[e] 1935.12–1936.02 omitted because of missing data
Source: See text.

floating (10 countries, excluding Germany) and 0.74 under managed floating (11 countries).[15]

[15] If we regress the sample average real exchange rate forecast error on the nominal exchange rate forecast error (and a constant term) for each cross-section of ten countries (Germany excluded), we can reject the hypothesis of no association at the 99% confidence level for the early 1920s and at the 95% confidence level for the early 1930s.

Table 5.4 Standard Deviations of Detrended Log Differences of Industrial Production

	Period 1: 1922–26	Period 2: 1927–31	Period 3: 1932–36
Belgium	.11528	.07632	.03040
Denmark	.08454	.08149	.07651
Finland	.09103	.06258	.03180
France	.11307	.10970	.09920
Germany	.32660	.06892	.11120
Italy	.07355	.10395	.10940
Netherlands	.06854	.12811	.07451
Switzerland	.08087	.09266	.03249
Norway	.10761	.14494	.01542
Sweden	.06492	.06277	.07056
U.S.	.07863	.06277	.07314
U.K.	.07279	.03554	.04229
12-country average	.10645	.08575	.06143
Average excluding Germany	.08644	.08728	.05641

Source: See text.

The behavior of these variables is strikingly different during the period of fixed exchange rates. The standard deviation of the log difference in the spot rate was an order of magnitude smaller, by definition (Table 5.1). The standard deviation of the risk premium was also smaller, by approximately the same proportion. Table 5.3 confirms that the greater stability of spot rates in the gold-exchange standard period enhanced the predictability of the spot rate. It also enhanced the predictability of the real rate. For all but two countries, the real rate was easier to predict in the fixed-rate period than in either period of floating rates. This is impressive given the momentous terms of trade shocks to which the world economy was subjected between 1929 and 1931.[16]

Evidence that the nominal exchange rate regime had implications for the variability and predictability of real exchange rates suggests that it also may have affected other real variables responsive to relative price movements. Table 5.4 shows the standard deviation of the first difference of annual detrended (log) differences in industrial production for all three periods.[17] (A separate linear trend is fitted

---

[16] The classic account of the period emphasizing these terms of trade disturbances is by Lewis (1949). The regression coefficients underlying the real exchange rate forecasts are provided in Table A2.

[17] Industrial production indices are drawn from the League of Nations' *Statistical Bulletins*, as supplemented by Thorp (1984) and Hilgerdt (1945).

for each subperiod.) The variability of industrial production fluctuations around trend was greatest on average in the period of freely floating exchange rates (1922–26). Variations around trend were about twice as pronounced in the period of free floating as in the period of managed floating (1932–36). But there exists no simple correlation between the nominal exchange rate regime and the variability of output fluctuations. In the period of fixed rates (1927–31), fluctuations of output around trend were more variable than in the subsequent period of managed floating rates. Obviously, factors in addition to the nominal exchange rate regime conditioned the severity of the cycle. The naive explanation is that the fixed-rate period coincides with the onset of the Great Depression. In fact, the Depression is split between the fixed-rate and managed-floating periods. In many countries, the upswing was initiated every bit as rapidly after 1931 as the downturn set in after 1928. The important difference between the three periods lies in the fact that 1922–26 and 1932–26 comprise expansion phases of the business cycle in most countries in the sample, while 1927–31 spans the end of an expansion phase and the beginning of contraction; thus a linear trend explains less of the variance in the middle period.

A more revealing characterization of the cyclical implications of different exchange rate regimes appears in Table 5.5. It reports the correlation between detrended changes in industrial output in each European country and detrended output changes in the United States.[18]

Table 5.5 Correlation between Detrended 1st Difference of Log Industrial Production for 11 Countries and Detrended 1st Difference of Log Industrial Production for the United States

	Period 1: 1922/23–25/26	Period 2: 1927/28–30/31	Period 3: 1932/33–35/36
Belgium	.11930	−.48938	.32412
Denmark	.02477	.54291	.93253
Finland	.86299	.58823	.66942
France	−.29325	.76677	.03120
Germany	−.77650	.96724	.59853
Italy	.31334	.92535	.75760
Netherlands	−.06323	.73139	.33509
Switzerland	.42824	.92194	−.66008
Norway	.45774	.70943	−.19172
Sweden	−.09080	−.01861	.17119
U.K.	.01989	.97713	.40347
Average	.09114	.60204	.30659

Source: See text.

[18] A similar analysis of post-World War II data has been carried out by Baxter and Stockman (1988).

Data definitions and detrending methods are the same as in Table 5.4. The hypothesis underlying this table is that countries were more susceptible to external disturbances under fixed exchange rates. Industrial production in the United States, the largest industrial power of the period, is taken as a proxy for the external disturbances to which the European economies were subjected. The contrasts among periods are striking. The average correlation of industrial production fluctuations in Europe with industrial production movements in the United States was three times as large under managed floating as under freely floating exchange rates, and twice as large again under fixed rates as under managed floating. It appears that vulnerability to external disturbances was an increasing function of the stability of nominal exchange rates under the prevailing international monetary regime.

A possibility suggested by the grouping of countries in Table 5.5 is that the synchronization of business cycle disturbances may have varied across currency blocs in the 1930s. Not only might have industrial production in countries that pegged to the dollar moved closely with industrial production in the United States, but industrial production in sterling area countries would have moved closed with production in Britain if a sterling peg was an important determinant of the direction of international business cycle disturbances, and similarly for the members of the gold bloc. To test this hypothesis, I expanded the sample of countries to all those for which reasonable time series on industrial production could be obtained and which were readily categorized as members of an international monetary bloc in the 1930s. I distinguish gold bloc countries, members of the sterling area, and the group of countries which, following Germany, adopted stringent exchange controls. The question is whether industrial production is more variable across currency blocs than within them.

To answer this question, I compute the relevant variance ratio. I first calculated the average variance within groups:

$$\text{Var}_{\text{within}} = (1/n) \sum_{i=1}^{n} [1/(N_i - 1)] \sum_{j=1}^{N_i} (X_{ij} - \bar{X}_i)^2$$

where i indexes the group or currency bloc (of which there are n) and j the member of that group. X_{ij} and $\bar{X}_i$ are the individual observation and the corresponding group mean. This is contrasted with the variance for the entire sample of N countries:

$$\text{Var}_{\text{tot}} = [1/(N - 1)] \sum_i \sum_j (X_{ij} - X)^2$$

where $N = \sum_{i=1}^{n} N_i$, and $\bar{X}$ is the sample mean.

If differences in output behavior are small within groups but large between groups, the ratio of Var_{within} to Var_{tot} should be significantly less than one.

The first column of Table 5.6 reports the components of the variance ratio. It shows that output variation within groups accounts for more than half of the total variation for the sample of 19 countries. (I calculate these statistics using one observation for each of the 19 countries: the average annual rate of growth of industrial production over the period.) One way to judge these ratios is to compare them with variance ratios for the same sample of countries for the immediately preceding fixed exchange rate period. The bottom panel of the table shows that the variance between groups explains almost none of the total variance in the gold standard period. It is striking how much less of the total variance is accounted for by variation within groups in the subsequent period 1932–36. These patterns can be assessed formally by computing the F-statistic testing that there are no bloc-specific growth effects. The F(2, 16) of 6.2 for the 1930s is borderline significant at the 99% confidence level. That for 1927–31 is insignificant.

Insofar as output fluctuations were linked internationally by the adoption of a common peg, the plausible explanation is that adherence to a currency area required convergence of monetary and fiscal policies

Table 5.6 Variance Ratio Decompositions (variance times 1,000)

	1932/33–1935/36		
	Industrial Production	Money Supply	Budget Balance
Variance Within	1.1317	0.3152	6.256
Variance Between	0.7976	0.4721	13.107
Total Variance	1.9292	0.7873	19.936
	1927/28–1930/31		
Variance Within	1.0547	0.8547	3.394
Variance Between	0.1272	0.0823	14.577
Total Variance	1.1819	0.9370	17.904

Notes: The countries are Belgium, France, the Netherlands and Switzerland (members of the gold bloc); Austria, Bulgaria, Czechoslovakia, Germany, Hungary, Italy, Poland and Yugoslavia (exchange control); and Australia, Denmark, Finland, New Zealand, Norway, Sweden, and the U.K. (sterling area). Belgium is not included in the money supply column. Australia, Italy and Bulgaria are not included in the industrial production column. Budget figures for Belgium, the Netherlands, Austria, Hungary, Poland, Bulgaria, Germany, Italy, Yugoslavia, Australia, Denmark and New Zealand are for 1928/29–1930/31 instead of 1927/28–1930/31.

Source: See text.

within currency blocs, while the maintenance of floating rates between sterling, the franc and the dollar, along with the adoption of exchange control elsewhere, permitted the divergence of policies across blocs. Table 5.6 therefore reports variance ratios for annual percentage changes in the money supply and the government budget deficit. Data for money supplies are taken from the same sources as above; those for the budget balance (adjusted to remove government borrowing from total revenues) are from various issues of the League of Nations' *Public Finances*. Table 5.6 confirms that adherence to a currency bloc induced monetary and fiscal policy convergence among its members. The variance between blocs accounts for the majority of the total variance of changes in money supplies in the sample. The F-statistic for money for 1932–36 is highly significant, but that for 1927–31 is totally insignificant. The evidence on fiscal policy is more difficult to interpret. While the F-statistic testing for bloc-specific fiscal policy effects is highly significant for 1932–36 (indicating convergence), so is that for 1927–31. A possible interpretation is that the pressures which led some countries to go off gold in 1931 were already evident in their fiscal stances in the immediately preceding years.

In summary, the nominal exchange rate regime in effect for different portions of the interwar period had a first-order impact on both asset and commodity markets. Nominal exchange rate variability was considerably greater under free than under managed floating. But the reduction of nominal variability under managed floating did not deliver a comparable reduction in nominal exchange rate uncertainty, whether measured by the exchange risk premium or by the accuracy of a naive exchange rate forecast. Neither did it uniformly enhance the predictability of real exchange rates. The move to fixed nominal rates, in contrast, significantly enhanced the predictability of real exchange rates. The nominal exchange rate regime also had implications for the synchronization of business cycle disturbances across countries. The degree of synchronization was greater under fixed than under floating rates, and greater within currency blocs in the 1930s than across them. Differences in the degree of synchronization in turn reflect differences in the degree of convergence of policies.

IV. Causes of International Monetary Disintegration

It had long been recognized that the sustainability of a fixed exchange rate depended on a willingness to adopt policies consistent with the exchange rate target. Since the essence of a fixed exchange rate under the gold-exchange standard was the maintenance of a stable domestic currency price of gold, the supply of domestic currency had to be adapted to variations in demand that obtained at the price fixed by statute. The price-specie flow mechanism brought about this result automatically under a gold coin standard. It continued to do so under a gold bullion standard so long as the authorities maintained the convertibility of domestic currency into gold and did not otherwise alter the money supply. Moreover, central banks could minimize the need for gold movements by altering domestic monetary conditions in the direction dictated by incipient gold flows. They could respond to a gold outflow with an open market sale, reducing the monetary base, or raise the discount rate, reducing the money multiplier. Either initiative would bring about the requisite stringency in domestic financial markets and minimize the need for further gold flows. This, following Keynes (1925), came to be known as playing by the rules of the game.

The first explanation for the inadequacies of the adjustment mechanism under the interwar gold standard and for that system's early demise was the failure of central banks to play by the rules of the game. Rather than reinforcing the effect on domestic money and credit conditions of incipient international gold flows, policymakers sterilized reserve movements instead. Nurkse (1944) tabulated the number of instances, in annual data, when the domestic and foreign assets of central banks moved in the same direction, as they would have if changes in foreign reserves were permitted to alter domestic money supplies, and the number of instances in which they moved in opposite directions, as they would have when central banks engaged in sterilization. He found that only a minority of central banks obeyed the rules of the game, 32% in 1927, 21% in 1928, 20% in 1929, 35% in 1930, and 19% in 1931.[19]

Arthur Bloomfield (1959) criticized Nurkse's conclusion on the grounds that by Nurkse's own measure, central banks violated the rules of the game every bit as often between 1880 and 1913. Therefore, he argued, violations of the rules could not explain the instability of the interwar gold standard, since they had been equally prevalent under its admirably stable prewar ancestor. But Bloomfield based his comparison on the entire interwar period and the years 1880–1914. When the comparison is limited to the two periods of fixed rates (1880–1913 and 1927–31), it is clear that violations of the rules were not equally prevalent before 1913. A rise in the incidence of those

[19] Nurkse (1944), 69.

violations can help to account for the instability of the interwar system.

Other historical developments lend plausibility to this argument. In many countries, the extent of the franchise was broadened as a result of World War I. It no longer was conscionable—or in any case feasible—to send members of the working class off to war without also entitling them to vote. The consequent growth of parliamentary labor parties created pressure to direct monetary policy toward the reduction of unemployment rather than to abstruse financial ends. The rise in recorded unemployment rates lent the matter additional urgency. Even before the Great Depression struck, industrial unemployment rates in many countries had reached unprecedented levels. For the first time, reputable experts such as Keynes advanced arguments of how monetary conditions could be systematically manipulated to improve the state of the domestic economy.

A standard approach to testing for violations of the rules of the game is to estimate reaction functions relating the change in domestic assets both to the change in foreign assets and to the change in other variables likely to influence the stance of monetary policy. Time series regressions are used to confirm or reject that particular central banks obeyed the rules.[20]

Here I adopt a slightly different approach, analyzing the behavior of a cross-section of 21 countries. Table 5.7 reports regressions relating the (percentage) change in domestic assets to the change in foreign assets and to the change in industrial production (a proxy for the state of the domestic economy).[21] The uniformly negative coefficients on the change in foreign assets confirm that central banks tended to sterilize reserve flows in each year of the system's operation, in violation of the rules. In contrast, the coefficients on the change in industrial production are unstable. In 1927–28 there seems to have been an

---

[20] Studies that adopt this approach using time series data for Great Britain are Goodhart (1972) for the pre-1914 period and Eichengreen, Watson, and Grossman (1985) for 1925–31. Roubini (1988) has shown that the standard interpretation is consistent with a model of an optimizing central bank. In response to most shocks, a central bank concerned mainly with domestic conditions (specifically, the stability of domestic interest rates) will adopt policies that result in negative comovements of domestic and foreign assets. Positive comovements will be observed if there is a relatively high weight on external targets (specifically, the stability of the level of reserves) in the central bank objective function.

[21] The change in domestic and foreign assets is taken from Nurkse (1944), Appendix 1, and from the League of Nations' *Monetary Reviews*. The equations are estimated by ordinary least squares. This creates potential problems of endogeneity bias, given that foreign reserves are likely to respond to domestic open market operations through the balance of payments. I plan to correct for this in future work.

Table 5.7 **The Rules of the Game: Determinants of the Change in Domestic Assets 1927–31 (Dependent variable: Percentage change in domestic assets of central banks)**

Years	Constant	Percentage Change in Foreign Assets	Percentage Change in Industrial Production	Percentage Change in Foreign Assets for Reserve Countries	n
1927–28	0.392	−0.101	−3.586		18
	(0.078)	(0.031)	(0.824)		
1928–29	0.065	−0.437	0.576		20
	(0.034)	(0.099)	(0.424)		
1929–30	−0.069	−0.176	0.367		21
	(0.024)	(0.044)	(0.394)		
1930–31	0.087	−0.212	−0.410		21
	(0.044)	(0.058)	(0.352)		
Pooled	0.045	−0.097	−0.354		80
	(0.019)	(0.028)	(0.195)		
1927–28	0.420	−0.107	−3.761	4.027	18
	(0.77)	(0.030)	(0.798)	(2.628)	
1928–29	−0.065	−0.437	0.578	−0.175	20
	(0.035)	(0.103)	(0.438)	(1.851)	
1929–30	−0.020	−0.259	0.341	0.945	21
	(0.021)	(0.076)	(0.278)	(1.019)	
1930–31	0.095	−0.212	−0.420	0.761	21
	(0.044)	(0.058)	(0.350)	(0.679)	
Pooled	0.045	−0.097	−0.354	0.028	80
	(0.019)	(0.028)	(0.197)	(0.749)	

Notes: Standard errors are in parentheses. *Source*: See text.

Country List
1. Austria
2. Hungary
3. Czechoslovakia
4. Poland
5. Colombia (industrial production missing 1927/28)
6. Mexico (domestic assets missing 1927/28, 1928/29)
7. Japan
8. Chile
9. Denmark
10. Finland
11. France
12. Germany
13. Greece (domestic assets missing 1927/28, 1928/29)
14. Italy
15. Netherlands
16. Norway
17. Sweden
18. U.S.
19. U.K.
20. Switzerland
21. Romania

Table 5.8 The Rules of the Game: Determinants of the Change in Domestic Assets, Further Results 1927–31 (Dependent variable: Percentage change in domestic assets of central banks)

	(1)	(2)
Constant	0.032	0.033
	(0.018)	(0.018)
Percentage Change in	−0.051	−0.051
Foreign Assets (%△FA)	(0.029)	(0.029)
Percentage Change in	−0.291	−0.292
Industrial Production	(0.186)	(0.187)
1928–29* %△FA	−0.377	−0.377
	(0.142)	(0.142)
1929–30* %△FA	−0.171	−0.172
	(0.157)	(0.158)
1930–31* %△FA	−0.205	−0.206
	(0.076)	(0.077)
%△FA for Reserve Countries		0.130
		(0.702)
Standard Error of the regression	0.156	0.157
n	80	80

Source: See Table 5.7 and text.

attempt to use monetary policy in countercyclical fashion. Subsequently, there is no clear relationship.

Can these findings help to explain the increasing difficulties of the interwar system as the fixed exchange rate period progressed? Table 5.8 shows that the coefficient on foreign assets tended to increase in absolute value after 1927–28. In effect, sterilization became more complete, consistent with the hypothesis that domestic monetary policies not directed toward external targets were a part of the problem. At the same time, it should be noted that the coefficient reaches its largest absolute value in 1928–29, not in 1930–31. Something else besides the growth of sterilization presumably contributed to the system's collapse in 1931.

A second explanation for the instability of the interwar system emphasizes inadequate leadership. Kindleberger (1973) argues that the stability of a system of fixed exchange rates requires management by a leading international financial power. This leading power, or hegemon, must serve as international lender of last resort, providing liquidity to weak links in the chain of fixed exchange rates. It must do so both by engaging in countercyclical, or at least stable, long-term lending and by providing emergency loans to foreign central banks in times of crisis. The hegemon can further ease balance-of-payments pressure on weak-currency countries by maintaining an open market for their exports. Absent such intervention, the weak links will be forced to devalue, permitting skepticism about the stability of other currencies to spread and threatening the viability of the system. Thus, by offering loans to the weak-currency countries, the hegemon supplies the international public good upon whose adequate provision the viability of a system of fixed exchange rates depends. This explanation differs from the preceding one in that the stability of the system of fixed rates depends not just on individual national policies, but also on the adequate provision of this international public good.

According to Kindleberger, Britain served as hegemon before 1913, as did the United States after 1945. The instability of the interwar gold exchange standard reflected the fact that Britain was no longer able to stabilize the system, whereas the United States was not yet willing to do so. Lending was procyclical rather than countercyclical. The provision of emergency liquidity to foreign central banks was inadequate. Rather than maintaining an open market, the United States adopted the Smoot-Hawley Tariff at the worst possible moment.

While this explanation contains a kernel of truth, its importance can be exaggerated. The period to which it best applies is the early years of the Bretton Woods System, when U.S. dominance of international financial and commodity markets was unrivaled.[22] By the 1960s, the stability of the Bretton Woods System hinged not on hegemonic leadership by the United States but rather on collective management by the industrial countries, through gold pooling, policy coordination, and the willingness to hold dollar reserves exclusively in order to stabilize the system. For the period before 1913, it is even more evident that the stability of the system depended on collective, not hegemonic, management. Notwithstanding Britain's preeminence in international markets, fending off convertibility crises required assistance by a group of central banks. On several occasions, the Bank of England was the international borrower of last resort, and Continental central banks, such as the Bank of France, were the international lenders. Insofar as the international economic difficulties of the 1920s and 1930s illustrated the importance of collective management, this was neither the first nor the last time when the observation would be pertinent.

The recognition that international monetary stability could be

[22] Even then, the stability of the international monetary system depended on other special factors, including the maintenance of inconvertibility as late as 1958. I evaluate the applicability of hegemonic stability theories to this experience in Eichengreen (1989b).

critically affected by the actions of the entire group of industrial countries provides the rationale for the third explanation, which emphasizes international cooperation. According to Clarke (1967), the collapse of the gold-exchange standard resulted from the failure of cooperation between the central banks of Britain, France, Germany, and the United States. Cooperation was adequate through the summer of 1928 but a dismal failure thereafter. The death of Benjamin Strong, who as Governor of the Federal Reserve Bank of New York played a leading role in the international economic affairs of the United States, dealt the fatal blow. Strong was on good personal terms with his British counterpart, Montague Norman, and with other foreign central bankers. This enabled them to negotiate a cooperative solution to the sterling crisis of 1927.[23] Strong's successor, Benjamin Harrison, attached less weight to the affairs of other nations, and cooperation was not forthcoming in 1929 or 1931.

Clarke's thesis has been objected to on grounds of timing and for its emphasis on personalities.[24] One can cite significant instances of failed cooperation before 1928 and successes thereafter. It is difficult to believe that the fate of the international monetary system would have differed fundamentally had Benajmin Strong's health been more robust.

Even if one rejects Clarke's definition of cooperation which focuses on negotiations among central bankers, and the sharp distinction he draws between the pre- and post-1928 years, it is still possible to argue that the failure of international cooperation contributed to the collapse of the fixed-rate system. The argument is that France and the United States, in particular, failed to coordinate their macroeconomic policies internationally. The two central banks had incompatibly large demands for the world's scarce gold reserves, and they pursued tight monetary policies in an effort to obtain gold from one another. As in a noncooperative game, their efforts were offsetting and resulted in a suboptimal equilibrium. The cooperative solution would have been a coordinated reduction in discount rates which left the international distribution of gold unchanged but exerted expansionary pressure on their economies. As Keynes wrote: "What helps each central bank is

---

[23] The New York Fed cooperated by lowering its discount rate, obviating the need for the Bank of England to raise its rate. Thus the pressure on sterling was ameliorated without a rise in interest rates when the world economy was poised on the verge of recession. Those who follow Clarke interpret this as an example of cooperation (although it also might be interpreted as a purely self-interested action by a Fed alarmed by the danger of an American recession).

[24] Kindleberger (1973), 298–99.

not a high Bank rate but a higher rate than the others. So that a raising of rates all round helps no one until, after an interregnum during which the economic activity of the whole world has been retarded, prices and wages have been forced to a lower level."[25] In this view, it was the failure of international economic policy coordination, and the inability or unwillingness of any one central bank to expand unilaterally in the presence of the external constraint, that brought about the post-1928 deflation.

France and the United States were not the only countries involved. For both to remain in surplus throughout the period, someone else had to be in deficit. The someone else was industrial countries with weak currencies, such as Britain and Germany, and the primary-product exporters. Not only were the noncooperative strategies pursued by the central banks of the surplus countries a source of deflationary pressure on the world economy, but they heightened the vulnerability of other central banks to speculative attack. By draining reserves from the coffers of the Reichsbank and the Bank of England, they increased the susceptibility of these central banks to destabilizing shocks. Inadequate international policy coordination thereby helps to account for the instability of the international monetary system and for the collapse of prices and economic activity.

This framework permits a reformulation of Kindleberger's emphasis on leadership. Leadership can be modeled as the Stackelberg strategy in a noncooperative policy game. The Stackelberg leader, say the United States, could lower its discount rate, despite the effect of such a policy on its reserve position, because it correctly anticipated that other countries would respond in kind. By internalizing at least some of the international externalities associated with national economic policies, the leader-follower solution could be Pareto superior to the Nash strategy described by Keynes.[26] But the gains from following exceed the gains from leading. The followers benefit from increased reserves and lower world interest rates. The leader, in contrast, benefits from lower interest rates but incurs a cost from lower reserves. Although there are plausible conditions under which both leader and followers gain, each player prefers someone else to lead. Moreover, as the leader grows smaller relative to the international market, the gains from adopting the role of leader tend to diminish. Thus, this formulation both provides an explanation for the absence of leader-

[25] Keynes (1929), 778–779.
[26] An explicit model that demonstrates circumstances under which these results obtain is sketched in Eichengreen (1985).

ship and helps one to understand why that problem was especially serious in the increasingly multipolar international economy of the 1920s. At the same time, it suggests that if leadership had advantages over other forms of noncooperative behavior, full international economic cooperation had greater advantages still.

At precisely the same time policy coordination was becoming more difficult, it was becoming more important. With the growing weight attached to internal targets, the credibility of the commitment to the exchange rate was no longer above question. Speculative capital was less likely to flow in stabilizing directions. Policies that led to a drain of reserves of a given magnitude could have more serious ramifications for the stability of the international monetary system than before the war.

Each of the three explanations discussed so far focuses on misguided national policies. A fourth emphasizes instead flaws in the structure of the system. In this view, the intrinsic problem of the interwar system was that it was a gold exchange standard rather than a pure gold standard.[27] In principle, the dual nature of reserves under the gold exchange standard could create problems of stability by relaxing the external constraint on the reserve-currency countries. These countries had no need to adjust to reserve losses, because they could finance them by providing domestic assets to foreign central bankers, who happily accumulated them as reserves. There would be no pressure to restore external balance.

This thesis would predict excessive creation of international reserves and inflation, where the opposite was the case. It holds little water for the United States, which strained the international system by running persistent surpluses, not persistent deficits. It would predict an even weaker response by the reserve-currency countries, principally Britain and the United States, to reserve inflows and outflows than was typical of other countries. Tables 5.7 and 5.8 test for this possibility by interacting the change in foreign assets with a dummy variable for the two reserve-currency countries. While the coefficient has the anticipated sign (suggesting that these countries took exceptionally feeble steps to alter domestic credit in response to changes in foreign assets), it is impossible to reject the hypothesis that these countries responded identically to the others in the sample.

A more plausible variant of the thesis emphasizes instabilities created by spontaneous portfolio shifts between alternative reserve assets.

---

[27] Two clear if skeptical formulations of this hypothesis are Mlynarski (1929, 75–76) and Nurkse (1944, p. 44).

The problem is similar to the one highlighted by Triffin (1960) in his critique of the Bretton Woods System. Triffin emphasized the dynamic instability of a system which relied for international liquidity on gold and dollars. The flow supply of new gold being relatively inelastic, the incremental liquidity of the expanding international economy took the form predominantly of dollars. Once the stock of dollar claims held by foreign central banks approached the value of U.S. gold reserves, the U.S. commitment to peg the dollar price of gold would no longer be credible. The danger was that a run on the dollar would lead to a sudden contraction of the supply of international liquidity and to the collapse of the system.

The problem for the interwar system was similar. While the U.S. gold stock was sufficiently large relative to foreign claims that a forced devaluation of the dollar could be fended off, loss of confidence still led to a massive liquidation of international reserves. The existence of two reserve currencies, sterling and the dollar, enhanced the ease with which central banks could shift between them. Once the suspension of convertibility by Austria and Germany in the summer of 1931 drove home the riskiness of exchange reserves, central banks and others began to shift out of sterling, the weakest reserve currency. Gresham's Law operated in reverse, with the good reserve driving out the bad. Britain's forced devaluation in September 1931 then shifted pressure toward the dollar. The Fed responded by tightening credit, which intensified pressure on foreign central banks already doing battle with weak payments positions and encouraged them to throw in the towel. In a counterfactual in which central banks held their reserves exclusively in gold, it would seem unlikely that the Austrian and German financial crises would have led to the liquidation of sterling on the same scale, or to the subsequent domino effects.

As noted above, the practice of holding foreign exchange reserves was not new. It had been encouraged and institutionalized precisely in the belief that the counterfactual of a pure gold-based system was not viable. The contemporary view was that the supply of gold had not increased over the first quarter of the 20th century at anything approaching the increase in demand. To preclude a costly deflation, at the Genoa Conference in 1922 the British proposed formalizing the practice of holding reserves in convertible foreign exchange. Although these proposals were not accepted, their spirit was incorporated into statutes adopted by central banks in subsequent years. The practice of holding foreign exchange reserves spread. This attempt to maintain diversified reserve portfolios of gold and foreign exchange created the possibility of a confidence-induced, spontaneous contraction in the reserve base, given the inability of any reserve country to unconditionally guarantee the convertibility of its currency into gold at a fixed price. And that spontaneous contraction of the supply of reserves could greatly intensify the pressure on central banks defending weak exchange rates. Thus, the hybrid nature of its reserve supply rendered the interwar system especially vulnerable to a destabilizing shock.[28]

This is where the Great Depression enters the story, since it was a destabilizing shock on a massive scale. The Depression led to a decline of nearly 50% in dividends and interest earnings on British foreign investments, which accounted for more of the deterioration in the British current account than any other single item. It thereby rendered one of the two leading reserve currencies ripe for speculative attack. The curtailment of U.S. and British foreign lending that coincided with the onset of the Depression contributed to the payments difficulties of Austria and Germany. Together with the deterioration of industrial performance, this created difficulties for the two countries' banking systems. The Depression thereby paved the way for the Austrian and German banking panics and for their suspension of convertibility, which further undermined confidence in sterling. The terms-of-trade deterioration suffered by primary-product exporters moved their payments balances into deficit, eroded their reserves, and increased their susceptibility to further external shocks. Thus, when the liquidation of foreign exchange reserves and the scramble for gold induced a tightening of credit conditions, exchange rates were already poised on the verge of collapse.

The Depression plays an equally central role in the other explanations for the disintegration of the international monetary system. The deterioration in domestic economic conditions intensified the pressure felt by central banks to bend the rules of the game. A remarkable feature of the period is the extent to which central bankers continued to direct policy toward the defense of the exchange rate, despite the collapse of money supplies, prices, and economic activity. But the deterioration in domestic economic conditions induced them to stretch the rules in ways that heightened the danger of a convertibility crisis.

Similarly, the Depression magnified the international monetary

---

[28] What mattered for the stability of the international monetary system was not that central banks liquidated their foreign exchange reserves, but that they attempted simultaneously to replace them with gold. Given the limited availability of monetary gold in the world economy, this could be accomplished only by increasing discount rates, tightening credit conditions and attempting to acquire specie from abroad, the consequence of which was to intensify the pressure on weak currency countries. See Eichengreen (1988b).

consequences of the failure of cooperation. With the shock imparted to the system by the deepening Depression, the need for loans to provide emergency liquidity to weak central banks grew more pressing. The need for international coordination of macroeconomic policies to counter the macroeconomic crisis that was undermining their position became all the more urgent.

What lessons are to be drawn from this experience for the optimal design and operation of fixed exchange rate systems? The circumspect answer is none. It is hard to imagine any fixed-rate system that could have withstood a disturbance on the scale of the Great Depression. At the risk of being inadequately circumspect, I would suggest three lessons. First, the sustainability of fixed-rate regimes rests on the credibility of policymakers' commitment to the system. If policymakers harbor reservations about the tradeoffs between exchange rate targets and other objectives, speculative pressures are sure to force the issue. Second, a fixed-rate system does not obviate the need for international policy coordination.[29] To the contrary, policy coordination is integral to the successful operation of fixed-rate systems. Third, the composition of international reserves is more than a technical detail in the design of fixed-rate systems. The stability of these systems may hinge on the adequacy of the reserve-supply mechanism.

The circumspect answer is predicated, implicitly, on the assumption that the Depression was exogenous to the operation of the international monetary system. It is to this assumption that I now turn.

V. *The Role of the International Monetary System in the Great Depression*

Imagine that a group of countries is subjected to a deflationary shock. For present purposes, it is largely irrelevant whether the initial disturbance is real or monetary. If it is monetary, real variables such as output and employment follow money and prices down. If it is real, the quantity of money contracts as the demand for it declines. The critical question is what options are available to the central banks of the countries affected. If the exchange rate was of no concern, any one central bank could unilaterally initiate expansionary open market operations to stem the contraction of money supply. If central banks

---

[29] The idea that fixed rates can function as surrogates for international policy coordination has been argued by Canzonari and Gray (1985), albeit in what they admit is a special case.

were committed to the maintenance of fixed exchange rates, it would be possible to initiate an internationally coordinated expansion of money supplies, arranged in such a way that no one exchange rate suffered undue weakness. But with a commitment to fixed rates and absent cooperation, reflationary action would be constrained. Expansionary open market operations or discount rate reductions would lead to a rise in imports, a capital outflow, a loss of reserves and, ultimately, an attack on the exchange rate.

The same external constraints would limit the use of fiscal policy. Except in the presence of high international capital mobility and asset substitutability, a unilateral increase in deficit spending weakens the exchange rate. By raising spending on imports and crowding out exports, it leads to a current account deficit, a loss of reserves and, ultimately, an attack on the exchange rate. Under these circumstances, a commitment to a fixed exchange rate requires that any significant fiscal expansion be coordinated internationally.[30]

This is the principal channel through which the gold exchange standard exacerbated the Great Depression. Given fixed rates, reflation required cooperation. Absent cooperation, reflation was impossible.

This thesis assumes that the effects of the international monetary system came into play only following the initial shock. The international monetary system contributed to the depth and duration of the Great Depression, not to its onset. One can construct an argument under which the same constraints contributed to the Depression's onset. For example, Hamilton (1987) argues that tight monetary policy in the United States played an important role in the onset of the Depression. Tight monetary policy also contributed to America's payments surpluses and to incipient reserve losses abroad, forcing other countries such as Britain and Germany to raise their discount rates in the first half of 1929. But the explanation for the onset of the Depression remains too controversial for this to be more than speculation.

In addition, the thesis assumes that gold standard countries maintained an unbending commitment to their fixed exchange rates. Reality was more complex. Once forced from the gold standard, countries like Britain luxuriated in their newfound freedom, adopting policies of cheap money and allowing their exchange rates to fall as needed rather than repegging at a lower parity. Others like Germany main-

---

[30] Sachs and Wyplosz (1984) show how the substitutability of domestic and foreign goods in consumption, the substitutability of domestic and foreign assets in portfolios, and the degree of international capital mobility interact to produce different exchange rate effects of fiscal policy. Most observers would agree that the case discussed in the text is the one relevant to the 1930s.

tained the pretense of a fixed exchange rate but adopted exchange controls that were tantamount to depreciation. Still others like Sweden took Britain's devaluation as an opportunity to reject the gold standard in favor of cheap money and a depreciated exchange rate. But fixed exchange rates remained a constraint for virtually every industrial country until the final months of 1931 and, for a significant subset of countries, for several subsequent years. Recognition that the exchange rate constraint might be incompatible with recovery took shape in the United States only in 1933, in Belgium only in 1935, in France, the Netherlands, and Switzerland in 1936.

Several factors explain this commitment. The gold standard was viewed as synonymous with financial stability, and financial stability was viewed as necessary for economic recovery. Financial centers such as London, New York, Amsterdam, and Switzerland saw the maintenance of fixed rates as essential to their ability to compete successfully in the financial services industry. In countries like France and Belgium, which had suffered persistent inflation in the 1920s, the public associated depreciation with inflation and social chaos, and politicians sought to resist it at any cost.

Finally, the thesis stated above assumes that the international coordination of reflationary initiatives proved impossible to achieve. Although it was suggested on more than one occasion that international coordination of policies could relax the external constraint, efforts at implementation proved unavailing. In 1930–31, Keynes urged the Bank of England to expand, in the hope that it could induce the Fed to follow. The British Treasury unsuccessfully pressured the Bank of France to expand. In 1933, at the World Economic Conference, it was the hope of a number of national delegations that a program of internationally coordinated reflation could be adopted.[31] There is no simple explanation for the failure of these initiatives. Some governments were beholden to the fallacious view that adherence to the gold standard obviated the need for cooperation. The standard model of the gold standard was one of a homeostatic system, with every boat floating on its own bottom. Efforts to coordinate policies were greatly complicated by the overhang of war debts and reparations. Sectoral interests blocked concessions that foreign countries would have required in return for monetary cooperation.[32]

[31] Keynes's efforts to influence policy in 1930–31 are analyzed in Cairncross and Eichengreen (1983), 59–61. Anglo-French discussions are recounted in Eichengreen (1986). A good summary of the World Economic Conference is provided by Kindleberger (1973), chapter 9.

[32] At the 1933 World Economic Conference, for example, France requested that

The external constraint was binding in significantly more instances than standard accounts of the period allow. The Bank of England was constrained in its efforts to expand in 1930 and 1931. The Reichsbank was prevented from expanding in the spring of 1931, when its reserves fell to their statutory minimum. Only with the help of window dressing and a transfer of deposits by the Bank of England did it manage to obey the letter of the gold standard law. The National Bank of Belgium attempted a more expansionary policy in August 1934. This led to a loss of reserves that forced retrenchment, exchange control and finally devaluation.[33]

More significant still was the extent to which the Federal Reserve and the Bank of France, the two central banks with the strongest reserve positions, were inhibited by the external constraint. The Fed was forced to raise its discount rate more quickly than ever before in its short history in the final months of 1931, when the devaluation of sterling increased the perceived riskiness of foreign dollar balances. Fearful of the implications of gold outflows for the defensibility of the exchange rate, the Fed limited its open market purchases of securities to a modest $50 million in a period when M2 was falling by more than $1 billion. Friedman and Schwartz (1963) criticize the Fed for worsening the Depression, but it is unclear what else a central bank committed to the gold standard parity could have done. Similarly, when in the spring of 1932 the Fed initiated large-scale open market purchases, the gold losses to which the program led quickly caused its abandonment.[34] There is much debate over the realism of the Fed's fears, on both occasions, that gold losses threatened an exchange-rate crisis. But there is no question that the fear profoundly influenced policymaking.

In France, developments followed a similar course, although they evolved more slowly. Policy ran up against the external constraint starting in 1934. The Flandin government, which came to power in November 1934, attempted to reflate and also to maintain the gold

---

the United States and Britain stabilize their exchange rates and that the three countries adopt a coordinated program of reflationary policies. But already having gone off the gold standard, the U.S. and Britain could reflate unilaterally. And France could offer little in return for a commitment by the U.S. and Britain to stabilize and coordinate. In principle, the French could have offered tariff reductions, but these were blocked by a domestic agricultural lobby that would have been adversely affected. Jackson (1985), 69.

[33] van der Wee and Tavernier (1975), 275–276.

[34] Although there are competing interpretations (see Epstein and Ferguson, 1984), I find the Fed's loss of reserves the most compelling explanation for the suspension of expansionary open market operations in 1932.

parity. The cornerstone of its program was a more liberal credit policy. The Bank of France was encouraged to discount Treasury bills on behalf of the fiscal authorities, whose budget was in substantial deficit. Predictably, the program led to a deterioration in the external accounts: the Bank of France lost 2% of its reserves in May 1935 and an alarming 11% in June. The central bank was forced to raise its discount rate from 2.5% to 6%, and the Flandin government fell.[35] The Laval government, which eventually replaced it, reverted to deflationary policies. But as opposition to its austerity measures mounted, it too reversed course. Instead of pushing for further cuts in public spending, it induced the Bank of France to again begin discounting Treasury bills as required to finance the budget deficit. The drain of reserves from the central bank accelerated. In April and May of 1936, the Bank of France lost 9% of its reserves. Once again it became clear that the conflict between reflation and the external constraint was fundamental. The difference was that by 1936, opposition to deflation had finally boiled over. Laval's difficulties contributed to the victory of the Popular Front in the spring 1936 elections. A new reflationary program was adopted. When its operation again compelled the authorities to choose between abandoning their recovery program and devaluing the currency, this time they opted for the latter.

Thus, fixed exchange rates represented a binding constraint on recovery policies even for the countries with the strongest reserve positions.

It was not only as a limit on the ability to adopt policies of cheap money and deficit spending, such as those of Britain and Sweden, respectively, that the effects of the external constraint were felt. The exchange-rate constraint also limited the ability of central banks to ensure the stability of banking systems. Several explanations for the depth and persistence of the Great Depression revolve around banking panics and their consequences. Friedman and Schwartz (1963) argue that bank failures induced a shift out of deposits and into currency; the consequent decline in money supply depressed output and prices. Bernanke (1983) argues that bank failures interrupted the provision of financial services; disintermediation disrupted resource allocation and depressed economic activity. Both sets of authors focus on the United States. But the phenomenon was quite general. In Austria, Germany, Hungary, Belgium and other countries, similar financial difficulties arose. In each case, banking panics led to further deterioration of an already critical economic situation.

[35] Sauvy (1984), 162–71.

Unfortunately, none of these authors places sufficient weight on the role of the exchange rate constraint in the banking panics. Stemming a run on the banks would have required intervention by the lender of last resort. Only by affirming its willingness to provide emergency liquidity to the banking system and by backing its words with deeds could central banks have contained bank runs. But a rapid increase in domestic credit threatened to produce a loss of international reserves. For central banks whose reserves were at the statutory minimum, this would have represented a breach of the gold standard statutes and a fatal blow to confidence in the exchange rate. Moreover, domestic bank runs tended to undermine exchange rate stability directly, even in the absence of central bank intervention. Foreign depositors who ran on domestic banks repatriated their funds. Domestic depositors concerned about financial stability moved their money abroad. The actions of both sets of agents produced a capital outflow and a decline in central bank reserves. For monetary authorities whose priority was defense of the exchange rate, this was the worst possible moment to expand the supply of domestic credit.

When panics erupted, therefore, the response of central banks tended to be hesitant and delayed. In Germany, the losses suffered by the big industrial banks became known at the end of 1930. But instead of injecting reserves into the system to bolster confidence, the Reichsbank stood idly by. When the situation reached crisis proportions, the Reichsbank's cover ratio had fallen to 40.1%, barely above the statutory 40% minimum. To defend its foreign reserves, the Reichsbank was forced to maintain a high discount rate and to ration credit. With the hands of the lender of last resort firmly tied, the smallest shock could topple the banking system. It took the form of the failure of the Nordwolle textile firm, which led to a run on the Darmstadter Bank, the Nordwolle's leading creditor.

A similar story can be told for several other countries. The gold standard constraints even came into play in the United States. The second wave of bank failures in the U.S. arose in August-September 1931, when uncertainty about the fate of sterling was at its height. The question of why the Fed did not intervene more aggressively is easily answered: fear for the gold parity. The gold cover ratio was not an immediate problem, but the drain of reserves—12% from September to November—was disquieting. Moreover, there was the problem of free gold: the Fed was required to hold a gold cover of 40% against Federal Reserve notes, and the other 60% had to take the form of gold and eligible securities (essentially excluding government bonds). Thus, the Fed could engage in open market purchases of government bonds only to the extent of its free gold, which had fallen to about $800 million in the wake of Britain's devaluation.[36] This left some room for maneuver, although the Fed wished to prevent free gold from falling to zero, at which point it would be wholly incapable of sterilizing the effects of reserve outflows. One can argue that the Fed made the wrong choice by failing to intervene more aggressively; but there is little question that the gold standard figured prominently in its decision.

By 1933, the Glass-Steagall Act had relaxed the free gold constraint. But the statutory gold cover ratio of 40% remained. When an even more serious wave of bank failures erupted in the early months of 1933, again the Fed was restrained from responding aggressively by the need to defend the exchange rate. As in Germany in 1931, bank failures led to the liquidation of foreign deposits and to a capital outflow. Sterling and other currencies rose relative to the dollar. The balance of gold imports and exports swung from surplus to deficit from February to March. Gold placed under earmark rose dramatically. For the week ending March 1, the Fed lost $116 million in gold because of earmarking. On March 3 alone, $109 million worth was placed under earmark in New York.[37] These numbers were small compared with a gold reserve of some $4 billion, and the gold reserve still amounted to 45% of the deposit and note liabilities of the Federal Reserve banks on March 3rd. But the trend was clear. By this time it was no longer appropriate to argue that causality ran unidirectionally from the banking panic to the foreign exchange market. There were apprehensions about President-Elect Roosevelt's commitment to the dollar parity, and foreigners began to withdraw their deposits from the United States in response to the possibility of devaluation and the instability of the banking system. But as long as the gold standard constraint remained in force, doubts about its sustainability only reinforced the pressure on the Fed. With the cover ratio falling toward the statutory minimum, the central bank felt there was little scope to inject liquidity into the collapsing banking system.

The point can be driven home by contrasting a country off the gold standard, in which the response to a potential banking panic was very different. The suicide of Ivar Krueger, the Swedish industrialist and financier, in March 1932, following revelations of financial fraud,

---

[36] The account I offer here conflicts with that of Friedman and Schwartz (1963), who deny that the Fed was constrained by the gold standard or by a lack of "free gold."

[37] These estimates are drawn from Hodson (1938, 211) and Nadler and Bogen (1933, 155).

raised doubts about the solvency of Krueger's banker, the Skandinaviska Kreditaktiebolag. But having devalued in 1931, the Riksbank was free to intervene. It conducted some 200 million kronor's worth of expansionary open market operations in response to the Krueger crisis. A banking panic was not allowed to delay Sweden's recovery from the Depression.

In much of the literature, the gold standard is portrayed as synonymous with financial stability. In the 1930s, as this account should make clear, the opposite was true. Far from being synonymous with stability, the decentralized gold exchange standard directly threatened financial stability between the wars.

Having analyzed channels through which the international monetary system contributed to the Depression, it is useful to mention some through which it did not. The competitive depreciation of currencies, often blamed for worsening the Depression, had on balance a salutary effect.[38] Elimination of the gold standard constraint permitted monetary policy to be enlisted on behalf of economic recovery. This package of policies accelerated recovery in devaluing countries through several complementary channels: promoting exports, raising prices relative to costs, permitting interest rates to be reduced, raising real share prices, and stimulating investment. Admittedly, devaluation was beggar-thy-neighbor, but these beggar-thy-neighbor effects could have been eliminated had countries remaining on gold emulated those that devalued. At worst, devaluation redistributed the Depression internationally. Insofar as it facilitated monetary expansion in at least some countries, it accelerated the recovery. My reading of the evidence is contrary to the view that devaluation did nothing for the initiating countries and only damaged their trading partners.

The uncoordinated way in which devaluation took place was not optimal. It created needless uncertainty. It encouraged the liquidation of foreign exchange reserves. The possibility of unilateral devaluation induced central banks to liquidate their foreign deposits. Insofar as they sought to replace these foreign exchange reserves, gold had to be acquired from abroad. To do so, central banks raised their discount rates, creating another competitive, mutually defeating scramble for gold, such as in the 1920s. The higher discount rates and more stringent domestic monetary conditions could have given the Depression another fillip. But in fact, the increase in global gold demand was minimal.[39]

---

[38] Having belabored this point on more than one occasion, I provide only the briefest summary here. For a complete analysis, see Eichengreen and Sachs (1985).

[39] Regression evidence and a more elaborate version of the argument are presented in Eichengreen (1988b).

In part, central banks simply liquidated their excess foreign exchange reserves. More important, devaluing countries could reduce their reserve ratios. The liquidation of foreign exchange reserves and the induced increase in discount rates in gold standard countries magnified devaluation's beggar-thy-neighbor effects. But there is no evidence that they eliminated its benefits.

There is another important caveat to the view that competitive depreciation was benign. Uncoordinated, haphazard devaluation contributed to the destruction of trade. Gold standard countries imposed exchange-dumping duties against goods exported by devaluing countries. Even countries with depreciated currencies imposed new tariffs against other producers off gold. As a result, the volume of trade recovered more slowly in the 1930s than the volume of domestic production. The implication is that international policy coordination, which would have minimized the likelihood of retaliation, would have been as advantageous following the gold standard's collapse as during its operation.

VI. Conclusion and Summary of Implications

Interwar experience underscores the difference the exchange rate system can make. It confirms the generality of several widely held interpretations of recent experience with floating. There is a positive association between nominal exchange rate flexibility and nominal exchange rate variability, and between nominal exchange rate variability and real exchange rate variability. But policies of intervention that reduce nominal exchange rate variability do not guarantee a proportionate reduction in nominal exchange rate risk or in real exchange rate variability and predictability. A credible commitment to a stable intervention rule—including but not limited to a commitment to peg the nominal rate—is needed to deliver these benefits.

Interwar experience also suggests what is needed to render such a commitment credible. It verges on the tautological to remind the reader that credibility, in this instance, requires of policymakers that they attach a heavy weight to exchange rate stability relative to other targets. As long as other targets retain a non-negligible weight, major disturbances affecting those targets can still raise questions about operational implications of policymakers' commitment to the exchange rate. But the credibility of the commitment can be greatly enhanced by international policy coordination. In the interwar period at least, policy coordination could have significantly relieved the conflict be-

Table 5.A1 Coefficients from Nominal Exchange Rate Forecasting Equation
Log Nominal Rates $E_t = \alpha + \beta E_{t-1} + e_t$

	Period 1 1922–26	Period 2 1927–31	Period 3 1932–36
	α	α	α
Denmark	2.6971	2.9003	3.8186
Finland	5.1989	5.2634	6.1390
Norway	3.0515	2.9004	3.6474
Sweden	2.8902	2.8975	3.6172
Switzerland	3.2204	3.2148	2.7155
U.S.	1.5878	1.5813	1.6827
France	7.3377	4.8205	4.3101
Netherlands	2.4924	2.4924	1.9786
Belgium	5.5270	3.5523	3.2988
Italy	7.1783	4.5221	4.0926
Germany	20.7137[a] 30.642[b]	30.6473	30.1390
	β	β	β
Denmark	.9990	.3709	.9669
Finland	.9038	.7220	.9751
Norway	.9883	.8865	.9654
Sweden	.9592	.4464	.9649
Switzerland	.8865	.9810	.9644
U.S.	.9674	.7241	.9642
France	.9923	.7229	.9650
Netherlands	.9719	.7750	.9648
Belgium	.9787	.7976	.9601
Italy	.9963	.6203	.9500
Germany	.9497[a] .9280[b]	.8404	.9620

Notes: [a] All observations except 1923.08–1923.11
[b] Leaving out the hyperinflation 1922.06–1923.12
[c] 1935.12–1936.01 omitted because of missing data

Source: See text.

tween the commitment to fix the exchange rate and the commitment to other targets.[40] Far from a surrogate for policy coordination, the desire to maintain a system of stable exchange rates rendered the need for coordination all the more pressing.

---

[40] Rogoff (1985b) has constructed an example where policy coordination can reduce credibility by exacerbating the time consistency problem facing policymakers. The statement in the text reflects my belief that this case has little applicability to the episodes with which this paper is concerned.

Table 5.A2 Coefficients from Real Exchange Rate Forecasting Equation
Log Real Rates $E_t = \alpha + \beta E_{t-1} + e_t$

	Period 1 1922–26	Period 2 1927–31	Period 3 1932–36
	α	α	α
Denmark	2.8799	2.8149	3.5708
Finland	5.6648[a]	5.1060	6.4406
Norway	2.9240	2.7560	3.4890
Sweden	2.8789	2.8429	3.5627
Switzerland	3.2270	3.1766	2.9196
U.S.	1.9811	1.9238	1.9415
France	3.3702	3.3087	3.1006
Netherlands	2.5296	7.5370	2.3933
Belgium	3.3599	1.7363	1.6938
Italy	7.1780	4.5221	4.0926[d]
Germany	8.1914[b] 30.752[c]	30.4990	30.2056
	β	β	β
Denmark	.8986	.3950	.9691
Finland	.8873[a]	.9947	.9791
Norway	.9192	.9584	.9683
Sweden	.9299	.9320	.9677
Switzerland	.9586	.8575	.8629
U.S.	.9143	.9245	.9474
France	.8698	.8083	.6647
Netherlands	.9313	.9997	.9117
Belgium	.8418	.8680	.9533
Italy	.9963	.6203	.9500[d]
Germany	.1575[b] .7373[c]	.9799	.9651

Notes: [a] From 1922.12 only
 [b] 1923.08–1924.11 omitted because of break in WPI
 [c] 1922.01–1924.01 omitted because of hyperinflation
 [d] 1935.12–1936.02 omitted because of missing data

Source: See text.

References

Artis, M.J. 1987. "The European Monetary System: An Evaluation." *Journal of Policy Modeling* 9: 175–98.

Baxter, M., and Stockman, A. 1988. "Business Cycles and the Exchange Rate System: Some International Evidence." NBER Working Paper No. 2689 (August).

Bernanke, B. 1983. "Nonmonetary Effects of the Financial Crisis in the Propagation of the Great Depression." *American Economic Review* 73: 257–76.

Bloomfield, A. 1959. *Monetary Policy Under the International Gold Standard: 1880–1914*. New York: Federal Reserve Bank of New York.

Cairncross, A., and Eichengreen, B. 1983. *Sterling in Decline*. Oxford: Blackwell.

Canzonari, M. and Gray, J.A. 1985. "Monetary Policy Games and the Consequences of Noncooperative Behavior." *International Economic Review* 26: 547–64.

Clarke, S.V.O. 1967. *Central Bank Cooperation, 1924–1931*. New York: Federal Reserve Bank of New York.

Eichengreen, B. 1985. "International Policy Coordination in Historical Perspective: A View from the Interwar Years." In Buiter, W., and Marston, R., eds. *International Economic Policy Coordination*. Cambridge: Cambridge University Press, 139–78.

———. 1986. "The Bank of France and the Sterilization of Gold, 1926–1932." *Explorations in Economic History* 23: 56–84.

———. 1988a. "Real Exchange Rate Behavior Under Alternative International Monetary Regimes: Interwar Evidence." *European Economic Review* 32: 363–71.

———. 1988b. "Did International Economic Forces Cause the Great Depression?" *Contemporary Policy Issues* IV: 90–113.

———. 1989a. "The Comparative Performance of Fixed and Flexible Exchange Rate Regimes: Interwar Evidence." Prepared for the International Economic Association Conference, Copenhagen, June.

———. 1989b. "Hegemonic Stability Theories of the International Monetary System." In Cooper, R., Eichengreen, B., Henning, R., Holtham, G., and Putnam, R. *Can Nations Agree? Issues in International Economic Cooperation*. Washington, D.C.: The Brookings Institution, 255–298.

———. and Sachs, J. 1985. "Exchange Rates and Economic Recovery in the 1930s." *Journal of Economic History* XLV: 925–46.

———, Watson, M., and Grossman, R. 1985. "Bank Rate Policy Under the Interwar Gold Standard: A Dynamic Probit Model." *Economic Journal* 95: 725–45.

Einzig, P. 1937, *The Theory of Forward Exchange*. London: Macmillan.

Epstein, G., and Ferguson, T. 1984. "Monetary Policy, Loan Liquidation and Industrial Conflict: The Federal Reserve and the Open Market Operations of 1932." *Journal of Economic History* XLIV: 957–84.

Friedman, M. 1953. "The Case for Flexible Exchange Rates." In *Essays in Positive Economics*. Chicago: University of Chicago Press.
Friedman, M., and Schwartz, A. 1963. *A Monetary History of the United States, 1867–1960*. Princeton: Princeton University Press.
Goodhart, C.A.E. 1972. *The Business of Banking*. London: Weidenfeld and Nicolson.
Hall, N.F. 1935. *The Exchange Equalisation Account*. London: Macmillan.
Hamilton, J. 1987. Monetary Factors in the Great Depression. *Journal of Monetary Economics* 13: 1–25.
Hilgerdt, F. 1945. *Industrialization and Foreign Trade*. Geneva: League of Nations.
Hodson, H.V. 1938. *Slump and Recovery, 1927–1937*. London: Oxford University Press.
Howson, S. 1980. "Sterling's Managed Float: The Operation of the Exchange Equalisation Account." *Princeton Studies in International Finance* no. 46. Princeton: Princeton University Press.
Jackson, J. 1985. *The Politics of Depression in France, 1932–1936*. Cambridge: Cambridge University Press.
Keynes, J.M. 1925. *The Economic Consequences of Mr. Churchill*, New York: Harcourt Brace.
Keynes, J.M. 1929. "Is There Enough Gold? The League of Nations Inquiry." In *The Collected Writings of John Maynard Keynes, Volume XIX: Activities, 1922–1929: The Return to Gold and Industrial Policy*, Moggridge, D., ed. New York: Cambridge University Press, 775–80.
Kindleberger, C. 1973. *The World in Depression, 1929–1939*. Berkeley: University of California Press.
League of Nations (various issues). *Monthly Statistical Bulletin*. Geneva: League of Nations.
League of Nations (various issues). *Monetary Review*. Geneva: League of Nations.
League of Nations (various issues). *Public Finances*. Geneva: League of Nations.
Lewis, W.A. 1949. *Economic Survey 1919–1939*. London: Allen & Unwin.
Lindert, P. 1969. "Key Currencies and Gold, 1900–1913." *Princeton Studies in International Finance* no. 24. Princeton: Princeton University Press.
Mlynarski, F. 1929. *Gold and Central Banks*. New York: Macmillan.
Nadler, M., and Bogen, J.I. 1933. *The Banking Crisis*. New York: Dodd, Mead & Co.

Nurkse, R. 1944. *International Currency Experience.* Geneva: League of Nations.
Rogoff, K. 1985a. "Can Exchange Rate Predictability Be Achieved without Monetary Convergence? Evidence from the EMS." *European Economic Review* 28: 93–116.
Rogoff, K. 1985b. "Can International Monetary Policy Coordination Be Counterproductive?" *Journal of International Economics* 18: 199–217.
Roubini, N. 1988. "Offset and Sterilization Under Fixed Exchange Rates with an Optimizing Central Bank." NBER Working Paper No. 2777 (November).
Sachs, J., and Wyplosz, C. 1984. "Real Exchange Rate Effects of Fiscal Policy." Harvard Institute of Economic Research Discussion Paper 1050 (April).
Sauvy, A. 1984. *Histoire économique de la France entre les deux guerres.* Paris: Economica (second edition).
Thorp, R. 1984. *Latin America in the 1930s.* London: Macmillan.
Triffin, R. 1960. *Gold and the Dollar Crisis.* New Haven: Yale University Press.
van der Wee, H., and Tavernier, K. 1975. *La Banque Nationale de Belgique et l'histoire monétaire entre les deux guerres mondiales.* Brussels: Banque Nationale de Belgique.

6

Evaluation of the Bretton Woods Regime and the Floating Exchange Rate System

Yoichi Shinkai*

I. Introduction

My assignment in this chapter is to evaluate the two international monetary arrangements after the war: the Bretton Woods regime and the floating exchange rate (non) system. As I understand the general aim of the conference, it seems to me that my paper should be organized in a forward-looking way so that the more important reform proposals can be examined in the light of our postwar experiences. Indeed, I am not interested in, nor am I qualified to write, a historical account *per se* of the postwar monetary arrangements; the paper will be concerned with a few selected topics of the two regimes.

The topics that seem to suggest themselves are, first, that the Bretton Woods regime collapsed, and second, that the floating exchange rate system that replaced it has performed poorly. Commentators mention, among other things, large trade imbalances that fuel protectionism, a large U.S. foreign debt that threatens the dollar's free fall, and the regime's poor performance in insulating a country from outside shocks. There is no denying the judgment that even a staunch defender of the present system cannot be complacent, and that any reform proposal should be examined in a humble, dogma-free manner. On the other hand, to advocate returning to the Bretton Woods regime takes a considerable amount of persuasion; after all, the pre-1971 regime collapsed on its own. We have much to learn from the postwar monetary developments, even when our primary purpose is to devise a better monetary arrangement.

Since the two postwar systems are diametrically opposite in the

---

* I would like to express my gratitude to the Ministry of Education for a grant (#63530004) and to the Bank of Japan staff for providing me with several documents. In preparing the final version of this paper, I have been helped by the numerous comments given by the conference participants.

exchange rate arrangement, I may be expected first of all to compare them, and I plan to do so in the next section. The Bretton Woods regime stipulated *adjustable* pegs, and the present floating rates are heavily *managed*: thus calling them diametrical may be an exaggeration. I plan to focus on the 1960s, when parity changes were infrequent, and to give an explicit account of official interventions when necessary. Anyway, the comparison of the two systems is difficult, as is well known. I shall do my best; I shall try to summarize macroeconomic performances, quote econometric comparisons, and discuss volatility and misalignments in exchange rates vs. resilience to shocks. But if the reader is left with the feeling that one cannot legitimately compare the two systems, I must accept that verdict and remind the reader that it is in the nature of a historical comparison.

Section III presents three case studies of macro policy cooperation (or lack of cooperation) among the United States, Germany, and Japan. I shall turn to case studies partly because the overall comparison of Section II is difficult and partly because the question of policy cooperation, an important topic in the conference, seems to be best examined in this way. One episode, President Nixon's new economic policy of 1971, is picked up from the Bretton Woods period. The other two episodes are chosen from the floating rate period: President Reagan's policy mix of the early 1980s and the policy cooperation after the Plaza agreement. As the reader may anticipate, the first two episodes will point out the difficulty of policy cooperation, and the last one will examine the nature of cooperative exercises. The three cases also shed light on the collapse of the adjustable peg system, the question of exchange rate misalignments, and the effectiveness of official intervention.

Section IV presents yet another approach to the postwar monetary experiences. I shall single out three issues that play important roles in any reform proposal: (1) Is our economic knowledge adequate? (2) What can we say about the question of macro adjustments vs. asset settlements? (3) Is the United States a benevolent despot? These are large issues, and one cannot expect a ready answer to any, but I shall try to answer them as well as I can in the light of postwar experiences. At the same time I shall take up the more important (and perhaps more interesting) reform proposals and try to assess them with the help of my discussion of the three issues. The proposals taken up include a fixed or pegged rates system based on the dollar, the target zones by Williamson and others, and the objective (quantitative) indicators and multilateral surveillance that is now practiced. My conclusion will be that they are all seriously flawed, but I suspect the conclusion *per se* is less important than the materials I shall have organized in a particular way in the present paper.

II. A Comparison of the Postwar Systems

This section will be concerned with a comparison of the pre-1971 IMF system with the (non)system of floating exchange rates. I shall not attempt, however, to compare them in a balanced and exhaustive way. To do so would take a better-informed economist, and, moreover, documents are readily available for that purpose, such as Crockett and Goldstein (1987). I may note too that a comparison is inherently difficult: we cannot differ only about the proper yardsticks; we must also quarrel over how to distinguish the effect of monetary arrangements from that of other exogenous shocks (see, e.g., Eichengreen [1985]). For these reasons, I shall confine myself to a few interesting topics, such as the simulation analysis of econometric models, exchange rate misalignments, and examples of exogenous shocks. But first, a few words may be proper concerning the overall macro performance under the two systems.

1. Macro Performance

To give the reader a rough idea (though he or she must have one already) of how the macro economies of the United States, Germany, and Japan performed under the pegged system and floating rates, I have prepared Table 6.1. No justification will be given for the indicators chosen, and I must apologize that only three countries are listed. Especially for the pre-1971 period, the United Kingdom, France, and other countries played more important roles than Germany and Japan and should have been listed in the comparison. I hope the reader refers to Marston (1988b, p. 80), for example, for reference to these countries.

The difference in macroeconomic performances between the two periods is large.[1] What will be troubling for those who favor the floating rates system will be that performances did not improve during the post-1973 period. Taken at face value, this must imply that the poor performances under floating rates cannot be explained by our

[1] However, see Baxter and Stockman (1988) where a great many countries are examined and where "there is little indication that these changes are related to the choice of exchange rate system." We should note, though, that the authors work mostly with detrended data.

Table 6.1 Macro Performance of U.S., Germany, and Japan (%, standard deviation)

	Unemployment rate	Inflation rate	GNP growth rate
1961–71			
U.S.	4.8	2.8	3.6
Germany	0.8	2.8	4.2
Japan	1.2	5.6	10.4
1973–87			
U.S.	7.2	6.8	2.4
	(1.4)	(3.6)	(1.1)
Germany	6.0	3.6	1.8
	(2.6)	(2.8)	(4.5)
Japan	2.2	6.0	4.0
	(0.5)	(0.8)	(3.4)
1973–79			
U.S.	6.6	8.6	2.3
Germany	3.8	4.6	2.3
Japan	1.9	9.8	3.5
1980–87			
U.S.	7.7	5.3	2.4
Germany	7.8	2.9	1.5
Japan	2.5	2.5	3.9

Source: Computed from the IMF, IFS.

inexperience of the new system. The table does not list balance-of-payments figures, but it is well known (see Table 6.3 below) that imbalances in the three countries' current accounts have become larger in the 1980s. The U.S. performance in this respect is unusual (Eichengreen, 1987), and we can claim at the very least that the floating rates system has not facilitated balancing the current accounts of major countries.

Of the three countries in Table 6.1, the performance of the U.S. appears to have deteriorated less under floating than the other two, especially in terms of growth rates. Is it because pre-1971 Germany and Japan were still in the process of postwar recovery and that they have since matured into the normal phase of moderate growth rates? This is but one example of the difficulty of a historical comparison. An obvious way to overcome it will be to construct an econometric model and simulate macro performances under alternative assumptions in regard to exchange rate arrangements. If the simulation employs exogenous shocks that are similar to our experiences, one may expect to derive reasonably realistic estimates of macro performances.

Taylor (1987) and McKibbin and Sachs (1986) are two representative examples of the simulation study of exchange rate regimes. Their models are broadly similar, though Taylor's is an econometric model and the McKibbin-Sachs model uses outside information in the estimates of coefficients. I do not intend to discuss their models in any detail, but to quote only the more interesting results (both produce very rich results). They measure macro performance in terms of the variability of real GNP and prices or a combined indicator. Taylor compares the fixed-rates system with the floating rates system and usually finds that the latter performs better. McKibbin and Sachs compare several exchange rate arrangements and usually find that a floating regime performs best; they also find that a managed floating regime and one based on the McKinnon proposal perform rather poorly. Though the specification of the models prevents a comparison of growth rates, it may be concluded that given the nature of shocks to the system, floating regimes do not necessarily perform poorly.

Taylor (1988) and McKibbin and Sachs (1988), whose papers came to my attention after I completed the first draft of the present paper, have revised their simulation studies. Taylor's conclusions are broadly similar to his previous results, though he now examines several monetary rules besides fixed and floating rate regimes, and "in general find[s] that monetary policy rules that focus on domestic price and output stability generate surprisingly stable exchange rate behavior." The McKibbin-Sachs paper does not permit an easy comparison of fixed and floating rate regimes, but the two now find that a version of the McKinnon proposal (which fixes nominal exchange rates) performs well for a range of shocks. It is interesting too that a target zone proposal by Williamson and Miller (which I take up in Section IV) works very well for all shocks except U.S. shocks. Thus it may be necessary to admit that their revised results are more favorable to fixed rate regimes. I also wish to point out for later reference that all the simulation results assume that the economic model is known to policymakers.

So much for comparing the performances of the two postwar systems. Since an overall comparison is difficult (a model revision sometimes changes the main result), it may be more fruitful to focus on the perceived major weakness and strength of the floating regime: exchange rate misalignments and resilience to large shocks.

2. *Volatility and Misalignments of Exchange Rates*

First a few words on the short-run volatility of exchange rates. It is true that volatility is large; the standard deviation of monthly percentage changes is about 0.025 in nominal bilateral terms and 0.015 in real effective terms (Marston [1988b], p. 83). Compared with interest rates these are very large numbers, but is volatility worrisome? Financiers welcome it: unless exchange rates are volatile, they cannot justify their huge investments in manpower and dealing rooms. Those engaged in international trade and long-term investments are not too worried. Changes on the order of two or three yen per dollar can be handled easily (unless volatility leads to misalignments). Indeed, econometric studies of the effect of exchange rate volatility on trade volume generally find either no effects or only small ones (see, however, Cushman [1988], who finds a sizable effect). Perhaps economists are the only ones worried about volatility, partly because it may lead to misalignments and partly because they believe large-scale resources have been invested in the financial sector.[2]

Will volatility (near-random changes in exchange rates) lead to large, persistent misalignments? Professor Takatoshi Ito tells me that the notion has not been well established, and being ignorant of works in the field, I must accept his judgment. Thus the only reason we have to be concerned with exchange rate volatility is that it may have caused investments of resources in the financial sector that were too large. This should be an important issue, but it is related to the volatility of all financial variables and could not be covered in the present paper, even if I were competent. I will therefore proceed to a discussion of misalignments, whatever may have produced them.

Prominent examples of misalignments—large, sustained departures of (real) exchange rates from their long-run equilibrium levels—include the high dollar in the first half of the 1980s and the high pound sterling from 1978 to 1981. It is true that in both cases export industry experienced a severe loss of competitiveness, and the economic cost in terms of dislocated factors of production must have been great. But to identify the approximate causes of these large movements in real exchange rates appears to be a complicated task (e.g., see works in Marston [1988]). In the case of the pound sterling's misalignment, the causes mentioned are the discovery of North Sea oil, Mrs. Thatcher's tight money policy, and so-called hysteresis phenomena in both demand and supply behaviors (Marston [1988a]). In the case of the dollar in the 1980s, economists usually cite President Reagan's policy mix, but there can be disagreements with this view (see Section III.2,

---

[2] Some participants found my view on the effect of exchange-rate volatility too sanguine. It may well be so that regardless of econometricans' findings, the exporters and importers whose margins are small are worried about volatile exchange rates.

below). I have nothing new to offer in the way of explaining misalignments. What I shall do below is to raise a few points on the interpretation of these large movements in real exchange rates.

The first point: Is there a large role to be attributed to speculative bubbles and to an overshooting in Dornbusch's sense (1980)? If a large movement is due to a bubble, then it must be the case that this part cannot be explained. Dornbusch's overshooting can in principle be accounted for by an econometric model, but I doubt how accurately that can be done (Section IV, below). On the other hand, large movements in real exchange rates because of speculative bubbles or overshootings are genuinely harmful. So it seems to me that the most interest should be in those movements that cannot easily be explained. I wonder how much of the dollar misalignment in the 1980s remains unexplained.

Next, let us suppose for the sake of argument that the dollar misalignment can be completely explained by President Reagan's policy of tight money and fiscal expansion. In that case, can we regard the high dollar as misaligned, that is, did it deviate from the long-run equilibrium level? The answer depends on what we mean by long-run equilibrium. And it will be futile to dispute over a definition unless we have some concrete points to make with its help. Two points that come to mind: (a) If the high dollar was judged as off equilibrium, could that have persuaded the United States to abandon the Reagan policy? (b) Was the dollar off equilibrium in the sense that it was not sustainable? Point (a) seems to me an interesting question, and I shall discuss it later in Sections III.2 and IV.3. Point (b) is taken up very briefly below.

There were respectable arguments that the high dollar was unsustainable (e.g., Krugman [1985] and Marris [1985]). They did not seem to imply that the large deficits in the U.S. current account that accompanied it were literally unsustainable; the ratio of its net debt to GNP is still about 10%, which is manageable, though we may find it worrisome that the interest rate is higher than the GNP growth rate (in view of the Domar theorem). Their arguments instead were that the foreign exchange market was mistaken and that once the market became aware of the mistake, the dollar would fall rapidly. And it appears that their view was vindicated by events after the Plaza agreement. But if the high dollar reflected a market mistake, it must have been a bubble, and we are back to where we were a moment ago; the high dollar was not fully accounted for by the Reagan policy.

My tentative position is that the dollar may have been on a bubble during the latter half of 1984 and the first half of 1985, but for the rest, it can be more or less accounted for by the Reagan policy (e.g.,

Branson [1988]). Can the post-Plaza dollar be explained, then? This is a more difficult question, but I submit that actual and expected changes in U.S. and Japanese policies will account for a large part of the dollar's fall (e.g., Dornbusch and Frankel [1987], Fig. 1; Fukao [1987]). The high dollar in 1984 and 1985 was undesirable, but *given* the dollar's value until the summer of 1984, was it something we should be alarmed about? I do not think so. Then the dollar misalignment problem boils down to this: If the high dollar in the 1980s was costly, could something have been done to alleviate the Reagan policy's effects? This will be a topic of my paper (Section III. 2).

3. Resilience of the Present System

One positive feature of the floating rate system often mentioned is that it has been efficient in dealing with real shocks, such as the oil crises. One might ask what would have happened if the fixed exchange rate system had been in effect when the oil crises hit the world economy. This is without doubt a pertinent question, though it will be difficult to answer how "efficient" the present system was because one would then need to evaluate the cost of exchange rate misalignments. I shall confine myself to the "what-if" part of the question.

Before proceeding to an examination of several shocks that hit the world economy since 1973, I will quote from a table of speculative crises in the pre-float period (Willett [1977], pp. 16–17). There were 20 cases of large short-term capital movements from October 1960 through March 1973. The size of each movement, if estimable at all, ranges from $212 million (June 1967, sterling into Swiss francs) to $3.7 billion (August 1971, dollar into European currencies). As many as six cases are recorded where more than $1 billion moved from one currency to another. I may also cite one Japanese example: about $4 billion flowed into yen in August 1971. It was these short-term capital movements that finally doomed the pre-1971 pegged-rate system to collapse. And except for President Nixon's policy change in August 1971, which will be a topic of Section III, these crises were not associated with such major shocks as the two oil-price increases. So it seems to me evident that a pegged-rate system could not have survived any of the major shocks in the post-1973 period.

Turning to the major shocks after 1973, I would like to quote from a chart of bilateral, real exchange rates (BIS (1988), Fig. 7.4). Since I am reading off a chart, the numbers I quote are rough approximations; none of my arguments in the present paper depends on exact numbers, anyway. Now, changes in real exchange rates after each shock were sizable. After the first oil shock of late 1973, the deutsch mark depreciated (against the dollar) 15%, the yen 8%, and the pound sterling 10%. The yen depreciation appears small, but in nominal terms it fell to 300, from 265, a 13% depreciation. During the second oil crisis, the mark fell by 20% and the yen by 30%, and the pound appreciated 40% (the North Sea discovery itself played a large part in this). The Reagan policy further shocked the mark to fall 30%, the yen 20%, and the pound 40%.

The changes in real exchange rates were sizable. Some parts of them may have been speculative bubbles, but I tend to believe that bubbles played relatively minor roles. The Reagan policy shock was discussed above in II.2, and I tentatively took the position there that if a dollar bubble were evident, it was confined to the period from the summer of 1984 to the summer of 1985. As for the two oil shocks, I note that the yen and the pound were under exchange controls, and bubbles could not have played a large role. Because both currencies changed as much as the mark (which was not under severe control), the implication is that those changes in real rates were necessary to restore equilibrium after the shocks.

If nominal exchange rates had been pegged, or if some type of target zones had been in force (with zones that were not too wide), could those changes in real rates have taken place? This is a different problem from the survival of a pegged-rate system; even if a peg system had survived major shocks by means of restrictions on trade and capital flows, the problem of adjusting real exchange rates would have had to be addressed. One may argue that a Smithsonian-type negotiation could have adjusted real exchange rates. Thus, whether policy cooperation succeeded after President Nixon's policy actions in 1971 and why the Smithsonian agreement survived only one year should be interesting issues, which I shall take up in Section III.1.

To anticipate my conclusion there, I submit that negotiated changes in real rates could have had little chance of surviving the crises. Cooperation would have been difficult because of the perceived conflict of interests among participants.[3] And the lack of adequate economic knowledge would have prevented any honest negotiations from arriving at enduring exchange rates. Indeed, the difficulty associated with our inadequate knowledge will be a topic of my paper. For ex-

---

[3] At the negotiations leading to the Smithsonian agreement, the United States wanted to see the yen up-valued substantially, while Japan regarded a small revaluation in its interest. Though both were supposed to propose an equilibrium parity, the outcome depended more on the respective bargaining power than on a rational calculation.

ample, a question often raised in the examination of international monetary systems concerns the international transmission of shocks under floating rates in contrast to the peg system. My position will be that macroeconomic models give results that are too divergent for a definite answer to this question. I already cited examples of econometric model simulations, and hinted that the answer must be: it depends. I shall have more to say on this and related issues in later sections.

III. Three Cases of Macro Policy Cooperation (or Lack Thereof)

This section presents three case studies of macro policy cooperation selected from the postwar monetary experiences. Although international cooperation in general is essential to the success of any monetary arrangement, how important the role of macropolicy cooperation should be, is debatable (see, e.g., Dornbusch and Frankel [1987]). And history seems to show that cooperation is not easy to achieve even if it is desirable. I plan to illustrate this point and to discuss several issues that accompany it by examining three well-known episodes: President Nixon's new economic policy of 1971, President Reagan's policy mix of the 1980s, and the so-called policy cooperation after the Plaza Agreement of 1985.

When I confine my attention to the three episodes, I know it would be more helpful if I could cover the postwar period entirely. I shall not attempt it partly because at present I am not prepared to discuss the whole period in any detail, and partly because some other episodes such as the Bonn Summit of 1978 have been examined extensively. In his compact review of international cooperation up to 1986, Higgins (1988) notes that there was successful cooperation in the 1960s, but that during the float period the Bonn Summit was the only prominent case of (*ex ante*) successful cooperation, the bargain being Germany's and Japan's expansionary policies in exchange for the U.S. promise of deregulation in its domestic oil price. I shall not comment on the Higgins review; I quote it to remind the reader that cooperation has been rare up to 1986. As for the 1960s, I shall turn to the final year of the decade without challenging Higgins's general assessment.

1. President Nixon's Policy of 1971

In August 1971, President Nixon unilaterally suspended the dollar's conversion into gold and introduced a 10% import surcharge. The latter measure, though in violation of GATT, was known to be a bargaining chip that would be withdrawn if other countries agreed to sizable adjustments in their exchange parities. It was a sobering reminder of how the United States could behave to coerce a policy "cooperation," but it did not seriously undermine GATT. The former measure, though, did undermine the international monetary system based on the gold-dollar standard. The pre-1971 regime did not survive what the Japanese named the "Nixon Shock."

An interesting question to be asked in the context of Section III is: Could the collapse of the gold-dollar system have been averted if the countries concerned coordinated their macro policies? It seems to me that two issues were involved, namely, the dollar confidence problem vis-a-vis gold and the U.S. balance of payments disequilibrium *per se*, issues that we can discuss separately. I shall take up the second one here, and postpone a detailed examination of the first issue to Section IV. The U.S. balance of payments disequilibrium could have doomed a pegged exchange rate system even if the dollar had been the sole international currency, that is, even if there had been no gold conversion problem. Thus my proposal to separate the two issues.

To facilitate the discussion of macro policy coordination, I refer to Table 6.2, which summarizes the economic scenes of the United States, Germany, and Japan until the summer of 1971 (budget deficits and current account balance of payments are annual figures and refer to all of 1971). First we note that Germany could have done little; it had already revalued the deutsche mark by 9.3% in October 1969, and its current accounts were almost balanced. With erratic growth rates and high (for Germany) inflation rates, it certainly could not have resorted to an overall reflation to help the United States. Indeed, the German policy in 1970 and 1971 was more restrictive than otherwise, though its 1971 budget was expansionary.

The Japanese situation was much different from Germany's. Its current accounts were in surplus, and the 1971 figure was to be a high 2.5% of GNP (not unforeseeable). The government budget was in the red throughout, so it could be argued that fiscal expansion was not in the cards. With inflation rates fairly high and the current account in large surpluses, however, Japan was in a textbook situation to revalue the yen. When we look back at those days from the vantage point of the 1980s, it is difficult to appreciate why the Japanese authorities and public were opposed to this remedy. But the fact is that they were prepared to do almost anything to "avoid being cornered into Germany's way (revaluation)."

Table 6.2 Several Economic Indicators for U.S., Germany, and Japan, 1969-71 (%)

	1969	1970 I	1970 II	1970 III	1970 IV	1971 I	1971 II
Real growth rates							
U.S.	2.6	−1.6	0.4	4.0	−3.2	10.0	2.0
Germany	8.2	−7.6	18.0	1.6	5.6	−0.8	2.8
Japan	10.1	3.6	12.8	7.6	−2.0	12.0	6.4
Yields on long-term government bonds							
U.S.	6.2	6.8	7.1	7.0	6.6	6.0	6.2
Germany	6.8	7.8	8.4	8.4	8.5	7.8	8.0
Japan	6.9	6.9		7.0		7.0	
CPI inflation rates							
U.S.	5.4	6.2	6.0	5.7	5.6	4.9	4.4
Germany	1.9	2.9	3.2	3.6	4.0	4.5	5.1
Japan	5.3	6.4	6.1	8.9	6.3	6.0	7.3
Budget deficits as percentages of GNP							
U.S.	−0.3	−2.0				−3.5[a]	
Germany	1.2	0.5				0.2	
Japan	−1.6	−0.8				−1.8	
Current account balance of payments as percentage of GNP							
U.S.	−0.4	−0.1				−1.3	
Germany	0.3	0.2				−0.2	
Japan	1.3	1.0				2.5	

Source: Statistical publications.
Note: [a] For entire 1971

The events up to the summer of 1971 seem to indicate that macro policy coordination is easier said than implemented. Germany did revalue its currency, but it did so mainly to avert the pressure of imported inflation. It will do what is called for in its best interest even if that collides with the interests of the United States. Japan announced a surplus-remedy package in 1971, but it did not revalue the yen; the package was too little, too late. The United States did not squeeze enough; the real interest rates were low and the 1971 budget was expansionary. Moreover, the U.S. could have devalued the dollar, but it did not. Macro policy cooperation might have been successful in the 1960s, as Higgins suggests, but at the critical moment of the gold-dollar system, cooperation was conspicuously absent.

What institutional arrangements could have prevented the collapse of the pegged-rate system? Let me first point out that I wrote above that the United States could have devalued the dollar. Though some commentators argue that the U.S. could not have effectively devalued because other countries would have followed suit (see, e.g., Houthakker in the *Wall Street Journal*, quoted by Moffitt [1983, p. 37]), this argument seems incorrect. The IMF articles implied that a surplus country could not propose devaluation or the Executive Directors would object to it. In the early 1970s, the United States did not want to devalue the dollar; instead of taking the politically painful step, it tried to coerce other countries to revalue. The episode seems to imply that in a different institutional arrangement, such as a target zone where policy changes are supposed to be encouraged, the United States would still be reluctant to take politically painful steps.

As for Japan's refusal to revalue the yen, I have no intention of defending its position by referring to the IMF articles that had no provision of encouraging a surplus country to adjust (except for the scarce currency clause). The articles did not prevent Japan from proposing a revaluation, and its failure to do so reflects either a lack of knowledge (unreasonable fear of revaluation) or the general difficulty of policy cooperation (mentioned already). Instead, I would like to raise a question: Could a revaluation of, say, 20%, by Japan have saved the pegged-rate system?

We know that the Smithsonian agreement, which President Nixon called the greatest monetary agreement in history, lasted only one year and was replaced by the floating rates (non)system. The agreement called for a parity change of the yen by about 17% against the dollar. The outcome was a result of horse-trading, but the bargaining was also based on the best technical evidence available. The IMF, it was said, expected that current account imbalances would be corrected within two years (de Vries [1987], p. 93). Thus we must conclude that a unilateral revaluation by Japan of about 20% would have been thought adequate, but it would have proved impotent in saving the pegged-rate system.

The experience is a reminder that our economic knowledge was severely limited. With the help of hindsight, we must admit that no one knew the magnitude of necessary changes in the parities that would have saved the peg system. Or was it impossible to save anyway? Given the extent of short-term capital mobility, large parity changes might have been inadequate. Indeed, Japan experienced an inflow of more than $4 billion of hot money (when its international reserves were about $6 billion) within the two weeks following the Nixon shock. The Japanese exchange control was among the tightest at that time, and it was helpless to stem the speculative tide. It was probably inevitable that the peg system would be replaced by floating exchange rates.

2. President Reagan's Policy Mix

The high value of the dollar and the large deficits in the U.S. current account in the 1980s are always cited when the topic of misalignments in exchange rates come up. Whether the dollar was in fact misaligned, given the Reagan policy in the early 1980s, was discussed in Section II. The present subsection will be concerned with the other side of the issue, namely, whether a macro policy coordination could have prevented the outcome.[4]

Let me first dispose of a relatively uninteresting case: given the Reagan policy, could Germany and Japan have changed their macro policies to prevent the high dollar and the accompanying large deficits from materializing? The Reagan policy is often characterized as one of tight money and an expansionary budget (see Sachs and Roubini [1988]). The German and Japanese policies are said to be typical of easy money and a tight budget. I am not persuaded that this was so; as Table 6.3 shows, the German and Japanese budget deficits, especially the Japanese, were fairly large in the first half of the 1980s. Moreover, the real interest rates in the two countries were not especially low. But I do not wish to press this point now. Let us accept the common assertion, understanding that they were comparing the German and Japanese stances with the U.S. stance.

What could Germany and Japan have done to "cooperate" with the United States to drive down the (real) value of the dollar? Since it is generally agreed that the dollar was high because of real interest differentials between the U.S. and the two countries, the latter should have raised their interest rates. Tighter money and a more expansionary fiscal stance would have produced that outcome. The budget deficits there were large without these policy changes, as noted above. Aside from the political cost of implementing such policy changes in order to cooperate with the United States, the overall result would have been disastrous. Interest differentials would have been smaller, thus driving down the dollar, but the level of interest rates in the three countries would have been higher. We would not have seen the in-

---

[4] The reader must have noticed that I am writing as if it were a foregone conclusion that the Reagan policy was undesirable. Actually this is not the case. On this point, see Shinkai (1989).

vestment boom in the United States, and the growth rates after 1983 would have been much lower.

I shall turn to examining the possibility of macro policy coordination in the true sense of the word, namely, the possibility of having had the United States reconsider the Reagan policy mix. This should have been the true policy coordination, but I submit that it would have been nearly impossible. We must first of all note that President Reagan had an indisputable mandate to embark on the policy of income-tax cut and defense build-up. A tight money policy to squeeze out inflation had also been his election pledge. (He even advocated a gold-based system; I present more on this point in Section IV.) If a U.S. President has been elected with a landslide on the platform of a macro policy mix, are Germany and Japan in a position to propose that he negate his policy pledge? The answer is obvious.

The next point to note is that it would have been difficult to argue against the Reagan policy mix on the basis of economic (technical) analysis. My personal feeling is that even if a U.S. President's platform has been a direct concern of Germany and Japan, he will nevertheless turn a deaf ear to their complaint. The 1988 Trade Act is a good example; this is how the United States, a hegemonic democracy, is run. But with the Reagan policy mix, its effect on the U.S. economy was not evident in the early 1980s, and that on Germany and Japan must have been far more debatable. That is, besides the political difficulty mentioned earlier, it would have been difficult on technical grounds to dissuade the United States from the macro policy of the 1980s.

As Table 6.3 shows, the U.S. current account was in surplus or almost balanced until 1984. The dollar had appreciated by then, but whether the real effective appreciation of about 20% (Figure 1) was alarming is not self-evident. In 1982, when the world was in a recession, some knowledgeable economists argued that a U.S. recovery would depreciate the dollar and called for a locomotive approach (Miller [1983], chapter 7). It was only after the data for four years had been gathered and sorted out that a consensus emerged among mainstream economists and non-American government officials concerning the effect of the Reagan policy mix. And the evidence was far from conclusive even then (see Islam [1986]).

But let us suppose, for the sake of argument, that technocrats from Germany and Japan had a well-functioning economic model in 1981, one which correctly predicted the Reagan policy would lead to a very high dollar and very large deficits in the U.S. current account. On the basis of their analysis, could the policymakers of Germany and Japan

Table 6.3 Several Economic Indicators for U.S., Garmany, and Japan, 1980–87 (%)

	1980	1981	1982	1983	1984	1985	1986	1987
Real growth rates								
U.S.	−0.2	1.9	−2.5	3.6	6.8	3.0	2.9	2.9
Germany	1.5	0.0	−1.0	1.9	3.3	2.0	2.5	1.7
Japan	4.3	3.7	3.1	3.2	5.1	4.9	2.4	4.3
Yields on long-term government bonds								
U.S.	11.4	13.7	12.9	11.3	12.4	10.8	7.8	8.6
Germany	8.5	10.4	9.0	7.9	7.8	6.9	5.9	5.9
Japan	9.2	8.7	8.1	7.4	6.8	6.3	4.9	7.2
CPI inflation rates								
U.S.	13.5	10.4	6.1	3.2	4.3	3.6	1.8	3.7
Germany	5.4	6.3	5.3	3.3	2.4	2.2	−0.2	0.2
Japan	7.8	4.8	2.9	1.8	2.4	2.0	0.6	0.1
Budget deficits as percentages of GNP								
U.S.	2.5	2.4	4.1	5.6	4.9	5.1	5.0	3.8
Germany	1.8	2.5	2.4	1.9	1.6	1.2	1.2	1.4
Japan	5.5	4.8	4.9	4.4	4.0	3.5	3.4	3.0
Current account balance of payments as percentage of GNP								
U.S.	+1.1	+1.1	+0.8	−0.1	−1.5	−2.0	−2.5	−2.7
Germany	−0.2	+1.0	+2.3	+2.2	+3.1	+4.4	+5.8	+5.5
Japan	−0.9	+0.6	+0.8	+1.9	+3.0	+3.7	+4.4	+3.8

Source: Bank of Japan, *Comparative Economic and Financial Statistics*, 1988.

have dissuaded President Reagan from his policy? No. President Reagan had his own technocrats; he was armed with an economic model named the Laffer curve. He would have replied that *his* model told him that the U.S. budget deficits would not grow, and that the larger deficits in 1982 and 1983 were aberrations brought about by the (Fed-produced, and unnecessary) recession. If he had had an economic model that differs from the model of Germany and Japan, the latter could not have dissuaded him on the basis of the model.

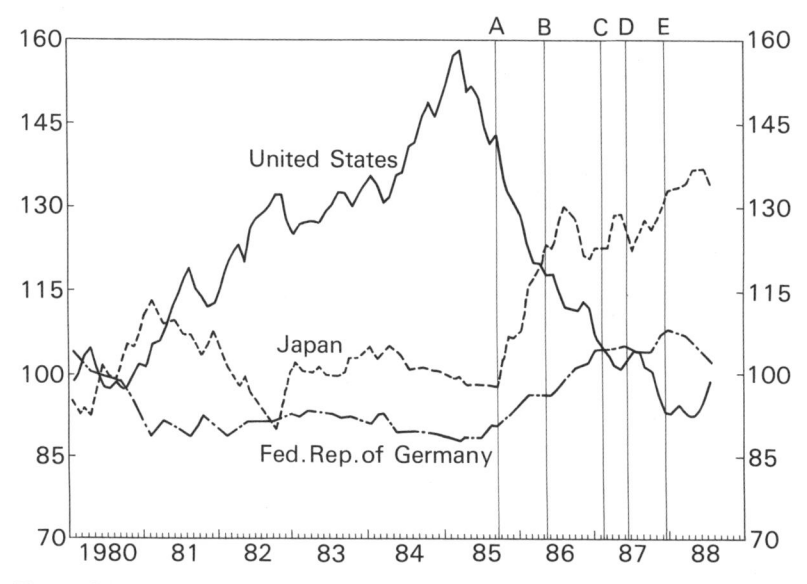

Figure 6.1
Major Industrial Countries: Real Effective Exchange Rates, 1980–88 (1980 = 100)
A: Plaza Agreement, September 22, 1985
B: Tokyo Economic Declaration, May 1–6, 1986
C: Louvre Accord, February 22, 1987
D: Venice Summit, June 8–10, 1987
E: Group of Seven Statement, December 22, 1987
Note: Real effective exchange rates based on normalized unit labor costs in manufacturing.
Source: Reproduced from Chart 1 of Frenkel and Goldstein (1988).

And when his model had finally been proven wrong in 1985, it was too late.

The lesson to be learned from this episode seems clear. Once a U.S. President is elected on an economic platform, he will proceed to implement it whatever Germany and Japan think of its wisdom. If the platform is concerned with a macro policy, the economists' knowledge of its effect is such that widely divergent answers can be produced. In other words, technocrats cannot agree on the correct macro model to analyze its impact. The President will naturally select a model that suits his preference, and reject others that disagree with his preferred analysis. If we remember that similar policy shocks are produced every four years and all the lags involved, we realize how difficult it will be for the major countries to coordinate their macro policies.[5]

3. The Plaza Agreement and After

The Plaza agreement in 1985 produced large appreciations of the yen and the deutsche mark (though the latter rose less sharply in terms of real, effective rates). Events after the Plaza, such as the Louvre agreement and economic summits, are said to testify successful policy cooperations among the major countries. As de Vries (1987, p. 278) once wrote, "all in all, by late 1986 coordination had become the central topic of international economic policy."

I tend to agree to the view that there have been successful policy bargains since 1985, and that the macroeconomic performances of the G-7 have been better than they would have been in the absence of cooperation. Exchange rates in 1988 were unusually stable, for example. The U.S. budget and trade deficits have been reduced appreciably when measured as ratios to the GNP. These are solid achievements, but when asked whether macro policy cooperation has been an unqualified success, I must think twice before answering in the affirmative. I am not sure, for example, whether the U.S. has done its fair part in the policy coordination exercises. It is also doubtful whether the policy bargains could have been realized if each participant had acted in its self-interest. In what follows, I shall discuss these and some related issues.

Let me first discuss the so-called cooperative intervention in the foreign exchange market. As for the effectiveness of official intervention, it has for some time been agreed that intervention will have only small effects, except in the case of a speculative bubble (e.g., Crockett and Goldstein [1987], p. 28). I argued in Section II that the year before the Plaza agreement must have been a period of speculative bubble. That the cooperative intervention initiated by the agreement had a dramatic effect, especially on the yen/dollar rate, seems to vindicate the conventional view that there had been a bubble and that intervention is effective in a situation of this kind. It is also said, and I tend

---

[5] Several participants argued that my view of policy cooperation and lack of adequate economic knowledge is too cynical, that cooperation may have been a substitute for (difficult-to-implement) domestic policies, and that we learn by experience and, in fact, have learned, as post-Plaza cooperation shows. I must admit the force of their arguments and would like to watch the future developments carefully to see whether history repeats itself or progresses.

to agree, that intervention was effective in this case because of U.S. participation.

Since then we have heard the authorities talk about cooperative intervention on several occasions. But the extent to which the United States has participated has been surprisingly small. According to a Bank of Tokyo study (1988), the total amount of U.S. intervention during the 1981–87 period was $18.6 billion ($9.1 billion in sales and $9.5 billion in purchases). This is a trifling amount; the authorities of other countries bought the dollar to the tune of $130 billion in 1987 alone. It may be argued that other countries were more interested than the United States in the stability of the dollar. It may also be argued that as far as the total amount of intervention is concerned, which authorities purchased the dollar is immaterial. But the fact remains that the U.S. did not do much; there have been few cooperative interventions. What this implies for the asset settlement problem will be taken up in Section IV.

Though there has been little cooperation in the past intervention, I am inclined to think it has been more or less effective. Let me confine myself to the yen because my knowledge about other currencies is not as broad. My back-of-an-envelope calculation shows that the Japanese intervention has been of the leaning-against-the-wind type,[6] and that monthly changes in money supply seem little affected by the intervention. In other words, the Japanese authorities have been engaged in more or less random smoothings. Their effect on the foreign exchange market must be to increase the (expected) cost of short-run speculation, and thus be similar to that of the Tobin tax. To the extent that the latter is effective in mitigating the volatility and misalignment of exchange rates, official intervention must likewise be viewed as effective.

Let me turn next to the Louvre agreement. What was really agreed on at the Louvre in February 1987 is not known to the public, but it is generally understood that the agreement included fairly narrow ranges for exchange rates and macro policy changes by the participants (BIS [1988], chap. 7). It is understood in particular that Japan agreed to a fiscal expansion in exchange for the U.S. promise to "cooperate" in yen stability. The bargains seem reasonable and resulted in a measure of successful macro performances. In this sense, I have no objection

---

[6] Since 1980, the sum of interventions is almost zero (relative to the variance), and dollar purchase is positively correlated with yen appreciation (the correlation coefficient is 0.37) in quarterly data.

to calling the agreement a success, but I am not persuaded that the bargains were necessary. I shall briefly explain why I am not persuaded that the Louvre agreement embodied what economists regard as a cooperative solution.

Japanese fiscal expansion was called for whether there was the Louvre agreement or not; its growth rate in 1986 was only 2.4%. A U.S. budget restraint, if included in the agreement, served the U.S. self-interest. The Gramm-Rudman Hollings Amendment had been under discussion since 1985, and no one will argue that the purpose of the Act was to please Germany and Japan. It is true that Japan desperately wanted to see the yen/dollar rate stabilized. But was it in the U.S. interest to have the yen/dollar rate go up further? Certainly not, because then its inflation would be rekindled and capital inflow would be threatened. Now economists advocate a macro policy cooperation when externality is involved, and I have argued that no externality was involved in the case of the Louvre agreement. To hail it as an outcome of cooperation might have discouraged speculative bubbles in the foreign exchange market. If so the whole exercise was a success after all. My point here is that it is good to remember that the Louvre agreement cannot be cited as an example of what economists mean by a cooperative solution.

Finally I shall have something to say on the objective (quantitative) indicators and the macro policy surveillance (Crockett and Goldstein [1987], pp. 15–16). These devices have been introduced under the U.S. leadership and have been in use for some time. They may be regarded as a partial realization of the long-standing U.S. position on the monetary reform that stresses prompt, symmetric and obligatory adjustments of macro policies (Cooper [1987], p. 28). Here symmetric adjustments mean, of course, that a surplus country should be forced to act. Whether a hegemonic deficit country is supposed to make prompt adjustments is not clear; the U.S. has been selective in the application of this principle. That it did almost nothing to correct the deficit in the first Reagan term was a conspicuous example, but I am concerned now with the post-Plaza period.

Germany and Japan have been reluctant participants in the surveillance exercise. They were afraid that the United States might be tempted to force them into actions they knew were harmful. The disastrous (to their eyes) consequence of the 1978 Bonn summit agreement was in their minds when they rejected the U.S. demand of a trigger mechanism. Indeed, on several occasions in 1987, the United States demanded that the two countries lower interest rates just as they were contemplating interest increases to nip inflationary pressures in the bud. It is not surprising then that the two countries were suspicious of the U.S. motive when in September 1987 it started advocating inclusion of a commodity price index in the set of quantitative indicators. Since commodity prices were generally depressed, they reasoned, the U.S. wanted to use the indicators to demand easy money of them. Ironically, though, commodity prices were rising at the time of the Toronto summit, and the indicators would have demanded that the United States raise its discount rate. Did it do that? It simply ignored the indicators.[7]

As I mentioned, I am not overly critical of the policy cooperation exercises in the post-Plaza period. But it seems to me that the several examples I cited imply that cooperation has not been symmetric. Broadly speaking, the U.S. acted as it wanted and demanded other countries to do what the U.S. wanted. The United States got others' cooperation only to a certain extent, but this is beside the point. What is important in the context of international monetary arrangements is that political and economic powers are distributed very unevenly among the major countries. In evaluating the present system or its reform proposals, we should keep this asymmetry in mind.

IV. A Critique of Reform Proposals in View of Postwar Experiences

In the previous two sections, I have been concerned with the postwar performance of international monetary arrangements. Through a general comparison of the pegged-rate system with the floating period and an examination of three episodes of policy cooperation, several issues of importance have emerged that should be taken into account when evaluating reform proposals of the international monetary system. Of these issues, I single out three here, namely, (a) Is our economic knowledge adequate? (b) What roles should asset settlements vis-a-vis macro adjustments play? and (c) Can the United States be kept a benevolent despot? Some aspects of the issues have been discussed already, but others have only been alluded to. It is the purpose of Section IV to organize my discussion in such a way that the three issues are addressed directly, and I also attempt a critical examination of the more important reform proposals.

---

[7] A participant argued that the U.S. motive behind its insistence on including a commodity price was not what I wrote in the text, but simply to have an anchor in the set of indicators.

1. Our Economic Knowledge and Macro Policy Adjustments

When I discussed the Reagan policy mix of the early 1980s, I emphasized that because our economic knowledge was inadequate, Germany and Japan could not have persuaded the U.S. to reconsider it. Some advocates of target zones, to be examined later, imply that Germany and Japan could object to the Reagan policy (Williamson and Miller [1987], pp. 5–6). Though I praise their sincerity and enthusiasm, it nevertheless seems to me that they underestimate the inadequacy of our economic knowledge. President Reagan, or any other U.S. President, could have invoked an economic model of his liking. And economics being no exact science, his own model would have had a good chance of withstanding "refutations" by rival models.[8]

If policy makers (or technocrats, for that matter) cannot (or do not intend to) agree on the correct economic model,[9] what does it imply for macro policy cooperation? Recent studies (especially Frankel and Rockett [1988]) have shown convincingly that cooperation based on incorrect models may lead to welfare losses. We are thus reminded that the naive notion that any cooperation, however ill-conceived, is better than no cooperation is false; it is sometimes better for each country to go it alone than to try striking policy cooperation bargains based on an inaccurate model. Frankel and Rockett also note that because our knowledge of policy multipliers is inaccurate in regard to their signs and magnitudes, we cannot be sure that a modest degree of cooperation marginally improves world welfare.[10]

The issue of our inadequate knowledge is important because some of the reform proposals of the international monetary system emphasize macro policy adjustments. I mentioned above that the United States has favored a prompt, symmetric and obligatory adjustment. In the words of Cohen (1977, chap. 4) the U.S. position in the reform debates has been diametrically opposite to the European position of "loose adjustment and tight (asset) settlements." The adjustment here

---

[8] The Laffer curve, which impressed almost no one. However, the economics profession is not without more respectable models that show that large U.S. budget deficits do not lead to high interest rates or to high values of the dollar. See Evans (1987) and (1986).

[9] In Shinkai (1989), I emphasized that policymakers have an incentive to cheat on the model to be used in a policy cooperation exercise. I referred above to a similar situation as a conflict-of-interest problem (see note 3), but it may be better referred to as a free-rider problem. See also Canzoneri and Gray (1985).

[10] More than one participant noted that in discussing policy cooperation, the problem of credibility should be addressed and that the Frankel-Rockett results I cited may be too extreme because studies exist that produce different results.

refers to correcting balance-of-payments imbalances (especially surpluses) by means of macro policy changes (which may or may not include changes in the exchange rate). A target zone proposal with its emphasis on tight adjustment and neglect of settlements,[11] for example, is a prominent offspring of the U.S. position. But can authorities adjust effectively if they do not know the way a policy change affects balance of payments? Frankel and Rockett note that the world's leading econometric models do *not* agree on the *sign* or magnitude of the effect of a monetary policy change on current account balances (see also Cooper [1988]).

I just referred to the asset settlement problem, and that gives me an occasion to make two remarks about it. One concerns the failure of the Smithsonian agreement, a topic taken up in Section III. There I noted that the parities agreed on survived only one year and indicated that this was one example of our inadequate knowledge exposed by reality. But it may be argued that the Smithsonian parities did not survive long because the inconvertible dollar was more vulnerable to speculative attacks than in the 1960s. The dollar convertibility is related to the asset settlement problem, and this argument implies that the Smithsonian agreement failed because it was of a loose settlement type, not necessarily because the new parities were wide of the mark. I raise this point to remind the reader of the settlement problem, but I personally believe that after August 1971, the United States could not have reintroduced the gold-dollar conversion at $38, $43, or whatever value was thought reasonable. The price of gold rose to more than $100 an ounce in 1974, and has remained above $200 since 1978. In the 1960s, the convertibility did not prevent speculative attacks (more on this below), or President Nixon's policy of 1971 would have been unnecessary.

My second remark is closely related to the first; it is concerned with the rationale of asset settlements. The European position vis-a-vis the U.S. position in the monetary reform debates must be that the introduction of asset settlements is essential for disciplining the United States. The Europeans must expect that this is the only way by which the U.S. will refrain from running a large deficit. Then we shall not need to worry much about macro adjustments, which if forced on them mechanically will do more harm than good. Thus their advocacy of "loose adjustment and tight settlements." I can be sympathetic to

---

[11] However, Cooper (1987, 144) quotes Williamson in 1975 when he advocated a reference-rate system and supported his advocacy by arguing that without it asset settlement could not be introduced.

their psychology, but I must judge that the reasoning ignores a lesson from the postwar experiences. The pre-1971 IMF system had the characteristics of loose adjustment and tight settlements; it had no provision to encourage adjustments by a surplus country. The United States was under a strict obligation to convert dollars held by foreign authorities into gold. But we know that the system did not discipline the U.S.; a hegemonic power simply refuses to subject itself to disciplines that an international institution imposes.

I started this subsection by emphasizing the inadequacy of our economic knowledge. As I proceeded, however, I found myself deriving some economic (or one may say political) lessons from the postwar experiences. Is our knowledge of economic history or general economic principles adequate? While I do not intend to be dogmatic in this respect, I submit that our economic knowledge is on shaky ground when we ask the magnitudes or signs—or both—of macro policy multipliers. But we are on sounder ground when it comes to deriving historical lessons or general economic principles. And I would like to conclude the subsection by citing one principle that is on solid ground.

I suggested above that the pre-1971 system collapsed because it was on the gold-dollar standard. It has been known since the days of the bimetallic standard that a system with two principal monies whose rate of exchange is fixed is inherently unstable. Thus the gold-silver standard of England degenerated into a gold standard despite Newton's best intentions. And we are told that Marshall devised a stable but multi-currency system in his symmetallism, where a standard contains fixed *quantities* of gold and silver, but their values fluctuate freely. Though Marshall's scheme was never adopted, we easily see why the pre-1971 IMF was inherently unstable, and that (incidentally) the present SDR promises to be a "symmetallic" standard.

2. The U.S. Hegemony and Dollar-based Systems

If it is known that multi-currency systems are unstable and fixed exchange rates are nevertheless desirable, we are led to the notion of a dollar-based, fixed-rate system (call one a dollar standard). Indeed, several economists have argued that the benefit of a common currency and the instability (or the diseconomy) of a multi-currency system logically call for a dollar standard. Kindleberger is a persistent advocate of a dollar-based system (Cohen [1977], chap. 7). McKinnon's proposal (1984 and 1988) appears more like a multi-currency system,

BRETTON WOODS AND FLOATING RATES 141

but given the asymmetric roles the dollar plays in private transactions, it may well be counted as a dollar standard.[12]

When other currencies are fixed tightly to the dollar, the system provides in effect a common currency. When they are merely pegged to it, as in the post-Smithsonian year, the system will fall short of the common currency ideal, but it will still be dollar-based. Even a target-zone regime may be counted as a dollar-based system because the (n-1) problem leaves one degree of freedom to the system, which will be used by a large country to set the *level* of money supply or prices. McKinnon does not ignore this problem; indeed, we may regard his proposal as one mainly concerned with addressing the problem of (world) money supply. So my evaluation of dollar-based systems below does not do justice to the spirit of his proposal.

Whatever the degree of fixity of exchange rates, the dollar-based systems belong to the hegemonic principle of organizing international monetary matters. Since it is based on the dollar, it has no such feature as gold standard automaticity. The other countries may have a limited voice in the conduct of American monetary policy, but the voice must be severely limited lest the U.S. degenerate into an unstable oligarchy (or democracy). Then the question to be asked must be: the world may reap the benefit of a common currency, but will the United States conduct its monetary policy in a benevolent way? As Kindleberger remarked, "Benevolent despotism is the best form of government. The difficulty is to keep it benevolent" (quoted by Cohen [1987], p. 228).

What can we learn on this question from the postwar monetary experiences? Let me cite several episodes that seem to indicate how the United States will behave, though some of them were already discussed. Take first the latter half of the 1960s when the gold-dollar system was in force. The U.S. experienced inflation, which was moderate by today's standard but worrisome at that time. Europeans complained of imported inflation, and Germany found it necessary to up-value its currency. The cause of U.S. inflation was the Vietnam War. Since I am not in a position to discuss the war itself, let me argue in the following way. Those who opposed U.S. involvement in Vietnam must have opposed it even if the authorities had been able to manage the economy more wisely. Those who supported the involvement must

---

[12] In the first version of the paper, I included Cooper's common currency proposal (1987, chap 13), but he rightly pointed out that his proposed regime is not a dollar-standard. A common currency managed multilaterally is not examined in the present paper, though I do not imply that it is uninteresting.

have supported it independent of its effect on inflation and balance of payments. In other words, macroeconomic considerations were irrelevant to both groups; I can argue that a major war is far more important a matter than inflation or balance of payments as long as it can be financed.

The U.S. chose involvement and chose to finance the war partly in an inflationary way. No country could oppose the U.S. involvement on *macroeconomic grounds*; the question of war or peace was more important. And, since the war effort was important, the United States proceeded to finance it in a way most convenient to it. As far as the economy is concerned, the U.S. did not feel bound by international considerations, even in the days of tight settlement. As a hegemonic power, the U.S. may very well find itself in a situation where a major war is inevitable. If the world should be on a dollar standard at that time, we can imagine the United States completely ignoring the international consequences of the way it finances its war effort.

I have already examined the Reagan policy of the early 1980s, but I did not explore fully its implications for the hegemonic behavior of the U.S. It can be argued that as a candidate, Reagan had no international economic perspective when he proposed his policy mix. What he had in mind was U.S. inflation and U.S. productivity growth. Even if he had known that the dollar would soar and the U.S. trade account would deteriorate, he would not have minded; witness his nonchalant attitude in the first term. Would he have felt restrained if, for example a target zone agreement had been in force? I do not think so; if he had found the agreement restraining, he would have run on the platform of *withdrawing* the United States from it. Remember, he advocated a return to the gold standard without considering its international consequences. And as I mentioned in Section III. 1, these kinds of policy shocks are bound to occur every four years.

I can cite several lesser events. I discussed the U.S. handling of the objective indicators, especially of commodity prices, and need not repeat it here. I also mentioned above that the supposedly "tight" settlement of the pre-1971 IMF did not discipline the U.S. In this respect, Germany and Japan may recall a minor episode: after the gold pool was closed in 1968, the United States pressured the two countries into holding dollars instead of converting them into gold. The two may also recall several occasions in 1987 and 1988 on which they were dissuaded by the U.S. from interest rate increases. If inflation had materialized, as they had feared, the episodes would have been a damaging experience, just as the 1978 Bonn summit poisoned the atmosphere of international policy debates.

In citing those examples, I have no intention of criticizing the United States. No one will deny that it has been a benevolent hegemonist in the broad political context. Even in terms of economic scores, its behavior in trade, technological transfer, aid, and so on has been generally benevolent. What I am arguing is that in the essentially short-term and technically controversial sphere of macro policies, a hegemonic power cannot be expected to behave benevolently. And I do not criticize the U.S. for this. A Japanese saying has it that you do not reason with a crying child or with your master. It is better to have an international monetary arrangement that does not unduly rely on the benevolent behavior of a hegemonic power.

3. Target Zones and Objective Indicators

If a fixed exchange rate system is either untenable (high capital mobility) or undesirable (the hegemonic principle), and if the present floating leaves something to be desired, can there be an arrangement in between that commends itself? A target zone proposal is assuredly among the most interesting. In this subsection, I shall examine a version of the proposal attributed primarily to Williamson (1985) and Williamson and Miller (1987). After that, I shall briefly discuss objective indicators that may be regarded as officially in use now.

The primary objective of a target zone proposal is to prevent misalignments in the exchange rate, and I can sympathize with the objective. Misaligned exchange rates are large, persistent deviations from equilibrium, and are harmful almost by definition. Two instruments that authorities are supposed to employ to prevent exchange rates from moving outside the zones are monetary policy and official intervention, but the advocates attach importance to the former (Crockett and Goldstein [1987], pp. 12–13). If intervention were important, they would need to address the question of which government does the job—that is, the question of settlements. As I indicated above, the target zone proposal is of a "tight adjustment and loose settlements" variety.

As such, it is not immune to the difficulty associated with our inadequate economic knowledge that plagues any macro policy cooperation. I may also add that the same conflict of interest problem arises here that will in a macro policy coordination.[13] The proponents will no doubt counter by contending that it is exactly to get around this difficulty that they advocate a fairly wide zone, say $\pm 10\%$ around

---

[13] See notes 3 and 8 above.

equilibrium. My argument against the target zone proposal is that the difficulty associated with our inadequate knowledge is simply too severe. One obvious point: when the exchange rate threatens to overshoot the zone, do we know whether money should be loosened or tightened? We apparently do not know if in the intermediate run the exchange rate is strongly influenced by changes in the current account.

Another point to raise will be the difficulty of arriving at an equilibrium exchange rate. Although I tend to think this difficulty is more involved with the conflict-of-interest problem—that is, the authorities working at cross-purposes—I shall not go into it. Let me confine myself to the technical difficulties, not the least of which derives from the need to estimate what Williamson names the underlying capital flow. Since (equilibrium) capital flow depends in general on an exchange rate outlook, the estimation involves finding a stable capital flow *function*. I really wonder whether this is practical. Anyway, the difficulty is well-known by the proponents themselves; their estimates of equilibrium exchange rates are highly divergent, over time and among individual proponents.

Table 6.4 lists some of the representative estimates. The figures refer to *nominal* yen/dollar rates, though the advocates of target zones usually define (correctly) equilibrium in real, effective rates. And I must admit that I do not know if Krause was a proponent when he made the estimate of ¥100 to the dollar. But no one can claim he should not have presented his estimate if he did not advocate a target zone. The 10% zone around ¥100 in 1986 was far below Williamson's 1987 zone around ¥145. Of course Williamson could argue (as he did in Marston [1988], pp. 163–64) that so low an estimate of equilibrium was wrong, but it was *his* view. The thrust of the Frankel and Rockett

Table 6.4 Examples of Equilibrium Exchange Rates (nominal yen/dollar)

Author, period	Yen/dollar
Willamson	
1983 I[a]	205
1984 IV[a]	198
1987	140–145
Krause	
1986[b]	100
Krugman	
1985 IV[b]	175
1988[c]	100–150

Notes: [a]: Williamson (1985), 34 and 79.
[b]: Loupesko and Johnson (1988), 110.
[c]: Frenkel and Goldstein (1988), 22.

paper (1988) is that any of the authors of the world's leading econometric models may claim that the others are wrong, and the Frankel-Rockett conclusion still holds unless the claimant *proves* his point. The same is true of the estimates of equilibrium rates.

The advocates of the proposal permit the equilibrium (that is, real effective) rate to move over time, which is reasonable. The figures in Table 6.4 are nominal, bilateral rates, so it may be argued that they reflect changes in price differentials as well as in the equilibrium rate itself. But I submit that the wide divergents in the table cannot be disposed of in this way. First, note that inflation differentials between the United States and Japan were not large after 1985. Next, suppose the target zone had been introduced in early 1985. The yen/dollar rate would have stayed above ¥180 for a while. But Williamson calculated that in 1987 the equilibrium rate was ¥145. Though I regret asking this question, I wonder whether he would have arrived at that value if the actual rate had stayed above ¥180 until, for example, 1986.

It seems to me that narrow 10% zones around an unknown equilibrium do not solve the problem associated with our inadequate knowledge. At any given time, estimates of equilibrium rates can diverge far more than 10%. And once a zone is introduced, it will be very difficult, and produce as divergent a result, to compute the movements of equilibrium rates. Perhaps because of this difficulty, Krugman (quoted by Frenkel and Goldstein [1988], p. 22) now advocates a wide zone of ¥100 to ¥150. This is a conscientious position, but a zone this wide though harmless, costs the proposal much of its attractiveness.

In conclusion, I turn briefly to objective indicators. For my purpose in this section, the best way to approach the multilateral surveillance through those indicators will be to regard it as an extension of a target zone (Crockett and Goldstein [1987], pp. 28–29). The latter monitors a single indicator[14] (an exchange rate, in the bilateral case), and the former monitors ten or so indicators that include semi-policy variables such as money supply. Will policy cooperation be made easier because ten indicators are monitored instead of one? I doubt it. I wish to point out three difficulties associated with the objective indicators approach. One is obvious: estimating the equilibrium values of ten indicators is less easy than estimating the value of one.

The second difficulty is how to handle a situation where, for example, three indicators are outside their zones, but the other seven are inside.

---

[14] The target zone proposal by Williamson and Miller includes nominal income targets.

Are policy changes called for, or should the authorities wait until most indicators are outside? This is the familiar problem of defining a diffusion index. Any diffusion index circumvents the difficulty by giving an equal weight to individual indicators and applying the majority rule. Will the authorities be satisfied with this arbitrary design? The third difficulty arises because two or more semi-policy variables (money supply, budget deficit) are included. Suppose seven endogenous indicators are outside their zones, but the semi-policy variables are inside. What should the authorities do? Should they try to change money supply and budget deficit and move them outside their zones? Or should they change the policy variables not included in the set of indicators?

These three difficulties (especially the last two) show the intrinsic arbitrariness of the objective indicators approach. Indicators may be objective by themselves, but there is no objective way to employ them in a policy cooperation exercise.[15] As such, such an exercise can easily be manipulated in an exploitative way by the hegemonic participant.

My conclusion can be briefly stated. Given the state of our economic knowledge and given the fact that the world consists of sovereign nations with a highly unequal distribution of political (and military) power, all the reform proposals, including that for tighter macro policy cooperation, must be viewed with caution. It seems to me that we must live with the present system of floating exchange rates with occasional official interventions, even though we may find this system's macro performance somewhat unsatisfactory.

References

Bank of Tokyo. 1988. "The U.S. Official Intervention in the Foreign Exchange Market" (in Japanese). *Tokyo Ginkou Geppo* (August 1988), pp. 4–21.

Baxter, M., and Stockman, A.C. 1988. "Business Cycles and the Exchange Rate System: Some International Evidence." NBER Working Paper No. 2689, August 1988.

BIS (Bank for International Settlements). 1988. *The 58th Annual Report*.

Branson, W.H. 1988. "Sources of Misalignment in the 1980s." In Marston, R.C., ed., pp. 9–38.

---

[15] In Shinkai (1989), I quoted Cooley and LeRoy's work to argue that this approach is not immune to the criticism of being atheoretical macroeconometrics, where policy multipliers are ill-defined.

Bryant, R.C., Henderson, D.W., Holtham, G., Hooper, P., and Symansky, S.A., eds. 1988. *Empirical Macroeconomics for Interdependent Economies*, Washington, D.C.: Brookings Institution.

Canzoneri, M.B., and Gray, J.A. 1985. "Monetary Policy Games and the Consequences of Noncooperative Behavior." *International Economic Review* 26: 547–64.

Cohen, B.J. 1977. *Organizing the World's Money*. London: Macmillan, 1977.

Cooper, R.N. 1987. *The International Monetary System*. Cambridge: MIT Press.

———. 1988. "U.S. Macroeconomic Policy, 1986–88: Are the Models Useful?" In Bryant et al., eds., pp. 255–66.

Crockett, A., and Goldstein, M. 1987. "Strengthening the International Monetary System: Exchange Rate, Surveillance, and Objective Indicators." IMF Occasional Papers, No. 50.

Cushman, D.O. 1988. "U.S. Bilateral Trade Flows and Exchange Risk During the Floating Period." *Journal of International Economics*. 24: 317–30.

de Vries, M.G. 1987. *Balance of Payments Adjustment, 1945 to 1986: The IMF Experience*. International Monetary Fund.

Dornbusch, R. 1980. *Open Economy Macroeconomics*. New York: Basic Books.

———, and Frankel, J. 1987. "The Flexible Exchange Rate System: Experience and Alternatives." NBER Working Paper, No. 2464.

Eichengreen, B. 1985. "Editor's Introduction." In B. Eichengreen, ed., *The Gold Standard in Theory and History*. London: Methuen, 1–35.

———. 1987. "Trade Deficits in the Long Run." NBER Working Paper No. 2437, November.

Evans, P. 1986. "Is the Dollar High Because of Large Budget Deficits?" *Journal of Monetary Economics*. 18: 227–49.

———. 1987. "Interest Rates and Expected Future Deficits in the United States." *Journal of Political Economy*. 95: 34–58.

Feldstein, M., ed. 1988. *International Economic Coodination*. Chicago: University of Chicago Press.

Frankel, J., and Rockett, K. 1988. "International Macroeconomic Policy Coordination When Policymakers Do Not Agree on the True Model." *American Economic Review*. 78: 318–40.

Frenkel, J.A., and Goldstein, M. 1988. "Exchange Rate Volatility and Misalignment: Evaluating Some Proposals for Reform." Paper prepared for Kansas Fed Symposium on Financial Market Volatility.

Fukao, M. 1987. "A Risk Premium Model of the Yen-Dollar and DM-Dollar Exchange Rates." *OECD Economic Studies*. 9: 79–104.
Higgins, C.I. 1988. "Empirical Analysis and Intergovernmental Policy Consultation." In Bryant et al., eds., pp. 285–302.
Islam, S. 1986. "The Dollar: Fickle Fundamentals or Misguided Markets?" *World Economy*. 9: 365–83.
Krugman, P. 1985. "Is the Strong Dollar Sustainable?" *The U.S. Dollar: Recent Developments, Outlook, and Policy Options*. Federal Reserve Bank of Kansas City.
Loopesko, B. and Johnson, R.A. 1988. "Realignment of the Yen-Dollar Rate: Aspects of the Adjustment Process in Japan." In Marston, R.C., ed. 105–44.
Marris, S. 1985. *Deficits and the Dollar: The World Economy at Risk*. Institute for International Economics.
Marston, R.C., ed. 1988. *Misalignment of Exchange Rates: Effects on Trade and Industry*. Chicago: University of Chicago Press.
———. 1988a. "Introduction." In Marston, R.C., ed., pp. 1–7.
———. 1988b. "Exchange Rate Policy Reconsidered." In Feldstein, M., ed., pp. 79–136.
McKibbin, W.J., and Sachs, J.D. 1986. "Comparing the Global Performance of Alternative Exchange Arrangements." NBER Working Papers, No. 2024.
———, and Sachs, J.D. 1988. "Implications of Policy Rules for the World Economy: Results from the MSG2 Model." Brookings Institution.
McKinnon, R.I. 1984, *A New International Standard for Monetary Stabilization*. Institute for International Economics.
———. 1988, "Monetary and Exchange Rate Policies for International Financial Stability: A Proposal." *Journal of Economic Perspectives*, 2, 1988, 83–103.
Miller, W., ed. 1983. *Regrowing the American Economy*. Englewood Cliffs: Prentice-Hall.
Moffitt, M. 1983. *The World's Money*. New York: Simon & Schuster.
Sachs, J.D., and Roubini, N. 1988. Sources of Macroeconomic Imbalances in the World Economy. In Suzuki, Y., and Okabe, M., eds. *Toward a World of Economic Stability: Optimal Monetary Framework and Policy*. Tokyo: University of Tokyo Press.
Shinkai, Y. 1989. "On the International Coordination of Macro Policies." *Economic Studies Quarterly*. 40: 1–13.
Taylor, J.B. 1987. "An Econometric Evaluation of International Monetary Rules: Fixed vs. Flexible Exchange Rates." processed.

―――. 1988. "Policy Analysis with a Multicountry Model." Washington: Brookings Institution.
Willett, T.D. 1977. *Floating Exchange Rates and International Monetary Reform.* Washington: American Enterprise Institute.
Williamson, J. 1985. *The Exchange Rate System.* Washington: Institute for International Economics.
―――. and Miller, M.H. 1987. *Targets and Indicators: A Blueprint for the International Coordination of Economic Policy.* Washington: Institute for International Economics.

Comments

Teh Kok Peng

I must begin with a disclaimer. I do not spend much of my working time thinking about how international policy coordination *should* be conducted or how the international monetary system *should* evolve. I suspect the same is true of other central bankers from small countries like Singapore. This is so even though such issues are much more important for small, open economies such as Singapore than for larger, more insular economies.

The reasons are simple. First, small countries such as Singapore are seldom seen, let alone heard, in the official forums that discuss these issues. Second, the spillover effect of Singapore's policy actions on the rest of the world is insignificant. I know it is fashionable these days to talk about the importance of the Asian NICs in the world economy and the need to involve them in international policy coordination. An examination of the relevant statistics for Singapore would suggest that the facts are otherwise.

In my comments, I will attempt first to summarize the views of Professors Eichengreen and Shinkai before proceeding to discuss them.

Professor Eichengreen's scholarly paper contains a wealth of statistical materials and has several strands of complex, interconnected arguments. His paper comprises two main parts. The second half provides an interpretation of the international monetary system between the two world wars. At the risk of some oversimplification, his arguments may be summarized as follows: the operation of the gold exchange standard was the cause of international monetary instability between these wars and worsened the Great Depression.

The key reason for this arose from misguided policies—more specifically, the absence of international policy coordination—instead of from any structural flaws caused by a gold exchange standard (as against a pure gold standard). The commitment to fixed exchange rates prevented each country from unilaterally engaging in expansionary monetary (or fiscal) policy. Yet in a depressed world economy, this commitment could have been maintained through an internationally coordinated monetary (or fiscal) expansion by the countries concerned. Such coordination would also have limited the extent of spontaneous, destabilizing portfolio shifts between reserve currencies by other central banks. In the absence of such international cooperation, the gold exchange standard limited the ability of both surplus and deficit countries to reflate and exacerbate the Great Depression.

The first part of Professor Eichengreen's paper examined exchange rate behavior under three distinct regimes—freely floating exchange rates from 1921 through 1926, fixed rates from 1927 through 1931, and managed floating rates during the rest of the 1930s—and provided certain policy implications which I interpret in the following way. There was little gain in moving from a freely floating exchange rate system to a managed floating rate system, in terms of reduction in nominal exchange rate risk or in real exchange rate variability and predictability. These can be achieved only by fixed nominal exchange rates. The resultant greater predictability of nominal and real exchange rates would have provided a greater stimulus to investment and exports. However, a fixed exchange rate regime can be sustained only if policymakers' commitment to it is credible, and it would be more readily achieved by international policy coordination.

In the second paper, in contrast, Professor Shinkai, based on his assessment of the postwar Bretton Woods and managed floating rate regimes, is skeptical, even cynical, about policy coordination. He questions its desirability but even more its attainability. On desirability, he is agnostic about whether the floating exchange rate regime we have had since 1973 has adversely affected growth, exports, and investment, compared with the Bretton Woods regime. On attainability, he considers that political leaders, principally in the United States, are most unlikely to sacrifice on the altar of international policy coordination the economic policy platforms, mostly domestic, on which they have been elected. In this, they are abetted by widely divergent results of different economic models and the lack of a consensus on the correct economic model. If the model used is an incorrect model, policy coordination could lead to a worse outcome. Even when the model is correct, the inadequate state of our economic knowledge makes it difficult to implement proposals such as target zones and multilateral surveillance using objective indicators. We therefore must continue to muddle along with the present managed floating rate system, despite its imperfections.

I do not know enough economic history to assess Professor Eichengreen's interpretation of the international monetary system between the wars. But if true, such an internationally coordinated monetary expansion would be a rare instance of an international macroeconomic policy free lunch. Little policy trade-off was involved. Why, then, was it not attempted? Professor Eichengreen quoted Keynes and wrote about his efforts to move policies in this direction. There were also similar initiatives by a few countries, which were unsuccessful.

So it appears we cannot plead ignorance. I am inclined to think that Kindleberger's explanation of the lack of leadership comes closer to the truth and that his explanation can be reconciled with Professor Eichengreen's. I would interpret leadership to involve taking a leading role in managing policy coordination and an ability and willingness to play by the rules of the game. On this view, Britain was the leader before 1913, and there was policy coordination. The United States was not prepared to assume leadership in the 1930s, and there was no policy coordination. The point I want to make is that policy coordination does not just evolve; it requires leadership to be successfully sustained. It was a role that the U.S., in its isolationist period in the 1930s, was unwilling to undertake.

The other dimension of leadership is the willingness and ability of the leader to observe the rules of the game. This affects credibility. The leader of the Bretton Woods regime was the United States. The regime came under siege in the late 1960s when the conduct of macroeconomic policies by the U.S. brought into serious question her ability to abide by its rules. More recently, the Plaza Accord of September 1985, of which the United States was the initiator, required the U.S. to reduce its budget deficit. This has not happened in any significant way and has strained G-7 policy coordination. The financial markets presently appear to be surprisingly benign over continued U.S. fiscal inaction. It would be interesting to see how long this phase can last.

Apart from leadership, what other lessons can we draw from the interwar experiences for international policy coordination today? I suspect not many. The principal lessons drawn were for domestic macroeconomic management, and these lessons were drawn long ago. They resulted in the post-World War II commitment to full employment and, correspondingly, a much weaker commitment to fixed exchange rates in most leading countries. Thus a repeat of the macroeconomic policy conduct of the interwar period is most unlikely. This is illustrated most vividly during the October 1987 stock market crash. Most of the principal countries responded by easing their monetary policies. There may have been some coordination among some of the leaders, but I would guess their monetary policies would have been in much the same direction even without coordination.

It could indeed be argued that it was the very success of the lessons drawn for domestic economic management by the countries which have best assimilated them that has given rise to the present global current account imbalances. This time, unlike the inter-war period, there is no macroeconomic policy free lunch for the world economy. For effective international policy coordination to reduce this global imbalance, domestic demand would need to be reduced in the deficit countries of the United States and United Kingdom and to be maintained, if not increased, in the surplus countries of Japan and West Germany. Further, far from maintaining exchange rate stability, it is likely that policy credibility may require the real exchange rates of the deficit countries to fall further against those of the surplus countries.

I now come to Professor Shinkai's paper, which is wide-ranging. I shall concentrate on a few points, since his paper covers areas I believe will be taken up in greater detail in other sessions. I respect Professor Shinkai's hard-nosed attitude about economic arguments in the face of political realities. It seems to be borne out by recent experiences. However, I do believe he is unduly pessimistic. Economic policy mistakes have political costs, and it is in the politicians' interest to learn from them. I referred earlier to the lessons learned from the Great Depression. Moving to a contemporary example: could the U.S. fiscal experiment of the early 1980s be sold again as a policy platform to the U.S. electorate at some point in the future, assuming that the current fiscal problem is somehow resolved? I doubt it. I also think that the lessons of this policy mistake have been learnt by other countries as well.

I have more sympathy with Professor Shinkai's view that recent policy actions, such as Japanese fiscal expansion, the U.S. Government's attempt to reduce its fiscal deficit, and U.S. action to avoid too rapid a fall in its dollar, are all in the interests of the countries concerned and need not involve any international policy coordination. Nevertheless, such coordination could improve the efficiency of domestic policy actions if there are externalities, as long as it does not distract each country from the pursuit of prudent domestic macroeconomic policies. Jacob Frenkel, in a survey last year of the international monetary system,[1] said that the floating exchange system, which

---

[1] Jacob A. Frenkel, "The International Monetary System: Developments and Prospects," IMF Working Paper, May 1988, page 14.

replaced the Bretton Woods system in 1973, could be said to have an implicit contract in which each country would adopt sound and stable macroeconomic policies at the national level, with the expectation that a stability of exchange markets would emerge as a useful by-product. Policy coordination in this setting would take care of small spillover effects of sound domestic policies. In the present policy environment, the risk is that policy coordination could be used as a substitute for good domestic policies. Professor Shinkai's skepticism would then be well founded.

Comments

Jan Michielsen

As a smaller European central banker, I am honored to be invited to take part in this discussion. At the international level, my country is primarily a policy taker, not a policymaker. I thus reflect more the interests of the consumer than of the producer. But even in the international monetary system, consumer interests are real and not unimportant.

In this short intervention, it is impossible to do justice to the work of the authors and to exploit fully their rich harvest of ideas. I therefore shall focus my remarks on three questions, which came to my mind as I read the stimulating papers presented by Professors Eichengreen and Shinkai.
1) Is there no ideal exchange rate system for all seasons?
2) Is international policy coordination an empty box, or is it a meaningful, operational strategy?
3) Is there a persistent and growing gap between the demands on the international monetary system and the available instruments?

I wish to make a few remarks about each of those issues.

I. On the Exchange Rate System

The combination of both papers offers a striking example of the recurrent and stubborn nature of problems related to the choice and the management of exchange rate regimes. In a long-term perspective, the often rapid succession of regimes—which allows us to apply the notion of variability to exchange rate movements as well as to the regimes—reflects a sense of dissatisfaction with the available options, or at least with their operating procedures. In this respect, I want to stress the following points, or lessons:

(a) Fixed rates or adjustable peg regimes appear clearly as the preferred system most conducive to the simultaneous achievement of internal *and* external stability and to the maintenance of an open trading system. This statement requires, however, some qualifications. Whereas the official support of misaligned parity structures poses a threat to monetary policies, appreciating floating currencies may make an important contribution to the anti-inflationary policies of individual countries. When such stabilization policies are conducted without a general cooperative framework, however, there is a clear risk that the problem of inflation will be exported to other countries.

One cannot deny that adjustable peg systems contain a bias toward rigidity. The exchange rate becomes a matter of political prestige and realignments a political contest. Moreover, the preservation of the existing parity grid may evolve as a prerequisite for the credibility of the system. Current account disequilibria then have to be absorbed by other measures conducive to a reallocation of resources with a particular emphasis on long-term capital flows. In this respect, it is not surprising that official blueprints for a European Monetary Union at the EEC level have come forward after a prolonged period of exchange rate stability.

b) Floating rate regimes have been introduced mainly as an act of surrender, or at least as a second-best solution. An exception could be made for the early 1980s when U.S. and U.K. authorities justified freely floating rates as a logical component of a free market system in which official intervention would only be counterproductive. This episode ended when the Plaza Agreement admitted the phenomenon and the dangers of overshooting.

In my view, monetary history does not support the proposition that the exchange rate function should be reduced to that of a pure market price. Exchange rate movements are subject to margins of tolerance, but we have seen that the distance between the two extremes may be large if the exchange rate constraint is not accepted as an effective policy instrument.

c) Managed floating has appeared as a hybrid concept that covers a wide range of objectives and strategies. The implementation of this concept seems to have suffered from two chief drawbacks: the rejection of a more ambitious regime, such as an adjustable peg, has raised doubts about the exchange rate commitment in a softer regime, and cooperative arrangements for managed floating have not been very successful. One may refer in this respect to the 1977 IMF guidelines on floating, which aimed at orderly markets through a smoothing out of daily fluctuations and at avoiding longer-term misalignments. The operational value of these guidelines has been questionable. Moreover, the usefulness of smoothing out short-term erratic movements has been disputed. More aggressive "leaning-with-the-wind" strategies have been defended as more promising avenues for intervention policies.

Past experience shows that the implementation of sound and officially endorsed principles has encountered practical obstacles. Although authoritative studies, such as the Jurgensen report of 1983, recognized the superiority of non-sterilized interventions, this type of official action has been applied exceptionally. Still more important is the gap between the need for exchange-rate adjustments to be supported by other policy measures in order to be effective and the practical achievements. At the risk of oversimplification, I would argue that significant devaluations have been the most efficient way of triggering unpopular accompanying measures. Most often, revaluing surplus countries have invoked an appropriate policy stance or used an exchange-rate adjustment only for internal stabilization purposes without accepting the need to offset stimulatory measures. Floating rates in general have a poor record as an incentive to the introduction of adjustment measures.

The international exchange rate regime has increasingly become dominated by the relationships between the G-3 currencies. According to the IMF list of exchange-rate arrangements, most IMF countries have pegged their currency to a major national currency. Those who preferred a composite currency have mostly constructed their own baskets. Recourse to the SDR at the international level or the ECU at the European level as an anchor of exchange-rate policies has so far been limited. Despite political reservations about dominant currencies, countries have thus favored an anchor with a concrete policy model. In this field too we have registered differences between the aim of promoting composite currencies as the center of the system and the practical developments.

II. On Policy Coordination

In his conclusions, Professor Eichengreen states that "in the interwar period at least, policy coordination could have significantly relieved the conflict between the commitment to fix the exchange rate and the commitment to other targets." If my interpretation is correct, the role that policy coordination failed to fulfill was one of implementing a program of concerted reflation in order to offset the depressing effects of an excessive exchange constraint, especially for countries with the strongest reserve positions. Thus lack of policy coordination and asymmetry are not new products of the 1980s, but old problems of the 1920s.

A possible explanation for this lack of policy coordination could have been the absence of multilateral surveillance and international institutions such as the IMF and the OECD. With the benefit of hindsight, one has to admit that the setting up of these prestigious institutions did not suffice to overcome the political and conceptual difficulties that are involved in policy coordination. I doubt that the strengthening of their ruling power would have done so. This assumption underpins the message of humbleness that is conveyed by Professor Shinkai when he mentions the state of economic knowledge as a major reason for caution in the field of macro policy cooperation.

One impediment to an internationally coordinated policy mix is the treatment of fiscal policies. Should one accept the proposition that their appropriate contribution to international adjustment is limited to a medium-term strategy which reduces the role of the public sector in the economy? Or is there still some leeway for fine tuning, that is, for discretionary short-term budgetary action to relieve the burden on monetary policy?

Unless the two authors correct me, their historical account is not very encouraging for those who are committed to international policy coordination. However, this should not lead to resignation. An assessment of the Louvre Agreement, which altogether constituted a valuable attempt at defining the responsibilities in a global strategy, remains very helpful. In this respect, I disagree with Professor Shinakai when he does not consider the Louvre Agreement as a cooperative solution because there is no externality involved. In my view, coordination aims at a common strategy based on a mutual self-interest of the participants.

III. On the Aims of the System

A judgment on the performance of the system requires an assessment of the changes in the general environment. These changes have been profound. The number of participants and their geographical diversification have been greatly increased, the boundaries between money and capital have come down, and the distinction between balance of payments and development assistance has narrowed.

The use of exchange controls in the industrial area has gradually eroded. The original Bretton Woods philosophy, which favored trade to capital, has been outpaced, and the choice between exchange rate stability and national monetary autonomy has become inescapable.

When drawing the lessons from the past and without reducing the vital need for historical analysis, these new facts must be duly taken into account. In contrast with the beginning of the interwar and postwar periods, the main challenge now is globalization, not reconstruction.

At the same time the tasks of monetary policies have become more complicated. Aside from the traditional functions and dilemmas, monetary policymakers have been confronted with the possible impact of their decisions on volatile financial markets and on international debt servicing. As an overburdening of monetary policies increases their exposure to political pressures, the question arises: does one not often expect too much from national and international monetary policies, including the answer to structural and development problems?

Past experience tells us that markets do not wait for committees. The prolonged negotiations in the 1960s that led to the introduction of the SDR did not prevent the collapse of Bretton Woods, and the Committee of Twenty was unable to restore it. The study of the G-10 on the functioning of the international monetary system, which was published around June 1985, did not predict the sudden change in the U.S. policy that led to Plaza and Louvre. Thus the success of blueprint reforms is not secured.

Finally, a fair record must have an eye for the achievements and for the shortcomings. In this respect, recovery from major political and economic shocks cannot be ignored. The industrial world is now enjoying a long-sustained economic expansion, and one should not forget the positive "non-events"—the crises that were expected to occur but did not happen. In my view the system performed quite well in its "fireman" function. One can, of course, argue that it is always easier to grant credit than to bring about economic adjustment. Nevertheless, one should concede that the needed amount of cooperation has been most often forthcoming. This allows me to end on a positive note, but I assume that the aims of this conference go beyond the mere implementation of crisis management.

Comments

William E. Norton

These papers by Professors Barry Eichengreen and Yoichi Shinkai discuss exchange rate policies for large industrial countries, those that have high levels of manufactured exports.

But what should other countries do about their exchange rates? What should commodity-exporting countries do?

Australia is such a country, although a high income one, and has tried many exchange rate regimes since World War II: fixed to sterling; fixed to U.S. dollar; fixed to a trade-weighted basket of currencies; adjustable link to a trade-weighted basket; and floating, as a "group of one," with varying degrees of intervention.

Terms-of-trade changes are a major reason for commodity-exporting countries to have some degree of exchange-rate flexibility. Australian experience can illustrate this point. In the early 1950s, Australia's terms of trade rose strongly because of the Korean War, but its exchange rates with the major currencies stayed fixed. The upshot was a substantial, even though temporary, increase in inflation. A flexible exchange rate for the Australian dollar could have dampened that burst of inflation. A second episode is illustrated by Figure 1. Australia's terms of trade fell sharply in 1985 and 1986, to their lowest level in real terms in 40 years, before rising strongly in 1987 and 1988. In this case, the exchange rate initially fell, which softened the 1986 recession, and subsequently rose, helping to restrain a cyclical upswing.

Thus commodity-exporting countries' exchange rates might need to be flexible because of terms-of-trade changes, even if industrial countries have fixed or, more likely, stable currencies. This was a lesson of the 1930s too, when devaluations in commodity-exporting countries moderated the effects of the depression.

Smaller terms of trade fluctuations in terms of trade would help. That would require steadier macroeconomic policies in the industrial countries because cycles in their levels of economic activity are a cause

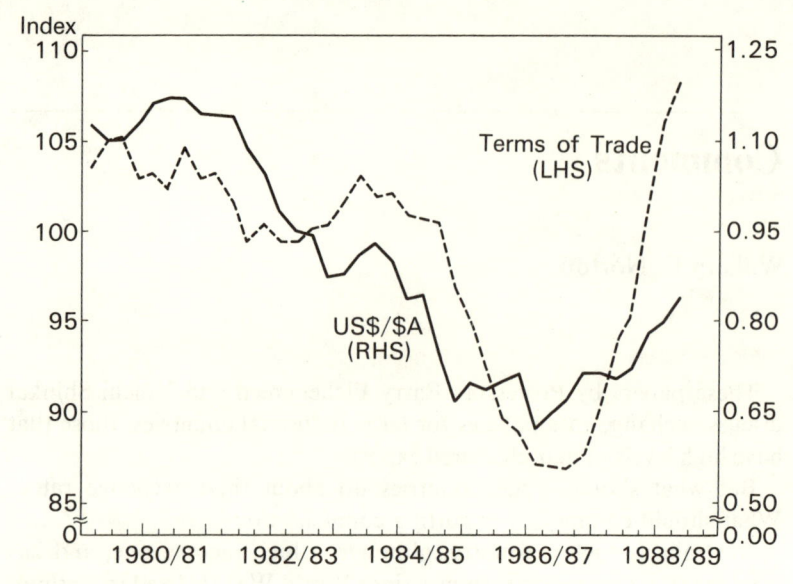

Figure 1
Terms of Trade and Exchange Rate

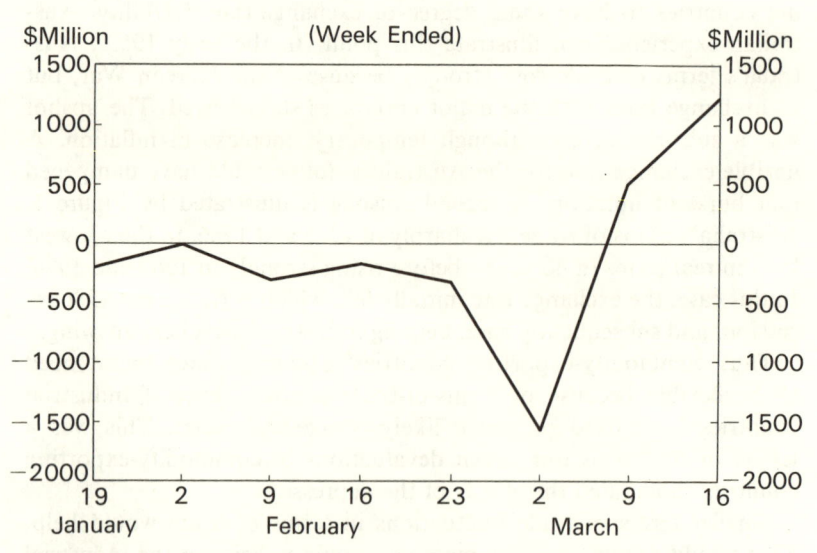

Figure 2
Changes in Foreign Exchange Reserves, 1983

of terms-of-trade fluctuations. More stability in commodity exporters' exchange rates depends therefore on greater steadiness in industrial countries' policies.

Capital flows are another influence on the degree of exchange rate flexibility. In 1983, capital flows overwhelmed Australia's exchange rate policy. At the start of that year there was a relatively fixed exchange rate—an adjustable link to a trade-weighted basket of currencies—and quite comprehensive exchange controls. During late February and early March of 1983, large capital outflows resulted in a devaluation (Figure 2). Late in the year, in contrast, there were substantial capital inflows, and this led to a decision to float the exchange rate and to abolish exchange controls. Since then, disturbances in industrial countries have at times caused portfolio shifts requiring flexibility in the exchange rate. For example, the share market crash in October 1987—which was seen as quite likely to precipitate a world recession and hence a fall in commodity prices—triggered sales of Australian-dollar assets and a sharp drop in the exchange rate, notwithstanding large foreign exchange sales by the authorities.

To sum up, commodity-exporter countries are likely to need flexible exchange rates because of terms of trade fluctuations and capital flows.

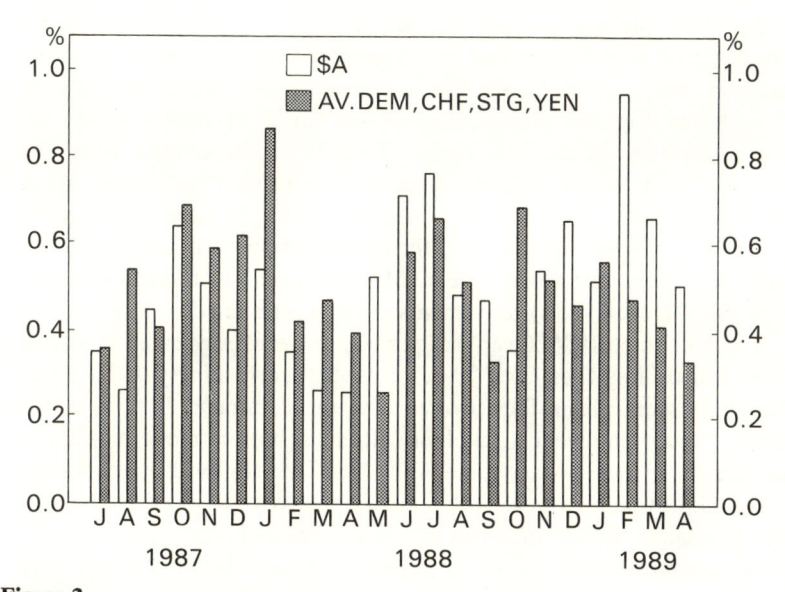

Figure 3
Volatility: Australian Dollar and Major Currencies (Average absolute daily change against U.S. dollar)

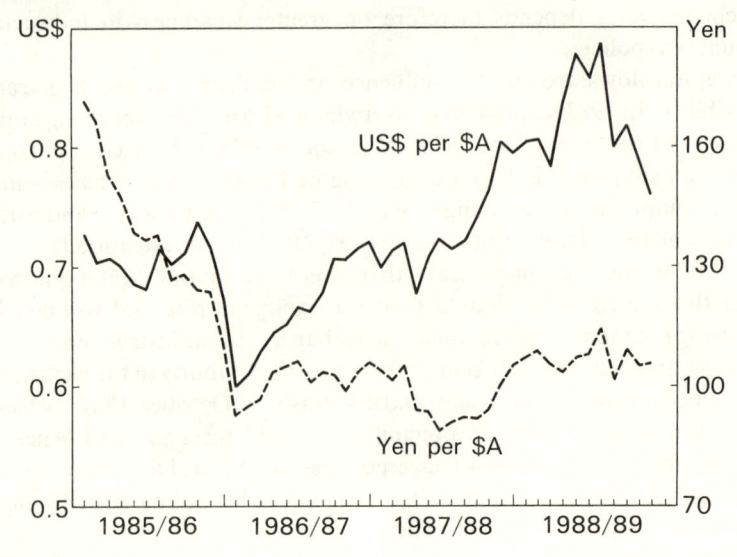

Figure 4
Exchange Rates

But does the market get the exchange rate right? Two problems are day-to-day volatility and misalignment. Figure 3 shows monthly data for average daily volatility in the Australian dollar against the U.S. dollar, together with a like measure for an average of other currencies in terms of the U.S. dollar. Volatility is larger than what was thought likely before floating. Business can protect itself from much of this volatility by the use of various hedging devices, but I would not want to underestimate the difficulties for some firms in coming to terms with this new environment. Misalignment is a more worrisome problem. Figure 4 shows movements of the Australian dollar against the U.S. dollar since 1986. Over that period, this exchange rate has varied from a little less than sixty U.S. cents to nearly ninety U.S. cents. This may seem prima facie evidence of misalignment. But, as noted earlier, that swing went in tandem with a substantial move in Australia's terms of trade. Also, some of the $A/$U.S. shift was due to moves in the U.S. dollar's value. Different perspectives are given by data on the Australian dollar in terms of the yen, as in Figure 4, and in the trade-weighted index, shown in Figure 5. A sounder conclusion may be that moods of excessive pessimism and optimism have at times put strong pressures on the exchange rate and required more management of the currency than was initially foreseen.

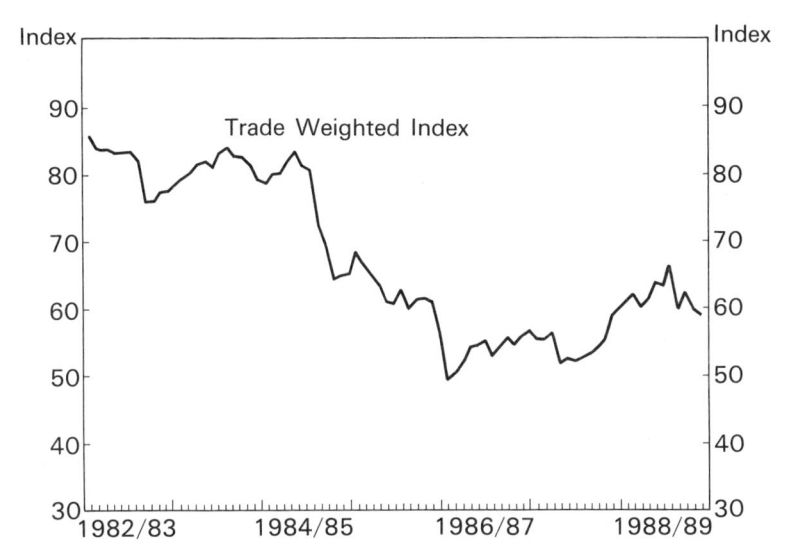

Figure 5
Australian Dollar, Trade-weighted Index

Finally, which exchange rate regime gives the best incentives to policymakers? In the 1950s and 1960s, the fixed rate regime served well, by and large, although it did better at inducing appropriate policy changes when there was a balance-of-payments deficit than when there was a surplus. With the floating rate in recent years, the incentives have worked in a broadly similar way from the viewpoint of economic stability. The floating rate regime, however, has led to greater community consciousness of the need to be efficient internationally and, in the presence of sharp movements in the terms of trade, has enabled adjustments in factor shares. All told, in present circumstances, the floating rate regime has done much for Australia, a commodity-exporting country, to encourage both stability and efficiency.

Comments

Richard Marston

The interwar period and the postwar period have both featured intervals of fixed and floating exchange rates. Barry Eichengreen has provided a thorough analysis of exchange rate regimes during the interwar period, which included a pure floating period (1922–26), a fixed-rate period (1927–31), and a period of managed floating (1932–36). Yoichi Shinkai has analyzed equally well the two regimes we have encountered in the postwar period. He focuses closely on the last years of the Bretton Woods system and the managed floating period since then. Both papers offer many insights into how exchange rate regimes help or hinder a country's performance.

It was once said that a wise statesman is someone who learns from the mistakes of his predecessors. This suggests that a close study of past experience with exchange rates might help us to avoid some of the pitfalls encountered in the past 70 years. Yet in some respects the problems we have recently faced are unlike any we previously encountered. In the 1980s, we have had to come up with new terms for these problems, like "misalignment" and "hysteresis."

When economists used to discuss exchange rate variability under flexible rates, they referred to what we now know as "volatility," the week-to-week, month-to-month variability of exchange rates with no necessary trend. (Imagine the yen-dollar rate moving around by 10% or 20%, a sizable movement, but moderate by the standards of the 1980s.) Now economists worry also about "misalignment," the sustained departure of *real* exchange rates from their equilibrium levels (however these are defined). That's because in the 1980s the pound and dollar have experienced medium-term swings of 40% to 50% in real terms. As far as I know, no such distinction was made in the interwar period or even in the 1960s and 1970s.

Eichengreen presents charts and tables showing that volatility was a chief factor in the two floating-rate periods, 1922–26 and 1932–36.

Shinkai presents similar evidence for the period since the breakdown of Bretton Woods. What problems are posed by such volatility? Firms complain that volatility raises the costs of international transactions. That must be so, but to what extent is international trade inhibited by such volatility? Shinkai rightly points out that the evidence is mixed on this question. Most studies are unable to show major effects of volatility on trade volumes. The reason that this might be the case is that firms have access to a variety of financial instruments which reduce the risks of currency positions. These instruments include forward and money market hedges, foreign exchange options, medium-term financing in a variety of currencies, and currency swaps. For companies with foreign exchange exposures, moreover, the risk associated with any specific transaction is likely to be attenuated by other positions the firm is simultaneously taking. Finally, the variability of a firm's overall earnings due to exchange rate volatility may or may not constitute additional risk for the shareholders owning the firm.

What are the corresponding costs associated with misalignment? In the cases of the real appreciation of sterling in 1980–83 and the real appreciation of the dollar until 1985, the misalignments led to sizable unemployment and loss of sales in each country's manufacturing sector. The decline of manufacturing was so steep in the United States that commentators spoke of "deindustrialization" taking place. The same was true of the industrial north of Britain several years earlier. But as long as these costs are *reversible*, the manufacturing sector should rebound once the real exchange rate returns to more normal levels.

Since the U.S. trade balance has failed to rebound to the decline of the dollar as quickly as expected, economists have begun to consider the possibility that the misalignment led to *irreversible* changes in the U.S. manufacturing sector. Baldwin and Krugman (1986) point out that the high dollar may have induced firms to enter the U.S. market that might never have done so if the dollar had not appreciated so much. Foreign firms may have incurred the fixed costs of setting up sales organizations, for example, because sales in the United States were so profitable at the then inflated exchange rates for the dollar. Once these fixed costs were incurred, firms may have elected to stay in the market even after the dollar depreciated. Baldwin and Krugman term such irreversible effects "hysteresis."[1] We have no hard evidence to establish the empirical importance of hysteresis, but anecdotal evidence suggests it may be the biggest cost of misalignment.

---

[1] Other recent studies of hysteresis include Dixit (1987) and Dumas (1988).

What are the drawbacks of the fixed rate system? One major one is its inability to contend with real shocks. Shinkai rightly asks whether a fixed rate system could have handled the shocks of the 1970s and 1980s. He cites three shocks: the two oil crises and the change in fiscal policy by the Reagan administration. Each shock brought with it changes in real exchange rates that facilitated the adjustment process. It's not evident that fixed rates would have been desirable in any of these three situations. In the Reagan fiscal shift, exchange rates could have remained fixed only by following a highly expansionary monetary policy that would have reignited U.S. inflation. Eichengreen cites another instance in which fixed exchange rates were not necessarily desirable, namely, when the downturn in U.S. industrial activity in the 1929–31 period was transmitted to other countries. Among other drawbacks of fixed rates is the loss of monetary independence so often complained about in the late 1960s.

So both systems have major drawbacks. The natural question is whether there is a middle path between rigidly fixed rates that cannot cope with real shocks and flexible rates where exchange rates are volatile and where misalignments occur. The solution usually offered is the coordination of national macroeconomic policies. I would like to address two questions about coordination. First, do we know enough about the cross-country effects of policies? Second, if we do, is coordination feasible?

A recent study by Frankel and Rockett (1988) cited by Shinkai suggests that our knowledge of cross-country effects may be quite limited. In examining the cross-country multipliers of several econometric models, they find the models provide different *qualitative* and quantitative results. This is especially true of monetary policy multipliers. In 1986, Secretary of the Treasury James Baker urged Germany and Japan to lower their interest rates to help improve the U.S. current account. Frankel and Rockett show that some econometric models predict positive transmission from foreign monetary policies of this type, with U.S. output rising as its current account improves, and others predict negative transmission.

When we turn to assessing the equilibrium value of the exchange rate, our knowledge may be even more limited. Yet proposals for refixing exchange rates or setting up target zones presuppose that we know what the equilibrium exchange rate should be. I would agree with Shinkai that gross misalignments are easy to spot, even though economists might not be able to agree on the magnitude of the misalignment. In 1984–85, when the dollar reached its peak, a strong case could have been made for a coordinated policy to bring it down.

But in more normal periods, such as the present, exchange rate policy represents fine-tuning. And we lack the empirical knowledge for it. As Shinkai observes, estimates of the equilibrium value of the yen or mark vary widely from one expert to another.

Even when we know which policies are desirable, we often find that coordination is not feasible. In 1984, a coordinated change in fiscal policies was called for, with the United States reducing its budget deficit and its large trading partners increasing theirs. Because U.S. fiscal policy remained nearly immobilized, coordination was delayed. And when the G-5 countries agreed to coordinate policy in September 1985, it was exchange rate policy, not fiscal policy, that was coordinated in the Plaza accord. I do not agree with Shinkai that uncertainty about the links between fiscal policy and the trade deficit immobilized fiscal policy in 1984–85. Most economists understood the need for a fiscal correction. It was the failure of politicians to act that prevented a better outcome.

Thus, the scope for coordination is quite limited. Given the above arguments, coordination is primarily needed to avoid a recurrence of the large misalignments experienced in the early 1980s. Yet fiscal coordination failed to materialize when it was needed. Coordination is proposed now to keep exchange rates close to targets, yet we lack the empirical knowledge to know what those targets should be. The only thing we can say for certain is that exchange rate arrangements alone, whatever they are, will not provide a panacea for the world's imbalances.

References

Baldwin, R., and Krugman, P. 1986. "Persistent Trade Effects of Large Exchange Rate Shocks." NBER Working Paper No. 2017, September.

Dixit, A. 1987. "Entry and Exit Decisions of Firms under Fluctuating Real Exchange Rates." Unpublished paper, forthcoming in the *Journal of Political Economy*.

Dumas, B. 1988. "Perishable Investment and Hysteresis in Capital Formation." Working paper, Rodney White Center, November.

Frankel, J. A., and Rockett, K. 1988. "International Macroeconomic Policy Coordination When Policymakers Do Not Agree on the True Model." *American Economic Review*, June, 318–40.

Theoretical and Empirical Issues Concerning International Currencies and the International Monetary System

7

The International Use of Currencies

Stanley W. Black

I. Introduction

In the 1980s, major changes have taken place in the structure of international assets and liabilities. Japan has swiftly become the world's largest net lender, with net assets of $240 billion at the end of 1987. Her banks are now acting as international financial intermediaries, with the country's short-term net liabilities of $169 billion balancing against long-term net assets of $410 billion. This position is analogous in some ways to that of American banks in the postwar period of 1945 to 1980 and to British banks in the 19th and early 20th centuries as bankers to the world, borrowing short and lending long. The British banks built up their intermediary position gradually over the 19th century, and by the turn of the century, the gold standard had effectively become a key currency system based on the pound sterling (Lindert, 1969). During the first half of the 20th century, culminating in the post-World War II period, American banks replaced British banks as financial intermediaries to the world, based on the strong U.S. external payments position. Also during that time, the dollar gradually took over the role of leading international currency from the pound sterling, both as reserve currency for monetary authorities and as vehicle currency in private exchange market transactions. It is obvious that Japanese banks are now the largest financial intermediaries internationally. The question underlying this paper is whether under current conditions there are reasons to believe that a similar process of evolution will lead the Japanese yen to rival the dollar as reserve currency and vehicle currency in foreign exchange markets.

Consideration of this question requires us to recall first the reasons for the existence of reserve currencies and vehicle currencies. Those steeped in neo-Walrasian general equilibrium theory often find the concept of international reserves mysterious, since the existence of perfect capital markets should enable the international extension of credit to fill any gaps between domestic income and expenditure with purchases or sales of goods and services to foreigners. To explain reserve currencies, we must rely on the concept of *convertibility*, which is required for most external transactions in goods and services. Whenever international transactions involve residents of countries using different currencies, assets must usually be converted from one currency to another, either by importers or by exporters, in the process of making payments. In fact, a much larger proportion of goods and services is purchased from or sold to foreigners as part of the international division of labor than would appear from examination of current account imbalances alone. The weighted average share of foreign trade in OECD countries' GDP during 1960–80 was 14.4%, and the average current account balance was 0.1%.

That maintenance of convertibility is a nontrivial matter is illustrated by the fact that in 1988, only 51 of the 151 members of the International Monetary Fund had currencies which were freely convertible for current account transactions without special charges or restrictions. Of these 51, only 15 had currencies that were also freely convertible for capital account transactions. The reasons that convertibility is so difficult to maintain are much the same as the reasons that inflation is so hard to control in many countries. In fact, maintenance of convertibility can be regarded as giving a currency purchasing power over foreign goods and services, much as maintenance of price stability assures purchasing power over domestic goods and services. Political commitments to full employment or excessive monetary financing of government deficits, or both, are often pursued to the detriment of the internal and external value of the currency. Various stratagems are then adopted to prevent residents from evading the inflation tax, usually involving some loss of convertibility of the domestic currency into other currencies. Under these conditions, central banks have found it essential to maintain a stock of reserve assets to ensure the maintenance of convertibility.

For countries with pegged exchange rates, the necessity for adequate stocks of international reserves to maintain the convertibility of their currencies is fairly obvious. A major surprise of the functioning of floating rates is the continued need for international reserves. Many central banks have continued to intervene frequently, even in floating exchange markets, for the purpose of reducing the degree of short-run fluctuation in exchange rates. Recent studies (Lizondo and Mathieson, 1987) have confirmed the continued stability of demand functions for international reserves, particularly for industrialized countries, but also for developing countries. Few industrialized countries, indeed, have been willing to leave the determination of the exchange rate at which their currency is convertible entirely to market forces.

The choice of currency in which to hold reserves has been shown to depend on portfolio risk and return, international monetary agreements, political considerations, and operational factors relating to the most useful currency for intervention purposes (de Macedo, 1982; Heller and Knight, 1978; Officer and Willett, 1974). The extent of use of different currencies in the interbank market is a key determinant of the usefulness of a currency for purposes of intervention. The turnover of currencies in the interbank market depends on customer demand, endogenous trading generated within the interbank market, and the extent to which a currency is used indirectly as a *vehicle* for invoicing transactions between other currencies. The demand for a vehicle currency in turn rests on economies of scale, transactions costs, and informational efficiencies in the interbank market for foreign currencies.

This paper will discuss the factors influencing the use of currencies as international reserve assets and vehicle currencies. It is organized as follows. Section two discusses trends in the international use of currencies, based on recent data. Section three then analyzes the choice of invoicing currency by exporters and borrowers in international markets. Given customer demands for currencies, section four first discusses the interbank market and the determination of bid-ask spreads for different currencies. Based on the analysis of bid-ask spreads, it then discusses a model of the evolution of the use of vehicle currencies. Section five offers some conclusions.

II. Trends in the Use of International Currencies

International Trade

Currencies may be used internationally as means of payment, store of value, and unit of account (Cohen, 1971, cited in Hamada and Horiuchi, 1987). Their use as means of payment arises from international transactions in goods and services, as noted above. The extent of use of different currencies for payments is related to both the *volume* of trade of different countries and the currencies in which that trade is *denominated*. Table 7.1 indicates three patterns of currency denomination of trade flows among industrialized countries: a European pattern with roughly three-fourths of exports and about two-fifths of imports denominated in domestic currency, the Japanese pattern with three-

Table 7.1. Currency distribution of world trade (%)

	Exports		Imports	
	U.S. dollar	National currency	U.S. dollar	National currency
United States	98	98	85	85
Japan	60.9	33.8	93.0	2.0
Germany	7.2	82.3	33.1	42.8
United Kingdom	17	76	29	38
France	11.6	62.4	28.7	35.8
World total	54.8	—	54.3	—

Sources: NIESR, *National Institute Economic Review*, and Bank of Japan, from Hamada and Horiuchi (1987).

Note: Figures for Japan's exports are for 1982 and for Japan's and Germany's imports for 1980. Figures for the United Kingdom and France are for 1979. Figures for the United States are estimated.

Table 7.2 Percentage of Japanese Total Trade Invoiced in Yen and Other Currencies, 1970–84

Currency	1970	1975	1980	1982	1983	1984	1985	1986	1987
Yen									
Export	0.9	17.5	29.4	32.2	34.5	33.7	35.9	35.3	33.4
Import	0.3	0.9	2.4	na	na	na	7.3	9.7	10.6
Dollar									
Export	90.4	78.0	65.7	62.3	60.4	61.4			
Import	80.0	89.9	93.1	na	na	na			
Pound sterling							EXPORT		
Export	7.1	1.9	1.1	1.4	1.0	0.9	64.1	64.7	66.6
Import	8.8	3.8	0.9	na	na	na			
Mark							IMPORT		
Export	0.5	1.1	1.9	2.1	2.1	1.9	92.7	90.3	89.4
Import	2.8	1.5	1.4	na	na	na			
Other									
Export	1.1	1.5	1.9	2.0	2.0	2.1			
Import	8.1	3.9	2.2	na	na	na			

Sources: Ministry of Finance, *Annual Report of the International Finance Bureau*, 1985, from Hamada and Horiuchi (1987); *Annual Report of the International Finance Bureau*, 1988.

fifths of exports and nine-tenths of imports denominated in U.S. dollars, and the U.S. pattern with most exports *and* imports denominated in dollars. Table 7.2 shows that the share of Japanese exports denominated in dollars has been falling over time, while the share denominated in yen has been rising. Thus Japan seems to be evolving in the direction of the European pattern, at least with respect to exports.

In addition, there is some indirect evidence that the share of U.S.

Table 7.3 Shares of World Exports (%)

	1975	1980	1984	1987
United States	13.2	11.7	12.3	10.8
Japan	6.8	6.9	9.6	9.8
Germany	11.0	10.2	9.7	12.5
United Kingdom	5.3	5.8	5.3	5.6
France	6.5	6.1	5.5	6.3
Oil-Exporting Countries	7.3	15.7	9.3	5.6

Source: IMF *International Financial Statistics*.

trade denominated in foreign currencies is rising. For example, the share of commercial liabilities to unaffiliated foreigners by U.S. nonbank enterprises payable in foreign currencies rose to 10.3% at the end of September 1988, from 6.8% at the end of 1984; the share of their *total* liabilities payable in foreign currencies rose to 16.8%, from 10.1%, in the same period.[1] Similarly, the share of bank liabilities to foreigners payable in foreign currencies has risen to 11.1%, from 2.7%, in that time. However, unlike the figures for commercial liabilities of nonbanking business enterprises, the external commercial *claims* of these firms (mostly trade receivables) remain overwhelmingly payable in dollars. The share of *banks'* claims on foreigners payable in foreign currencies has, on the other hand, risen to 11.3%, from 2.9%, matching the increase in banks' liabilities in foreign currency.

According to Table 7.3, the U.S. share of world exports has been declining in recent years, and the Japanese and German shares have been rising. Since the high Japanese share of exports denominated in dollars is declining, this strongly suggests that the share of world trade denominated in dollars has been declining, even without taking into account the drastic drop in the OPEC share of world exports, which is denominated entirely in dollars. During this same period, the share of world trade denominated in Deutsche marks and yen has been rising.

Long-Term Capital

Turning to the use of international currencies as store of value and unit of account in the international bond markets, we notice similar trends from Table 7.4. While the dollar remains the largest currency of issue at 43% of the total in 1987, its share has declined 13 percentage points; the share of the yen has doubled to 12%, from 6%. The increasing share of yen-denominated bonds appears to be due to the increasing

---

[1] *Federal Reserve Bulletin* 75 (3), March 1989, Table 3.22.

Table 7.4 International Bonds Outstanding, by Currency of Issue

In billions of US dollars (%)	1982		1985		1986		1987	
U.S. dollar	144.0	(56.5)	316.7	(56.8)	393.8	(50.1)	423.8	(43.2)
Yen	16.5	(6.5)	42.7	(7.7)	75.0	(9.7)	121.7	(12.4)
Swiss franc	43.0	(16.9)	78.9	(14.2)	117.5	(15.2)	157.0	(16.0)
Deutsche mark	31.0	(12.2)	50.4	(9.0)	76.4	(9.9)	98.5	(10.0)
Sterling	4.0	(1.6)	19.2	(3.4)	30.0	(3.9)	54.2	(5.5)
ECU	2.0	(0.8)	16.5	(3.0)	24.5	(3.2)	38.3	(3.9)
Other	14.5	(5.7)	33.9	(6.1)	55.4	(7.2)	87.8	(9.0)
Total	255.0	(100.0)	557.4	(100.0)	772.6	(100.0)	981.3	(100.0)

Source: Bank for International Settlements, *Annual Report*, 1988.

willingness of Japanese borrowers to tap the Euroyen bond market and to some increased use of the samurai bond market by foreigners. The liberalization of Japanese foreign exchange regulations has permitted these developments.

Short-Term Capital

The market for international bank loans and deposits is increasingly becoming a multi-currency market as well. A major factor here has been the increased foreign asset position of Japanese banks, as shown in Table 7.5. Of course the 62% increase in the dollar value of the yen from the end of 1985 to the end of 1987 plays some role in the doubling of the Japanese banks' foreign assets over the period. Table 7.6 examines the growth of international bank assets by market center excluding exchange rate changes, indicating that the United Kingdom remains by far the largest individual market. But in the past few years, Japan has emerged as the second leading center, followed by the United States and the various offshore centers. The increased financial clout of Tokyo and of Japanese banks has begun to influence the currency

Table 7.5 International Bank Assets by Nationality of Bank

In billions of US dollars (%)	1985		1986		1987	
Germany	191.2	(7.0)	270.5	(7.8)	347.9	(7.9)
Japan	707.2	(26.1)	1120.1	(32.4)	1552.1	(35.4)
United Kingdom	192.9	(7.1)	211.5	(6.1)	253.9	(5.8)
United States	590.2	(21.7)	599.2	(17.3)	647.6	(14.8)
Other	1033.3	(38.1)	1252.7	(36.3)	1579.8	(36.1)
Total	2714.8	(100.0)	3454.0	(100.0)	4381.3	(100.0)

Source: Bank for International Settlements, *Annual Report*, 1988.

Table 7.6 International Bank Assets by Location of Bank

In billions of US dollars (%)	Changes, excluding exchange-rate effects				Stocks
	1984	1985	1986	1987	1987
Germany	7.4	19.4	38.8	17.0	206.0 (5.0)
Japan	21.9	53.4	126.6	166.6	576.9 (13.9)
United Kingdom	23.1	30.7	87.5	89.1	875.6 (21.1)
United States	14.6	3.0	50.3	29.4	508.9 (12.2)
Offshore centers	13.4	54.9	122.5	147.2	878.5 (21.1)
Other	43.7	72.1	91.6	118.5	1111.3 (26.7)
Total	124.1	233.5	517.3	567.8	4157.2 (100.0)

Source: Bank for International Settlements, *Annual Report*, 1988.

Table 7.7 The Currency Composition of Banks' External Assets

In billions of US dollars (%)	Changes, excluding exchange-rate effects				Stocks
	1984	1985	1986	1987	1987
U.S. dollars	30.8	54.3	232.0	199.9	1696.4 (56.9)
Deutsche marks	14.8	29.0	27.5	37.8	445.6 (14.9)
Swiss francs	4.5	18.1	11.1	1.7	205.6 (6.9)
Yen	18.3	43.1	64.8	123.5	436.4 (14.6)
Sterling	11.7	7.1	17.5	14.1	290.5 (4.0)
ECUs	12.8	13.7	7.4	9.9	78.5 (2.6)
Total	92.9	165.3	360.3	386.9	2983.0 (100.0)

Source: Bank for International Settlements, *Annual Report*, 1988.

composition of the international assets of banks in industrialized countries. Table 7.7, which excludes the effects of exchange rate changes, shows that the U.S. dollar retains the largest currency share at 57%, but that the Deutsche mark and yen amount to about 15% each.

The Interbank Market

Information on the use of currencies in the interbank market is available from surveys conducted by central banks in New York, London, and Tokyo in March 1986 and at earlier dates in New York.[2]

---

[2] Another survey was undertaken in April 1989, but the results were not available for this paper.

Table 7.8 The Currency Composition of Banks' Foreign Exchange Market Turnover (%)

	New York			London	Tokyo
	March 1980	April 1983	March 1986	March 1986	March 1986
Deutsche marks	31.7	32.5	34.2	28	10.4
Yen	10.2	22.0	23.0	14	77.0
Sterling	22.8	16.6	18.6	30	3.4
Swiss francs	10.1	12.2	9.7	9	5.6
French francs	6.9	4.4	3.6	4	0.3
Canadian dollars	12.3	7.5	5.2	2	
Other currencies	6.0	4.6	5.8	10	3.3
Cross-currency	—	0.2	na	3	
Daily volume (bil $)	18.0	26.0	50.0	90	45.7

Sources: Federal Reserve Bank of New York; Bank of England *Quarterly Bulletin*, 1986: 379–82.

The surveys summarized in Table 7.8 show that the interbank market in these centers remains a dollar-based market, with almost all transactions taking place between the dollar and another currency. Only 3% of trades reported by banks in London did not involve the dollar, mostly between the mark and the pound. New York did not report such a figure, but it is understood that cross-currency trading in New York is growing significantly. Since all accounts are held and settled in dollars, however, trades involve "writing two tickets," for example dollar/mark and dollar/sterling for a sterling/mark trade. Thus the data in Table 7.8 may not reflect the extent of cross-trading in New York. Within these dollar-based markets, the share of the yen has increased sizably in recent years, up from 10% in New York in 1980 to 23% in 1986; the D-mark share has remained roughly stable. According to Table 7.8, in Tokyo dollar/yen trading accounted for 77% of interbank transactions in 1986, with the balance mainly in Deutsche marks and Swiss francs.

Information obtained from interviews in Milan indicate that interbank trading in a typical smaller market center in which there are exchange controls may involve the domestic currency in only about 25% to 30% of the total volume, which is comparable to the sterling share in London, shown in Table 7.8. In these markets, up to 70% of volume would involve cross-currency trades from the point of view of the local currency. Thus the question of the use of a vehicle currency arises all the time. Information gained in Milan suggested that the dollar share of such business has fallen sharply in the past few years, to the point where it is now roughly comparable to the Deutschemark share. Bid-ask spreads on the dollar/lira were quoted at 0.04%, compared with 0.01% on the mark/lira. The lower spread on the mark is presumably related to the existence of the European Monetary System and to competitive pricing by German banks bidding for market share. In general, improved communications facilities, such as video quote screens, for the major currencies have reduced the need for vehicle currencies by reducing information costs. Where direct cross-currency quotations are not readily available in the local market, they can often be obtained by working with a correspondent bank in the market of one of the two currencies involved. For example, escudo/krone quotations could be obtained from either Lisbon or Copenhagen.

International Reserves and Central Bank Intervention

The shifting patterns of use of international currencies in private markets discussed above has its reflection in the changing patterns of holdings and the use of international reserves by central banks. Table 7.9 indicates that the share of the U.S. dollar in official foreign exchange holdings of industrial countries has declined to 70.6%, from 77.6%, since 1980; the share of the yen has risen to 6.6%, from 3.3%, and the share of the mark has risen to 16.5%, from 14.3%. There is little

Table 7.9 Share of National Currencies in Total Identified Official Holdings of Foreign Exchange, End of Year 1979–87 (%)

	1979	1980	1981	1982	1983	1984	1985	1986	1987
Industrial countries									
U.S. dollar	83.5	77.6	78.7	77.1	77.4	73.6	65.4	68.4	70.6
Pound sterling	0.7	0.7	0.7	0.8	0.8	1.6	2.1	1.6	1.5
Deutsche mark	9.4	14.3	12.8	12.2	12.8	14.8	19.4	17.5	16.5
French franc	0.6	0.5	0.4	0.3	0.3	0.4	0.5	0.6	0.8
Swiss franc	1.4	1.7	1.7	1.7	1.4	1.4	1.8	1.4	1.1
Netherlands guilder	0.6	0.7	0.8	0.7	0.5	0.6	1.0	1.1	1.1
Yen	2.6	3.3	3.7	4.4	5.1	6.3	8.8	8.2	6.6
Unspecified currencies	1.2	1.2	1.2	2.8	1.7	1.2	1.1	1.2	1.8

Source: International Monetary Fund, *Annual Report*, 1988

Table 7.10 Currency Distribution of Foreign Exchange Intervention by Countries in the EMS Exchange Rate Arrangements

(%)		1979–82	1983–85	1986–87
U.S. dollars	P	17.2	15.1	20.9
	S	54.3	38.6	5.4
EMS currencies				
–at the limits		11.2	10.5	15.2
–intramarginal	P	5.8	19.7	22.2
	S	10.2	13.3	34.3
Others	P	0.1	2.2	0.9
	S	1.2	0.6	1.1
Total		100.0	100.0	100.0

Source: EMCF, BIS, from Mastropasqua, et al. (1988). P = purchases; S = sales.

Table 7.11 Currency Distribution and Amount of Foreign Exchange Intervention by U.S. Federal Reserve and Treasury

Year (beginning Feb. 1)	Amount (bil $)	Deutsche marks (%)	Year (%)
1976	0.9	100.0	0.0
1977	1.7	100.0	0.0
1978	10.2	98.0	2.0
1979	17.3	99.7	0.3
1980	17.4	98.5	1.5
1981	0.9	100.0	0.0
1982	0.1	46.5	53.5
1983	0.5	78.8	21.2
1984	0.5	100.0	0.0
1985	3.7	62.3	37.7
1986	0.1	0.0	100.0
1987	10.7	40.1	59.9
1988	10.4	75.4	24.6

Source: *Federal Reserve Bulletin*, various issues. Amount is sum of purchases and sales in absolute value.

information available on the *use* of currencies in intervention by central banks, but Table 7.10 shows that the share of the dollar in interventions in the European Monetary System has declined to 26.3% during 1986–87, from 71.5% during 1979–82. This is consistent with the indications that the dollar is playing a smaller role in private markets in Europe. Table 7.11 shows that yen intervention has become significant for the United States since the Plaza Agreement of 1985.

III. Factors Affecting the Choice of Currency by Traders and Borrowers

Choice of Invoice Currency

While the patterns of currency use in international trade shown in Table 7.1 have been known for some time (Grassman, 1973; Page, 1981), our understanding of the reasons for their existence and their evolution has been inadequate. McKinnon (1979) explained that the European pattern arose because exporters of industrial products desire to minimize risk in their home currency by denominating exports in the home currency. Bilson (1983) further pointed out that "the importer's price risk is likely to be both larger and more highly correlated with the exchange rate than the exporter's cost risks. Hence, by accepting the foreign exchange risk, the importer obtains an important hedge against the price risk of the transaction." Rao and Magee (1980) argued that if the exporting firm were free to set the price, it would be set to make the firm indifferent to exchange risk.

Recently, Bissaro and Hamaui (1988) have advanced understanding of these matters significantly by constructing a model of risk-averse firms that explains the setting of prices, the choice of invoice currency, and the determination of the contract period. The key assumptions of the model are that (1) the exporter's risk on sales denominated in foreign currency increases with the length of the contract period and the variability of exchange rates; (2) the importer's risk on sales denominated in the exporter's currency *decreases* with the length of the contract period while increasing with exchange rate variability; and (3) sales adjust gradually to changes in prices, following Phelps and Winter (1970). The longer settlement period reduces risk for the importer because it shortens the lag between payment and resale of the goods and also increases the chance of being able to prepay at a favorable exchange rate. It increases risk for the exporter who faces an increased risk of default or repayment at an unfavorable exchange rate.

The results of Bissaro and Hamaui imply that p < ep* as long as there is exchange risk, where p is the price in domestic currency and ep* is the domestic currency equivalent to the price in foreign currency. Therefore, pricing does respond by offsetting the effect of exchange risk to some extent. There is, however, an optimal share of invoicing in each currency, as long as neither risk aversion by both parties nor expected change in the exchange rate is too large. The results show that the share of exports denominated in domestic currency declines with expected depreciation in the domestic currency and rises with an increase in variability. Thus, the exporter seeks to avoid the effects of anticipated depreciation by shifting to the importer's currency in the first case and to shift increased risk to the importer in the second.

Using this framework, Bissaro and Hamaui show that the share of Italian exports denominated in lira versus other currencies fluctuated over the period 1977–86 in accordance with expected depreciation and variability as implied by the model. Their results need to be replicated with other countries' data. But with that qualification, their model seems to explain the rise in the share of Japanese exports denominated in yen and the apparent rise in the share of U.S. imports denominated in foreign currencies discussed in section two above. Furthermore, it suggests further evolution in those trends, since the incentives for Japanese exporters to denominate in yen and the incentives for all exporters to the United States to denominate in their own currencies remain unabated. What about the incentives for U.S. exporters to denominate in other currencies? During the past few years, one would have expected a significant shift to have occurred as the dollar has trended downward. But the data on commercial claims by U.S. nonbanking enterprises on foreigners cited in section two suggest no shift.

Choice of Borrowing Currency

Some writers on corporate finance have suggested that firms might be indifferent to the currency in which their debt is denominated if they were willing to rely on the uncovered interest parity condition that the interest differential just compensates for expected exchange rate changes (Aliber, 1978: 137–39). Unfortunately, the exact form of this condition and its equivalent, the unbiasedness of the forward exchange rate as a forecast of the future spot rate, have been pretty thoroughly rejected by the data for reasons not completely understood (Hodrick, 1987). Aliber suggests more active strategies for firms which seek to take advantage of apparently systematic deviations from uncovered interest parity. The share of bonds issued in domestic versus foreign currency would then depend directly on the differential expected return as measured by the uncovered interest differential (adjusted for the expected change in the exchange rate) and inversely on the variability of the exchange rate as a measure of exchange risk. Johnson (1988) has shown that the currency denomination of Canadian long-term corporate bonds over the period 1970–1979 fluctuated in response to the uncovered interest differential. Areskoug (1980) has found a similar relationship between exchange risk and the currency denomination of Eurobonds.

These findings are not inconsistent with the evidence cited above in section two on the changing currency denomination of external bond issues and bank lending. However, the more significant factor affecting the rising share of yen-denominated bonds and bank loans appears to be the increasing wealth position of agents whose preferred currency habitat, in McKinnon's phrase, is the yen.

IV. The Interbank Market

There have been few attempts to model the interbank currency market. Krugman (1980) and Chrystal (1984) have each discussed the emergence of vehicle currencies in the interbank market based on transactions costs, using different models. Each assumes an underlying structure of payments based on transactions in goods and capital markets. Each assumes that transactions costs will be inversely proportional to volume in each bilateral currency market. Each then shows that a vehicle currency will emerge whenever *indirect* exchange costs through the vehicle are less than direct exchange costs between two non-vehicle currencies. In contrast to their work, this paper will *derive* the structure of transactions costs. We will then modify the approach of Chrystal, who used a model of uninformed traders based on the origin of currencies in barter exchange. In contrast, we use a model of liquidity traders who know exactly *where* to trade, but who must rely on dealers and speculators to set the price at which they may trade.

Bid-Ask Spreads

The basic transactions cost in the interbank market is the bid-ask spread (Levich, 1985). Banks which are active in the market quote bid and offer prices at which they are prepared to deal with each other and with (large) customers. From 10% to 15% of transactions reported by banks arise through dealings with nonbank customers, the rest through dealings with other banks, either directly or through brokers. The basic problem for the bank trader is to maximize trading profits without becoming overexposed to risk in any one currency. Since banks are committed to trading at the prices they quote, their positions are continually becoming unbalanced via trades with each other and with customers. As this happens, they seek to square up their positions by further transactions, thus generating additional volume in the market. Finally, banks will actively take positions by trading at what they regard as favorable prices, expecting to close out the position later at a profit.

Allen (1977) and Booth (1984) have discussed the determination of bid-ask spreads in the foreign exchange market; Demsetz (1968) and more recently Cohen et al. (1986) have discussed bid-ask spreads in securities markets. Both Allen and Booth assume that the dealer is risk averse and analyze the problem as a type of portfolio choice. In Allen, the portfolio choice variables are the bid and ask prices, which are assumed to influence the probabilities of transacting at those prices. The relationship between prices and probabilities seems intuitively plausible but empirically difficult to estimate. In Booth, interaction between a risk-averse monopolistic dealer and risk-averse customers leads to a bid-ask spread, which depends only on differences in the exchange rate expectations of customers on the buying and selling sides of the market, implausibly independent of degrees of risk aversion and of exchange risk.

The following analysis assumes random buy and sell orders placed by liquidity traders "at the market" with a representative competitive risk-neutral dealer who then clears the market in deals with price-sensitive speculative traders. Let $\tilde{Q}_s$ and $\tilde{Q}_d$ be random sell and buy orders in a specific bilateral currency market from liquidity traders, each with mean $\bar{Q}$. Let P_b and P_a be the dealer's posted bid and asked prices, with mean $\bar{P}$. The mean itself may be determined according to a random walk, but it reflects public information that is available to all parties.

$$\tilde{Q}_s + b(\tilde{P} - \bar{P}) = \tilde{Q}_d - a(\tilde{P} - \bar{P}). \tag{1}$$

The representative dealer's profit can then be defined as

$$\tilde{\pi} = \tilde{Q}_d(P_a - \tilde{P}) + \tilde{Q}_s(\tilde{P} - P_b). \tag{2}$$

If we define the spread $t = P_a - P_b$ and the expected value of $\tilde{P} = \bar{P}$, then the expected value of the dealer's profit is

$$\bar{\pi} = \text{cov}(\tilde{Q}_s - \tilde{Q}_d)(\tilde{P} - \bar{P}) + \bar{Q}t. \tag{3}$$

Using (1) above, we can write (3) as

$$\bar{\pi} = -(a + b)\,\sigma_p^2 + \bar{Q}t. \tag{4}$$

The assumption of competitive risk-neutral dealers will force expected profit to zero (or to a level just sufficient to cover dealer costs). As a result we find

$$t = (a + b)\, \sigma_p^2/\bar{Q}. \tag{5}$$

The implication of this analysis is that spreads in the interbank market will vary directly with riskiness as measured by the variability of the exchange rate in the very short run and inversely with the expected volume of transactions in the market. Thus wider spreads will be expected in low-volume markets and narrower spreads in markets where the authorities enforce narrow bands of short-term fluctuation, as in the EMS. Imperfect competition would be reflected in wider spreads, which would just tempt new entrants to reduce spreads to earn profits and gain market share. Where bank dealers expect to have multiple relationships with customers, price competition in the exchange market might be used to attract business that would bring profits in other areas.

The discussion so far relates to spreads quoted by bank dealers to customers. But Cohen *et al.* (1986) make clear that in securities markets, observed *market* spreads will frequently be less than dealer spreads. Close observation of exchange market behavior confirms their conclusion. In active markets, dealers will be constantly changing quotes with the arrival of new information and new orders from customers. Overlapping quotes from different dealers each using the same spread will create a narrower *market* spread during periods of significant market activity. Thus observed market spreads will also vary from (5) inversely with the *current* volume of transactions.

Vehicle Currencies

According to Krugman (1980) and Chrystal (1984), the use of vehicle currencies arises whenever indirect transactions costs through the vehicle are less than direct transactions costs between two non-vehicle currencies. Armed with the above analysis of transactions costs, we will now consider this question, following the approach of Chrystal based on Jones (1976).

$T = (t_{ij})$ is a matrix of transactions costs or bid-ask spreads between currencies defined by equation (5) above. Assume

$$t_{ij} > t_{in} + t_{nj}, \tag{6}$$

for some $i, j \neq n$.

$U = (u_{ij})$ is a matrix of the fraction of customers entering on a given day who wish to exchange currency i for currency j directly ($u_{ii} = 0$). For simplicity, assume that U is symmetric.

$u = (u_1, \ldots, u_n)$ is a vector of the row or column sums of U representing the fractions of customers wanting to transact in currency i directly.

$q = (q_1, \ldots, q_n)$ is a vector of customers who transact in currency i, taking account of both direct and vehicle use of each currency.

s is the fraction of currency exchanges occurring indirectly through the medium of currency n. The second transaction is assumed to take place on the same day.

m is the number of individuals entering the market each day to make either direct or indirect transactions, assumed constant for the purposes of this analysis. Each individual transaction is assumed to be of equal size.

The number of customers demanding currency i on a given day is then mu_i if $i = 1, \ldots, n - 1$, and $mu_n + ms$ if $i = n$. Since the total number of participants is $m + ms$, we find q_i related to u_i as

$$q_i = \frac{mu_i}{m + ms} = \frac{u_i}{1 + s} \qquad (7)$$

for $i = 1, \ldots, n - 1$ and

$$q_i = \frac{mu_n + ms}{m + ms} = \frac{u_n + s}{1 + s} \qquad (8)$$

for $i = n$.

Equations (7) and (8) can be written in vector form as

$$q = u + \frac{s}{1 + s}(e_n - u), \qquad (9)$$

where $e_n = (0, 0, \ldots, 0, 1)$.

The analysis, which differs up to this point only slightly from that offered by Jones and Chrystal, is completed by specifying s as the sum of u_{ij} over all i, j such that condition (6) holds. Consider a matrix U for which the matrix T indicates that at least one bilateral currency market is dominated in the sense of (6) by a vehicle. Then $s > 0$ and (9) indicates that q_i falls for all $i \neq n$ and rises for $i = n$. We can now see from (5) how this will increase t_{ij} for all $i, j \neq n$ and reduce t_{in} and

t_{nj}, through the changes in volume shown in (9). Further extension of the use of the vehicle is likely as transactions costs through it fall and costs of direct transactions through non-vehicle currencies rise.

There is nothing in this analysis to prevent the emergence of multiple vehicle currencies, especially if transactions costs rise in the dominant vehicle currency because of increased exchange rate variability or reduced transactions volume. Nor is there anything to prevent technological change in communications from reducing dealers' costs, omitted from (5), in such a way as to mitigate the need for vehicle currencies altogether.

The fact that evolution seems to be led by the private market rather than by official users should make it gradual. It would be interesting to pursue a stability analysis of the process described above to examine this question.

V. Conclusions

The evolution of the international monetary system has its roots in the response of participants in private markets to the changing properties of internationally convertible currencies and to the changing relative importance of different groups of participants. As we have seen, both changing trade patterns and changing patterns of currency denomination of trade have had an effect on the use of currencies in international trade. Continued evolution of currency denomination appears particularly likely, given the incentives faced by traders and the historical patterns which still exist. With respect to the use of currencies in the capital markets, although comparative risk-adjusted borrowing costs appear to be an important factor, the changing balance of external asset positions of borrowers with different currency habitats may be even more so. Further evolution in external asset positions are predictable on the basis of sluggish adjustment of current external imbalances, implying further evolution in the use of currencies in capital markets.

With international traders and investors changing their uses of international currencies, the interbank foreign exchange market is bound to evolve in the same direction. As the volume of dollar-based trade and investment flows drops back from dominance to merely *primus inter pares*, so will the dollar's role in the foreign exchange market. It seems quite likely that as intraregional trade and investment links grow tighter within Europe, the EMS will further promote the use of European currencies in international trade already clear from

Table 7.1. To some extent, similar developments may be expected within East Asia, but the absence of the European degree of political and economic integration will inevitably limit the development of EMS-type arrangements in Asia. But to the extent that Japan's exports to East Asia are significantly invoiced in yen, there will be a natural tendency for yen financing. Most of the other Pacific Basin currencies are not, however, completely convertible for current *and* capital transactions, thus limiting the potential for the development of an interbank foreign exchange market among East Asian currencies.

Beyond the question of regional use of specific international currencies lies the overall structure of international payments and the international monetary system. Inevitably, the evolution in the structure of payments discussed above will have its effect on the markets and on the institutions of the international monetary system. The multi-reserve currency system appears to be a reality, even if the data in Table 7.9 show the dollar still to be the dominant element in foreign exchange reserves. It has been suggested by some writers (Bergsten and Williamson, 1983) that evolution toward a multi-reserve currency system, if led by official use of currencies, might be destabilizing. Others, such as Kenen (1981), have dismissed this possibility. Gyooten (1986) has suggested that the multi-reserve currency system will promote exchange rate stability, if accompanied by policy coordination among the reserve currency countries.

My tentative conclusion is that the effect of reserve diversification on exchange rate stability will depend on its effect on policy in the reserve centers. If diversification promotes discipline in reserve centers, it will be stabilizing. If, however, reserve centers seek to avoid the consequences of their exposures to discipline by limiting access to their markets and reducing the convertibility of their currencies, it could lead to withdrawal of funds and destabilizing behavior.

References

Aliber, R.Z. 1978. *Exchange Risk and Corporate International Finance.* New York: John Wiley & Sons.

Allen, W.A. 1977. "A Note on Uncertainty, Transactions Costs and Interest Parity." *Journal of Monetary Economics*, 3: 367–73.

Areskoug, K. 1980. "Exchange Rates and the Currency Denomination of International Bonds." *Economica*, 47: 159–63.

Bergsten, C.F. and Williamson, J. 1983. *The Multiple Reserve Cur-*

rency System: Evolution, Consequences, and Alternatives. Washington: Institute for International Economics.

Bilson, J.F.O. 1983. "The Choice of an Invoice Currency in International Transactions." In Bhandari, J.S. and Putnam, B.H., eds., *Economic Interdependence and Flexible Exchange Rates.* Cambridge: MIT Press.

Bissaro, G., and Hamaui, R. 1988. "The Choice of Invoice Currency in an Inter-temporal Model of Price Setting." *Giornale degli Economisti,* 47: 139–161.

Booth, L.D. 1984. "Bid-Ask Spreads in the Market for Foreign Exchange." *Journal of International Money and Finance,* 3: 209–22.

Chrystal, K.A. 1984. "On the Theory of International Money." In Black, J., and Dorrance, G.S., eds., *Problems of International Finance.* New York: St. Martin's Press.

Cohen, B.J. 1971. *The Future of Sterling as an International Currency.* London: Macmillan.

Cohen, K.J., et al. 1986. *The Microstructure of Securities Markets.* Englewood Cliffs, N.J.: Prentice-Hall.

De Macedo, J.B. 1982. "Portfolio Diversification Across Currencies." In Cooper, R.N., ed., *The International Monetary System under Flexible Exchange Rates.* Cambridge: Ballinger.

Demsetz, H. 1968. "The Cost of Transacting." *Quarterly Journal of Economics,* 83: 33–53.

Grassman, S. 1973. "A Fundamental Symmetry in International Payments Patterns." *Journal of International Economics,* 3: 105–16.

Gyooten, T. 1986. "Internationalization of the Yen: Its Implications for the US-Japan Relationship." In Patrick, H.T. and Tachi, R., eds., *Japan and the United States Today: Exchange Rates, Macroeconomic Policies, and Financial Market Innovations.* New York: Center on Japanese Economy and Business, Columbia University.

Hamada, K., and Horiuchi, A. 1987. "Monetary, Financial and Real Effects of Yen Internationalization." In Arndt, S.W. and Richardson, J.D., eds., *Real-Financial Linkages among Open Economies.* Cambridge: MIT Press.

Heller, H.R., and Knight, M. 1978. "Reserve Currency Preferences of Central Banks." *Princeton Essays in International Finance,* 131.

Hodrick, R.J. 1987. *The Empirical Evidence on the Efficiency of Forward and Futures Foreign Exchange Markets.* Chur, Switzerland: Harwood Academic Publishers.

Johnson, D. 1988. "The Currency Denomination of Long-Term Debt in the Canadian Corporate Sector: An Empirical Analysis." *Jour-*

nal of International Money and Finance, 7: 77–80.
Jones, R.A. 1976. "The Origin and Development of Media of Exchange." *Journal of Political Economy*, 84: 757–75.
Kenen, P.B. 1981. "The Analytics of a Substitution Account." *Banca Nazionale del Lavoro Quarterly Review*, 139: 403–26.
Krugman, P. 1980. "Vehicle Currencies and the Structure of International Exchange." *Journal of Money, Credit, and Banking*, 12: pp. 513–26.
Levich, R.M. 1985. "Empirical Studies of Exchange Rates: Price Behavior, Rate Determination and Market Efficiency. "In Jones, R.W., and Kenen, P.B., eds., *Handbook of International Economics*, Vol. II. Amsterdam: North-Holland.
Lindert, P.B. 1969. "Key Currencies and Gold." *Princeton Studies in International Finance*, 24.
Lizondo, J.S., and Mathieson, D.J. 1987. "The Stability of the Demand for International Reserves." *Journal of International Money and Finance*, 6: 251–82.
Mastropasqua, C., Microssi, S., and Rinaldi, R. 1988. "Interventions, Sterilization and Monetary Policy in EMS Countries, 1979–1987." In Giavazzi, F., Micossi, S., and Miller, M., eds., *The European Monetary System*. New York: Cambridge University Press.
McKinnon, R.I. 1979. *Money In International Exchange*. New York: Oxford Uversity Press.
Officer, L.H., and Willett, T.D. 1974. "Reserve-asset Preferences in the Crisis Zones, 1958–67." *Journal of Money Credit, and Banking*, 6: 191–211.
Page, S.A.B. 1981. "The Choice of Invoicing Currency in Merchandise Trade." *National Institute Economic Review*, 85: pp. 60–72.
Phelps, E.S., and Winter, S.G. 1970. "Optimal Price Policy under Atomistic Competition." In Phelps, E.S., *et al.*, *Microeconomic Foundations of Employment and Inflation Theory*. New York: W.W. Norton.
Rao, R.K.S. and Magee, S.P. 1980. "The Currency of Denomination of International Trade Contracts." In Levich, R.M., and Wihlborg, C.G., eds., *Exchange Risk and Exposure*. Lexington, Mass.: Lexington Books.
Suzuki, Y., ed. 1987. *The Japanese Financial System*. Oxford: Clarendon Press.

8

Financial Integration and International Monetary Arrangements

Alexander K. Swoboda

To quote from this conference's program outline, "one of the distinctive features of today's world economy is the increasing trend toward global unification both in trade and financial transactions." Innovation, globalization, securitization, and deregulation are the catchwords usually employed to describe current trends towards increased competition and integration in the world's financial markets. At the same time it appears that a number of currencies are beginning to challenge the dollar's role as the dominant vehicle and reserve currency in the world economy and the role of New York as the world's dominant financial center. These developments raise numerous questions and have many implications for the international financial and monetary system. This paper takes up a few of them.

More specifically, and in keeping with the organizers' brief, I will raise three questions in what follows. First, is there a place for several international financial centers in an integrated financial system, and will these also be at the center of new currency areas or blocs? Second, what are some of the implications of increased economic integration for the conduct of macroeconomic policy in a world where several important international currencies exist? Third, what are the merits and prospects of various alternative international monetary arrangements in a financially integrated world economy?

The first of these questions will be discussed only briefly as it is highly speculative, is partly the object of Stanley Black's paper for this conference, and goes somewhat beyond the macroeconomic focus of this paper. The second question will again only be taken up briefly, as the implications of capital mobility and asset substitutability for the conduct of macroeconomic policy in the open economy are the object of an abundant literature; nevertheless a few remarks under this heading will be useful if only as background for discussion of the third question, to which the third and major part of this paper is devoted.

That third part of the paper is divided into six sections. The first summarizes succinctly the function of alternative monetary arrangements and the criteria by which their merits can be judged. The next three sections consider in turn three alternatives for the future: limiting capital flows among major currency blocs; maintaining the present system of floating with occasional management of exchange rates; and adopting more ambitious schemes for international policy coordination. The conclusion of these three sections is that limitations on capital flows are undesirable, that the present system is unlikely to endure much beyond the next few years, and that most current proposals for more ambitious policy coordination are flawed. The fifth section of the third part of the paper therefore outlines a few basic principles that any scheme for macroeconomic coordination should respect if it is to be viable. The last section briefly makes the case for (and discusses some of the difficulties of implementing) a common currency as perhaps the economically most suitable international monetary arrangement in a highly integrated world economy.

I. Financial Integration and Financial Centers

There are national and international financial centers, and some that combine both functions. Among the latter, New York, London, and Tokyo are the main ones today, with Zurich and Frankfurt quite a way behind. Of these centers, New York and London are clearly the dominant ones at an international level. A first question we may ask is whether Tokyo is likely to become equally important and whether there are some other candidates in the wings. To address this question it will be useful to ask briefly what the requirements for becoming (and remaining) an international financial center are. Some of these conditions are also required in order for the currency of the country to become an important international vehicle and reserve currency.

1. International Financial Centers and Currencies

Becoming an international financial center is usually a long process in which geography and historical accident have important roles to play. In general, however, a prerequisite is an appropriate general national social, political, and economic system that offers guarantees of stability, freedom of transactions, and the endowments in physical and human capital required to sustain a competitive financial industry. The commitment to freedom of transactions and to stability must be credible; investors must believe that it will be adhered to in the future. One element in gaining such credibility is simply a past history of stability and respect for the freedom of transactions; another, more specific factor is a stable legal framework defining property rights credibly and durably. Without the second prerequisite, economic stability, existing property rights may be put in question. A stable fiscal and monetary environment is particularly important here. The likelihood that freedom of capital movements will be maintained and exchange controls and arbitrary taxation avoided in the future depends crucially on a tradition of fiscal and monetary conservatism, lest one expect the government to have recourse to an inflation tax to finance budget deficits and to the imposition of exchange controls (which could easily spread from residents to non-residents) to protect the inflation tax base. It would thus be difficult for a country that suffers from large government budget deficits, is a heavy borrower in international capital markets, or has a habit of having an inflationary monetary policy to become an international financial center.

There are additional requirements not only for a country to become an important financial center but also for its currency to be used as an international reserve asset by foreign central banks and as a vehicle for private transactions. One is that the country be economically important enough for a broad internal market for securities denominated in its currency to exist. Another is that the country not have persistent current account deficit (or have had sizable surpluses over an extended period of time) so that one does not, again, expect its authorities to impose capital controls in order to protect its balance of payments. The important thing here is not that a current account surplus enables the country to accumulate net assets in the rest of the world but that the surplus diminishes the likelihood of exchange controls in the future and thus allows for the building up of sizable gross assets in, and liabilities to, the rest of the world. That is, it is not so much net transfers of resources abroad as having an important role in international financial markets in terms of gross assets and liabilities that matters here.

Obviously, Japan and the yen are increasingly fulfilling the preconditions for becoming an international financial center and an international currency, respectively. The rapid growth of the Japanese economy means that its relative economic size has increased substantially over the past two decades, with Japanese GNP reaching roughly 60% the size of that of the United States in 1987 at current prices and exchange rates. Nor is the importance of Japan in the world economy just a matter of relative GNP size: high per capita income, a high savings rate, developing capital markets, and a large value of exports and imports in absolute terms have all contributed to making Japan the world's second most important industrialized country (if one does not lump the EEC economies together). Macroeconomic policy has been quite stable over the past two decades, and Japanese financial markets have begun to broaden. In addition, liberalization of capital markets, both internal and external, has been significant. Finally, the large current account surplus makes it unlikely that exchange controls (at least additional restrictions) should be imposed. Most of the conditions for becoming an international financial center thus seem to have been gradually fulfilled.

Yet Japan is not yet a dominant international financial center, nor is the yen yet a dominant international currency: even though the yen is increasingly used on capital markets, less than 60% of Japan's exports and only some 10% of its imports are invoiced in yen. One reason is perhaps that the stability of property rights mentioned above has, in one sense, not yet been achieved. Most foreigners do not yet have a full understanding of what is going on in Japan, and there remain questions about whether access to various financial transactions is and will be on equal terms for everybody and of whether there are not risks of future (implicit) expropriation of at least partial property rights by local groups. This factor is, however, diminishing in importance as transparency increases, and the question becomes how far and how fast Japan is likely to become a dominant financial center.

Although the preconditions mentioned above are increasingly being fulfilled, neither history nor present circumstances suggest that the yen will rapidly become an international currency of the importance of the dollar, or that Tokyo is likely to become the dominant financial center that New York still is. A first reason for this conclusion is that currencies gain—and lose—international status slowly. The evolution of the world currency system into a sterling era and from a sterling to a dollar standard took well over a century. Sterling lost its status as the dominant currency only long after its relative economic power had declined significantly; similarly, the dollar is likely to remain the most used international currency for a while even though the relative economic power of the United States has declined steadily over the past two or three decades. The "depth, breadth, and resiliency" of the United States internal securities market is one reason why it is likely to take some time for the dominance of the dollar to wane, though the process might accelerate unless the two U.S. deficits are brought under control.

Second, today's world is not one in which one can expect hegemony of a single power. Even if Japan manages to catch up in economic size with the United States over the next twenty years, it will not be the single dominant economic power: the United States will still exist, and the European Economic Community, if it manages to get its act together, will dwarf both in terms of economic size—and this without even mentioning the Eastern bloc or Asia outside Japan. In short, we are moving to a multipolar world in which the yen cannot play the role that the dollar used to play (and to some extent still does). This being said, there is little doubt that Japan and the yen will be one of the major poles of that world and will come to play an increasingly important role reflecting not only its size but also its high growth rate.

2. Prospects

In looking to the future, one may ask which of the following two scenarios is more likely: (1) a world with a dominant currency and financial center around which "satellite" centers and currencies gravitate; or (2) a multipolar world with several international financial centers and currency areas which, incidentally, need not overlap. The preceding analysis suggests that the second of these scenarios is more likely than the first in the medium run. For the long term, and for the main industrial countries, I suspect and will briefly argue at the end of this paper that the choice will be between two alternatives: disintegration of the world economy into hostile blocs, or a trend toward a single jointly managed currency.

The reasons for this forecast are as given above: the hegemonic role of the dollar is slowly eroding, but the new configuration of some three economic blocs of roughly equal power among industrialized countries should prevent a new hegemon from emerging. But the shape of this new multipolar system is likely to be different from what it has been in the recent past. Part of the reason is integration, deregulation, and innovation in financial markets and the revolution in telecommunications. The result is a global market for financial assets and services. This does not mean that financial centers will be replaced by the linking of individual institutions, wherever located, into a worldwide computer network ("home inter-banking," as it were); time-zone differences suffice to insure that this will not be the case. Rather, a number of international financial centers are likely to coexist and be located in places offering attractive packages of capital, skilled labor, technology, communications services, and regulation. Regarding this last factor, an attractive regulatory framework is not the most permissive one, but one that offers clear rules and the amount of freedom that is compatible with a supervisory system capable of inspiring confidence in the soundness of those it regulates.

Note that these financial centers need not be located in countries that have a dominant influence on the world economy or are issuers of an important reserve or vehicle currency. London and Zurich are contemporary examples. Sterling plays a disproportionately minor role in the denomination of external assets of banks or in official reserve holdings in relation to the importance of London as an international financial center. Although the Swiss franc is a relatively important international currency (at least in relation to Switzerland's size), Swiss economic policy has practically no influence on the rest of the world. A relatively large economy, though it helps, is not a sufficient condition for a country's currency to become an important official reserve asset, though it is sufficient for its macroeconomic policy to matter to the rest of the world. By the joint criteria of size and international importance of currencies, it is the relation between the United States, Japan, and Germany (or the EEC, once it has progressed further toward economic and monetary union) that matters for international monetary arrangements in the industrialized countries, which form the core of the system at large. Before turning to these arrangements we briefly consider a few issues for macroeconomic policy in an integrated world economy.

II. Macroeconomic Policy in an Integrated World Economy

The consequences of internationally integrated capital markets for the effectiveness of macroeconomic policies in open economies have been thoroughly investigated in the international macroeconomic literature in the wake of the original Mundell-Fleming models. The conclusions for the effectiveness of monetary and fiscal policy in the *small* open economy are stark.

Under fixed exchange rates, monetary policy will have hardly any effect on economic activity, as any change in domestic credit is rapidly (even instantaneously) offset by an equal and opposite change in the stock of international reserves of the monetary authorities. Fiscal policy, on the other hand, appears to be effective; but note that its effectiveness depends on the existence of idle resources that can be re-employed without requiring any change in the price level in the "ultra"-Keynesian versions of these models or, if the expansion in demand is accompanied by an increase in the domestic price level, on constant nominal wages, i.e., on the existence of a money illusion in the labor market (a fall in the real wage can be achieved through price increases but not through decreases in nominal wages). Note further that, in the last case, it must be assumed either that the country is not a price-taker in the market for its exportables or that there is significant scope for an increase in the price of non-traded goods relative to that of traded goods. With goods market integration, the scope for such increases, as will be noted below, is relatively limited, and hence also the effectiveness of fiscal policy as a counter-cyclical device.

Under floating exchange rates, capital mobility renders fiscal policy rather ineffective (in the limit totally so) in terms of its effects on real output. The reason is that a fiscal expansion, by putting upward pressure on the domestic interest rate, leads to an incipient capital inflow that appreciates the domestic currency, crowds out net exports, and keeps the domestic rate of interest in line with foreign rates. As for monetary policy, it appears to become very effective as a form of monetary expansion by depreciating the home currency, increasing net exports and output at the prevailing world interest rate. Note, however, that the effectiveness of monetary policy is entirely dependent on the existence of a money illusion on the labor market: workers are willing to accept a cut in real wages brought about by an increase in traded goods prices at a given nominal wage.

Money illusion is a shaky assumption on which to rely in the conduct of macroeconomic policy, especially in an integrated world economy in which information circulates freely and extremely fast and, for diversified small open economies, with typically high ratios of tradable goods in total consumption and production. With such high ratios, substitutability with non-traded goods is likely to be high under fixed exchange rates; and, under flexible exchange rates, the heavy weight of traded goods in overall price indices will make for a rapid reaction of such indices to depreciation of the national currency.

As a matter of fact, in an integrated world economy, "goods mobility" may be as important as capital mobility in reducing the effectiveness of macroeconomic policy in a small open economy. Consider, for instance, an economy which is a price taker in the markets for both its importables and its exportables and where domestic goods are close substitutes in consumption and production for traded goods.

At the limit, the price level in such an economy is equal to the foreign price level times the exchange rate. The limiting case is illustrated in Figure 8.1. Output and absorption are measured on the horizontal axis, the price level on the vertical axis. The short-run aggregate supply curve which assumes a fixed nominal wage is labelled SSR. It is similar to the marginal cost curve of a perfectly competitive firm. Aggregate demand is equal to the sum of absorption and net exports; as we are considering a small open economy which is a price taker, the excess demand for net exports (and hence the aggregate demand curve, AD) is infinitely elastic at the given world price level, P*. Absorption, i.e. expenditure by residents, is,—given the money stock, taxes, government spending, and wealth,—an inverse function of the price level and is initially given by AB_0. Initial equilibrium is at C, with output equal to absorption at Y_0, and hence trade and payments are balanced.

Consider the fixed exchange-rate case first and assume, for the moment, that capital is immobile internationally. A monetary or fiscal expansion shifts the absorption schedule to the right to, say, AB_1. The result is a trade deficit of CD as output stays at Y_0 while absorption rises to Y_1. In the case of a monetary (fiscal) expansion, the move to Y_1 is accompanied by a fall (rise) in the interest rate. The deficit, unless sterilized, will result in a fall in the money stock, and A shifts back to its initial position. An expansionary fiscal policy thus creates a temporary rise in absorption and a transitory trade deficit, both of which are eliminated by the monetary contraction created by the deficit. Assuming perfect capital mobility makes for two differences in the story. First, a monetary expansion would be undone immediately, as the capital account deficit it entails returns AB_1 to AB_0 immediately. Second, a fiscal expansion results in a "permanent" (until wealth effects come into play) trade deficit of CD financed by a capital inflow induced by the upward pressure on the domestic rate of interest. In fact, with goods and asset substitutability, fiscal policy has the same effect under fixed as under floating rates: it does not affect output but creates a matching trade imbalance.

The reason policy is ineffective when domestic goods are close substitutes for foreign ones is that in that case fixing the exchange rate fixes the price level and, given the aggregate supply curve, the level of output. There are only two possible ways of affecting output in this framework: a supply-side policy that shifts the aggregate supply curve or a devaluation that increases the price level and, given the nominal wage, reduces real wages and increases the demand for labor. Consider a devaluation that raises the aggregate demand curve to AD' and the price level to P_1. Output has risen to Y_2, absorption has fallen to P_1F,

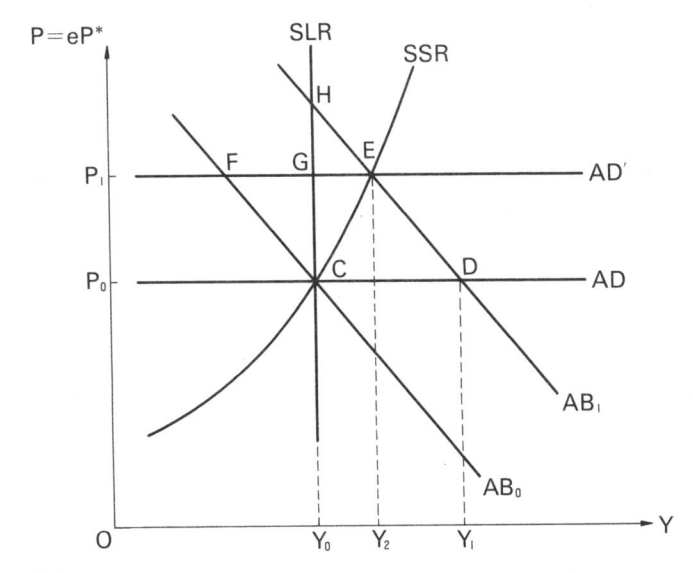

Figure 8.1

and there is a trade surplus of FE. In the absence of sterilization, the money stock increases and AB_0 shifts to AB_1, eliminating the trade surplus. With capital mobility, this shift occurs very rapidly as the initial trade surplus is accompanied by a capital account surplus. This is not the end of the story, however, as with the passage of time wage contracts are renegotiated and output falls back to its long-run equilibrium level on the long-run supply curve SLR. The final equilibrium is at G.

Consider now the case of flexible exchange rates. Initial equilibrium is again at C. Assume capital immobility for the moment. An expansionary monetary or fiscal policy shifts AB_0 to AB_1. The result is a depreciation of the currency sufficient to bring the price level to P_1, and the economy comes in the short run to rest at E where the increase in output matches the increase in absorption. With time, as nominal wages adjust, SSR begins to shift up, output falls and the currency depreciates further (AD shifts further up) until the economy comes to rest at H. Introducing perfect capital mobility makes it necessary to distinguish the source of the initial upward shift in the absorption schedule. Capital mobility reinforces the short-run effect of monetary policy: a given increase in the money stock shifts the AB schedule out further than when there are no capital movements since the interest rate is prevented from falling and the whole of the initial excess supply of money must be absorbed into so-called transactions balances. On the other hand, capital mobility works against fiscal policy: the upward pressure on domestic interest rates caused by fiscal expansion tends to appreciate the domestic currency, counteracting the tendency towards depreciation due to the initial excess demand for goods, and the economy stays at P_0, with the increase in government spending matched by a trade deficit financed by a capital inflow.[1]

The general conclusion from this discussion of the effectiveness of macroeconomic policy in a small open economy is that it buys less and less in terms of effective control over real economic activity in a world where both goods and capital markets are becoming increasingly integrated and where money illusion cannot be relied on for long.[2] Large countries, in contrast, retain some effective control over real economic variables since they can affect world output, relative prices, and world interest rates (and the world price level under fixed exchange rates) even with integrated markets.

In view of the preceding discussion one might well want to ask why small countries should not peg their currencies to that of a major country or currency block since floating does not buy them all that much effective policy autonomy except with respect to nominal variables such as their price level, rate of inflation, and nominal interest rates. The answer is partly that many of them do. Pegging to a low-inflation block allows them to import monetary stability; this is one motivation for participating in the EMS, for instance in the case of Belgium. Other countries do not peg either because they do not want to adopt the monetary policy of any of the major countries or blocs or because they cannot do so. The countries in the last group are mainly those whose fiscal system has traditionally relied on the inflation tax to finance budget deficits and where switching to a low inflation rate and the required fiscal discipline would prove politically difficult.

One may thus well imagine a gradual evolution toward a world of a few currency areas toward which smaller countries will slowly gravitate.

---

[1] This last result, together with a number of previous ones, holds exactly only for specific formulations of asset market equilibrium and of the expenditure and import functions.

[2] In addition, flexibility of exchange rates is unlikely to provide much insulation of real economic activity in an integrated world economy where there are many additional channels of transmission to those traditionally considered in macroeconomic models. For instance, shocks may well be to industrial sectors, wherever located, or to expectations about the profitability of investment, wherever undertaken. For a discussion of some of those channels and of the notion of world business cycles to which they give rise, see Swoboda (1983).

Relations between the smaller and larger countries within these blocs will depend largely on political cohesiveness. Where such cohesiveness is (or will be) present, as in the case of the European Community, one would expect some degree of joint management of the area's monetary and exchange rate policies. Where it is not, the countries on the periphery would simply peg their currency to the area's dominant one and the system would be operated very much as the *de facto* dollar standard of the 1960s was.

This, however, leaves open the arrangements which will or should rule the relations between the major currency areas—the dollar, yen, and ECU areas, to name the most important ones for the foreseeable future.

III. Alternative International Monetary Arrangements

The institutions and arrangements governing international monetary relations can take many different forms and have done so in the past. It is not the task of this part of the paper to enumerate them all. Instead, it will examine briefly three alternatives that are often discussed and have been singled out by the organizers of this conference: controls on capital movements, the maintenance of the present managed floating system, and more ambitious schemes for international coordination of macroeconomic policies. It then proceeds to discuss the broad principles that should govern "policy coordination" under alternative exchange-rate regimes and concludes with a brief discussion of the common currency alternative. In keeping with the conclusions of the preceding part of the paper, the discussion focuses on the arrangements governing relations between major currency areas in a highly integrated world economy. First, however, we begin with a brief mention of the functions of alternative monetary arrangements and of the criteria by which their merits are to be judged.

1. Functions of International Monetary Systems

The main function of an international monetary system is to be as unobtrusive as possible. The best system is neither heard nor seen. In classical language, money should serve to grease the wheels of commerce and otherwise be neutral—a veil, if you wish. It should facilitate an efficient international transfer of resources, should not interfere with the forces of productivity and thrift, and should allow trade in goods and assets to take place on the basis of comparative advantage determined by tastes, endowments, and technology.

At a more mundane level, the monetary system should not add sources of uncertainty to those that are inherent in any forward-looking economic activity. More specifically, it should not generate exchange-rate variability (uncertainty) beyond that which is unavoidable in view of the variability of fundamentals; nor should it lead to large medium-run swings in exchange rates that are not needed for an optimal allocation of resources through time. Furthermore, the monetary system should not contain systematic biases towards inflation or deflation. It must also provide for an efficient adjustment mechanism (a way of restoring external equilibrium when the latter has been disturbed) that is also sufficiently "equitable" for member countries not to opt out, or corrupt the nature, of the system. In short, it should foster efficiency, facilitate adjustment, and insure stability.

2. Capital Controls and Financial Transactions Taxes

The motivations for controls on capital movements, on the one hand, and for the taxation of international financial transactions, on the other, are somewhat different. The first are mainly designed to restore autonomy and effectiveness to macroeconomic policy; the second, to reduce exchange-rate variability and "misalignments," though it, too, is sometimes advocated to reduce interdependence.

There is little to recommend controls on capital movements among major currency areas (with perhaps freedom of movements within the areas)—be they of the interest-equalization type or outright exchange controls—in terms of efficiency, stability, or effectiveness. They don't buy much policy autonomy; what they buy may not be worth having, and the efficiency costs are likely to be large. Under fixed exchange rates, controls serve mainly to allow domestic interest rates to diverge from international ones and thus to restore some freedom of action to monetary policy. To the extent that goods markets are closely integrated, however, variations in the money stock will rapidly be offset through international reserve changes due to the trade account disequilibria the money stock variations engender. Moreover, capital controls serve here to prevent or slow down the adjustment of external disequilibria; these adjustments will eventually have to occur and may be all the more painful and destabilizing for having been postponed with the help of the controls. Note also that a given level of the tax rate on capital movements produces a given interest rate differential; further insulation of the domestic economy and of the balance of payments will require ever-rising tax rates. As such controls distort the relative prices of goods as well as of assets and interfere with the transfer of real resources across countries and over time, their efficiency costs are obvious. Their effectiveness and feasibility in integrated world financial markets is less obvious unless the imposing countries or areas are willing to adopt severe policing measures.

The rationale for imposing capital controls under floating exchange rates is even less obvious. Under that regime, as we have seen, capital controls weaken the effectiveness of monetary policy. The rationale must therefore be elsewhere. Two reasons for the use of controls come to mind. The first would be to lessen exchange-rate variability or to prevent wide cyclical swings in exchange rates. To the extent that they thin out markets and confirm the existence of inconsistencies in the goals and means of economic policy, their effect may well be in the opposite direction. The second possible reason is their use for current account control in cases where the authorities are not willing or not able to use fiscal policy for that purpose. It should be noted, however, that use of capital controls for that purpose is distinctly second best as they do not attack the basic problem (saving-investment imbalances) at its source. Moreover, to be effective, controls on capital outflows (inflows) to improve (worsen) the current account will work only if they increase (reduce) saving or reduce (increase) investment. To the extent that controls on outflows raise domestic relative to foreign rates of interest, domestic investment will suffer, thus threatening internal balance. The remarks about feasibility and effectiveness of controls under fixed exchange rates apply here too.

The basic criticism of capital controls is that they seek to solve national macroeconomic problems at the expense of the world economy. Round-trip taxes on financial transactions are less prone to this criticism to the extent that they seek to reduce the short-run volatility of asset prices and of exchange rates in particular, and to nip speculative bubbles in the bud. The "sand in the wheels" proposal of Tobin (1982) is an early example of such proposals; more recently, Dornbusch (1989) has suggested the introduction of a "moderate, worldwide tax on all financial transactions," thus extending Tobin's proposal from international to all financial transactions.

Such schemes, according to their advocates, should reduce the short-run volatility of exchange rates since they deem such volatility to be due to trading on short-run trends that is unrelated to fundamentals; such trading would become unprofitable as the transactions tax raises the (annualized) cost of financial roundtrips to levels that escalate as the holding period gets shorter. Whether the tax would succeed in its aim depends on whether volatility is actually caused by bubbles unrelated to fundamentals and on whether roundtrip transactions are undertaken by bubble traders or by market makers whose dealing reduces the volatility of asset prices. As both participants are likely to be in the market, the transactions tax is as likely to increase as to reduce volatility, at least over certain periods of time. There are also well-known problems of enforcement of such schemes, notably in terms of universality of application, and potentially large administration costs. Be that as it may, such schemes do not solve the medium- and long-run problems of international monetary organization. To which one may add that if the goal is to stabilize exchange rates, an alternative is to fix them.

3. Maintaining the Present System

There are reasons to believe that maintaining the present system as it functions today may not be a realistic alternative for the medium run. One of the virtues of the floating rate system when it was introduced in 1973 was that it resolved, by default as it were, a number of policy conflicts that had arisen in the last days of the Bretton Woods system. The resolution, however, has not proved entirely satisfactory as old problems have reappeared in new guises and the floating rate regime has brought with it some additional ones. The most commonly cited include the volatility of both nominal and real exchange rates, so-called misalignments of exchange rates over extended periods of time, a failure to provide an adequate mechanism for current-account adjustment, and national policy mixes that have proved inadequate from an international perspective and may have exacerbated the transmission of economic shocks across countries. Partly as a result, protectionism seems to be on the rise again. It would therefore seem that the present system is unlikely to continue in its present form. Unless some improvement takes place, international monetary (and more generally economic) relations are likely to take the road of economic disintegration through the adoption of trade and exchange controls by relatively hostile blocs of countries.

Improvement could take the form either of a "better" float among major currencies or of more ambitious schemes of policy coordination including a return to some form of a fixed exchange rate regime. As a matter of fact, a "better" float among the emerging three currency blocks may be not only an attractive alternative but also a necessary intermediate step on the way to a fixed exchange rate, or ultimately a common currency, system to rule the relations among them. In that sense, maintaining some of the central features of the present system while improving the way in which it is run ranks high on a list of priorities for reform of the international monetary system.

Further down the road—say, in a span of five to fifteen years—the choice may become a fairly radical one: it may well be between disintegration and a fixed exchange rate system among major currencies. The reason is that a pure float, to work properly, requires in one sense as much if not more discipline and more difficult-to-implement policy coordination than a fixed exchange rate system would.

The general requirements for any type of improvement will be taken up below. First, however, I discuss some specific recent reform proposals of a more ambitious type.

4. Proposals for Policy Coordination

Of the more ambitious schemes for policy coordination, the two proposals that have probably received most attention are target zone proposal(s) and the "international standard for monetary stabilization" advocated by McKinnon (1984). One important distinction between these proposals is that the first relies on a good dose of discretionary policy and continuous explicit coordination, the second on rules for the conduct of policy.

The original target zone proposal by Williamson (1985) centered on calculating a "fundamental equilibrium real exchange rate," defined as that rate which would yield a current account balance compatible with underlying (sustainable) capital flows and with internal balance defined as a reasonable approximation to full employment and price stability. Governments would then attempt to keep the actual real exchange rate within a 10% band on either side of this equilibrium rate. The band could have either hard or soft shoulders (depending on whether there was an obligation or just a presumption that the authorities should keep the rate within the band); it could be preannounced or not, and would need to be periodically recalculated to take into account changes in fundamentals. As an exchange rate involves two countries, international agreement would have to be reached on the level of the equilibrium rate and hence on the limits of the band. These limits could be gradually reduced over time.

Among the many possible objections to this scheme, I will list only a few. First, calculating the fundamental equilibrium rate is fraught with both statistical and conceptual difficulties; different analysts may legitimately have widely differing views of its value, all the more so when the exchange rate is a forward looking variable and that calculating, or revising, the rate thus involves guessing the future impact of current changes in underlying fundamentals. Moreover, calculating that rate as defined by Williamson would involve defining the value of the macroeconomic policies that are to bring about internal balance since the equilibrium rate will be different for various policy mixes for internal balance. Second, and related, it is not clear by what means the target rate is to be achieved given that a particular policy mix for internal balance is being pursued. Presumably the target real rate is to be achieved by manipulation of the nominal exchange rate, and the latter by monetary policy. This raises a third and fundamental objection to the proposal, namely that it is self-defeating in the long run, and potentially destabilizing in the short run, to seek to target a real variable with the help of a nominal instrument. Fourth, it is not clear that, if the target is the current account, the real exchange rate is the appropriate instrument or indicator to achieve it. In fact, as will be argued below, there are good reasons to believe that it is not. Finally, seeking international agreement on what the equilibrium rate is may exacerbate conflict rather than reduce it; even if agreement on the rate could be secured, achieving it would require continuous discretionary action that would demand more from the capacity for internal and international coordination of policies either than is available or than would be required under fixed exchange rates.

Partly in response to criticism, Williamson and his colleagues have recently extended the target zone proposal to a more general scheme linking targets and indicators, or targets and instruments (see Edison, Miller and Williamson, 1987, and Williamson and Miller, 1987). Their blueprint for the international coordination of economic policy is an ambitious proposal that has the advantage of indicating fairly clearly what the targets for policy coordination should be and how these authors envisage that they be achieved. For instance, the implications of Edison, Miller, and Williamson (1987) for the conduct of policies in today's circumstances would seem to involve the need for the following steps: lower U.S. real interest rates to depreciate the dollar in real terms and achieve current account equilibrium; increase money supplies to lower world interest rates and thus raise world nominal output; and let countries adjust their individual fiscal policies to achieve their own internal balance target.

Though I have much sympathy with the general approach (it relies much more explicitly on policy rules of the assignment type than the initial version of the target zone proposal), and although the extended proposal does take care of some of the criticisms above, it still suffers from serious defects. We are not told how real interest rates are to be lowered in the United States. The real exchange rate is still the indicator or instrument of choice for achieving current account balance. Nor, as this paper has argued, is it obvious that fiscal policy is the appropriate instrument for achieving internal balance under flexible nominal exchange rates and capital and goods market integration. In fact, the proposal may well prove destabilizing rather than stabilizing for the world economy.

While target zone proposals assume flexible nominal exchange rates and seek to target real exchange rates, McKinnon's proposal targets nominal exchange rates and seeks to stabilize prices. To oversimplify, there are two key elements in his plan, which is aimed at the relations between the three main currencies in international markets, the dollar, the yen, and the deutsche mark (or possibly, one day, the ECU). The first is that the exchange rate should be the main indicator for monetary policy in the three participating countries. McKinnon identifies shifts in currency preferences from one of the three currencies to one or both of the other two as the main source of instability in their foreign exchange value. Hence, an appropriate response would seem to be a decrease in the money supply of the country with the depreciating currency and an increase in that of the country with the appreciating currency relative to trend. The second main element concerns what that trend should be. Here agreement would be sought on a formula defining the world money stock as a weighted average of the three countries' money stocks, with weights basically reflecting relative economic size, and on a rate of growth of that stock. That rate, and the weights, should be set so as to stabilize an index of traded goods prices in each currency and on average.

McKinnon's schemes (there are several variants) are in many ways attractive and coherent in the way in which they assign instruments to targets and in which they solve the n-1 problem and set rules for the growth of international monetary aggregates. The scheme outlined above is also ingenious in that it basically simulates a jointly managed fixed exchange-rate system without requiring complete fixing or the deliberate choice of an international reserve asset. The scheme does, however, have at least two drawbacks. It requires a great deal of commitment and agreement among the participating countries, probably as much as would be required to run a true fixed exchange-rate system among the three currencies. And the targeting of changes in national money stocks on changes in the exchange rate may be inappropriate if the source of the exchange-rate change is not a shift in currency preferences. In particular, McKinnon's scheme takes no account of fiscal shocks or of fiscal policy coordination. That this may pose problems can be seen by considering what the consequences of the

Federal Reserve following McKinnon's first rule would have been in the 1982–85 period: a monetization of the U.S. budget deficit and a resumption of rapid inflation in that country. Still, McKinnon's scheme goes some way towards meeting the requirements for effective and viable policy coordination outlined in the next section.

5. Effective and Viable Monetary Arrangements

We have just argued that some of the major proposals for improving international monetary arrangements are, in one way or another, flawed. Our task would thus seem now to be to outline the main requirements for effective and viable international monetary arrangements in general and for international policy coordination in particular. Such a task is far too vast to be undertaken thoroughly in this paper. It would include consideration of such topics as credibility, commitment, incentive compatibility, and strategic behavior. Instead, I will confine myself to asking what we can learn from the simplest of basic principles as to the functioning of fixed and flexible exchange-rate systems for appropriate international monetary arrangements. By the latter is meant here mainly what instruments of policy should be assigned to what targets under the two regimes. In an integrated world economy it turns out that some variables, for instance real interest rates, will tend to move together in all countries, and are thus world variables. To the extent that such variables are targets of policy, the appropriate instruments to achieve them are "world" instruments (aggregates of national instruments in our examples), and setting the instruments at the appropriate level then clearly requires policy coordination.

Consider a very simple setting. There are two large countries, each of which has two instruments at its disposal, monetary and fiscal policy. The targets at which these four instruments should (or can) be aimed will depend on which of the two exchange rate regimes is in force and on whether the perspective is a long- or short-run one. Four possible targets for each regime and the instruments which should be assigned to them are listed, in a long-run perspective, in Table 8.1.

Take first the targets for the fixed exchange rate system. National price levels are not targets individually since they are tied together by the fixed exchange rate (this would be true in the short run as well with a high degree of goods market integration). Instead, it is the world price level that is a target under fixed rates. Maintaining fixed nominal parity is of course a requirement of the regime, and the nominal exchange rate is thus a target to which an instrument must be devoted.

Table 8.1 Long-run Assignments

TARGET	INSTRUMENT	
	Fixed E	Floating E
P		M
P*		M*
P_w	$M_w = M + M^*$	
E	$M - M^*$	
CA	$G - G^*$	$G - G^*$
r_w	$G + G^*$	$G + G^*$

Definition of variables:
  G ... government spending
  M ... money stock
  P ... price level
  E ... nominal exchange rate
  CA ... current account
  r_w ... world interest rate
Note: An asterisk identifies foreign variables, the subscript w identifies world variables; the real exchange rate, e = EP*/P is endogenous under both exchange-rate regimes.
Source: Swoboda (1988), p. 10.

The remaining two variables are more controversial candidates for target-of-policy status. I will assume that the current account is a target of policy as it seems to have become, without questioning here—as one should—the legitimacy of its elevation to that status.[3] Including the world real rate of interest in the list of targets reflects current concerns that it is too high and thus may be detrimental to economic growth. Note that no national variable enters the list of targets for the fixed exchange rate case. In the short run, world nominal income may replace the world price level in the list. In contrast, the price level targets are national ones under floating exchange rates, the nominal exchange rate drops out by definition, and the world price level loses its meaning. In the short run, one could have replaced national price with nominal income levels in the list of targets.

Table 8.1 contains specific assignments of instruments to targets. Genberg and Swoboda (1987) develop the rationale for those assignments under floating exchange rates in some detail and show them

---

[3] It is possible to argue that there are few good general reasons to treat the current account as a target of policy as it should be the outcome of saving and investment processes that optimize the distribution of real resources across countries and through time. It is, however, possible to argue for trying to reduce imbalances that are considered too glaring on pragmatic grounds: not correcting them could fuel protectionist sentiment and action. It can further be argued that perceived current account imbalances are often the result of inappropriate fiscal policies and that

to be valid in the short (sticky nominal wages) as well as in the long (flexible prices and wages) run. However, to understand the proposed assignments, notably that of fiscal policy to the current account, it will be enough here to consider the long-run case. That case is particularly simple since, with fully flexible prices and wages, monetary policy affects only nominal variables, i.e., national price levels and the nominal exchange rate under flexible rates, the world price level under fixed rates. Fiscal policy, on the other hand, affects real variables. But note that, if we assume perfect capital mobility, as is done in the table, it is the sum of fiscal stances in the two regions that determines the level of the real rate of interest in the world while the difference between these stances determines the current account. In the long-run context illustrated in Table 8.1, it is obvious that assigning monetary policy under floating exchange rates to the current account, on the idea that a monetary expansion depreciates the domestic currency in real terms and hence improves the trade balance, is self-defeating. It turns out, however, that even in the short run where price rigidities are assumed, fiscal policy has a comparative advantage over monetary policy in affecting the current account as contrasted with the two policies' effects on national output levels. This is obvious in the simple Mundell-Fleming small-country model under perfect capital mobility since, in that case, the effect of an increase in government spending is to leave the level of output unaffected and to deteriorate the current account by the same amount while the effect of a monetary expansion is to increase output and improve the trade balance.[4]

Table 8.1 also contains lessons, some of them familiar, for the implications of alternative exchange-rate regimes for policy coordination. Fixed exchange rates require that national monetary policies (or, in the table, the difference between money stocks) be devoted to fixing the nominal exchange rate, to external balance if you wish, while the overall stance of monetary policy in the world economy (the sum

---

targeting the current account may force a correction of these fiscal policies in the appropriate direction (at least to the extent that fiscal policy is the instrument used to redress current account imbalances).

[4] Fiscal policy has a comparative advantage over monetary policy with respect to the current account relative to the output target if the expression R below is positive:

$$R = (dCA/dG)/(dY/dG) / (dCA/dM)/(dY/dM).$$

For the special case in the text the first left-hand term tends toward infinity, the second toward zero. Genberg and Swoboda (1989) show that R is positive for more general models of the open economy under floating exchange rates.

of national money stocks, dubbed the world money supply) determines the world price level in the long run (or, in the short run and together with fiscal policy, world nominal output). Coordination therefore requires that some agreement be reached on an appropriate level for the world price and the world money stock and on some mechanism for achieving that level. Coordination of the regional distribution of fiscal policies is required if a specific distribution of current account deficits and surpluses is to be achieved; coordination of the over-all stance of fiscal policy in the world economy is required to reach a particular level of real interest rates. Note again that some agreement on the desirable pattern of current accounts and level of interest rates as well as some institutional mechanism (e.g., assignment rules) for reaching the agreed targets is required in order for the coordination of fiscal policies to be effective.

The same principles govern the coordination of fiscal policies under flexible as well as under fixed exchange rates. What does change, of course, is monetary policy coordination. In the long run, no coordination of national monetary policies is required, each country being free to pursue its own price level and inflation targets; indeed, this autonomy of monetary policy is one of the main advantages claimed for flexible exchange-rate regimes. Things are, however, more complicated in the short run. For, in an integrated world economy, national monetary and fiscal policies have real (notably output) spillover effects abroad. Analytically, it is possible to aggregate individual countries into a world "IS-LM" type model when capital is perfectly mobile internationally. Overall output will be determined by the sum of fiscal and monetary stances, its distribution by the differences between them. The scope for strategic interaction and conflict is clearly there.

Coming back to the fixed exchange-rate case, the institutional requirements for returning to such a regime are fairly obvious on the monetary side. There must first be a mechanism for fixing exchange rates and that inescapably requires that monetary autonomy be sacrificed in n-1 of the participating countries. Second, there must be some agreement as to the mechanism governing the growth and composition of international reserves and hence the growth of the world money stock. A wide variety of choices are available here, ranging from various "outside" reserve systems (gold, SDRs, etc.) to various "inside" reserve systems (dollar standard, multi-currency reserves, etc.). Once these two requirements are credibly met, overall payments adjustment should not be a major problem insofar as it would be achieved by the automatic monetary mechanism of adjustment inherent in any fixed exchange-rate system. "Credibly" is a key word in the preceding sentence. Adoption of a number of simple, monitorable rules of behavior could help achieve credibility. Among these rules, the assignment of monetary policy to overall payments equilibrium (less than complete sterilization of reserve flows is the key here) is a crucial one. A second crucial rule would have to concern the rate of growth of international reserves and of system-wide monetary aggregates; various alternatives suggest themselves, among them some variants of McKinnon's proposals.

Does a return to fixed exchange rates put requirements on the running and coordination of fiscal policies beyond the assignment questions raised above? The answer depends on whether member countries wish to pursue internal balance policies in the short run or a real interest-rate target in the long run and on whether a particular pattern of current accounts is being pursued or not. Note that, as far as longrun outcomes are concerned, the issues raised for fiscal policy are in one sense independent of the exchange rate regime, as Table 8.1 indicates.

The types of issues that arise for fiscal policy coordination are illustrated in Figures 8.2 and 8.3. G and G* represent government spending (or more generally the fiscal stances) in the United States and the rest of the world respectively.[5] The line CA represents those combinations of (those differences between) levels of government spending which yield a specific current account level; for simplicity, assume that countries agree to target current account balance and that it is reached on CA. The r_w lines show those combinations of government spending levels which yield a given world real rate of interest. The sum of government spending is constant along a given r_w line which thus has a slope of 45 degrees; the further up and to the right the line, the higher is the rate of interest.

Consider Figure 8.2. Where are we today? One answer is to argue, as most people would, that the U.S. current account deficit is too large, which implies that we are below the line CA; and that the level of interest rates is too high, that is that we are above the r_w line which would yield an "appropriate" interest rate level, say r_{w0}. In other words, current U.S. government spending, at G_1 is too high and we are somewhere between B and D on the vertical line above G_1. Assume for simplicity that we are at C, i.e., that the current level of government spending in the rest of the world, G_0^*, is that which, in combination with G_0, would yield the targeted current account and interest rate.

Assume first that no change in fiscal stance takes place; that is, G

---

[5] For a fuller explanation of the type of diagram used in Figures 8.2 and 8.3, see Genberg and Swoboda (1987).

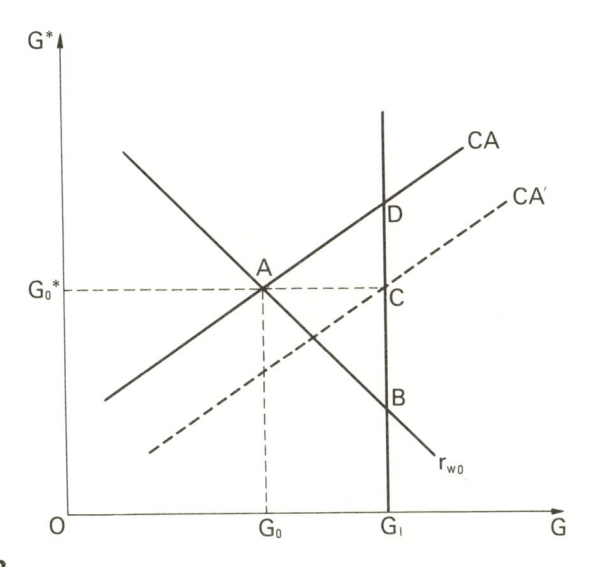

Figure 8.2

stays at G_1 and G^* at G_0^*. What would happen? Presumably current-account equilibrium would eventually be reestablished by the "debt-dynamics" mechanism. Increasing indebtedness in the United States would lead to a risk premium on the dollar; real interest rates would rise in the United States and fall in the rest of the world. Net private saving would rise in the United States and fall abroad; the CA line would gradually shift to the right to CA' and the system would come to rest at point C. However, the average level of interest rates in the world would be too high in terms of the target initially set. (The average level would stay roughly at its initial excessive level.)

The only way to achieve the two (CA and r_w) targets simultaneously is to change fiscal policy so that point A is reached. A number of recent proposals as to how to get there can be illustrated in terms of Figure 8.3.[6] There is an additional line in Figure 8.3, r_{w1}, which indicates those combinations of government spending which would maintain the world rate of interest at its present excessive level. The issue is how to move from C to A. One suggestion, made notably by Branson (1988), would amount to moving directly from C to A, leaving it to expansionary monetary policy in Germany and Japan both to cushion the pos-

[6] The remainder of this paragraph is adapted from Swoboda (1988).

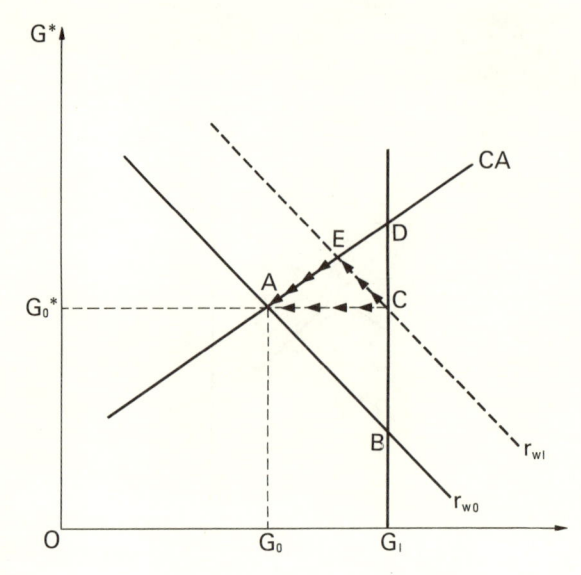

Figure 8.3

sible recessionary impact of a reduction in U.S. government spending in the short run and to avoid too sharp a nominal depreciation of the dollar. The Louvre Accord, with its emphasis on fiscal policy and suggestion that exchange rates are about right, would seem to call for a movement from C to E, where the matching of the decrease in U.S. government spending by an increase in government spending abroad would result in a return to current account equilibrium at the currently high level of real interest rates. The matching increase in government spending abroad is justified, as in the Branson proposal, by fear of the recessionary impact of the fall in U.S. absorption, now coupled with a fear of the inflationary consequences of monetary expansion in the surplus countries (and a general disbelief in the effectiveness of monetary expansion). A third possibility would be to combine the U.S. budget cut with a temporary fiscal stimulus abroad, if possible of the supply-side variety. This would amount to moving from C to E and then to A as the temporary stimulus is withdrawn.

Coordination of fiscal policy of the type suggested above is difficult not only because fiscal stances are a matter as much of politics as of economics but also because the degree of ignorance about the structure of economies (the exact slopes and locations of curves such as CA and r) is such that one does not know the appropriate long-run values of instrument variables with any precision. This suggests that some simple and robust contingent rules governing national policies, notably fiscal ones, be devised and adhered to. This suggestion is of course in the spirit of Mundell's famed assignment problem. One such rule, already mentioned above, is that under floating exchange rates monetary policy be assigned to national internal balance targets and fiscal policy to current account targets; and that, under fixed exchange rates, monetary policy be devoted to over-all payments equilibrium. It is more difficult to devise an assignment rule for fiscal policies which would allow simultaneous convergence to current account equilibrium and to the appropriate level of world interest rates. In one sense, this raises a problem that is analogous to the n-1 problem in the context of monetary policies and exchange rates. One suggestion, made by Genberg and Swoboda (1987) in a two-country context, is to let the larger country aim its fiscal policy to the real rate of interest, the smaller one to its current account. This would suggest that, in a U.S.-versus-rest-of-the-world framework, U.S. fiscal policy look after the current account, the rest of the world after the real rate of interest. The problem with this suggestion is of course that the rest of the world is composed of a great many countries. It may, however, be easier to solve if one considers only three major currency blocs. An alternative rule might be that the burden of current account adjustment fall on the fiscal policy of deficit countries when real interest rates are too high, on that of surplus countries when they are too low.

6. A Common Currency

In principle, any number of specific institutional arrangements could satisfy the principles outlined above, ranging from a properly run floating exchange rate system among major currency areas to fixed exchange rates or to a jointly managed common currency. In conclusion, I would like briefly to make a case for the last regime as the long-run alternative most appropriate in an integrated world economy, at least at the core. The argument is close in spirit to that of Cooper (1984).

The case for a single currency for the industrialized countries is a simple one. In a world where not only financial markets but also goods and factor markets are becoming increasingly integrated, there is very little to be gained by monetary autonomy, provided that the monetary policy governing the issue of the common currency is a reasonable one. A common currency is the best, and perhaps the only viable, solution to the types of problems that proponents of a tax on financial transactions are trying to solve. In a world in which output levels, relative prices, and interest rates are increasingly determined in worldwide markets for similar goods, services, and assets, a single currency would seem to provide the best way of maximizing the value of the services that money provides in its many functions.

The case for joint management of the supply of the common money seems equally obvious. Since it is the aggregate supply of money in the fixed exchange rate world economy that affects those economic variables that are shared by all countries in an integrated world economy—interest rates, prices, and real economic activity—it is control of that aggregate that matters. Control of one part does not help if it is offset by variations in the other parts. Of course control of the world supply could be taken over by a hegemon, but such entities are currently in short supply at a world level. Since all countries have a joint stake in the conditions of supply of world money, it seems natural that they should share in its control.

There are problems, of course. A first problem concerns the proviso made above: "provided that the monetary policy governing the issue of the common currency is a reasonable one." Joint management is one condition for meeting the proviso; separation of the monetary authority from fiscal authorities and shielding it from political meddling is the other.

A second issue concerns the relationship between the exchange-rate regime and fiscal discipline. A floating exchange rate does seem to provide some discipline for fiscal policy since irresponsible spending should in principle result in an exchange crisis. Potential exchange crises should thus impose some constraint on government (although one may wonder whether such discipline is operative for a large reserve currency country). The fear has recently been expressed that in a world of integrated capital markets no such discipline would be provided under a fixed exchange rate regime (cf. the case of Italy after 1990). On the other hand, the example of federal countries like the United States or especially Switzerland would indicate that such fears may be much overdone. Presumably national fiscal autonomy need not be given up just because the same world currency served as legal tender in member countries of the monetary union. Market-determined risk premia should in principle be able to discipline individual national authorities, although here, as elsewhere, there may be serious initial adjustments to be made. In this respect, there would be a gain in having several, not too large, competing fiscal agents. This indeed is an additional problem of world economic arrangements: to avoid their becoming dominated by a few all too powerful actors. It is also the seduction of competing currencies. But if the competition is limited to a few hostile blocs, a jointly managed common currency may well be a preferable alternative.

References

Branson, William H. 1988. "International Adjustment and the Dollar: Policy Illusions and Economic Constraints," in *Economic Policy Coordination*, Guth Wilfried, moderator. Washington: International Monetary Fund.
Cooper, Richard N. 1984. "A Monetary System for the Future," *Foreign Affairs*, Fall.
Dornbusch, Rudiger. 1989. "The Adjustment Mechanism: Theory and Problems," in *The International Monetary System*. Boston: Federal Reserve Bank of Boston.
Edison, Hali J., Miller, Marcus H., and Williamson, John. 1987. "On Evaluating and Extending the Target Zone Proposal," *Journal of Policy Modeling* 9: 189–224.
Genberg, Hans, and Swoboda, Alexander K. 1987. "The Current Account and the Policy Mix under Flexible Exchange Rates." *IMF Working Paper*, WP/87/70.
―――. 1989. "Policy and Current Account Determination under Floating Exchange Rates." International Monetary Fund *Staff Papers* 36: 1–30.
McKinnon, Ronald I. 1984. *An International Standard for Monetary Stabilization*. Washington: Institute for International Economics.
Swoboda, Alexander K. 1983. "Exchange rate Regimes and U.S.-European Policy Interdependence." International Monetary Fund *Staff Papers* 30: 75–102.
―――. 1988. "The Changing Role of Central Banks in the Context of International Policy Coordination." Background paper prepared for the Israeli International Institute conference, Paris (mimeo).
Tobin, James. 1982. "A Proposal for International Monetary Reform," in his *Essays in Economics*. Cambridge, Mass.: MIT Press.
Williamson, John. 1985. *The Exchange Rate System*. Washington: Institute for International Economics.
―――, and Miller, Marcus H. 1987. *Targets and Indicators: A Blueprint for International Coordination of Economic Policy*. Washington: Institute for International Economics.

Comments

Michael J. Prell*

I must confess at the outset, as one who is not a specialist in the field, that the challenge of understanding multi-country economic and financial behavior appears to me to be as daunting as that of solving the three-body problem in physics. And although the papers prepared for this conference certainly have added to my appreciation of the issues, I cannot say they have persuaded me that economists have found the answers to the many important questions confronting them in the sphere of international monetary arrangements. My impression is that, at this stage, our analytical tools perhaps can do more by way of telling us what *won't* work than by telling us what *will*. This probably is true of any field of political economy, when one recognizes the complexities of the real world, but those complexities seem especially great in the international context.

With that preamble, let me turn to the two papers prepared by Black and Swoboda.

I found Stanley Black's paper useful in two respects: first, as a presentation of some facts about the use of the dollar and other currencies internationally, and, second, as an effort to provide an analytical framework for understanding at least some facets of the role of vehicle currencies.

On the vehicle currency issue, perhaps Black's potentially most interesting observation is his last, which is that there is nothing "to prevent technological change in communications from reducing dealers' costs... in such a way as to mitigate the need for vehicle currencies altogether." The same thought had occurred to me, but in the transition period between now and that possible future date

---

*Director, Division of Research and Statistics, Board of Governors of the Federal Reserve System. The opinions expressed are those of the author and do not necessarily reflect the views of the Board of Governors or other members of the staff.

when the concept of vehicle currencies has become irrelevant, there still may be a variety of phenomena warranting our attention. One that crossed my mind as I read Black's paper, and that he did not address, is the implications of changing international uses of currencies for the stability of traditional domestic money demand relations. I cannot say that in our work at the Federal Reserve we have found much evidence that exchange rates or foreign interest rates contribute significantly to the explanation of U.S. monetary aggregate behavior, but the facts Black reports suggest that we should keep an open and inquiring mind on the matter, perhaps looking for other indicators of the external influences on money.

In this connection, it may be noted that a few months ago the Federal Reserve changed its longstanding position on the issuance of foreign currency deposits by U.S. banking institutions. As of the end of this year, banks will be free to issue such instruments in the United States. We currently are modifying our reporting forms so that we shall, among other things, be in a position to exclude the foreign currency deposits from our monetary measures—a step we are taking on the assumption that such balances will have little bearing on spending decisions by U.S. residents. Time will tell whether that assumption is, in fact, appropriate.

I'd like also to comment briefly on the matter of the use of the dollar as an official reserve currency. My first observation is that, while there has been a tendency over the longer haul for some reduction in the relative importance of the dollar in this capacity, the trend has not been especially marked in the past few years. Indeed, if one considers a broader collection of countries than the industrial nations in Black's Table 7.9, it is not clear that there has been any further erosion of the role of the dollar since 1980.

My impression is that there is a fairly general view that some increase in the official role of the yen and other currencies is to be expected. From a policy standpoint, I should think that one concern would be that such change occur in a manner that does not work at cross-purposes with international efforts aimed at fostering stability in the markets. It would be illogical, if not silly-looking, for authorities to be adjusting their reserve asset portfolios in one way when they are intervening in the opposite direction.

I will make just one more comment about Black's paper. As he correctly observes, Japan's balance sheet shows a substantial net "short-term" liability that is more than offset by a large net "long-term" asset total. The situation appears to be one in which Japanese banks, being constrained by domestic regulation, have been sizable net takers of funds from the international markets, while nonbank investors have, in effect, "overfinanced" the Japanese current account surplus. Presumably, the ongoing deregulation of the banking sector could have some effect on this pattern.

I shall now turn to Swoboda's paper, which I found to be a helpful survey of a number of analytical issues. The first of these was the question of what conditions need to prevail for a country to become a major international financial center or for a currency to assume a major role as a reserve asset or international transactions vehicle. Professor Swoboda notes that these are separable phenomena; as he indicates, one can envision—and cite examples of—a nation being a main center of international financial activity without its currency playing a correspondingly prominent role in official reserves. I have no reason to take issue with his observation that Japan and the yen can be expected to assume more importance; however, this is an opportunity to suggest again that the evolution of Japan's role as a financial center may be linked importantly to ongoing developments in the regulatory sphere.

In the second part of his paper, Swoboda argues that, based on the macroeconomics of small open economies, "One may thus well imagine a gradual evolution toward a world of a few currency areas toward which smaller countries will slowly gravitate." However, this statement immediately follows a passage in which he explains why, because of their different policy goals and economic structures, some countries might perceive there to be serious drawbacks in joining such a bloc. The logical tension between the two thoughts effectively highlights a very real issue regarding the reluctance to surrender economic sovereignty, which stands as an impediment to strict international monetary arrangements. We perhaps can watch the progress of discussions in the EC to see how good a forecaster Professor Swoboda is.

Having discussed the small economy case, Swoboda turns to the question of alternative international monetary arrangements, which might shape the behavior of larger economies or blocs of smaller economies. He concludes that a jointly managed currency is "the long-run alternative most appropriate in an integrated world economy at least at the core." I must say that I am skeptical about how germane the assertion is in the present circumstances. Perhaps the trick is in Swoboda's use of the words "long-run" and "integrated."

I may be suffering from the traditional American insularity, but it seems to me that, setting aside issues of differing policy tastes, the world's labor and product markets are still sufficiently unintegrated and far enough from frictionless that to eliminate the possibility of relative price adjustment through exchange rate movement might be seen as imposing greater costs than nations would deem it reasonable to accept. That being the case, it is difficult to take the common currency idea seriously as a practical option for the foreseeable future.

What, then, is the alternative? One could begin answering that question by exploring in some depth what objectives people have for the international monetary system. And Swoboda has given us a good discussion of that issue. He also provides a persuasive critique of the Williamson and McKinnon proposals. But would it really be farfetched simply to suggest that the system that has evolved in the past couple of years isn't so bad after all?

To be sure, we have seen neither absolute exchange rate stability nor the elimination of external imbalances. And policy developments, perhaps especially U.S. fiscal policy, have not consistently met all expectations. But has the outcome in terms of such fundamental and crucial objectives as economic growth and movement toward price stability really been disappointing? I think one can reasonably say no, it has not. I certainly don't want to be Pollyanna-ish: one must feel some insecurity in a circumstance where, in particular, the United States is rapidly building a large external liability, soaking up world savings and probably contributing to higher real interest rates without an obviously exceptional rate of productive capital accumulation. And the large U.S. trade deficit does provide political ammunition for those seeking to achieve a competitive edge through trade protection. However, it is important not to exaggerate the ills of the present system.[1]

For all its flaws, the current system is arguably a very reasonable one, given not only the political realities of the desire for national sovereignty, but also the state of economic knowledge. As elegant as his theoretical presentation is, I believe Swoboda would find himself, as I do, in considerable agreement with the view that Professor Shinkai expresses so forcefully in his paper: that, on an empirical level, we don't really know the signs, let alone the magnitudes, of many key effects in our open economy models. I can't help but think when I read the IS-LM analysis in Swoboda's paper that economists continue to debate how even to define and measure the monetary and fiscal variables in his models.

Traditionally, faced with such uncertainty, economists have argued

---

[1] I suspect that the discomfort economists have been exprsssing recently about exchange rate "volatility" has been enhanced more than a little by the tendency of the markets to confound our expert analyses of how they *ought* to be behaving!

about the virtues of rules versus discretion. My own inclination is toward the latter. Those who feel rules will minimize policy errors not only must put a great deal of faith in the stability of some basic economic relation (or perhaps some small, manageable set of relations); they must also ignore the proven ability of those policymakers to circumvent or discard the rules when they deem it desirable. I find such flexibility reassuring in light of the fact that, historically, simple rules would have pointed at times in directions that most analysts would think incorrect. Of course, the potential for deviations from rules also limits the beneficial "credibility" effects to which proponents of rules often like to point.

In any event, the religious pursuit of tightly prescribed rules seems likely to be inconsistent with the full use of available information. The current consultative process, involving the discussion of a wide range of economic data and policy objectives and options, seems to be a far more reasonable approach. Assuming that this exercise is not undertaken cynically, the process should yield such benefits as are realistically achievable through cooperative behavior. Even if there is not strict coordination of policies, potentially a good deal may be gained simply from being better informed about the assessments and intentions of one's chief trading partners. In the end, I conclude that economists might make a greater contribution to the achievement of a stable and efficient world financial system by devoting their energies to filling the gaps in knowledge we all admit exist, instead of attempting to devise simple rules to govern international monetary policy.

Comments

Masahiro Kawai

Stanley Black's paper [1989] discusses the factors affecting the choice and use of a particular currency (or set of currencies) as an international currency. Alexander Swoboda's paper [1989] focuses on the broader issue of the implications of globalized economic activities and increased economic integration for the international monetary system. I will first take up Black's paper, then Swoboda's paper.*

Black attempts to examine the conditions under which a national currency plays an international role, specifically as an invoice currency, a borrowing currency, a vehicle currency, and an intervention and reserve currency.

Invoice Currency. Citing Bissaro and Hamaui's work, Black states that "the share of exports denominated in domestic currency declines with expected depreciation in the domestic currency and rises with an increase in variability," and that their theoretical prediction is confirmed in the case of the Italian lira. But a simple application of this result may be misleading, because this argument applies only to one side of a trade contract which is made by *both* exporters and importers. (If the domestic currency is expected to depreciate, other things being equal, exporters will wish to receive export revenues in the foreign currency, and importers will wish to pay in the domestic currency.) The trade-invoice currency is selected as a result of bargaining between exporters and importers, and the factors affecting such bargaining include not only exchange rate expectations and variability, but also tradition and habit, differences in attitudes toward risk, the characteristics of the goods traded, market power, and financial convenience (Magee, 1974; McKinnon, 1979). Table 7.2 of Black's paper clearly indicates that the share of Japanese exports denominated in yen was rising in the early 1980s but started to decline in 1986. One

---

* I am thankful to David Campbell for his suggestions on an earlier version.

explanation for this is that foreign importers did not want their imports to be denominated in yen, which was appreciating in value and was expected to continue to appreciate. To the extent that this reasoning is correct, it would appear that foreign importers had stronger bargaining power than did Japanese exporters in selecting an invoice currency.

The above, however, ignores the more important question of how exchange risk is actually shared between exporters and importers, given that a certain currency is chosen for invoicing. Here, a long-term implicit contract may be used as an effective device for optimal exchange risk sharing. For example, suppose Japan's exports to a foreign country are invoiced in yen and the yen appreciates unexpectedly. If the exporter has a strong incentive to maintain the sales network and other related intangible assets abroad that are costly to replace, he may not necessarily insist that his exports be paid fully in yen, but instead may allow the importers to pay only partially in yen, permitting *ex post* price reductions and risk sharing. In such a case, the selection of an invoice currency is a relatively minor issue, and the way in which actual exchange risk sharing is arranged is more important (see Shavell (1976) for a model of this kind).

Borrowing Currency. Black notes that the shares of yen-denominated bonds and bank loans have recently been rising. He concludes that the rising shares are the result of the increasing wealth position of agents whose preferred currency habitat is the yen. I believe there are other reasons for the rising share of the yen in international bond issues. First, the recent development of financial techniques such as swaps enables business corporations and firms to borrow funds in U.S. dollars by means of issuing yen bonds. The reason this is done is that issuing Euro-yen bonds and swapping them into dollar bonds is often less costly than issuing dollar bonds because of the low yen interest rate. This means the yen is used only as a transit currency, rather than as a borrowing currency.

Second, the frequent use of the yen in the international market reflects partly the "hollowing out" of the Japanese bond and capital market: Japanese borrowers issue yen-denominated bonds in Eurobond and/or external bond markets, and Japanese investors purchase them. They do so because of the existence of regulations, restrictions, and various business practices that raise the cost of using the domestic market. (This practice appears more pronounced with regard to the issuance and purchase of dollar bonds.) In this sense, the internationalization of the yen in capital transactions is highly exaggerated.

Vehicle Currency. A currency is chosen to be a vehicle in the interbank market when its use economizes on transactions and information costs in comparison to direct exchange of two non-vehicle currencies. Black's contribution here is to characterize bid-ask spreads as transactions costs and explicitly demonstrate that as more currency exchanges occur through the medium of a vehicle, the volume of transactions rises and the transactions costs decline. Thus, the model offers a microeconomic foundation for Krugman's (1980) argument concerning the importance of the role of economies of scale in the use of a vehicle currency. Once a vehicle is chosen, it becomes the basis for interbank transactions, official intervention, and, hence, official reserve holdings. Needless to say, the selection of a reserve currency is affected also by portfolio (return-risk) considerations, among other factors.

The Role of the Yen. An interesting question, which Black mentions only briefly in his conclusion, is whether the yen is likely to become an international currency in Southeast Asia, if not in the world as a whole. In Southeast Asia, the yen-denominated shares of Japanese exports and imports in 1988 were 41.2% and 17.5%, respectively (see Table 1). These shares are lower than those for the EC countries. In Japan's trade with Southeast Asia, the yen is not used as extensively as one might think. But the yen share of trade, particularly in Southeast Asia, will likely rise over time given the expanding volumes of Japan's trade and direct investment flows in this region.

With regard to the yen's role as a reserve currency in the Pacific-Asia region, proposals to establish a regional basket of currencies in the form of the ACU (Asian Currency Unit, excluding the dollar) or the PACU (Pacific Asian Currency Unit, including the dollar) have been advanced by some economists. My opinion is that Southeast Asia, which is a de facto dollar area today, is likely to become a PACU area rather than a yen or ACU area. This is suggested by the fact that since 1985, when the yen started to appreciate against the U.S. dollar, the currencies of Korea, Taiwan, and Hong Kong have risen in value, but not by as much as the yen has. In essence, these newly industrializ-

Table 1 The Share of Japan's Yen-Denominated Trade in 1988 (%)

	U.S.	E.C.	Southeast Asia	Total
Exports	16.4	43.9	41.2	34.3
Imports	10.0	26.9	17.5	13.3

Source: Ministry of Finance, *International Finance Bureau Annual Report*, 1989.

ing countries have been attempting to stabilize the value of their currencies against a basket of the dollar and the yen. In order for a multi-reserve currency system to become viable in Asia or elsewhere, however, the Japanese financial market must be perceived as a market that offers easy access, freedom of transactions, and transparency. This is indeed one main topic Swoboda examines.

International Financial Center. Swoboda first points out three preconditions for an international financial center:

1. A commitment to economic stability and transparency in the sense of legal framework.
2. A commitment to the freedom of transactions.
3. The maintenance of a competitive financial industry.

To gain credibility, an established history of stability and respect for the freedom of transactions is important. With regard to Japan's financial system, I am sympathetic with Swoboda's concern that "Most foreigners do not yet have a full understanding of what is going on in Japan, and there remain questions about whether access to various financial transactions is and will be on equal terms for everybody or whether there are not risks of future expropriation of at least partial property rights by local groups." I believe, however, that the possibility of future expropriation in Japan is as remote as in other major developed countries.

Future of the International Monetary System. In his discussion of the future of the international monetary system, Swoboda envisions a "single jointly managed currency" (Cooper, 1989) and a "multipolar world of a few currency areas (Dollar, Yen, ECU)" as probable scenarios for, respectively, the long run and the medium run. There have been extensive discussions concerning the long-run scenario throughout this conference. His medium-run scenario is similar to the one proposed by Black.

I like Swoboda's way of looking at the future of the international monetary system from long-run and medium-run perspectives, though we must recognize that we are in the short-run reality. The long-run scenario of establishing a single common currency and a single common central bank for the industrialized economies may be an impossible dream. Nevertheless, it is a dream that cannot be easily dismissed. It is a much more "credible" commitment to irrevocable fixed exchange rates, economic integration, and the elimination of inflation taxes by local authorities than the usual fixed exchange rate arrangements, and it therefore maximizes the usefulness of money for international transactions. In order to establish a single, common currency area, the preconditions for an optimum currency area must be satisfied, and further coordinated policy measures to facilitate smooth adjustment must be adopted. These measures include fiscal transfers and industrial and supply-side policies to promote faster structural changes in the economy. In addition, changes in tradable/nontradable relative prices and in wealth positions will also facilitate adjustment.

In the medium run, Swoboda regards a "multipolar world" with the Genberg-Swoboda policy assignment or McKinnon's "symmetric gold standard without gold" as likely international monetary arrangements. He dismisses other medium-run scenarios, such as the Worldwide EMS (Kenen) and the Target Zones system (Williamson-Miller).

Asymmetry. It seems that the long-run and medium-run scenarios envisioned by Swoboda are all "symmetric" in the sense that the selection of an international currency is considered unimportant and the burden of adjustment is distributed evenly between surplus and deficit countries. But in reality, the present international monetary (non)system is asymmetric; that is, the U.S. dollar plays the role of the dominant international currency, and the United States is in a special position where macroeconomic policy is not always constrained by external considerations. Essentially, U.S. policy makers often do not find the need to adopt disciplined macroeconomic policy, given that U.S. current account deficits are financed relatively easily by borrowing in dollars.

The question remains how we could move from the present short run to the medium and long run. Several recommendations can be made. One would be to diversify international reserves, which could be expected to impose macroeconomic policy discipline on the center country, that is, the United States. However, this may not be easy when the economies-of-scale argument (see Black's paper) dictates that it is more resource-economizing to choose a single vehicle and, hence, a single reserve currency than having multiple vehicles and reserve assets. Although high exchange rate volatility should reduce the attractiveness of a currency as a vehicle and a reserve, it is not clear that the recent dollar volatility has indeed reduced the use of the dollar as an international vehicle and reserve currency.

Another recommendation would be to introduce asset settlements or rigid target zones, or a combination of the two, which should impose macroeconomic policy discipline on the United States. Asset settlements and rigid target zones, however, appear unacceptable to the United States. This suggests that it is difficult to find a smooth path toward the medium and long run.

Finally, I should like to point out that in a forthcoming multipolar world, a large degree of asymmetry will continue to remain between the United States and Japan. As Swoboda emphasizes, it takes a long time for a currency to achieve the status of an international currency (an established "brand name," using Meltzer's (1989) word). Japan lifted its exchange controls only in 1980, but other explicit and tacit regulations and business practices still remain, making it more costly to use the Japanese financial and capital markets than the Euro market and other markets. Japan depends heavily on the dollar for international trade invoicing (note that about 50% of Japan's exports and 80% of its imports are still denominated in the dollar) and for capital transactions (Japan borrows short and lends long, mostly in U.S. dollars). The latter type of dependence reflects the fact that the U.S. or offshore dollar market is much more efficient and convenient than the yen market. This suggests that for the foreseeable future, the yen will not be able to gain the international status the dollar currently enjoys. The yen will be used increasingly by third countries in Asia as an international currency (possibly as part of a basket, such as the PACU), but in order for this process to be accelerated, significant progress must be made in guaranteeing easy access to the market, freedom of transactions, and transparency.

References

Black, S.W. 1989. "The International Use of Currencies." In this volume.

Cooper, R.N. 1989. "What Future for the International Monetary System?" In this volume.

Krugman, P. August, 1980. Vehicle Currencies and the Structure of International Exchange. *Journal of Money, Credit, and Banking.* 12: 513–26.

Magee, S.P. 1974. U.S. Import Prices in the Currency-Contract Period. *Brookings Papers on Economic Activity.* 1: 117–64.

McKinnon, R.I. 1979. *Money in International Exchange: The Convertible Currency System.* New York: Oxford University Press.

Meltzer, A.H. 1989. "Efficiency and Stability in World Finance." In this volume.

Shavell, S. February, 1976. "Sharing Risks of Deferred Payment." *Journal of Political Economy.* 84: 161–68.

Swoboda, A. 1989. "Financial Inegration and International Monetary Arrangements." In this volume.

Comments

John Murray

I. Introduction

The papers that Professors Black and Swoboda have prepared for this conference are insightful and interesting, and address many of the major issues that have been raised in recent years concerning the functioning of the international financial system and the use of international currencies. Since I agree with most of the authors' observations, as well as their description of recent economic events, there is little that I can add by way of criticicm or advice. Instead, my comments will focus on a few related topics that I feel might have been given greater attention in their papers. These are briefly summarized in the following sections of this note.

II. S.W. Black, "The International Use of Currencies"

The principal purpose of Black's paper is to "discuss the factors influencing the use of currencies as international reserve assets and vehicle currencies." Black begins his analysis by documenting the decline of the U.S. dollar and the emergence of the yen and the Deutsche mark as possible contenders for the role of dominant world currency. He notes, however, that neither currency is likely to supplant the dollar in the near future, or return us to the sort of hegemonic state that was observed prior to World War I (under the sterling standard) and in the immediate post World War II period (under the dollar standard).

Later sections of the paper examine the various economic factors that might account for the rise and subsequent decline of different international currencies. A formal model is presented, highlighting the importance of transactions costs, trading volumes, and exchange risk in the "internationalization" process. The model is then used to show how more than one currency could serve as a medium of exchange in international trade. Contrary to the impression created by several earlier studies, Black suggests that the international financial system need not gravitate toward a single vehicle currency.

Although I have no difficulty with the descriptive and analytic portions of Black's paper, I was surprised that government regulations and controls were not included among those factors that could either inhibit or facilitate the internationalization of a currency. The importance of these restrictions is perhaps most evident in the case of Japan, the host country for our conference. While Japan's growing economic influence in world trade and investment have no doubt contributed to the yen's popularity in recent years, there is reason to believe that deregulation of Japanese financial markets and the removal of foreign capital controls have also played a critical role.[1]

Two other potentially important influences that could have been given greater attention in the paper are technological change and financial innovation. These changes and innovations have presumably reduced the importance of economies of scale and transactions costs as factors determining the currency composition of international trade and investment. Lower transactions costs, for example, likely encourage more direct forms of international exchange, limiting the need for "two-ticket" transactions and the use of vehicle currencies.

Recent financial innovations might also cause interested readers to question the descriptive analyses that are presented in Sections II and III of the paper. Historical comparisons of changes in the currency composition of international trade and investment may not be very revealing in a world where agents can quickly alter the denomination of their assets and liabilities through a series of swap transactions.

Unlike the limited treatment accorded government regulations and technological change, exchange rate risk seems to have received considerable attention in Black's paper. I worry, however, that its influence may have been overemphasized—both in the model that is presented in Section IV and in some of the other studies that are referenced (for example, Bissaro and Hamaui [1988]). No recogni-

---

[1] Swoboda's paper complements Black's in this regard, by emphasizing the importance of what Swoboda terms "the freedom of transactions," and the the supportive role that goverments can play in providing an open and stable economic environment.

tion is given to the fact that exporters, importers and investors might be able to minimize, if not completely eliminate, the uncertainty arising from unexpected exchange rate movements through forward exchange transactions and other hedging strategies.[2]

Finally, as a possible extension to his work, it might have been interesting if Black had investigated some of the policy implications of current and prospective changes in the international use of currencies. A few of the questions that could have been examined are noted below.

(1) Should authorities regard the internationalization of their currencies as a positive or a negative development? What benefits might the country whose currency is being internationalized derive (increased seigniorage, a lower cost of capital, or possibly increased flexibility with regard to financing its deficits)?

(2) Should the internationalization of currencies be actively encouraged or discouraged by governments and/or multilateral institutions? If so, what steps should be taken to influence the process?

(3) Should other countries care if the yen or the Deutsche mark usurps the dollar's role as dominant currency? Would the international system be made more or less stable? Are there any positive spillovers or externalities that might be realized?

To help put some of these issues in context, Black might have drawn on Japan's experience during the past twenty years. Through the 1970s and early 1980s Japanese officials were apparently reluctant to see the yen assume a larger international role, and in fact took steps to actively discourage its use. The officials may have been concerned that a more open and less regulated domestic capital market would complicate the implementation of monetary policy. In the event, their position appears to have changed, and a number of measures have been introduced to help open Japanese financial markets.[3] Interestingly, the yen's new international status does not seem to have had any adverse effect on Japan's ability to control monetary conditions or foster non-inflationary growth.

---

[2] See Krugman (1984).
[3] This may have been in part a response to some encouragement from the United States, via the U.S.-Japan Ad Hoc Committee on the Yen-Dollar Exchange Rate (May 1984). Evidently the United States felt that increasing the international role of the yen might take some of the pressure off the dollar, at a time when the dollar was generally believed to have been overvalued.

III. A.K. Swoboda, "Financial Integration and International Monetary Arrangements"

While Swoboda's paper touches on a number of different topics, the various sections are organized around three central questions: (1) Can an integrated world economy accommodate more than one international currency and more than one international financial center? (2) What problems might increased economic integration pose for macro stabilization policies under alternative exchange rate regimes? (3) How might the problems of the present floating rate system be minimized or overcome through alternative monetary arrangements?

Swoboda, like Black, doubts that we will see the emergence of a new "currency hegemon" in the near future. Rather, he anticipates a continuation of recent trends and the development of a multicurrency/multipolar international financial system.

He is also not very optimistic about the prospects for macro economic stabilization under the present floating exchange rate system, and believes that increased international interdependence and integration has probably limited the effectiveness of both fiscal and monetary policies. Swoboda notes that the performance of the floating rate system has fallen far short of its proponents' original expectations, and that promises of stabilizing speculation and automatic correction of external imbalances have given way to the reality of excess volatility and persistent currency misalignment.

Two alternatives are offered to the status quo in the medium term: (1) a system of international capital controls and taxes to eliminate excess volatility; and (2) more ambitious forms of policy coordination. Swoboda concludes that each of these proposals is seriously flawed, however, and offers his own solution for a more "effective and viable monetary arrangement." The latter involves assigning target values to real interest rates and current account deficits, under a fixed exchange rate system, and using the world money supply and government deficits as policy instruments.

As a long-run solution, Swoboda indicates that he would favor the adoption of a single world currency.[4] If this does not happen, he warns, the international monetary system will become increasingly unstable and be dominated by a "few hostile trading blocks."

While the analysis in these sections is intriguing, I have some res-

---

[4] A similar recommendation is put forward and developed in greater detail by Cooper (1984, 1989).

ervations concerning the observations and recommendations that are made toward the end of the paper. In particular, I worry that Swoboda has perhaps given too much weight to the downside of deregulation and greater market integration—emphasizing only the constraints that this might impose on policymakers' ability to stabilize the macro economy. As a consequence, there is a risk that readers will overlook the upside or positive elements of the futuristic world that he has described (characterized by free trade, frictionless markets and rational, forward-looking agents). These positive elements are not limited simply to the improved efficiency that would result from eliminating market distortions. Recognition should also be given to the fact that stabilization policies would be unnecessary in such a world, and that consequently one would not need to worry about whether policy effectiveness had been reduced.

Unfortunately, unlike Swoboda, I believe that we are still some distance from this idyllic state; so I am less dismissive of the potential importance and effectiveness of macro policies. Moreover, I would tend to place greater emphasis on controlling nominal magnitudes, such as prices and interest rates ("In view of the preceding discussion one might well want to ask why small countries should not peg their currencies to that of a major country or currency block since floating does not buy them all that much effective policy autonomy *except with respect to nominal variables such as their price level, rate of inflation, and nominal interest rates*" [Swoboda (1989)]).

Swoboda seems to have drawn too sharp a distinction between the behavior of nominal and real variables. Indeed, it is the presumed dependence of real economic performance on the behavior of nominal magnitudes that provides the rationale for central banks' primary function, viz. the achievement and maintenance of domestic price stability. Because of this dependence, the choice between fixed and flexible exchange rates is not a matter of indifference. Indeed, many countries continue to favor flexible currency arrangements precisely because of the increased independence the latter provide with respect to controlling prices and interest rates. Though exchange rate variability may impose real costs on the international economy in the form of reduced trade and distorted price signals, the advantages that flexible rates provide in terms of assisting macroeconomic adjustment and preserving monetary policy autonomy are often thought to be worth the potential microeconomic costs.

In this regard, it is also worth noting that I am not as pessimistic as Swoboda about the present and future performance of the current international monetary system—an eclectic blend of fixed and flexible exchange rates. There is an important difference between arguing that "the present system... has not proved *entirely* satisfactory," and suggesting that it "is not a realistic alternative." I believe that the costs of short-run exchange rate volatility are often overstated and that many of the persistent swings in exchange rates that we have observed in recent years can be explained by market fundamentals, including, on occasion, (misdirected) macro policies.

A single world currency has much to recommend it in terms of reducing transactions costs, and the world may well gravitate toward such a system as part of a natural evolutionary process. Nevertheless, I am not convinced that such a move would be advantageous from a short-run macroeconomic perspective.

Proponents of a single currency often point to large, regionally diverse economies like those of Canada and the United States as proof that such a system would be workable. It would be a mistake, however, to minimize the adjustment costs that are frequently borne by the different sectors and regions of these countries. Indeed, Mundell first applied his concept of optimal currency areas to the North American economy, demonstrating that national political boundaries did not necessarily correspond to the currency blocks that would have been preferred on economic grounds.

Research at the Bank of Canada has shown that the implied real exchange rate movements between some of Canada's provinces during the past ten years have been as large as (or larger than) those experienced by most European economies vis-à-vis their major trading partners (See Table 1 and Figure 1). Particularly noteworthy in this regard is the close correspondence between the numbers that are reported for the province of Alberta, using Ontario as a base, and those for the United Kingdom, relative to Germany. Both Alberta and the United Kingdom are oil exporters and have experienced comparable movements in their real exchange rates over time.

One could interpret these results in several different ways. Those who support the creation of a European Monetary Union, for example,

Table 1 Real Exchange Rate Movements: 1980, Q1–1987, Q4

	Standard Deviation
Canada	
Alberta/Ontario	11.3
EEC	
France/Germany	3.5
Italy/Germany	5.9
U.K./Germany	11.2

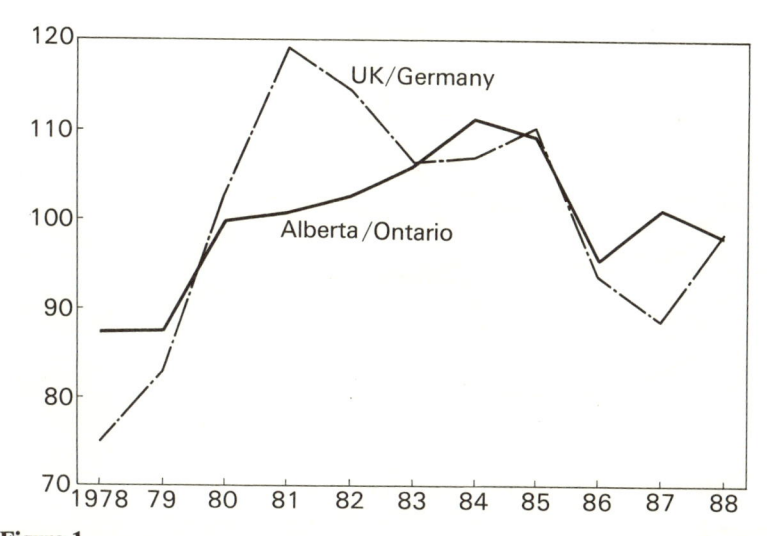

Figure 1
Real Exchange Rates

	Alberta/Ontario	U.K./Germany
78: 1	87.333	74.898
79: 1	87.525	83.202
80: 1	99.949	103.548
81: 1	100.827	119.474
82: 1	102.661	114.540
83: 1	106.074	106.428
84: 1	111.412	106.965
85: 1	109.504	110.466
86: 1	95.414	93.297
87: 1	101.204	88.471
88: 1	98.099	98.734

might argue that the evident viability of Canada's "monetary union" and its ability to cope with large swings in regional real exchange rates augurs well for the eventual success of the EMU and other fixed exchange rate systems. Others might argue, as Mundell did, that based on economic considerations alone Canada should perhaps be divided into at least two separate currency areas.

Recent economic developments in Canada help illuminate the serious dislocation and adjustment costs that can result when a common monetary policy must be applied to economically diverse regions. Differences in unemployment rates between regions have varied con-

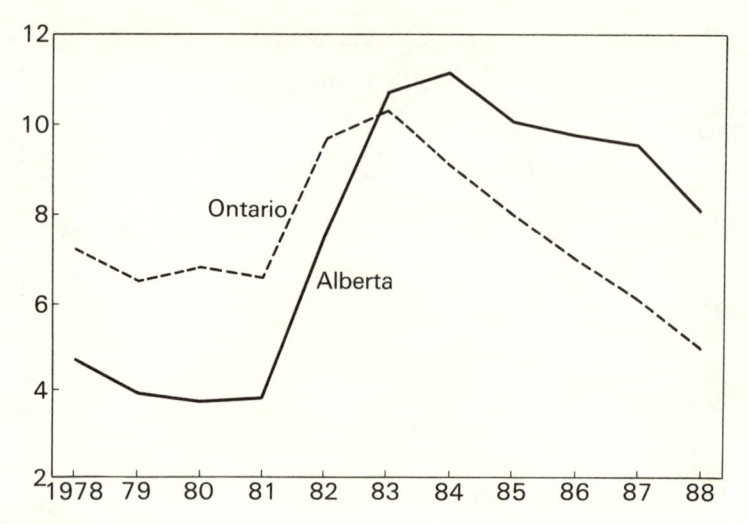

Figure 2
Unemployment Rates

Ontario	Alberta
7.20000	4.70000
6.50000	3.90000
6.80000	3.70000
6.60000	3.80000
9.80000	7.70000
10.4000	10.8000
9.10000	11.2000
8.00000	10.1000
7.00000	9.80000
6.10000	9.60000
5.00000	8.00000

siderably over the last ten years, and on occasion have been as large as 13.3%.[5] Inflation and real growth differentials have been as high as 17.1% and 8.9% respectively, and have displayed remarkable persistence over time (See Figures 2, 3, and 4).[6] Clearly, re-equilibrating regional economies via adjustments to nominal wages and prices as

---

[5] All of the percentages reported in this section have been calculated on a year-over-year basis.

[6] The unemployment differential that is cited here is based on data from the province of Newfoundland, as opposed to Alberta, and does not correspond to the data shown in Figure 2.

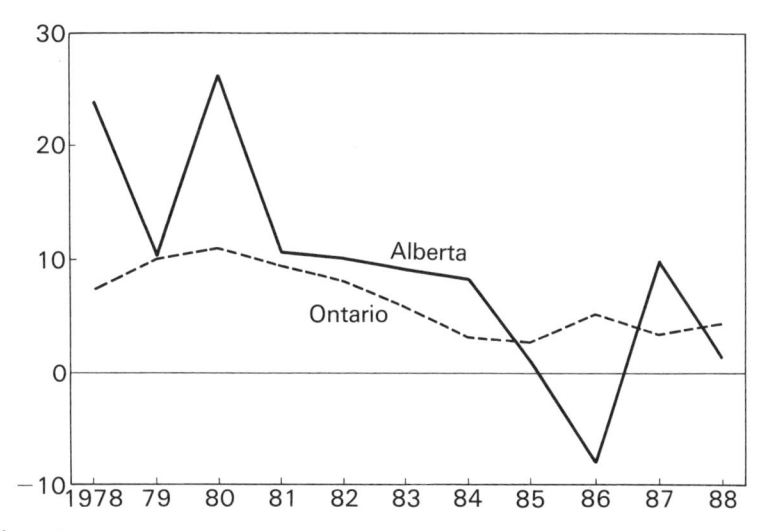

Figure 3
Inflation Rates

ONTARIO	ALBERTA
7.43294	23.8661
10.0624	10.2974
10.9756	26.7668
9.49215	10.6110
8.16377	10.1412
5.72979	9.17764
3.12082	8.33525
2.66362	.905358
5.16234	−8.37923
3.40501	9.73051
4.40073	1.20117

opposed to changes in nominal exchange rates can be a painful process. Flexible exchange rates offer policymakers an extra degree of freedom, and Canada's experience would suggest that other countries should not abandon them too readily. Instead, attention should probably be concentrated on improving the present system.

With regard to the alternatives examined by Swoboda, most observers would agree with his conclusion that capital controls and transactions taxes ought to be avoided. His treatment of policy coordination is more contentious, however. By relating this alternative to more extreme forms of coordination such as Williamson and

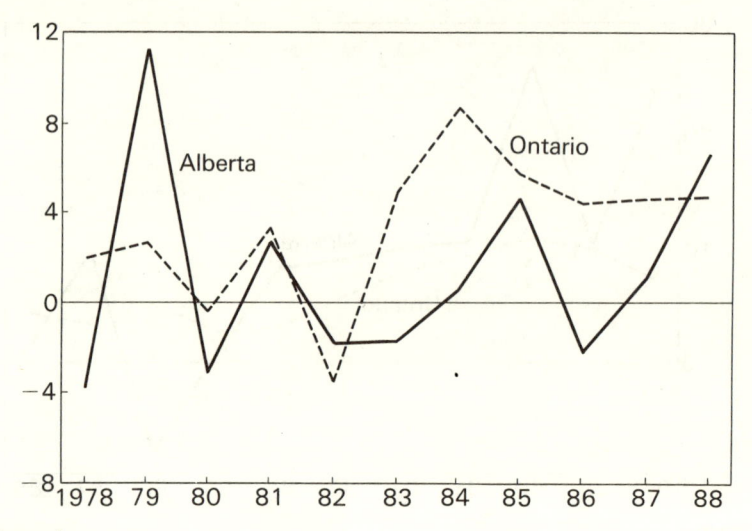

Figure 4
Real Growth Rates

Ontario	Alberta
1.99000	−3.30000
2.68000	11.5400
−.390000	−3.27000
3.28000	2.78000
−3.65000	−1.87000
5.27000	−1.73000
8.82000	.680000
5.69000	4.86000
4.43000	−2.16000
4.69000	1.18000
4.80000	6.80000

Miller's target zone proposal or McKinnon's PPP standard for international stabilization, Swoboda may not have shown policy coordination to its best advantage. A less ambitious proposal, along the lines of Frankel's nominal income targeting, might have been more appropriate.[7]

Swoboda's own "medium-term" recommendation for an effective and viable monetary arrangement is imaginative, but might also be subject to a number of pitfalls, among them, his choice of target

[7] Frankel (1988).

variables. While concern has frequently been expressed over the current level of world real interest rates and the large external imbalances that exist among the major industrial countries, it is not clear that these variables should be treated as policy targets.

The attention that is given in Swoboda's analysis to budget deficits, as distinct from more fundamental concerns such as the productivity or desirability of government expenditures, is also troublesome. Deficits, whether they are internal or external, need not pose a problem unless they are associated with wasteful public and private activities.

Targeting the world money supply, as Swoboda has suggested, may also present serious difficulties, given the demonstrated instability of monetary aggregates in most industrial countries.

IV. Conclusion

While there is near unanimity with regard to the national policy objectives of most countries—price stability, full employment, and sustainable economic growth—opinions vary on whether these can best be achieved within a fixed or a flexible exchange rate system. This divergence of views reflects the differing economic circumstances of various countries as well as their disparate assessments of the benefits and costs of alternative systems.

Those who believe that exchange rate variability is a primary concern, and would like to link their monetary policy to those of other countries with reputations for sound financial management, will opt for fixed exchange rate systems such as the EMS. Others, whose industrial structures display greater diversity and who are perhaps more dependent on exports of raw materials (e.g., oil), will typically prefer more flexible systems.

Ideally, countries should be able to select the system that best suits their needs and inclinations, provided that there are no significant negative spillovers from such a mixed approach. Policymakers should not feel obliged to actively promote or impose a more comprehensive and radical system on the international economy, but should instead adopt a more benign and flexible stance.

A similar view was voiced by Black in the final section of his paper, with regard to the evolution of a multicurrency reserve and payments system. Here, he suggested that there may be some advantage to letting markets take the lead, while governments play more of a supporting, or reactive role.

References

Bissaro, Ginanantonio, and R. Hamui. 1988. "The Choice of Invoice Currency in an Inter-Temporal Model of Price Setting," processed, Bocconi University, Milan.

Cooper, R. 1984. "A Monetary System for the Future," *Foreign Affairs*, Fall, reprinted in *The International Monetary System*, MIT Press, 1987.

———. 1989. "What Future for the International Monetary System?" This volume.

Frankel, J. 1988. "A Modest Proposal for International Nominal Income Targeting," International Policy Coordination and Exchange Rate Fluctuations, NBER, Kiawah Island, October.

Krugman, P. 1984. "The International Role of the Dollar: Theory and Prospect," *Exchange Rate Theory and Practice*, eds. J. Bilson and R. Marston, NBER.

McKinnon, R. 1963. "Optimum Currency Areas," *American Economic Review*, vol. LIII (September).

Mundell, R. 1961. "A Theory of Optimum Currency Areas," *American Economic Review*, vol. LI (September).

Towards a Better International Monetary System

9

The EMS Experience

Francesco Giavazzi*

I. Introduction

When the EMS was launched in 1978, the new plan for exchange rate stability in Europe was accepted with much skepticism. Policymakers still were influenced by the collapse of Bretton Woods, and concentrated on learning how to live with flexible exchange rates. Because economists were also attempting to understand the working of flexible exchange rates, there was no analysis of the EMS until the mid-1980s. Now the situation is quite different. According to conventional wisdom, the EMS has been a success. In stark contrast with the gyrations of the dollar, European currencies and intra-European competitiveness indices have remained remarkably stable over the past ten years;[1] during the same period, inflation rates and inflation-rate differentials across Europe have been dramatically reduced. Hence the shift in public opinion and the renewed interest in the EMS.

Meanwhile, outside Europe the reform of the international monetary system is no longer an unfashionable topic: "target zones" and the simple return to fixed exchange rates have taken center stage in policy discussions and, to some extent, also in economic analyses.[2] There are at least five views on the future of the international monetary system. Some of them advocate reforms which would limit the degree of exchange rate flexibility; others concentrate on "fundamentals" and play down the effectiveness of exchange rate management. Ronald McKinnon (e.g., 1988) is responsible for one set of proposals. He argues for fixed nominal exchange rates. The system he envisages

---

* I am especially indebted to Alberto Giovannini because I draw freely in this paper on material contained in our book (Giavazzi and Giovannini, 1989).
[1] An important exception is the United Kingdom, which remained outside the EMS.
[2] See, for instance, Krugman (1988a).

is similar to a symmetric gold standard: central banks would use domestic credit policies to peg the price of a common basket of internationally traded goods. Fiscal policy would target external balance; deficits and surpluses would be corrected by changes in the level of spending in the various countries, at given relative prices. The second proposal, for "target zones," was originally formulated by John Williamson (1985) and later elaborated in Miller and Williamson (1988). The central point of the plan is the assignment of monetary policy to a real exchange rate target: interest rate differences among countries would keep the real effective exchange rate of each country within a preassigned band. Nominal variables (nominal GDP) would be controlled by the average level of world real interest rates and by domestic fiscal policy in each country.

The most radical view is Richard Cooper's suggestion (originally formulated in Cooper (1984)) that "the time has come to begin contemplating a common currency among the industrialized democracies." The least orthodox is James Tobin's proposal (1982) to put some "sand in the wheels" of international financial markets: a transactions tax would discourage short-term speculation and presumably reduce exchange rate volatility.

A very different view seems to be favored by the staff of the International Monetary Fund. It begins with the premise that "a reform of the international monetary system should be viewed as a constitutional change that should not be taken lightly . . . [and] not viewed as an instrument for crisis management" (Frenkel, 1987, p. 11). Policymakers should concentrate on eliminating the "fundamental" sources of imbalance in the world economy: "the use of monetary policy to sustain exchange rate stability has definite drawbacks as a longer term strategy. . . . Monetary policy is no more than a temporary substitute for changes in underlying fiscal positions." (IMF, 1987, p. 17).

In the debate that surrounds these proposals, the EMS experience is often referenced. Some—McKinnon, for instance—point to the success of the system at limiting exchange-rate volatility. Others—Miller and Williamson—point to the evidence that the EMS has operated as a Deutsche-mark zone as an indication of how difficult it is to build symmetric exchange rate regimes. Still others—for example, Fischer (1987)—point to the apparently crucial role played by capital controls in keeping the system together. These frequent references to the EMS have so far lacked the rigor of a thorough review of the system, one aimed at identifying which lessons—if any—can be drawn from this experiment at limiting exchange rate flexibility.

Analyses of the EMS have been limited to Europe and have never been brought to bear on the wider questions of world monetary arrangements.

Two issues are especially relevant. The first is the formal resolution of the so-called N-1 problem—that is, the issue of *symmetry*. Mundell (1968, p. 195) pointed out the importance of this problem in any plan for the reform of the international monetary system, and Frenkel (1987) has recently reminded us: "It is essential to ask how the various proposals, including those for target zones, deal with the extra degree of freedom." The second is the extent to which the exchange rate system can impose constraints on domestic policies—that is, the issue of *discipline*. The discipline question was central in discussions over the reform of the Bretton Woods system in the 1960s[3] and has been raised recently by Fischer (1988). That question has two sides: one is the effect of exchange-rate rules on inflation expectations—this is the way the "discipline" argument is usually understood; the other is related to the constraint that the exchange-rate regime imposes on fiscal policy.

This paper is organized in six sections. Section II discusses symmetry. Section III the credibility of exchange rate targets. Section IV discusses exchange rate rules and fiscal policy. In Section V, I ask what Germany gained from the EMS. In Section VI, I summarize the main lessons of the EMS experience.

II. The EMS as (Imperfect) Greater Deutsche Mark Area

Ten years of operation of the European Monetary System provide an important case study for those interested in designing new forms of international monetary policy coordination. In any fixed exchange-rate regime, the task of running monetary policy is not *explicitly* assigned to any one country. Supporters of the hypothesis that international monetary policy coordination is feasible claim that in commodity standard systems, such as the gold standard or the Bretton Woods regime, the establishment of nominal parities in terms of an external numerary forces all countries to pursue the nominal target in a symmetric fashion. The mechanism, it is claimed, imposes an implicit coordination of monetary policies. In a fiat currency system

---

[3] See, for example, Johnson (1965), p. 28.

such as the EMS, systematic cooperation by monetary authorities could help to define common monetary targets, to be pursued jointly by all countries.[4]

Are the uses of an external numerary—like gold in the earlier fixed exchange rate regimes—or the institution of consultative bodies—like the EEC Monetary Committee and the Committee of Central Bank Governors—effective enough measures to induce monetary policy cooperation? The evidence from the EMS suggests a negative answer to that question. The EMS, like the gold standard and the Bretton Woods system, is characterized by a "center" country—West Germany—whose central bank pursues its own monetary targets independent of the policies pursued by the other members. The other countries, which have—to a significant extent—converged to West Germany's monetary targets, have maintained limited independence by the systematic use of capital controls and the adoption of periodic exchange rate devaluations.

The strongest evidence in support of the hypothesis that the EMS works as a (imperfect) Deutsche-mark area comes from the study of interest rates. West German interest rates are unaffected by most intra-EMS shocks, such as expectations of parity realignments; interest rates on assets denominated in other EMS currencies are those that bear the full impact of intra-European portfolio disturbances. Countries such as Ireland, Italy, Belgium, and France have used capital controls to shelter their domestic economies from the wide fluctuations in interest rates on assets denominated in their own currencies oberved in the (unregulated) Euromarkets.

This evidence[5] is similar to that of the gold standard and the Bretton Woods period, when countries other than Great Britain (in the first case) and the United States (in the second) sought to defend their policies from the influence of the "center" country by imposing various forms of regulatory hurdles on the international transmission of monetary policies.[6]

---

[4] This issue is analyzed in Russo and Tullio (1988).

[5] Giovannini (1988) provides a historical comparison of the gold standard, Bretton Woods, and the EMS; a formal statement of the "asymmetry" hypothesis; and an analysis of the empirical evidence. The asymmetric working of the EMS is documented in Giavazzi and Giovannini (1989, chap. 4).

[6] In the form of changes in the regulations affecting the gold market and controls on international capital flows. The following quote from J. W. Birch, governor of the Bank of England, complaining about capital controls in France and Germany during the classical gold standard (when England was the central country), provides a striking analogy to the current situation: "In the Banks of France and Germany the money box seems to have two slits, the one a tolerably broad one, and if you

III. The Credibility of Exchange Rate Targets

A popular argument to explain why regimes of fixed exchange rates tend to work asymmetrically points to the efficiency of solving the overdeterminacy associated with the n-1 problem by allocating the task of providing the "nominal anchor" for the whole system to one country. The center country should be chosen from those whose monetary authorities have the highest "anti-inflationary reputation." The argument dates back to Mundell's (1968) "optimal burden of adjustment" argument.[7] More recently, it has acquired new fame, along with the emergence of a new and influential view of the inflation process. Inflation is seen simply as the inefficient outcome of a non-cooperative "game" between the public and the monetary authorities. If inflation is just a source of inefficiency, then the inflation standard in an international monetary system should be set by the country where the "game" produces the least inefficiency—that is, the lowest equilibrium rate of inflation. There is an incentive to build monetary areas centered on low-inflation countries.

This view rests on the assumption that exchange rate rules provide "discipline," that is, that the exchange rate system can influence inflation expectations because exchange rate targets are more credible than monetary targets. Professional opinions of the role of the exchange rate regime in a disinflation and the actual experiences differ widely. On the one hand, the experiences of a number of Southern-Cone countries, where the exchange rate was used to stop very high inflation rates, were often disappointing. Critics (Dornbusch (1982) for instance) pointed to the effects of the lack of credibility of the exchange rate targets: failure of price and wage behavior to adjust to the exchange rate target produced large real appreciations that eventually became unsustainable. On the other hand, Bruno (1986) suggested that exchange rate policy might have had an important role in the successful Israeli stabilization. The positive role of exchange rate policy in the Bolivian stabilization is also stressed by Sachs (1986).

The EMS provides an important case study. The ten years of operation of the system have witnessed a dramatic convergence of inflation

---

turn the box on a certain corner, the gold comes out: this slit is marked 'For Home Use'; but the other is an uncommonly narrow one, and that is marked 'For Export,' and very difficult it is to get the gold out through this slit." From the *Journal of the Institute of Bankers* (1887, pp. 509-10), quoted in Ford (1962).

[7] There is also an influential view (Johnson [1973] and Yeager [1976, p. 643]) maintaining that the Bretton Woods system collapsed when the United States stopped providing price stability to the world economy.

rates across its members: when the EMS started, in the wake of the second oil shock, inflation differentials *vis-à-vis* West Germany were as large as 16% in Italy, 13% in Ireland, 8% in France, and 7% in Denmark. From 1980 to 1988, while German inflation was falling to 1%, from 6%, inflation differentials *vis-à-vis* Germany fell much more dramatically: to 0% in Ireland, 1% in France, 2.5% in Italy, and 3.5% in Denmark. In this section, I discuss the empirical evidence on the European disinflation. The question I address is whether the decision to join an exchange-rate system centered on a low-inflation country affected price and wage expectations, thus lowering the output cost of the disinflation.

1. *Breaking the Inflation Inertia*

One fundamental feature of the inflationary process in modern industrial economies appears to be its persistence, a phenomenon that has been linked to the mechanics of wage and price setting. Firms and unions—for a number of reasons we need not explore here[8]—find it more convenient to set prices and wages much less frequently than the rate of arrival of economic news. Therefore, wages and prices are crucially affected by workers' and firms' expectations. Workers and firms attempt to preserve the purchasing power of their incomes by incorporating in pricing policies their forecasts of the evolution of the general price level. Indirectly, wage and price setters concerned about the evolution of the general price level need to forecast the stance of monetary policy.

The special nature of wage and price setting therefore creates a problem of coordination between the central bank and the public. The central bank might want to use monetary policy to steer the economy toward a higher output path, but the public, anticipating future expansionary policies, can sterilize them fully by incorporating in its current pricing decisions the expectations of future monetary expansion and higher inflation. This process, by itself, generates inflation and tends to force the central bank to accommodate the higher rate of growth of prices to avoid a recession. Hence, in equilibrium there is higher inflation, and less output growth, than initially desired by both the public and the central bank. This is the inflationary bias of monetary policy in the presence of price and wage inertia, first described and analyzed by Barro and Gordon (1983).

Figure 9.1 further illustrates this point. The CC schedule describes

---

[8] See, for example, Blanchard (1988) and Rotemberg (1987).

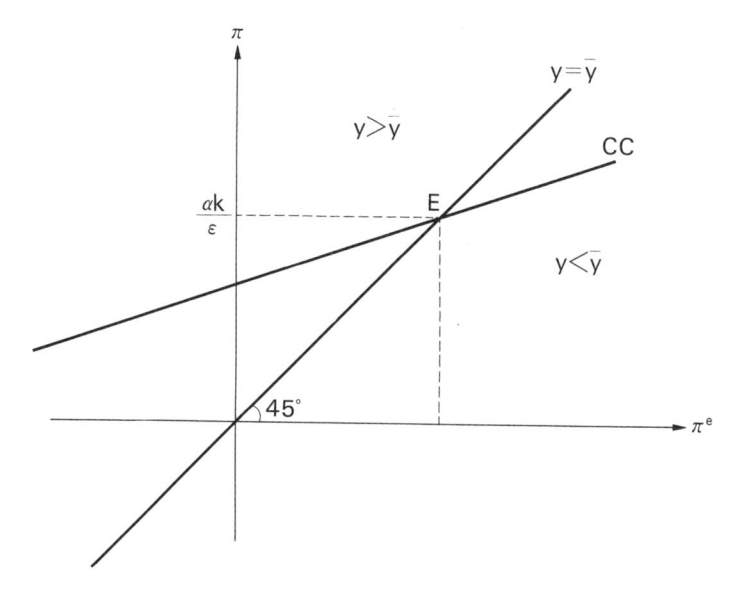

Figure 9.1

the central bank's reaction function: given the inflation expectations of the private sector, π^e, the central bank sets the actual inflation rate, π:

$$\pi = \alpha k/(\alpha^2 + \epsilon) + \alpha^2/(\alpha^2 + \epsilon)\pi^e \qquad (1)$$

The parameter α describes the real effects of unanticipated inflation, and ϵ measures the weight of inflation volatility, relative to output volatility, in the central bank's loss function; k is the central bank's target level of output. (The derivation of equation (1) is shown in the Appendix.) The 45° line describes all rational expectations equilibria (it is in fact the private sector's reaction function): above the line, inflation is higher than expected, and output is above the natural rate; the converse is true at all points below the 45° line. The interaction between the 45° line and the CC schedule characterizes the equilibrium: the private sector is effective at eliminating the chance of being caught by surprise inflation; the central bank is frustrated in its attempt to raise output, and inflation is "too high."

The coordination problem between the central bank and the public is at the core of the issue of disinflation. An interesting situation—and one directly relevant to our discussion—is the case of a new incoming

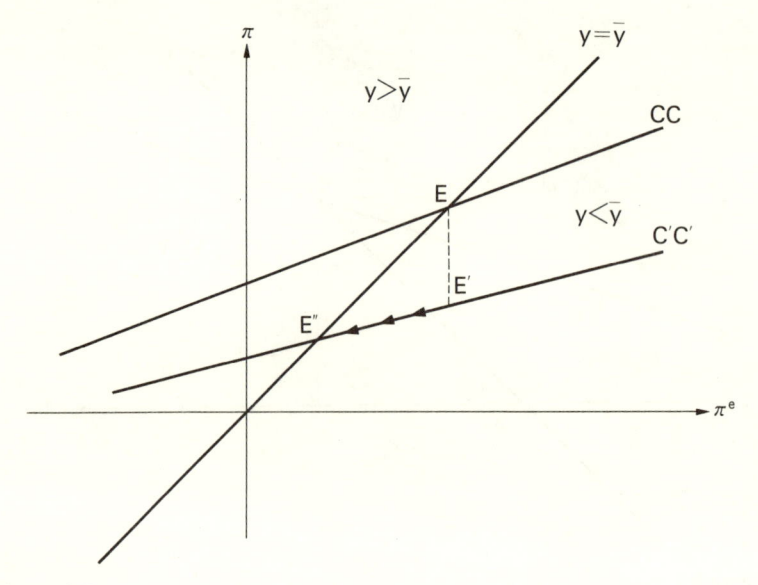

Figure 9.2

government that wants to bring inflation down. When the new administration takes office, the public is uncertain about its true preferences—that is, whether this is really a "tough" government or just another "wet" government pretending to be tough. The uncertainty comes from the fact that a wet government might also have an incentive to act tough for some time to try to fool the public, postponing the day when it creates a big inflation. The only thing the truly tough government can do is to reduce the growth rate of money and stick to it, waiting for the public to convince itself that it really is tough. The cost of acquiring that reputation is a recession, which occurs because money is tight, but expectations have not adjusted fully. This is illustrated in Figure 9.2. When a "tough" government takes office, the central bank's reaction function shifts down (to $C'C'$.) If inflation expectations do not fully adjust, output falls below the natural rate. The slower the public in revising its expectations, along the E'-E'' path, the longer the recession.

Alternatively, the new administration could avoid going through this prolonged "initiation" period by seeking a way to influence expectations with some institutional reform. The institutional reform of interest for us is a change in the exchange rate regime. How can the decision to fix the exchange rate shift expectations and thus reduce the output cost of bringing down inflation? Under fixed exchange rates, a central bank tends to loose control on the domestic supply of money, since the changes in international reserves needed to support the exchange rate parity produce changes in the domestic supply of money which, in principle, the monetary authority cannot influence.

Now, suppose a country decides to passively peg its exchange rate to another country, whose monetary authority enjoys the reputation of being an inflation-buster. By "passive peg" we mean that the former country's monetary authority, after announcing the exchange-rate parity, simply accommodates the latter country's monetary policies, with no attempt to directly influence their choice of targets. What happens to the inflation expectations of the private sector? Wage and price setters need to evaluate the credibility of this institutional reform; that is, they need to determine the likelihood that the announced exchange rate target will be pursued consistently. If, and only if, the exchange-rate target is credible, expectations will adjust and the process of disinflation will be facilitated.

In practice, the EMS has not completely eliminated the ability of peripheral central banks to control the supply of money. Countries with higher inflation rates have resorted to periodic exchange-rate realignments to recover the losses in competitiveness caused by persisting inflation differentials and fixed exchange rates. The disruptions caused by speculators' expectations of these exchange-rate realignments have been limited through the systematic use of capital controls.[9] Even when exchange rates are periodically realigned, though, pegging to a low inflation country can improve the output-inflation trade-off. This happens because the terms-of-trade fluctuations that occur during the intervals when exchange rates are not changed provide sufficient deterrent to central banks to deviate from the center country's monetary policies as much as they would under a pure floating rate regime.[10] With periodic realignments, however, the center country's output-inflation tradeoff also is affected. During the intervals when exchange rates are kept fixed, the center country's terms of trade worsen because the partner's inflation rate is higher than its own. As a consequence, the center country's output-inflation tradeoff also worsens: the inflation-buster exports reputation and imports inflation.

In summary, the argument that pegging to West Germany has helped

[9] This argument is formally analyzed in Giavazzi and Pagano (1988).
[10] The role of capital controls and parity realignments in allowing peripheral countries to maintain some degree of monetary sovereignty is stressed by De Grauwe (1989).

high-inflation countries in the disinflation efforts of the 1980s rests crucially on the assumption that exchange-rate targets are more credible than monetary targets. The argument also suggests that the central country may be the loser in an agreement in which it provides the nominal anchor that helps its partners to disinflate. In the next section, I present estimates of the effects of the EMS on inflation expectations and on the short-run output-inflation tradeoff of member countries.

2. Measuring the Shifts in Expectations

Our discussion in the previous section suggests that one important macroeconomic benefit of the EMS for countries other than West Germany could have been associated with a shift in inflationary expectations originating from the public's awareness that in a fixed-exchange-rate regime, such as the EMS, monetary policy is run, by and large, by the Bundesbank. To assess the empirical relevance of these effects, we need to measure these shifts of expectations. Consider the dynamics of wages and prices. As we argued above, private agents (firms and unions) set prices and wages by forming expectations on future macroeconomic variables, such as the overall rate of inflation. These expectations are necessarily a function of agents' available information, reflected in current and past realization of all relevant macroeconomic variables. If a monetary reform such as the EMS is put in place, private agents who believe the reform will actually change monetary policies in the way described above must reevaluate the methods they use to extrapolate from past macroeconomic variables their expectations about future inflation and economic activity. Hence the shift in expectations and its effect on the inflationary process will be reflected in a shift of statistical equations relating wages and prices to available information. In this section we study the process of disinflation in Denmark, France, Germany, Ireland, and Italy by analyzing how the relation between price and wage inflation and output has shifted since the start of the EMS. For comparison, we study also the United Kingdom, where the start of the EMS—which the U.K. did not join—corresponds to the beginning of the Thatcher era. We are concerned both with the timing of the shifts and with their magnitude.

In Giavazzi and Giovannini (1989), we estimate a (quarterly) system of three equations specifying the dynamics of CPI inflation, wage inflation, and output growth, which we measure by using industrial production indices. Each equation includes, on the right-hand side, a time trend, seasonal dummy variables, four lags of wage inflation, CPI inflation and industrial production growth, and dummy variables representing country-specific events that the model cannot explain.[11] We also include four lags of M1 growth rates, as well as changes in the relative price of imported intermediate and final goods. This last set of variables is assumed to be determined outside the system: though innovations in wage and price inflation are plausibly correlated with money growth and changes in relative prices of intermediate and final goods, we assume this latter set of variables affects inflation and output growth only with a one-quarter lag.[12]

The first question we address is whether there is evidence of a significant shift in these statistical equations after early 1979. A test of stability of the parameter estimates was performed for each equation and each country using as a cutting point the first quarter of 1979.[13] The results indicate the presence of a structural shift only in France: in no other country are the shifts of wage-price dynamics after 1979 statistically significant. Although this evidence is against the hypothesis that the decision to join the EMS has been associated with a shift in expectations, this negative result is very likely to be caused by the low power of the parameter stability tests we employ.

The next question we address regards the timing and the direction of shifts in the inflation processes. Using parameter estimates obtained over the 60–79 sample and the actual realizations of the forcing variables (money growth and relative prices of intermediate and final goods), we compute dynamic simulations of wage and price inflation and output growth. Table 9.1 reports the timing and the direction of estimated shifts in inflation and output dynamics obtained from the simulations. For every country, we report the date when the simulated paths of inflation and output growth start diverging in a persistent way from the actual paths, and the sign of the divergence. The words "higher" and "lower" reported in parentheses under each date indicate that the actual realizations of the variables were respectively higher and lower than their simulated values.

The table shows several impressive regularities. First, for all coun-

---

[11] The dummies are the following. For all countries, from 1971:3 to the end of the sample, the fall of Bretton Woods. For Italy, 69:2–70:1 *Autunno Caldo*, and 73:3–74:1, the price freeze. For France, 63:4–64:4 and 69:1–70:4, the price freeze; 68:2–68:3, "May '68"; 74:1–74:4, 77:1–77:4, 82:3–83:4, wage and price controls. For the United Kingdom, 67:4, sterling devaluation, and 73:4–74:4, wage controls.

[12] The estimates are obtained assuming that superneutrality holds, that is, the sum of the coefficients of nominal variables is equal to 1 in the equations explaining wage and price inflation, and it is zero in the equation explaining output growth. These constraints were not rejected in the largest majority of cases.

[13] In Giavazzi and Giovannini (1989, chap. 5), we report a more detailed analysis of the model and all the statistical results. Detailed statistics for Ireland, which do not appear there, are available on request.

Table 9.1 The Timing and Direction of the Shift in Expectations

	Denmark	France	Germany	Ireland	Italy	U. Kingdom
Price Inflation (direction)	80:1 (lower)	83:2 (lower)	79:2 (higher)	82:3 (lower)	85:1 (lower)	81:3 (lower)
Wage Inflation (direction)	80:2 (lower)	83:2 (lower)	79:2 (higher)	80:2 (lower)	85:1 (lower)	81:1 (lower)
Output Growth (direction)	80:3 (higher)	none	79:2 (lower)	none	none	none

Note: The words "higher" and "lower" indicate that the actual realization of the variables are respectively higher and lower than their simulated values. The word "none" indicates that no systematic divergence between actual and simulated values can be detected. In the case of Italy, the divergence between actual and simulated variables occurs close to the end of the simulation period.

tries except West Germany, and possibly Denmark, actual and simulated inflation and output paths start diverging long after the beginning of the EMS. Second, simulations for output growth tend to be less clear-cut than simulations for inflation. Third, the directions of the divergence are opposite for West Germany and the other countries in the table: in Germany, actual inflation after 1979 is higher than its simulated value, and output growth is lower.

Table 9.2 provides evidence on the magnitudes of the shifts in the output-inflation tradeoffs. The table reports the actual changes in

Table 9.2 The Shift in the Output-Inflation Tradeoff

	Denmark	France	Germany	Ireland	Italy	United Kingdom
End of the Simulations	84:4	85:4	86:4	88:1	86:4	87:1
Change in Inflation	−1.83	−4.86	−3.37	−9.72	−12.87	−6.23
Predicted Change in Inflation	−2.57	6.78	−5.51	−8.57	−8.38	6.63
Cumulative Change in Output	19.43	5.06	13.82	39.84	18.30	12.10
Predicted Cumulative Change in Output	−3.45	26.18	58.95	59.60	8.25	9.98

inflation and cumulative output growth that occurred in the five countries in our sample since 1979 and compares them with simulations of the same variables obtained from the model described above. Contrast, for example, the experiences of Germany and Italy. According to our simulations, every percentage point of inflation reduction since 1979 would have afforded Germany 10.7% output growth: in contrast, the output growth for every point of inflation reduction was only 4.1%. In the case of Italy, our simulations predict that every point of inflation reduction could have afforded 0.98% growth; but in reality, real growth for every point of inflation reduction was higher: 1.4%. Similarly, our simulations predicted a fall of 1.3% in output for every percent point reduction of inflation in Denmark, whereas the actual change in output was positive ($+10.6\%$) for every percent point reduction of inflation. The results for France are more difficult to interpret, since our simulations predicted higher inflation and higher output, and inflation actually fell. Ireland is the only country in our sample where the output-inflation tradeoff appears to have worsened after 1979. The results for Great Britain, however, raise the question of the nature of the shift in expectations and the role played by the EMS. Our simulation model predicted higher inflation and higher output for the United Kingdom (and for France): actual output growth was very similar, but it was associated with a reduction of inflation.

3. *Summary of the Empirical Findings*

What do we learn from the EMS experience about the role of the exchange-rate regime in a disinflation? Three important findings emerge from the empirical results discussed above.

(i) First, price and wage expectations seem to have adjusted with a long lag. The effects of the new exchange-rate regime on expectations were not as direct as predicted by the model of imported reputation.

(ii) Second, our estimates of the timing of the shifts in expectations suggest that these shifts were prompted by shifts in domestic policies. In Italy, we estimate a shift in expectations in the first quarter of 1985 in the aftermath of a government decree that had set a ceiling on wage indexation. That decree had been challenged by the unions and was eventually ratified by a national referendum. The referendum occurred in June 1984. In Ireland, a major turnaround in economic policies took place in the summer of 1982, marked by an announcement of tighter guidelines for monetary policy, a decision not to devalue the central parity of the punt in the February and June 1982 EMS realignments, and a decision to freeze pay increases in the public sector. In

France, the turnaround in macroeconomic policies occurred in March 1983, after the expansionary experiment of the first Mitterand government had produced a large current account deficit (3.5% of GDP) and a speculative attack on the franc. The government accompanied the EMS realignment with a freeze in budgetary expenses, an increase in income taxes, and a dramatic tightening of credit.

What was the linkage between these policies and the EMS constraint? In the case of France, the linkage is apparent. French authorities justified the unpopular policies as a necessary step if France were to remain in the EMS and linked the decision to stay in the EMS to the participation in the European Community (EC), arguing that EMS membership is an integral part of EC membership. This is an important point that I shall discuss in the conclusions.[14] With Italy, we were unable to find any important reference to the EMS in the government pronouncements after the decree on wage indexation, but we cannot exclude that the external constraint might have motivated that unpopular policy.[15] In conclusion, EMS membership might have helped countries other than West Germany in their disinflation efforts only to the extent that it provided a justification *vis-à-vis* the domestic public for unpopular policies, which in turn helped to strengthen the credibility of the exchange-rate targets. The role of domestic policies in prompting a shift in expectations may also explain the results for the United Kingdom, where we observe a similar shift in the output-inflation tradeoff two years after the election of Mrs. Thatcher.

(iii) The third important finding is the uneven distribution of the shifts in expectations between West Germany and other EMS members. This raises the question of what incentives West Germany has to belong to such a system. I shall address that question in Section V.

IV. Exchange Rate Rules and Fiscal Policy

Proposals aimed at (re)introducing "exchange rate rules" among the leading currencies are often criticized[16] on the grounds that they cannot substitute for changes in underlying fiscal positions. Policymakers should first concentrate on eliminating the fundamental sources of imbalances in the world economy. In this section, I review the ex-

---

[14] Sachs and Wyplosz (1986).
[15] Giavazzi and Spaventa (1989).
[16] See, for instance, IMF (1987), quoted in the introduction.

perience of Italy in the EMS: this experience provides an illustration of the inability of exchange rate rules per se to impose "fiscal discipline."

1. The Fiscal Implications of Monetary Convergence

The decision to peg to a low-inflation country has implications for fiscal policy. The monetary contraction reduces the portion of the budget that can be financed by printing money, and the increase in real interest rates associated with the disinflation raises the cost of servicing the public debt. It is well known[17] that monetary and fiscal policies cannot be set independently: failure to adjust fiscal policy to the new monetary regime can set public debt along an unstable path and eventually undermine the credibility of the exchange rate targets.

Instability of the public debt would be sufficient to make the new monetary regime eventually unsustainable. However, the macroeconomic variable that is more likely to trigger a confidence crisis is the current account. If the monetary contraction not only raises the stock of public debt, but also worsens the current account, thus adding to external indebtedness, the credibility of the exchange rate target will not last long. There are two channels through which the decision to peg to a low-inflation currency can worsen the current account: the more traditional one works through the real appreciation produced by the lack of credibility of the exchange rate target. (This is the channel usually emphasized in the analysis of the failed Southern-Cone stabilizations experiments.) But even a nominal exchange rate target that is fully credible—and thus affects domestic inflation directly—can produce a current account deficit.

A shift from money to debt financing is a shift from current to future taxes: seigniorage and the inflation tax fall and are replaced by taxes that will be levied to service the public debt. If individuals fully discount future tax liabilities, a switch in the path of taxes has no real effect (provided government spending remains unchanged.) But if Ricardian equivalence does not hold—for example because the time-horizon of taxpayers is shorter than that of the government—a switch from money to debt financing raises private wealth and thus private spending. In an open economy, the increase in spending worsens the current account.

This argument suggests that pending the fiscal correction required by the new exchange rate regime, the ability to control the current

---

[17] See, for example, Helpman and Razin (1987) and Buiter (1986).

Table 9.3 Ireland: Monetary Contraction, the Budget and the Current Account (percent of GDP)

	1972–78	1979–82	1983–88
Public debt (end of period)	88.3	110.3	148.8
Money financing of the PSBR	2.2	0.9	0.8
Budget surplus net of interest payments	−4.1	−6.5	0.0
Current account surplus	−4.9	−12.6	−2.5

Source: Dornbusch (1989) and *European Economy*.

account may be an important condition for the temporary sustainability of the new exchange rate targets. The experiences of Ireland (recently studied by Dornbusch [1989]) and of Italy offer some support for this view. During the first three years of EMS membership, Ireland made no corrections to the budget. By 1982, the Irish public debt had grown to 110% of GDP, from 88%, and the current account deficit was more than 10% of GDP (Table 9.3). The acceleration of Ireland's external indebtedness prompted a major crisis that eventually produced a sharp turnaround in fiscal policy.

In Italy too, EMS membership was associated with growing public debt, but unlike what happened in Ireland, the growth of domestic debt was not accompanied by a worsening of the current account. Table 9.4 compares the Italian budget in 1978 with that ten years later. At the start of the EMS, the debt-to-GDP ratio was almost stable: the primary deficit exceeded the revenue from money financing, but real interest rates were below the growth rate of real income. By 1988, money financing had vanished and real interest rates had climbed above the growth rate of real income. The surprising fact, however, is the persistence of the primary deficit: ten years after the start of the EMS, the shift in monetary regime has not yet been accompanied by a consistent shift in fiscal policy. We would expect that postponing

Table 9.4 Italy: The Fiscal Consequences of the Disinflation (percent of GDP)

	1978	1988
Public debt (end of period)	40.1	80.6
Money financing of the PSBR	2.1	0.0
Budget surplus net of interest payments	−4.4	−3.4
Real interest rate	2.0	6.0
Real interest rate minus growth rate of real GDP	−2.8	2.1

Definitions: Debt level is the stock of public debt on the market, i.e., total debt net of debt held by the central bank. Money financing corresponds to the public-sector borrowing requirement financed by the central bank.
Source: Giavazzi and Spaventa (1989).

the fiscal correction would have undermined the credibility of the exchange rate target. This does not seem to have happened: in the empirical results discussed in Section III, Italy was one of the countries for which we did find evidence of a shift in expectations.

How did Italy avoid the association between internal and external indebtedness? The answer is exchange controls. Table 9.5 shows interest rate differentials between the onshore and the offshore market: a measure of the effectiveness of exchange controls. The surprising finding is the frequency of occasions when we observe a covered interest rate differential in favor of the domestic market (20% of all observations in the sample): these were days when it would have been profitable to borrow lire in the Euromarket to invest in the domestic money market. The regulation mainly responsible for such a differential was the ceiling on net foreign borrowing by domestic banks. Exchange controls in Italy thus worked both ways: they prevented capital *outflows* at the time of crises in the system (for example, in the first subsample shown in Table 9.5, which corresponds to the four months preceding the March 1983 realignment) and capital *inflows* during periods of calm in the system (second subsample). The motivation for the first type of regulation—those preventing capital outflows—is well understood (namely, to defend the central bank from the effects of a speculative attack); the second type of regulation has seldom been discussed. It appears to have been crucial to uphold the credibility

Table 9.5 Italy: Onshore-Offshore Differentials (November 1980–December 1987)

Sample	1980:11–1987:12 (173)			1982:10–1983:3 (27)			1983:4–1985:11 (138)		
No. of observations Direction	Out	In	Neither	Out	In	Neither	Out	In	Neither
Number of weeks	112	75	185	25	1	1	1	58	79
Frequency (%)	30	20	50	92	4	4	1	42	57
Mean rate of return (%)	2.7	0.6		3.2	–		0.1	0.6	

Direction indicates the direction in which unexploited arbitrage profits are observed. The *mean rate of return* represents the instantaneous profit that could have been earned on each riskless and costless arbitrage operation if there had been no exchange controls. *Out* signals an incentive for capital outflows, *in* for capital inflows. Data are collected on Friday each week.
Source: Giavazzi and Giovannini (1989), chap. 7.

of the exchange rate target in the absence of any shift in fiscal policy. There is no evidence, at least in the experience of Italy, that exchange-rate rules are enough to impose fiscal discipline.

V. Costs and Benefits for West Germany

The view of the EMS as a system designed to enhance the credibility of inflation-prone countries leaves us with one big puzzle. What incentives does Germany have to belong to such a system? The imported credibility model discussed in Section III suggests that the central country may be the loser in an agreement in which it provides the nominal anchor that helps its partners to disinflate. If the decision to peg to a stable currency produced an instanteneous adjustment of expectations, the central country would be unaffected by the decisions of others to peg to its currency. But if learning takes time and disinflation is a dynamic process, during the transition the terms of trade of the central country worsen, and so does its output-inflation tradeoff. These effects are obviously smaller the larger the central country is relative to its partners: the United States was not concerned when Grenada and Belize decided to peg to the dollar. But even if we consider Germany and the Netherlands a de facto monetary union and thus sum their economic sizes, the joint GDP of the two countries is still only two thirds of the joint GDP of the other members of the EMS. The EMS area also accounts for some 30% of total German and Dutch trade.

The empirical results described in Section III seem to confirm that Germany's output-inflation tradeoff has worsened since the start of the EMS. The evidence would thus seem to justify the initial reluctance of the Deutsche Bundesbank to join the system. It remains to be explained, however, why German policymakers tried, since the late 1960s, to avoid an uncoordinated response of European countries to the fall of Bretton Woods. As it became clear that the Bretton Woods system was approaching its final days, German policymakers became increasingly worried that other European currencies might not be able to follow the appreciation of the DM vis-a-vis the dollar: they were preoccupied that the realignment of intra-European parities would disrupt the European customs union and the common agricultural market—two institutions they considered important for the German economy.[18]

---

[18] For an account of the German position in those years, see Emminger (1977) and Kloten (1978).

In this section, we look for evidence of Germany's incentives to stay in the EMS, analyzing the behavior of Germany's terms-of-trade from the Bretton Woods era to the 1980s. The terms-of-trade index we use is the real effective exchange rate of the Deutsche mark built by using relative wholesale prices and the IMF-MERM weights that are designed to measure a country's competitiveness relative to its trading partners. We are interested in finding out whether the EMS has stabilized Germany's terms of trade relative to previous periods.

The definition of "stability," however, is not unambiguous. One possibility is to look at the variability of unanticipated changes in the real effective exchange rate. This measure, however, eliminates most of the low-frequency components of the series. Indeed, it could be argued that those low-frequency components are worthy of special attention. Williamson (1985) suggests that while exchange rate *volatility* (measured by the standard deviation of unanticipated exchange rate changes) might have a negative impact on trade and welfare, exchange rate *misalignments* (that is, prolonged deviations of the exchange rate from some fundamental level) are likely to bring about the largest costs.[19]

Table 9.6 reports the simplest possible measure of the variability of the real effective exchange rate: its standard error. The data are monthly, from 1960 to 1985. Standard errors are computed for the EMS years and the years preceding them, including the Bretton Woods years, from January 1960 to August 1971. (The numbers in the table are standard errors of the log of the real exchange rate.) A remarkable fact emerges: for all countries except West Germany, there has been

Table 9.6 Standard Errors of Real Effective Exchange Rates (in percent per month)

Currency	60:1–71:8	60:1–79:2	79:3–85:12
Deutsche mark	3.5	12.3	10.9
Belgian franc	1.8	3.4	14.1
Deutch guilder	6.6	8.1	9.2
French franc	2.9	5.2	11.1
Italian lira	2.7	3.8	6.1

Sources: IMF, *IFS*. Real exchange rates are constructed by using wholesale prices. Effective exchange-rate weights are the IMF-MERM weights for 1977.

[19] Recent research by Krugman and Baldwin (1989), Baldwin and Krugman (1986), Dixit (1987), and especially Krugman (1988b) provides the first attempt at formalizing the linkage between the uncertainty and slow mean-reversion in exchange rate movements and the speed of adjustment of intersectoral factor movements and investment.

Table 9.7 Correlations between "Global" and "EMS" Real Effective Exchange Rates

Currency	1960:1–1979:2	1979:3–1987:9
Deutsche mark	0.910	−0.051
Belgian franc	0.295	0.958
Dutch guilder	0.922	−0.160
French franc	0.848	0.423
Italian lira	0.795	−0.657

Sources: As in Table 9.6. Computed EMS real effective rates include only Belgium, France, Germany, Italy, and the Netherlands.

an increase in the volatility of real effective exchange rates in recent years. In the case of the DM, the volatility of the effective rate decreases about 11% when the EMS period is compared with the 20 years preceding it. Thus, the table indicates that in West Germany, unlike the other EMS countries, fluctuations of the real effective exchange rate are smaller in the period after 1979 than in the previous 20 years.

Table 9.7 helps to interpret the results from the previous Table. We compute the correlation between the effective rates used in Table 9.6 and the effective rates that include only EMS partner countries, also obtained from the original MERM weights. Table 9.7 shows that in the 1960s and 1970s, the correlation between the index of competitiveness vis-a-vis EMS members only and the global index is highest for West Germany and the Netherlands. The high correlation for West Germany indicates that the other EMS currencies, with the exception of the Dutch guilder, did not follow the large appreciation of the DM vis-a-vis the dollar during the collapse of the Bretton Woods system. This phenomenon is clearly attenuated in the recent years. The correlation between the EMS and the global index for Germany turns negative, indicating that the EMS might have limited the effects of the fluctuations of the dollar/DM rate on Germany's competitiveness.

The German experience contrasts sharply with that of Belgium. In Belgium, the standard error of the log of the real effective exchange rate has increased by a factor of four since the start of the EMS. Part of this increase in volatility can be attributed to the increase in the correlation between the global and the EMS real exchange rate indices for Belgium. Given that Belgium is one of Germany's chief trading partners (accounting for 12% of Germany's intra-European trade), this has been an important factor in stabilizing Germany's real exchange rate.

The French and Italian experiences fall somewhere in the middle.

The reduction in the correlation between the global and the EMS indices—Italy's even becoming negative—is consistent with the observation that during the EMS, these countries found their currencies placed between the dollar and the DM.[20] But apparently this has not been enough to stabilize their overall competitiveness.

The evidence on Germany's terms-of-trade seems to support the "European Alliance" view of the EMS: the system has protected Germany from the effects of dollar fluctuations. A comparison between two episodes of sharp dollar depreciation, in the late 1960s and after 1985, shows the extent to which the EMS has stabilized Germany's overall competitiveness. From November 1969 to March 1973, the Deutsche mark appreciated 25% vis-a-vis the dollar; this was accompanied by an 18.6% worsening of Germany's overall competitiveness. From January 1985 to December 1987, the DM appreciation vis-a-vis the dollar was similar—27%—but this time it was accompanied by a loss of competitiveness only half as large—9%.

VI. Conclusions: Why Did Europeans Set Up the EMS?

Discussing the EMS experience, most observers tend to conclude that the exchange rate regime helped the high-inflation countries. Fischer (1987) describes the EMS as "an arrangement for France and Italy to purchase a commitment to low inflation by accepting German monetary policy." Even in countries considering EMS membership, the main advantages of membership are associated with Germany's reputation. *The Economist* (September 21, 1985) writes: "If sterling does join, the biggest change will be the transfer of responsibility for Britain's monetary policy from the Bank of England to the Bundesbank which, as the central bank keenest on sound money, sets the pace for others to follow. This would be a blessing: Tory governments may like appointing City gents as governors of the Bank, but Mr. Karl Otto Poehl would do a better job." *The Financial Times* (September 28, 1987) writes: "In place of money supply targetry, long since discredited, we would have that unflinching guardian of monetary rectitude, the Bundesbank, standing as guarantor against Britain's endemic propensity to genererate double-figure rates of inflation."

---

[20] The asymmetric behavior of European exchange rates relative to the dollar is documented and analyzed in Giavazzi and Giovannini (1986).

Despite its popularity, the view that European countries may have joined the EMS simply to buy the anti-inflationary reputation of the Bundesbank is narrow. First of all, the discipline argument was not prominent when the EMS was designed. By neglecting the incentives to stabilize intra-European exchange rates, the reputation view overlooks the main motivations that brought about the establishment of the EMS. Moreover, we found very weak evidence of a shift in expectations associated with the institution of the EMS. Inflationary expectations seem to have adjusted with a long lag: 2–3 years. One explanation might be that learning takes time. Another and more appealing explanation is that some European governments used the EMS to justify unpopular domestic policies. These policies, in turn, shifted expectations.

Using the exchange rate regime to justify being tough is an indirect, albeit effective, way to impose discipline. If it worked in Europe—and our evidence suggests that it might have—then it did so under *very special* circumstances. The EMS is just one element of a much richer set of agreements among European countries in the trade, industrial, and agricultural areas. These agreements rest on exchange rate stability in Europe. Leaving the EMS is perceived as a move that would endanger other spheres of cooperation as well. Failure to understand the importance of intra-European agreements and institutions may result in a very misleading assessment of the role of the exchange rate regime in Europe. In this concluding section of the paper, I discuss why Europeans are especially averse to exchange rate fluctuations and what the links are between the exchange rate regime and other EC institutions.

Europeans dislike exchange rate fluctuations for three main reasons. The first is rooted in Europe's recent history. In the 1920s and 1930s, many European countries had sought to defend themselves against external shocks through competitive exchange rate depreciations. Many in Europe today hold those policies responsible for the disruption of international trade and economic activity and the ensuing collapse of European democracies.[21] The experience of the 1920s and 1930s is important to understand the postwar quest for exchange rate stability, which led to the Bretton Woods system.

Openness is the second explanation for the European distaste for exchange rate fluctuations. The EC as a whole is not a particularly open region—no more, for example, than the United States or Japan:

---

[21] The memory of these events is kept alive by Nurske's illuminating account of the effects of the exchange-rate policies of the 1920s. See Nurske (1944).

the share of imports in GDP was—in 1987—12.3% in the EC, 10.1% in the United States, and 11.4% in Japan. Therefore, no particular reason why Europeans should worry about the fluctuations of the ECU relative to the dollar or the yen—no more, at least, than Americans and Japanese worry about fluctuations of their own currencies. But what is special in the EC is that the region is not a common-currency area. Individual countries have different currencies and are also much more open than the region as a whole. Even before the creation of the customs union, the share of imports in GDP was as high as 40% in Belgium and the Netherlands and 16% in Germany. The trade creation and trade diversion effects of the union rapidly raised these figures: now they are around 60% to 70% in the small northern countries and 25% to 30% in Germany, France, Italy, and the United Kingdom. Openness, however, is mostly an intra-European affair: thus, to the extent that exchange rate fluctuations pose problems for an economy, it is the fluctuation of intra-EC exchange rates that Europeans view as worrisome.

The third explanation for the European aversion to exchange rate fluctuations lies in the very institutions set up with the Treaty of Rome, and in the common agricultural market in particular. The survival of the common agricultural market depends on the stability of intra-European exchange rates. Consider French and German grains, for example: they are almost perfect substitutes. Thus in the common EC market for cereals, purchasing power parity (PPP) holds. However, input prices in agriculture—labor costs in particular—do not follow PPP: exchange-rate realignments could thus produce large shifts in the profitability of the farming sector across Europe and induce swings in agricultural trade in the region. The problem is aggravated by the fact that across European agricultural markets PPP rules by law. This is so because the European Commission regulates the cereals' market, setting an EC-wide price for each product. The price is set in ECUs and translated in local currencies at the ongoing exchange rate.

Europeans have agonized over the difficulty of running a common market in a region that does not use a common currency, at least since the early 1960s. The rules of Bretton Woods permitted excursions of up to 3% between any two European currencies.[22] Such excursions were big enough to interfere with the functioning of the cereals market.

---

[22] The rules set 1% margins around the dollar parity of each currency, thus in principle permitting bilateral excursions of up to 4%. European countries, however, had agreed to maintain their dollar parities within smaller margins: 0.75%.

The problem was precipitated in 1969 at the time of the devaluation of the French franc, in August, and of the revaluation of the Deutsche mark, in October. The response to the realignments was the temporary suspension of the free cereals market. France prevented a jump in the prices of cereals on the home market by converting the common ECU price at an artificial exchange rate—that did not reflect the devaluation. Germany avoided being flooded with French cereals by imposing a tariff on imports and granting an export subsidy to its own farmers. After the fall of Bretton Woods, responding to realignments with the introduction of tariffs and subsidies became common practice. By 1974, a German farmer exporting butter to Italy received a subsidy equal to 28.3% of the price; if the butter was shipped the other way, a corresponding tax was levied on the Italian exporter.

Beyond infringing on the basic principle on which the EC was set up, the tariffs and subsidies introduced to cope with realignments have also been costly for the EC budget, for two reasons. The first is that it proved easier to remove the tariffs by letting agricultural prices rise in the devaluing country than to remove the subsidies by cutting prices in the revaluing country. Therefore the revenue from the tariffs did not match the expenditure on the subsidies. The persistence of export subsidies in strong-currency countries aggravated Europe's chronic overproduction of food. By the mid-1970s two thirds of the financial resources available to the EC were absorbed by the cost of running the agricultural market—leaving very little room for action in other areas. Exchange-rate stability then became a vital issue for the EC, and it thus was natural that the Commission would become a strong supporter of schemes designed to limit intra-European exchange rate fluctuations. The problem has not disappeared in the EMS. The "agri-monetary" consequences of a realignment are an important item in the negotiations, as documented by the realignment communiques that always carefully spell out the provisions for agricultural markets—such as the timing of price adjustments.

For many years, the common agricultural policy has been the only real activity of the EC and the only reason for its existence. In the early 1970s, the agricultural market absorbed 90% of the total EC budget; in 1985, the figure was still as high as 73%. It is most unlikely that the EC would still be there had it failed to keep the common agricultural market alive. Over the years, the operation of this market provided the testing ground for cooperation in other areas. The EC is now moving in new directions. The planned liberalization of 1992 is its first major initiative outside agriculture: if successful, it will reduce the importance of agriculture among the activities of the EC and enhance the role of this institution in the coordination of economic policies across Europe. To some extent, the evolution of the EC has been possible because this institution survived the difficulties of operating the cereals market. Exchange rate stability has thus been an important condition for institutional developments in Europe.

Trying to understand the European Monetary System without considering the grounds for the particular European aversion to exchange rate fluctuations would give a very biased picture of the system. In the countries that belong to the EMS, leaving the system is a step that many would associate with the abandonment of other areas of cooperation as well. This view is important because on some crucial occasions (in the French turnaround of March 1983, for example), it has been instrumental to force policy shifts that in turn have made the survival of the EMS possible.

References

Baldwin, R., and Krugman, P. 1989. "Persistent Trade Effects of Large Exchange Rate Shocks." M.I.T. mimeo.

Barro, R.J., and Gordon, D. 1983. "A Positive Theory of Monetary Policy in a Natural Rate Model." *Journal of Political Economy* 91: 589–610.

Blanchard, O.J. 1988. "Why Does Money Affect Output? A Survey." Forthcoming in Friedman, B.M., and Hahn, F.H. eds. *Handbook of Monetary Economics*. Amsterdam: North Holland.

Bruno, M. 1986. "Sharp Disinflation Strategy: Israel 1985." *Economic Policy* 2: 379–408.

Buiter, W.H. 1986. "Fiscal Prerequisites for a Viable Managed Exchange Rate Regime." NBER W.P. no. 2041.

Cooper, R.N. 1984. "A Monetary System for the Future." *Foreign Affairs*, Fall.

Dixit, A. 1987. "Entry and Exit Decisions of Firms under Fluctuating Real Exchange Rates." Princeton University. Mimeo.

De Grauwe, P. 1989. "Is the EMS a DM-Zone?" CEPR Discussion Paper no. 297.

Dornbusch, R. 1982. "Stabilization Policies in Developing Countries: What Have We Learned?" *World Development* 10: 701–08.

———. 1989. "Ireland's Failed Stabilization." *Economic Policy* 8: 173–209.

Emminger, O. 1977. "The D-Mark in the Conflict Between Internal and External Equilibrium, 1948–75." *Essays in International Fi-*

nance, No. 122. International Finance Section, Princeton University.

Fischer, S. 1987. "International Macroeconomic Policy Coordination." NBER W.P. no. 2244.

———. 1988. "Comments to Miller and Williamson." *European Economic Review* 32: 1048–51.

Frenkel, J.A. 1987. "The International Monetary System: Should It be Reformed?" *American Economic Review—Papers and Proceedings* 77: 205–10.

Ford, A.G. 1962. *The Gold Standard: 1880–1914. Britain and Argentina*. Oxford: Clarendon Press.

Giavazzi, F., "and Giovannini, A. 1986. The Dollar and the EMS." *Economic Policy* 2: 455–85.

———. 1989. *Limiting Exchange Rate Flexibility: The European Monetary System*. Cambridge: MIT Press.

Giavazzi, F., and Pagano, M. 1988. "The Advantage of Tying One's Hands: EMS Discipline and Central Bank Credibility." *European Economic Review* 32: 1055–82.

Giavazzi, F., and Spaventa, L. 1989. "Italy: The Real Effects of Inflation and Disinflation." *Economic Policy* 8: 133–71.

Giovannini, A. 1988. "How Do Fixed-Exchange-Rate Regimes Work: The Evidence from the Gold Standard, Bretton Woods and the EMS." NBER W.P. no. 2766.

Helpman, E., and Razin, A. 1987. "Exchange Rate Management: Intertemporal Tradeoffs." *American Economic Review* 77: 107–23.

International Monetary Fund. 1987. *World Economic Outlook*.

Johnson, H.G., 1973. "The Exchange-rate Question for a United Europe." In Krause, M.B., ed. *The Economics of Integration*. London: George Allen.

———, 1965. *The World Economy at the Crossroads*. New York: Oxford University Press.

Kloten, N. 1978. "Germany's Monetary and Financial Policy and the European Economic Community." In Kohl, W.L., and Basevi, G. eds. *West Germany: A European and Global Power*. Lexington, Mass.: Lexington Books.

Krugman, P. 1988a. "Target Zones and Exchange Rate Dynamics." NBER W.P. no. 2481.

———, 1988b. "Deindustrialization, Reindustrialization, and the Real Exchange Rate," NBER W.P. no. 2586.

McKinnon, R.I. 1988. "Monetary and Exchange Rate Policies for International Financial Stability: A Proposal." *Journal of Economic Perspectives*, 2: 83–103.

Miller, M., and Williamson, J. 1988. "The International Monetary System: An Analysis of Alternative Regimes." *European Economic Review* 32: 1031–54.

Mundell, R.A. 1968. *International Economics*. New York: Macmillan.

Nurske, R. 1944. *International Currency Experience*. Geneva: League of Nations.

Rotemberg, J. 1987. "The New Keynesian Microfoundations." *NBER Macroeconomic Annual* pp. 69–116. Cambridge: MIT Press.

Russo, M., and Tullio, G. 1988. "Monetary Policy Coordination in the EMS: Is There a Rule?" In F. Giavazzi, F., Micossi, S., and Miller, M. eds. *The European Monetary System*. Cambridge: CUP.

Sachs, J. 1986. The Bolivian Hyperinflation and Stabilization. NBER W.P. No. 2073.

———, and Wyplosz, C. 1986. "The Economic Consequences of President Mitterand." *Economic Policy* 2: 261–313.

Tobin, J. 1982. "A Proposal for International Monetary Reform, In *Essays in Economics*. Cambridge: MIT Press.

Yaeger, L.E. 1976. *International Monetary Relations: Theory, History and Policy*. New York: Harper and Row.

Williamson, J. 1985. *The Exchange Rate System*. Washington, D.C.: Institute for International Economics.

Appendix: Derivation of Equation (1)

Consider the economy described by equations (A1) through (A4). There are three actors in this economy: firms, unions, and a central bank. Lowercase letters indicate variables expressed in logs and in deviations from equilibrium. Uppercase letters indicate the level of the same variables. Labor is the only factor of production, and the technology is Cobb-Douglas with decreasing returns.

$$y = \alpha n, \quad 0 < \alpha < 1 \tag{A1}$$

$$V_F = PY - WN \tag{A2}$$

$$V_U = -(n)^2 \tag{A3}$$

$$V_B = -(n - k)^2 - \epsilon(p)^2, \quad \epsilon > 0 \tag{A4}$$

(A1) is the output-supply equation: (the log of) output is an increasing function of (the log of) employment. Equations (A2), (A3), and (A4) describe the objectives of the three actors in the economy: firms maximize one-period profits, and unions aim at stabilizing employment around its natural rate ($n=0$). The central bank has two objectives: it minimizes price-level fluctuations and the deviation of domestic employment from a target, k, that exceeds the natural rate. This assumes that the natural rate of output lies within the country's production possibility frontier—for example, because of the presence of distortions or externalities. The inefficiency of the natural rate of output is the motivation of the game that takes place between the union and the central bank: if the natural rates of output were socially optimal, central bankers would have no incentive to affect real variables, and the game would vanish.

The economy works as follows. First, unions set nominal wages; then firms decide the levels of output and employment, and the central bank sets the price level (by deciding the level of the money stock). The existence of nominal contracts gives the central bank the power to affect real variables ex-post; unions, however, anticipate the power and the incentives of the central bank: it is straightforward to show that maximization of the union's objective function implies the following wage-setting rule:

$$w = p^e. \qquad (A5)$$

The wage is equal to the expected price level. Equation (1) in the text is the central bank's reaction function ($\delta V_B/\delta p$), given price expectations. The only difference is that equation (1) is written in deviations from an initial price level.

10

What Future for the International Monetary System?

Richard N. Cooper

This paper discusses some problems with present international arrangements and suggests that the time has come to begin contemplating a common currency among the industrialized democracies. This idea is much too radical to garner much political support in the near future. But it does offer a way to overcome a number of difficulties that these economies now face, and which are likely to become more, not less, serious in the coming years. So despite its novelty, a common currency provides a focal point for analysis, which may in turn suggest intermediate steps that accomplish some of the same results with less political commitment.

Before we turn to the present and the future, it is worth considering past international monetary arrangements and how they performed. The first section of the paper, therefore, reviews briefly six types of international monetary arrangement that have existed during the past century. It then turns to an evaluation of the strengths and weaknesses of the current arrangement of floating exchange rates subject to ad hoc management. Throughout, the focus will be on the arrangements among the major economies of the day, basically Europe, North America, and, in the past 30 years, Japan. During the earlier period, these arrangements encompassed many "peripheral" areas as well, by virtue of their colonial status. How peripheral countries relate to the international monetary core is an interesting and important topic, but it is necessary first to be clear on relationships at the core.

I. Past International Monetary Systems

History is complex, and it would take us too far afield to enter into a detailed exposition of the workings of different international monetary systems. But every system must address two fundamental questions, and it is worthwhile to sketch how different systems addressed these questions, both in theory and in the way the theory was modified in practice. The two fundamental questions concern how the international monetary system envisions that countries will adjust to "disturbances" to economic relations among countries (the adjustment problem) and how it envisions adequate, internationally acceptable means of payment will be provided (the liquidity problem).

The history of the past century can be divided roughly into six periods, excluding the two world wars and their immediate aftermath, each of which involved a somewhat different international monetary system covering the major countries. Of course, this division inevitably involves some stylization, since history evolves continuously; in some cases the shift from one system to another is gradual and involves antecedents, and not all countries move together.

The six systems are the gold specie standard (1879–1913); the gold exchange standard (1925–31); freely floating exchange rates (1919–25, 1933–36), the Bretton Woods system, early phase (1947–59); the Bretton Woods system, late phase (1959–73); managed flexible exchange rates (1973-present).

Gold-Specie Standard. Under the gold-specie standard, national money and acceptable means of payment were the same, namely, gold coins of standard weight and fineness. These might be re-minted into different national coins, although foreign coins sometimes also circulated domestically. Thus both domestic and international liquidity were satisfied in principle from new gold production. If this proved inadequate, as it did for prolonged periods, most notably from the 1870s to the mid-1890s, the increased liquidity was supplemented domestically by a rapid expansion of new forms of payment, notably banknotes and demand deposits in banks (Triffin, 1964) and by a prolonged decline in the price level, which raised the real value (in commodities) of a given volume of gold money. Wholesale prices fell by 40% to 55% in all the major countries between 1873 and 1896 (Cooper, 1982).

The theory of the adjustment mechanism under the gold standard was simple, and it was clearly and concisely stated by David Hume in 1752 (Cooper, 1969). A transfer (for example, reparations, or a capital investment) from country A to country B raised the money stock in B and lowered it in A. As a result, prices would fall in A and rise in B, and A would in consequence enlarge its trade surplus (or reduce its deficit), make the real transfer in goods, and earn the gold back until monetary and payments equilibrium was restored.

How the adjustment mechanism worked in practice is still controversial. First, much less gold actually moved internationally than the theory would suggest (Bloomfield, 1959). Second, Viner's (1924) classic study of large capital inflows into Canada before World War I suggested that although price movements could be discerned, especially of non-tradable goods against tradable goods, the price movements were far smaller and worked to accomplish changes in trade flows more rapidly, than he and his teacher Taussig expected. Later analysis suggested that a substantial part of the adjustment was accomplished by changes in spending—up in the receiving country, down in the sending country—associated with the transfer itself. Recently, McKinnon (1988) has argued that there is no presumption one way or the other about which way the sending country's terms of trade will change, and with a fully integrated capital market, there need not even be any change in domestic (that is, non-tradable) prices. The key point is that adjustment is accomplished partly through changes in spending, or absorption, and partly through changes in prices, especially the prices of non-tradables.

Gold Exchange Standard. The adjustment mechanism under the gold exchange is similar to that under the gold standard. In this case, the downward pressure on prices in the sending country is mediated by the banking system, which operates on fractional gold reserves. In fact, the period of the gold exchange standard was dominated by economic stagnation in the leading country, Britain, but that was related to the exchange rate at which Britain returned to gold convertibility rather than to the nature of the standard itself. Its period was too short to discover if adjustment eventually would have taken place.

The novelty of the gold exchange standard was to conserve gold by removing it from circulation and concentrating it in the hands of the leading banks, even going beyond that by encouraging banks, including smaller central banks, to hold short-term claims on other countries, mostly in sterling, secondarily in dollars. Thus national currencies began to play a role as international means of payment. Moreover, this period also saw extensive use of loans from one central bank to another as a temporary source of liquidity. Again, the period was too short to reveal the potential problem of relying on growth of the ratio of the gold-convertible currency holdings relative to a more slowly growing stock of monetary gold, a problem underlined later by Triffin (1960).

Floating Exchange Rates. Floating exchange rates during the interwar period were not thought of as a "system" at all, but rather as an unavoidable but temporary expedient during a turbulent time until a more stable system could be reestablished. The "adjustment process" worked by a market price—the exchange rate—clearing the market for foreign exchange, much as the price of strawberries clears the market for strawberries. If for any reason home demand for a foreign currency rose, the exchange rate of that currency would appreciate to ration the demand to what was available at the new price. The most comprehensive examination of floating exchange rates during this period (Nurkse, 1944) found them to be a major source of disturbance rather than a source of smooth adjustment, and that view strongly influenced the reestablishment of fixed exchange rates under the Bretton Woods system.

International liquidity in the sense of an internationally accepted means of payment was not necessary under these arrangements, since residents would buy the foreign currencies they needed in the foreign exchange markets, and the banks need not hold international reserves. Because this arrangement was considered temporary, however, central banks had their eye on the longer term and continued to hold gold. In 1919–20 and again in 1929–33 there was a sharp drop in wholesale prices, so the real value of monetary gold rose. In addition, both Britain and the United States devalued their currencies against gold (that is, they redefined the gold content of a pound and a dollar) in the 1930s, and that also increased the monetary value of gold reserves.

Bretton Woods, early phase. The Bretton Woods system was the first international monetary system to be designed from scratch. It stipulated fixed exchange rates, but recognized that with national full employment commitments, "fundamental disequilibria" might arise from time to time and it called for a discrete change in exchange rates, with international approval. It was taken for granted that monetary and fiscal policy would be used to achieve domestic equilibrium, as defined by each country. International disequilibria were to be financed in the short run, drawing if necessary from the new International Monetary Fund.

There was an adjustment in exchange rates in 1949, but thereafter exchange-rate changes of leading currencies were rare. Instead, adjustment was achieved by differential liberalization of trade and payments. Many countries were in a suppressed disequilibrium following World War II and maintained tight restrictions over trade and payments. These restrictions were gradually relaxed, country by country, as conditions permitted. Not until the end of 1958 did Western European countries abandon controls on current account transactions, and many maintained restrictions on outward capital movements long after that.

Curiously, the Bretton Woods system made no provision for a secular rise in international liquidity. Since the United States held a disproportionate share of the world's monetary gold reserves (more than 70%) in the late 1940s, the gold reserves of other countries could be built up in part by drawing on those of the United States, as well as from new production. In addition, however, countries accrued substantial balances of U.S. dollars, as under the gold exchange standard. It should be noted that the world economy grew much more rapidly in the 1950s than anyone dared to expect in the 1940s. The rapid growth in production and trade seemed to call forth a corresponding growth in demand for international reserves, which was satisfied in large part by U.S. Treasury bills, thought to be better than gold since they bore interest and for monetary authorities were convertible into gold at the U.S. Treasury on demand. These circumstances gave rise to the celebrated Triffin (1960) dilemma: how could the world economy grow without additional dollars, yet how could the gold-convertibility of the dollar remain credible as U.S. liabilities to foreign monetary authorities grew continually relative to the U.S. gold stock?

Bretton Woods, late phase. The conceptual underpinnings of the Bretton Woods system remained the same, but the scope for differential payments liberalization as the mechanism of adjustment diminished. Some modest exchange rate adjustments among major currencies occurred during the 1960s (DM in 1961, pound in 1967, French franc in 1969), but for the most part, countries were spared the need to adjust by a large and growing U.S. payments deficit, financed by a buildup in dollars held by central banks. When this buildup became unacceptably great, the Bretton Woods system broke down. It broke down basically because discrete changes in exchange rates, the key feature of its adjustment mechanism, are incompatible with the high mobility of private capital, which had resumed by the late 1960s. Any anticipated change in official exchange rates evoked a huge movement of speculative capital, which played havoc with domestic monetary policy. The emergence of any "fundamental disequilibrium," especially if it was in the world's largest economy, was bound to be financially destabilizing under these circumstances.

In the late phase of Bretton Woods, the question of international liquidity, omitted earlier, was addressed systematically, and the result was creation of a new kind of international fiat money, the SDR, to be held and used by central banks. The SDR was designated to become the centerpiece of the international monetary system, to be created as needed to serve the world's need for international liquidity. In fact, total SDR creation has amounted so far to only about $25 billion, less than 10% of official foreign exchange reserves.

Managed Floating, 1973—present. Since 1973 the major currencies have been floating with respect to one another, but the floating has been subject to market intervention by the monetary authorities—sometimes heavy intervention—to influence the movement of exchange rates. And most European currencies since March 1979 have been linked through the European Monetary System (EMS) in a Bretton Woods type system combined with permissible variation in market exchange rates around the central rates, and occasional changes (11 in all from 1979 through 1989) in central rates.

Under floating exchange-rate arrangements, it is supposed that the main mechanism of adjustment will be changes in real exchange rates brought about by market-induced changes in nominal rates, supported as appropriate by changes in fiscal policy designed to maintain overall balance in the economy. (Within the EMS, of course, adjustment is similar to what it was supposed to be under the Bretton Woods system.) In fact, it is difficult to interpret the period of floating as behaving in this way, since manifestly exchange rates did not always move in such a way as to reduce current account imbalances. But interpretation of the historical record is complicated by two factors. First, macroeconomic policy, and especially fiscal actions, were not always conducive of international balance. On the contrary, in the early 1980s the United States pursued a markedly expansionist fiscal policy, combined with a tight monetary policy, while Japan, Germany, and Britain introduced strong fiscal contraction. The combination produced heavy upward pressure on the U.S. dollar, which in turn led to a sharp deterioration of the U.S. current account and corresponding increases in the surpluses of Japan, Germany, and, for a period, Britain (which was also influenced by increasing production of North Sea oil). In this instance, exchange rate movements "disequilibrated" the current account.

But in doing so, perhaps they were serving the broader role of equilibrating economies. That brings us to the second problem of interpretation: in an integrated world economy, there is no special merit in assuring balance in each country's current account position. On the contrary, for a variety of reasons at particular times some countries will be net savers and others net investors, and one of the useful functions of an integrated economy is to channel savings to investment. If the integrated economy crosses national boundaries, the savings may also be expected to cross national boundaries, and sometimes for substantial periods of time. As a consequence, we do

FUTURE OF THE SYSTEM   283

not have a clear, operational definition of international equilibrium. At a minimum, "sustainable" capital movements should be set against the current account, but unfortunately the actual purchases of foreign assets do not carry labels that tell us whether they are sustainable or not. Drawing the line at "long-term" investments will not do, since the definition of short-term (with original maturities under one year) is itself arbitrary, and in an integrated market many financial instruments, whatever their original maturity, may be purchased for short-term or speculative motives, while some short-term credits (for example, trade credits) may be expected to grow predictably in total over time.

Another dividing line often suggested is between official monetary transactions and all others. This suggestion introduces the other characteristic of a monetary system, international liquidity. Under a system of freely floating exchange rates, there should be no need for international liquidity, i.e., officially held international means of payment. But in fact we have not had free floating, and the growth of official foreign exchange reserves during the period of floating has been phenomenal (Table 10. 1), despite the widespread view that liquidity was excessive at the end of 1972 before floating began.

The growth in international liquidity has been satisfied overwhelmingly by the acquisition of foreign exchange reserves. There has been only one allocation of SDRs (in three tranches) since 1973, amounting to less than $15 billion. The dollar has continued to be the preferred currency, but the official holdings of German marks and Japanese yen have grown even more rapidly, starting from a much lower base. In addition, the members of the European Monetary Compensation

Table 10.1   End-of-Year International Reserves ($ Billion Equivalent)

Holdings	1945	1960	1970	1980	1985
Gold[1]	33.3	38.0	37.2	41.8	40.1
U.S. gold holdings	20.1	17.8	11.1	11.2	11.1
Foreign Exchange[2]	14.3	18.6	44.6	370.8	378.7
U.S. liabilities	4.2	11.1	23.8	157.1	172.8
Other[3]	—	3.6	10.8	36.5	62.5
Total Reserves	47.6	60.2	92.5	449.1	477.7
Addendum: World exports	34.2	113.4	280.3	1844.6	1783.

[1] At official prices of $ 35/oz before 1980 and $ 42/oz in 1980 and 1985.

[2] Reported assets differ from U.S. reported liabilities by minor differences in concept, by measurement error, by official holdings of foreign exchange other than dollars, and by official deposits in the Eurocurrency market.

[3] Special Drawing Rights (SDRs) and reserve positions in the IMF.

Sources: Federal Reserve Bulletin; International Financial Statistics.

Fund have opened unlimited lines of short-term credit for one another. Gold, the traditional reserve asset, continues to be held by many monetary authorities, but it is virtually never used. Indeed, there is no generally accepted method of valuation, since the official price remains $42 an ounce, while the market price has ranged from $200 to $800 and has remained in the vicinity of $400 an ounce for several years.

Much of the explosive growth in reserve holdings has been voluntary and desired, lending support to Harrod's long contention that demand for reserves would be higher under floating exchange rates, not lower as economic theorists generally contended. The voluntary acquisition of reserves makes it inappropriate to consider a balance on current account plus net private capital movements a suitable measure of payments equilibrium. Some of the reserve acquisition, particularly the large official acquisition of U.S. dollars in 1987, took place not to satisfy a growing demand for reserves, but to brake the depreciation of the dollar against other leading currencies, especially the yen and the DM. So increases in official foreign exchange holdings reflect a mixture of motives, being partly a consequence of defensive exchange-rate actions under managed floating.

II. A Brief Evaluation

What do we want of an international monetary system? I suggest (1) that it should contribute to our basic economic objectives of growth

Table 10.2 Variance of Quarterly Forecast Errors (Times 1,000) for the United States

	Nominal GNP	Price Level	Real GNP
Gold Standard			
1890(1)–1914(4)	2.98	.25	2.83
1915(1)–1931(3)	1.80	.60	1.41
No Clear Standard			
1931(4)–1941(4)	5.64	.24	4.02
1942(1)–1951(1)	.67	.60	.78
Bretton Woods, 1951(2)–1971(3)	.13	.02	.11
Fluctuating Rates, 1971(4)–1980(4)	.13	.02	.14

Note: Quarterly forecasts are made by using a Kalman filter with respect to expected level and expected rate of change on past data for each series.
Source: Meltzer (1986, p. 141).

with low inflation, (2) that to that end and for its own sake it should help reduce the uncertainties economic agents face as close as possible to the minimum intrinsic in nature and the economic system, (3) that it should permit diversity in the national pursuit of economic and social objectives with a view to maintaining harmonious relations among nations, and (4) that it should do all this as unobtrusively as possible.

In terms of such aggregate indicators as real economic growth, variability of inflation, and predictability of growth and inflation, the Bretton Woods system, while it lasted, was a superior performer compared with previous periods and compared with the current managed float (Table 10.2). In terms of long-term price stability, the gold standard performed best, although the reasons remain poorly understood, since both short- and medium-term price variability was sizable.

III. The Case for Flexible Exchange Rates

Two quite different traditions argue in favor of flexible exchange rates. The Monetarist tradition (Friedman, 1953) emphasizes the feature of flexible exchange rates that insulates a national economy from external monetary disturbances, from inflationary impulses that may be coming from abroad. This tradition emphasizes that under fixed exchange rates or market intervention, monetary expansion abroad will lead to reserve outflows for the expanding country, but it will also lead to reserve inflows, hence monetary expansion, for the country that is not expanding. If the economy is operating at full capacity, this expansion will lead to domestic inflation. By eschewing exchange market intervention and allowing the currency to appreciate, this imported inflation can be avoided. In the smooth and frictionless world of economic models, flexible exchange rates provide perfect insulation against monetary impulses, positive or negative, coming from the rest of the world.

There is also a Keynesian tradition that supports flexible exchange rates, or, more accurately, changes in exchange rates. It operates on the assumption that the economic system will be hit by "exogenous" disturbances from time to time; that for any single country, these disturbances may include the policies of other countries; and that the country will need to "adjust" to these disturbances. Under a competitive market system with continuous market clearing, any needed adjustment is spread throughout the system via price signals, and the loss of output will be minimal and short-lived. But with various rigidities in the formation of prices and wages, such as exist in all modern economies, some of the need for adjustment will be thrown on output and employment, thus producing economic waste. The possibility of changing exchange rates introduces an element of price flexibility into this system replete with price rigidities. Under some circumstances, movements in exchange rates may substitute for product or labor market price flexibility, achieve adjustments in real wages and prices, and thereby avoid some of the loss in output. On this view of the world, the possibility of exchange-rate movements introduces an additional element of flexibility into the economy. It is noteworthy that while the Monetarist and the Keynesian schools emphasize different aspects of exchange rate flexibility and the Monetarist school in particular underlines the need for full flexibility rather than merely for changes in the exchange rate, the two schools at this level of generalization are quite compatible.

IV. Problems with Flexible Rates

In spite of these arguments for exchange-rate flexibility, there are several worrisome features about the present arrangements of floating exchange rates subject to occasional official management. First, as Tobin (1988) has pointed out, major adjustments to external disturbances may require changes in the overall price level between one country and another. To the extent that governments treat their price levels as policy targets, adjustment via this mechanism is thwarted. If price-level targeting is wholly successful, and if relative prices are sticky—which was the starting point of the Keynesian rationale for floating rates—national action will offset the effect of exchange-rate movements. Thus, for example, if the U.S. dollar depreciates in response to some external disturbance, leading to price increases in the United States, the Fed may tighten money in order to avoid "inflation." The Bundesbank, in contrast, eases monetary action in order to avoid "deflation." In this way, adjustment is shifted to output after all.

Second, the imperfect competition that leads to sticky prices may have a further implication, as Krugman (1989), elaborating an analysis by Dixit, has recently pointed out. Fixed market entry costs not only will slow the process of adjustment to changes in the exchange rate, but will actually create a band of variation in which, for the relevant industries, no adjustment will take place. The profit incentive must exceed a certain threshhold before entry is worthwhile. Once entry has taken place and the costs of entry have been sunk, the profit disincentive must move correspondingly far to make exit the proper strategy. This difference between marginal cost on entry and on exit will be reinforced by uncertainty about future exchange rates. It may make sense for a firm to hold onto its market at prices even below its current marginal costs if the costs of reentry after exiting the market are high and if there is a sufficient probability that the conditions for reentry—for example, a sufficiently large movement in the exchange rate—will recur.

The implication of this market feature is that exchange rates may have to swing very far in order to achieve real adjustment, since industries subject to significant entry and exit costs will be unresponsive to movements in exchange rates of a relatively minor character. In this respect, flexible exchange rates are not an especially efficient mechanism of adjustment since, when measured against long-run comparative advantage, misallocations of resources may be induced, and then persist for a long period of time, in response to exchange rate fluctuations. One might have in mind the United States in the mid-1980s, for instance, when many foreign companies, attracted by the profit possibilities created by an exceptionally strong dollar, entered the U.S. market profitably and then hung on tenaciously even after the dollar depreciated substantially, in some cases beyond the point at which profitability continued.

Third, a high variability of real exchange rates may reduce total investment in the sectors of the economy open to international competition. When a currency has depreciated strongly, profits in tradables will be high and cash flow will be good, but firms will be reluctant to invest in productive capacity because the cheap currency is not expected to last. They will simply enjoy their windfall profits and perhaps invest more in market opening, as discussed above. When a currency is strongly appreciated, on the other hand, even though the situation is expected by management to be temporary, profits and cash flow will be low, leading to low investment because of credit rationing and because of skeptical, risk-averse boards of directors. Although many other factors have undoubtedly also played a role, it is perhaps not a mere coincidence that investment in plant and equipment throughout the OECD area has been depressed since the inauguration of floating exchange rates in 1973, compared with the 1950s and 1960s. In particular, Europe failed to invest much when profits were high and rising as a result of a strong dollar in the period from 1983 to 1985.

Fourth, since firms cannot hedge their investments in future production—as distinguished from a particular sale—through financial markets they will do so by investing abroad, across currency zones, even if that means giving up some of the advantages of cost and scale associated with exporting from their home bases or some other lower-cost location. Because some of this diversification takes place through takeovers and buyouts, one possible further consequence is greater world concentration in certain industries, leading to a reduction of worldwide competition.

Fifth, at the national level businesses will seek to blunt what they consider unequal competition by urging an increase in trade barriers. Business firms generally feel they can cope with the market uncertainty that attends any growing, dynamic economy, as long as their competitors are subject to the same ups and downs. What they find intolerable is being placed at a competitive disadvantage with respect to their leading competitors for reasons unrelated to decision-making in the firms, or indeed in the industry. Present exchange-rate arrangements violate this strong desire, insofar as a firm can suddenly find itself facing much stiffer competition (or much less, but that is rarely a cause for concern) as a result of an exchange rate movement, which has its origins in the arcane world of finance. Certainly American firms, and organized labor, greatly increased their pressure on the U.S. government in the period 1983–85 for some form of relief against over-competitive imports during the period of an exceptionally strong dollar. It is noteworthy that under the gold standard, while national price levels moved substantially, they tended to move in parallel instead of moving relative to one another.

These factors involve a misallocation of resources arising from the uncertainties associated with exchange rate flexibility. Whether monetary arrangements can be improved is a complex question, which depends in part on whether exchange rate uncertainty is simply the surface manifestation of uncertainties intrinsic to the economic system as a whole, or whether exchange rate dynamics actually add to the uncertainties faced by those who must make decisions on production and investment, that is, on present and future output of the economy. It also depends on whether a superior set of arrangements can be found, one that reduces whatever incremental uncertainties market-determined exchange rates contribute to the economic system while preserving or finding an adequate substitute for the contribution that changes in exchange rates may make to reducing the costs of adjustment to those changes which dynamic economies will inevitably have to make from time to time.

Whether high volatility in floating exchange rates reflects the uncertainties in the economic system and instabilities in economic policies or adds to them is a source of unresolved controversy. It is difficult to sustain the view, however, that foreign exchange markets reflect accurately and faithfully only the disturbances exogenous to the economic system, plus the net impact of governmental actions, which may themselves either dampen volatility or augment it. Figure 10.1 shows the monthly changes in the dollar-DM exchange rate, corrected for differential movements in wholesale prices, 1960-88. The increase in volatility following the inauguration of floating in 1973 is dramatic.

There is a growing body of evidence to support the view that practitioners have long held, namely, that financial markets have a dynamic of their own and are occasionally subject to bandwagon effects, or speculative bubbles, whether these be rational or irrational. Shiller (1984) has shown that U.S. stock prices have frequently followed paths that are very difficult to explain except in terms of fashion or social psychological dynamics. Indeed, one of the principal bases for stock selection by some specialists, chartism, presupposes that stock prices follow distinctive patterns that are basically unrelated to what

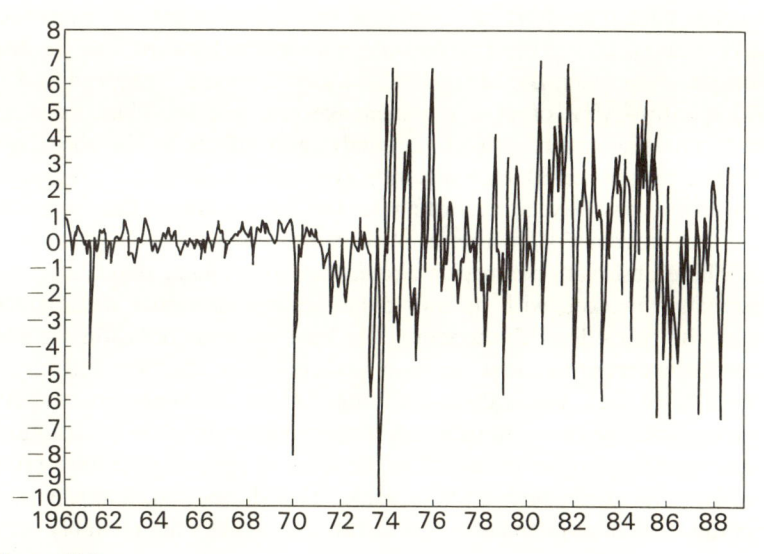

Figure 10.1
U.S.-Germany: Real Exchange Rate Changes (percent/month)
Source: Dornbusch (1988).

is happening in the economy. To the extent that substantial numbers of investors adopt this basis of stock selection, chartism can become self-fulfilling, provided the chartist prices stay within the wide bounds set by liquidation value of the firms and the competition for funds provided by yields on long-term bonds.

More recently, Krugman (1985, 1989) has shown that the appreciation of the dollar in 1983–85 cannot have been based on fundamentals alone, even though some appreciation could have been expected on the basis of the configuration of monetary and fiscal policies in the United States, on the one hand, and in Japan, Germany, and Britain on the other. Krugman's analysis starts with the observation that the "market" must have expected a subsequent depreciation of the dollar at a rate no greater than the interest differential between comparable assets denominated in dollars, yen, and DM. On generous assumptions about the effect of such expected depreciation on trade flows, Krugman shows that U.S. external debt would have grown explosively, that is, unsustainably. This simple calculation suggests that market participants were not paying adequate attention to the underlying fundamentals, but instead were following their own lead in a bubble, until it burst in early 1985, with encouragement from heavy purchases of DM by the Bundesbank.

Moreover, Frankel and Froot (1987) have shown on the basis of survey data that short-run exchange rate expectations are extrapolative, that is, they project recent rate movements forward into the near future, even when the movement is away from the "long-run"—6 to 12 months—view of what the exchange rate will be. Thus, exchange rate movements are subject to bandwagon effects in the short run. Over a longer period, exchange rate expectations seem to be regressive to recent past levels, according to the survey data. But of course market movements are a series of short runs.

These observations provide circumstantial evidence that the foreign exchange market, with its own dynamic, can introduce disturbances into the real side of the economy. At least on some occasions, it adds to the uncertainties that decision makers on production and investment must face. But is there anything that can be done about it? Are there exchange rate arrangements that are superior to the unstructured managed floating we have had, in the sense of reducing the uncertainty without incurring high costs in some other dimension, and especially in the costs of adjustment to the disturbances that will inevitably occur from time to time?

V. Proposals for Reform

A number of suggestions have been put forward. Tobin (1982) has suggested a modest tax on foreign exchange transactions to discourage short-term transactions of low social utility, with the presumption that that will reduce exchange rate volatility. Williamson and Miller (1987), Kenen (1988), McKinnon (1984, 1988), and Cooper (1984) have made proposals for introducing greater stability into exchange rate movements directly, but with different techniques and emphases.

1. A Transactions Tax

A small tax, say 25 basis points (0.25%), could be imposed on all transactions that involve converting one currency into another, including forward transactions. (Some go further and suggest a small tax on all financial transactions, but that is not discussed here.) Such a tax would raise the cost of all cross-currency transactions, but it would be so small that it could be expected to have virtually no effect on trade in goods and services and on long-term capital flows. But the tax would impose a relatively large cost on short-term in-and-out transactions. For instance, 50 basis points for a two-way transaction would require an interest differential of more than 25% per annum to cover it for a weekly turnaround and over 100% per annum for a daily turnaround. Such a tax would greatly reduce the huge volume of foreign exchange transactions that now occurs ($700 billion a day in New York alone), most of which are interbank transactions. The aim of the tax would be to reduce short-term exchange rate volatility and to encourage greater emphasis on longer-term transactions, which presumably are socially more valuable.

In fact, however, the impact of such a tax on short-term volatility is entirely unclear. To the extent that banks, corporate treasurers, and other short-term traders are "market makers," such as securities specialists, their activities should be stabilizing and reduce short-run volatility. Taxing them out of short-term transactions would in that event lead to an increase in volatility. But to the extent that these traders seek quick short-term gains, must guess very short-run market developments, and therefore are subject to bandwagon effects, their activities may increase short-run volatility, and a transaction tax would reduce it.

In either case, a transactions tax would not prevent the emergence of major misalignments, such as those that occurred in the mid-1980s, except insofar as those arise from the cumulative effect of a series of short-run extrapolative expectations, which might not get started in the presence of a tax. Presumably one characteristic of a cumulative exchange rate movement in the "wrong" direction is that each participant feels he can reverse his position at the right moment, before the crowd turns, or at least ahead of it. The crowd could turn at any time, even in the near future. To that extent, a transactions tax could inhibit major speculative currency movements, but it is unclear that it would be enough to prevent them.

To be effective, the transactions tax would have to be introduced in all leading financial centers; otherwise, transactions would move to the tax-free centers, something that is increasingly possible with modern communications. But it would not be necessary to get universal agreement on the tax. It would suffice to stipulate that disputes arising over foreign exchange transactions could not be adjudicated in countries of the leading financial centers unless the tax had been paid. Since it takes years to establish a reputation for fair and impartial dispute settlements, a small tax would be unlikely to drive transactions to tax-free countries without such reputations.

A tax represents one proposal for reducing exchange-rate volatility. That is not a certain outcome, however, nor is the avoidance of significant misalignment. Other proposals focus on commitments to affect exchange rate movements directly.

2. Target zones

Williamson and Miller have proposed that the major countries establish "target zones" for their exchange rates. The basis for establishing the target zones would be a calculation for each country of a "fundamental equilibrium exchange rate," which in turn would be based on mutually agreed-upon current account targets for each country. These equilibrium rates would be recalculated at regular intervals so they could move in response to new information, but presumably they would move slowly. They in turn would be translated into a set of mutually consistent nominal exchange rates, which would represent the center of the target zone. At first, the zone around these central rates would be wide, say $\pm 10\%$, to encompass substantial initial deviation from the target current-account positions, but the zones could gradually be narrowed over time, once the current-account targets were achieved.

Monetary authorities would intervene in exchange markets—and, more important, adjust their monetary policies—as exchange rates reached the edges of the target zone. These edges could be either hard—well-defined rates, which are not to be surpassed—or soft—presumptive points of intervention and "leaning" by authorities, but without a firm commitment that the boundaries will never be crossed.

With n countries and only n-1 exchange rates among them, there would be a degree of freedom in monetary policy. This would be directed toward aggregate demand in the community as a whole. Put another way, if a given exchange rate approached the edge of the zone, whether one country tightened its monetary policy to affect the rate or the other country loosened would depend on the overall state of aggregate demand. Each country, in addition to having a current account target, would also have a target for growth in nominal demand, chosen in a way to be mutually consistent with those of other countries, and national fiscal policies would be directed toward achieving these aggregate demand targets.

The effect of this system in operation would be to limit the movement of exchange rates and thus prevent the emergence of major misalignments of the kind that occurred in the 1980s. It would not, however, eliminate short-run volatility of exchange rates, and the uncertainties they create, unless the target zones were quite narrow, which is not envisaged. While it is possible for businessmen to hedge against unexpected exchange rate movements for particular transactions, it is not possible to hedge for an investment or a commitment to a marketing strategy that will take a number of years to mature. So this source of uncertainty would remain.

The Williamson-Miller proposal is ambitious in its demands on policy coordination among major countries and on the skillful manipulation of monetary and fiscal instruments by national authorities. It is especially ambitious with respect to the coordination of policy targets—real effective equilibrium exchange rates and growth in national nominal aggregate demand. Agreement on the key underpinnings for calculation of real effective equilibrium exchange rates—current account targets, plus the bearing of exchange rates on their achievement—is especially demanding, not least because the setting of current account targets would be an intrinsically arbitrary exercise in a world of high capital mobility and open markets for goods and services. For concreteness, consider Canada. As a high-income country, it should perhaps run a current account surplus, contributing to the transfer of real resources to the lower-income developing countries. But in every respect except income, Canada itself is a "developing country," and indeed Canada has run current account deficits throughout most of its existence as an independent state. How should we determine what Canada's current account position should be in the future? Or, for that matter, the current account position of the United States, which by comparison with Europe and Japan is also a developing country, with its population growing relatively rapidly, increasingly through immigration, as in the 19th century.

Kenen (1988) advocates something like an extension of the European Monetary System to include the United States, Japan, and possibly other countries. He supports hard exchange rate margins with a band width of at least 10%, much larger than the EMS band, so that changes in central rates, which must occasionally be made, need not affect market rates and hence would not provide a one-way speculative option when accurately anticipated. Kenen would also increase the visible reserves available for intervention, by analogy with the EMS, especially for the United States, by creating a modified substitution account into which the United States would deposit gold and others would deposit dollars.

On the choice of central rates, Kenen takes the view that that is less relevant than the procedures for changing them. If they are not right, i.e., are needed for adjustment, they should be altered. He would give weight (but not mechanically) to a host of indicators, especially changes in relative price competitiveness, as in the EMS, but in the end, changes in central rates would be discretionary, to be negotiated among all the relevant parties.

3. Key Currency Monetary Coordination

McKinnon (1984, 1988) concentrates on just three countries and their currencies: the United States, Japan, and the federal Republic of Germany, although he assumes several other currencies will be linked to the German mark through the EMS. He would at first confine movement of exchange rates among the three key currencies within a 10% band, like Kenen, but over time he would gradually reduce the width of the band so that the exchange rates among the three key currencies eventually showed little or no movement. In addition, McKinnon departs from the other two proposals by selecting the central rates to which the exchange rates are to converge on the basis of purchasing power parity. Concretely, McKinnon would construct broad-based indices of tradable goods, and would choose exchange rates that equate the value of a comparable basket of these goods (McKinnon and Ohno, 1988). Nominal exchange rates would then remain fixed except insofar as changes were required to offset relative changes in purchasing power parity as defined by the baskets. Monetary policy in each of the countries would be dedicated to maintaining the fixed exchange rates; monetary policy in the three countries taken together—close coordination would be required—would be dedicated to maintaining stability in the prices of the baskets of tradable goods, as was advocated over half a century ago by Keynes (1930). Such a target implies moderate inflation as measured by the consumer price index, because of its component of services.

4. A Common Currency

Cooper (1984) would go a step further than McKinnon by institutionalizing the close monetary cooperation in coherent management of a single currency for the industrialized democracies. So long as national currencies are distinct, under distinct management, the possibility of major changes in nominal and real exchange rates exists, and that possibility is itself a source of uncertainty to investors so long as memories of the 1970s and 1980s persist. The most effective way to eradicate exchange rate uncertainty is to eradicate exchange rates, that is, to introduce a single currency. A single currency would require a single monetary authority, which would represent a bold, even radical step—one that governments and their publics are not yet ready to contemplate seriously, much less undertake. So unlike the proposals discussed above, which are put forward with the near future in mind, this proposal must be envisioned in a longer time frame, into the next century. Still, it carries the logic of a return to fixed exchange rates to its full conclusion, and for that reason it is worth exploring more fully.

The institutional aspects of a common currency are not so difficult to imagine: they could be constructed by analogy with the U.S. Federal Reserve System, which is an amalgam of 12 separate Reserve Banks, each issuing its own currency. One could imagine an open-market committee for all or any subset of the industrial democracies that would decide the basic thrust of monetary policy for the group as a whole. On it could sit representatives of all member countries, with votes proportional to GNP. At one extreme the representatives could be ministers of finance; at the other they could be outstanding citizens chosen by their governments for long terms solely for the purpose of managing the monetary system. An obvious interim (and possibly permanent) step would be to appoint the senior governors of existing central banks.

National central banks could continue as the national components and agents of the new international Board of Bank Governors, and indeed they could remain the issuers of currency, just as the 12 District Federal Reserve Banks do in the United States. If national sentiment called for it, currency designations—pounds, marks, yen, francs, dollars—could even be retained on nationally issued currency. The central point is that monetary policy would be out of the hands of any single government. Governments could not finance their budget deficits through monetary expansion, and the national currencies would exchange at fixed exchange rates. Most commercial transactions do not involve currency at all, so all commercial and bank transactions could take place in a common unit of account. A common currency would of course eliminate exchange rate uncertainty not only for commercial transactions, but also for financial transactions, so a unified capital market would develop throughout the area covered by the currency. By the same token, however, changes in nominal exchange rates could not be used any longer as part of the adjustment process. More will be said about this below.

A common currency could create serious adjustment problems if the exchange rates among the precedent currencies were not right at the time of conversion into the common currency. For this reason also, such a move cannot be consummated until major disequilibria have been eliminated. Purchasing power parity conditions, such as those suggested by McKinnon, must be met at least approximately; in addition, uncovered interest parity over all maturities should obtain at least approximately, implying no expectation of future changes in exchange rates.

For the participating countries, international and national currency would become identical, and liquidity needs would be satisfied by decisions by the Board of Bank Governors to increase the money supply.

VI. Evaluation of the Single-Currency Proposal

One objection that will be raised immediately against a single money for the industrialized democracies is that it involves ceding too much sovereignty to an international entity (in this case, the Board of Bank Governors). This is a misguided objection. Ultimate sovereignty continues to reside with the national governments. It is an exercise of sovereignty, not an abrogation of sovereignty, to agree on a common endeavor with other sovereign nations. The key question that should be asked is whether, on balance, the particular exercise of sovereignty leaves the participants better or worse off. It would limit the freedom of action of individual governments in the monetary arena. But the economies of these nations are becoming increasingly interdependent, and that economic interdependency increasingly limits the efficacy of individual actions in the areas of macroeconomic policy, taxation, and financial regulation. So retaining full freedom of action may turn out to be largely empty short of withdrawal into autarky, which would be extremely costly. A cooperative endeavor, while reducing national freedom of action, will restore effectiveness to joint action.

What of the adjustment process? The principal argument for exchange rate flexibility is that it may reduce the costs of adjustment to various economic disturbances. It should be kept in mind, however, that the requirements for efficient adjustment depend on the nature of the disturbances; and the nature of the disturbances in turn depend in part on the nature of the monetary system.

In particular, disturbances to national economics that are wholly or largely monetary in nature will be greatly diminished or eliminated altogether when the nations share a common currency, with no chance (short of major political disturbance) of changes in exchange rates among national monies. This would apply, for instance, to shifts in asset preferences among national financial claims motivated by expected changes in exchange rates or to differential inflation among nations in tradable goods. Differences in national wage settlements not based on changes in productivity cannot be ruled out under a common currency, but they are much less likely in the presence of a common currency and extensive trade between nations. So at least some disturbances for which changes in exchange rates might be helpful hardly exist under a common currency.

What about disturbances to the real side of the economy, such as the discovery or exhaustion of natural resources, the technological changes that have differential effects among sectors, or the divergent rates of growth between demand and supply among nations?

With respect to technological change and discovery or exhaustion of resources, three observations can be made concerning economic adjustment in the industrialized democracies. First, most of the adjustment will have to take place within the three regions of the United States, Japan, and the European Community. Sectors, especially resource-based sectors, are often concentrated geographically, and changes in technology or the pattern of demand will require consequential adjustment among them. Such adjustments now take place within these economic areas. But exchange rate changes facilitate adjustment between countries, not within them. Yet these three economies taken as a whole are large and diversified; so little adjustment is likely to be required between them. Second, major disturbances at the global level, such as the oil price increases of the 1970s, are likely to affect all three regions in roughly the same way, although not identically. Third, the differential effects that remain once the first two points are taken into account are likely to be manageable within the parameters established by the natural growth and retirement of the labor force and the capital stock. Changes in real income and in domestic relative prices (for example, between tradables and nontradables) will help to bring about the adjustment without substantial changes in output.[1]

With respect to differential growth in national (or regional) demand and output, such discrepancies, whether merely cyclical or reflecting more durable changes in saving behavior, can easily be accommodated by capital movements motivated by relatively small differences in yield within an integrated capital market, such as would obtain over a common currency area under modern conditions.

Possibly the greatest source of disturbance between large and diversified economies would arise from significant and opposite changes in fiscal policy. If one country pursued fiscal expansion while another was contracting substantially, that could create significant adjustment problems, and changes in exchange rates might assist the adjustment. But two things should be said about this possibility. First, it is desirable to be able to use fiscal action, within limits, to affect aggregate demand at the national or regional level. The adoption of a common currency, far from preventing this, would enhance the desirability of fiscal flexibility. Thus, it may be undesirable to allow or encourage exchange rates to adjust in response to discrepant fiscal actions, since such adjustment both affects the structure of output (for example, between tradables and nontradables) and weakens the demand effects of the fiscal actions (for example, by leading to a fall in net exports attendent upon a fiscal expansion).

Second, however, fiscal deficits would have to be financed exclusively in the (integrated) capital market. So long as a government's credit was good, it would have no trouble borrowing. As the ratio of public debt to tax revenues grew, however, the market would require higher

---

[1] In this regard, Krugman (1989) exaggerates the changes in output—or under flexible rates, in the real exchange rate—required to achieve a given adjustment between two large and diversified economies. McKinnon (1988b), based on Jones (1975), argues persuasively that change in the terms of trade need not be large to accommodate a disturbance between two multisectored economies that are reasonably flexible, and it may not be necessary at all.

yields to be willing to take that government's securities. There would be market signals indicating when one government was markedly out of line with the others in terms of growing indebtedness. Thus, while fiscal freedom of action would be unimpaired, it would be limited by the ability to service public debt. It would undoubtedly be useful to have informal discussions concerning the framing of fiscal action among all the participants; but formal coordination of fiscal action would not be necessary, and full harmonization would not be desirable.

The above points can be summed up briefly by saying that in the not very distant future nominal exchange rate flexibility among major currencies may create more disturbances for the real productive side of national economies than it corrects.

References

Bloomfield, A.I. 1959. *Monetary Policy under the International Gold Standard, 1880–1914*. New York: Federal Reserve Bank of New York.

Cooper, R. "A Monetary System for the Future," in *Foreign Affairs*, Fall 1984. Reprinted in *The International Monetary System*, 1987.

———, ed. *International Finance*. Baltimore: Penguin Books, 1969.

———. 1987. The Gold Standard: Historical Facts and Future Prospects, in *Brookings Papers on Economic Activity*, 1982, pp. 1–43. Reprinted in *The International Monetary System*. Cambridge: MIT Press.

Dornbusch, R. Fall 1988. "The McKinnon Standard: How Persuasive?" In *The CATO Journal*, No. 8, pp. 375–83.

Frankel, J., and Froot, K. March 1987. "Using Survey Data to Test Standard Propositions Regarding Exchange Rate Expectations." *American Economic Review*, No. 97, pp. 133–53.

Friedman, M. 1953. "The Case for Flexible Exchange Rates." In *Essays in Positive Economics*. Chicago: University of Chicago Press.

Jones, R.W. August 1975. Presumption and the Transfer Problem. In *Journal of International Economics*, No. 5, pp. 263–74.

Kenen, P.B. 1988. *Managing Exchange Rates*. London: Routledge.

Keynes, J.M. 1930. *A Treatise on Money*, Vol. 2. London: Macmillan.

Krugman, Paul. *Exchange-rate Instability*. Cambridge: MIT Press, 1989.

———. 1985. "Is the Strong Dollar Sustainable?" In *The U.S. Dollar:*

Prospects and Policy Options. Kansas City: Federal Reserve Bank of Kansas City.

McKinnon, R.I. Fall 1988. "An International Gold Standard Without Gold." *The Cato Journal*, No. 8, pp. 351–73.

———. 1984. *An International Standard for Monetary Stabilization* Washington D.C.: Institute for International Economics.

———. 1988. "Monetary and Exchange Rate Policies for International Financial Stability: A Proposal." *Journal of Economic Perspectives*, No. 2, pp. 83–103.

———, and Kenichi Ohno. "Purchasing Power Parity as a Monetary Standard." San Francisco: Federal Reserve Bank of San Francisco, processed October 1988.

Meltzer, A.H. 1986. "Some Evidence on Comparative Uncertainty Experienced under Different Monetary Regimes." In Campbell, C., and Dougan, W., eds. *Alternative Monetary Regimes*. Baltimore: Johns Hopkins University Press.

Nurkse, R. 1944. *International Currency Experience*. Geneva: League of Nations.

Schiller, R.J. 1984. "Stock Prices and Social Dynamics." In *Brookings Papers on Economic Activity*, No. 2. Washington, D.C.: Brookings Institution, pp. 457–98.

Tobin, J. 1982. "A Proposal for International Monetary Reform." In *Essays in Economics*. Cambridge: MIT Press.

———. 1988. "Are There Reliable Adjustment Mechanisms?" In Suzuki, Y., and Mitsuaki Okabe, M., *Toward a World of Economic Stability: Optimal Monetary Framework and Policy*. Tokyo: University of Tokyo Press.

Triffin, R. 1960. *Gold and the Dollar Crisis*. New Haven: Yale University Press.

Viner, J. 1924. *Canada's Balance of International Indebtedness*. Cambridge: Harvard University Press.

Williamson, J., and Miller, M.H. 1987. *Targets and Indicators: A Blueprint for the International Coordination of Economic Policy*. Washington, D.C.: Institute for International Economics.

Comments

Philippe Lagayette

Let me say first that those papers provided an excellent basis for discussing the possibility of improving the present organization. I will first refer to Giavazzi's paper. As he clearly demonstrated, the EMS has been an undeniable success, above all in stabilizing exchange rates and reducing rates of inflation. And as far as exchange rate stabilization is concerned, there has been a reduction of variability, and this has not been accompanied by the kind of misalignments observed in the case of the principal floating currencies. In the field of inflation, to give a brief summary, there has been a marked convergence in the rate of price increase. For instance, the inflation differential between Germany and France was 6.6% at the beginning of the system in March 1979, and it is now less than 1%. Even if this did not come rapidly, I think as a matter of fact that it is significant if one remembers that during the end of the '70s and the beginning of the '80s there was a particular situation with a high rate of inflation in many countries.

But this success is less evident in other areas, such as the level of activity. The rate of growth has converged at a lower average level than the one we have just seen in the countries outside the EMS, even if the situation is improving now; for instance, the rate of unemployment is presently around 2.5%, in Japan 5.5%, in the United States, and 10% in the whole EEC. The situation is less than satisfactory in balance of payments, largely because of the very sizable growth of the surpluses of West Germany: in 1988, nearly two thirds of this trade surplus originated in trade with other EEC countries.

Therefore, the EMS can be improved. The requirement in regard to economic policy coordination should be extended beyond the convergence of anti-inflationary policies. By its very design, the EMS tends to exercise a greater pressure on inflationary trends than it does on the lack of progress in achieving balanced and stable growth. It is this point that probably underlies Giavazzi's criticism of the EMS. In his paper, indeed, the EMS is presented as a deutsche mark zone. This raises the question of arriving at a common definition, for member countries of the EMS, of economic policy objectives regarding price movements and also growth and balance of payments.

This then raises the question of setting monetary objectives jointly and on an ex ante basis, in reference to the situation of Europe as a whole, instead of by simply deriving these objectives in the other countries from the ones set in the country with the strongest currency. And we should probably also use fiscal policy as an additional tool to harmonize the economic situation.

If such improvements were made, and I do not doubt that they will sometime be made, greater symmetry could be introduced within the EMS as regards both exchange rate determination and even intervention, when necessary. Even if, in agreement with Giavazzi, I do not believe the EMS could simply be transposed to the world level as it stands, I think there are ideas that can be drawn from the EMS for international monetary relations. I shall now turn to Cooper's paper.

The example of the EMS raises the questions of the advantages of exchange rate stability. Obviously this is necessary when economies are very deeply integrated. Maybe it is less necessary at the world level, but the specifics of the EEC do not solve the question, and we should not forget the problem of stability in the international field. Even if the thinking about the international monetary system deals first with the adjustment question and the liquidity question, as Mr. Cooper did in his whole presentation, in which he gave very useful remarks on the value of stability, we can add other things. Do we consider, for instance, that the relative stability of exchange rates we have experienced for two years has nothing to do with the higher level of growth and investment worldwide? And the question of asking who gains at any time, even within a system like the EMS, does not explain the whole of the thing. There is certainly a collective gain in exchange rate stability, and you may add that, as Mr. Cooper said, there are other ways of adjustment that are operating: either within our economies or also between diversified economies.

So we can say that the more economies are diversified and integrated, the less possible it is to have an attitude of benign neglect about exchange rate fluctuation, and the less possible it is not to consider stability as a collective gain. We can also add that exchange rates are a synthetic indicator; any domestic problem that reduces competitiveness has consequences on the exchange rate. Therefore, an exchange rate discipline is a good way for everybody to maintain discipline in the conduct of sound domestic monetary and economic policies oriented toward domestic stability, which is in industrial economies the first basis of competitiveness. And if we think that some organization in the field of exchange rate is useful, this leads to the coordination of policies as a basis for any progress.

It may be difficult, but we must not forget that this is the necessary ingredient. For instance, we must not forget that in the Louvre agreement, the coordination of economic policies was the main tool before intervention or before the declaration of intentions about the level of relative exchange rates. And also, as I tried to point out yesterday, we must coordinate policies to avoid large uncertainties and disequilibria, if we want the global financial market we have created to operate without overreactions and disorders.

Mr. Chairman, one last word. Maybe the common currency is far away, even for Europe, but it is certainly in the logic of the single market, as the Delors report points out. Maybe it is far away, but if we want to go in that direction, there is also a prerequisite condition, which is to be able to coordinate policies. So whatever we are envisaging in the near future as improvements in the present state of exchange rates in the international monetary system, policy coordination is a necessary instrument.

This is my last point: scepticism has been permanently around the European monetary construction, as Giavazzi said at the beginning. When the EMS was created, many people, and sometimes experts, said it could not last, but it has resisted and even been strengthened. So what does not seem to be realistic at some times can be natural a few years later. Thank you.

Comments

Leonhard Gleske

Because of the time limit I will concentrate my comments on Professor Giavazzi's paper. What I would have liked to have said about Professor Cooper's paper has been said by Professor Fischer in the opening meeting. I widely share his views and conclusions.

May I begin with the question Giavazzi asks in his concluding chapter: "Why did the Europeans set up the EMS?"

The reasons, I believe, were not only economic, but also to a large degree political. Giscard d'Estaing and Helmut Schmidt felt strongly that Europe should be able to speak with a stronger voice and put a greater weight into its reaction to the American policy of benign neglect of the dollar and of the U.S. balance of payments situation of the 1970s. This met with a desire, which was then perhaps stronger on the French than on the German side, to make some progress in European monetary integration, a desire that was frustrated in the early 1970s when France had to leave the "snake" arrangement that preceded the EMS. Giscard and Schmidt agreed that the European Community needed a new push, and it seemed that the monetary field offered the opportunity for it.

The economic arguments listed by Professor Giavazzi are well taken. The argument relating to the great openness of the European economies should probably come first, together with the realization that a large share of foreign trade of all European countries is with one another, and it is trade in goods and services with a high value-added that is sensitive to exchange rate fluctuations.

The renewed interest in exchange rate stability was reinforced by the view that exchange rates could in fact be stabilized among partners that shared important and far-reaching integration objectives and were willing to pursue appropriate policies, whereas exchange rate stabilization relative to the dollar, in particular, looked far less feasible. There were several reasons to support this view, among them the fact that financial flows had become so important for dollar exchange rates of major currencies that their stabilization seemed less easy, if not impossible, even if the United States joined in the effort.

Giavazzi mentions the common agricultural policy (CAP) as a special reason for stable exchange rates between Community currencies. The CAP indeed posed a problem and continues to do so. For a time, the EMS functioned on the hypothesis that realignments should not be affected, prevented, or delayed by their possible implications for farm prices, subsidies, and agricultural policies if such realignments were considered necessary by all partners in the EMS. After all, agriculture accounts for only a very small share in the GDP. But this intention proved to be an illusion. At each major realignment, the implications for the CAP ranked high on the agenda and made agreement difficult. The current insistence on existing parities in the EMS is in good part due to this factor.

In recent years, for some important countries the credibility aspect of exchange rate policy has become equally important if not more important. The fixed-rate commitment has been a basic element of their stabilization effort. Arguing that the achievement of greater domestic price stability in these countries depended on the commitment to fixed, though adjustable, exchange rates would perhaps overstate the case. The need to regain control over inflation was felt all around by the end of the 1970s. But pegging to a currency whose internal value was more stable as a means to achieve greater price stability at home became a preferred strategy not only within the EMS, but also for some European non-EMS countries, for example, Austria and Switzerland. The United Kingdom, though within the EMS but outside the ERM, also at times indicated a preference for a DM-oriented policy, though adoption of the fixed rate commitment of the EMS has been left for later "when the time is ripe."

Giavazzi speaks of the EMS as "an (imperfect) greater D-mark area." On the one hand, it is widely recognized that the key currency role of the Deutsche mark and the monetary policy of the Bundesbank have provided the EMS with a stable anchor. The tricky n-th currency problem inherent in any fixed-rate system has thus been solved. On the other hand, there have at times been complaints that the German policy mix imposes a deflationary bias on the system.

Some critics simply advise Germany to accept a somewhat higher inflation rate if this is necessary to allow for faster growth of domestic demand, but also because it would ease the pressure on their own policies. The end result would be higher inflation all around with no assurance of the growth benefits sought by the proponents of the "moderate inflation strategy." Targeting for a higher inflation rate than is within the Bundesbank's reach is unlikely to be acceptable in Germany. Moreover, the likely implications for exchange-rate stability within the EMS also argue against this option.

The "greater D-mark bloc" image suggests asymmetries within the EMS. These may involve the balance of cost and benefits for individual countries and among countries, that of rights and obligations under the existing rules, or the adjustment and financing burdens deriving from these rules and their applications. The current asymmetry debate appears to be mostly about the last point.

It is well known that the Bundesbank enjoys relative policy autonomy in its area of responsibility and competence within Germany. It also enjoys a greater degree of autonomy than other countries' central banks within the EMS, owing to the economic weight of Germany and the key currency role of the D-mark in the system. There is evidence that German interest rates are less affected by intra-EMS shocks than those of other countries are. The monetary aggregates are relatively unaffected by intervention undertaken by its partners in D-marks within the margins, which is the technique preferred by our partners in recent years.

But this ignores the fact that current account surpluses and capital inflows will affect the aggregates directly. To the extent there is no automatic offset through less rapid domestic credit expansion, the central bank will be compelled to satisfy the additional reserve demand of the system. Action taken to slow the monetary expansion is likely to be ineffective or even counterproductive in an environment of quasi-fixed exchange rates and highly mobile capital. Higher interest rates may discourage recourse to domestic credit, but they will tend to attract more capital inflows. In today's world, the potential inflationary consequences for surplus countries are likely to be more serious than the corresponding constraining effects on deficit countries arising from the loss of exchange reserves through intervention.

The D-mark is also exposed to currency competition with the dollar especially, which reduces the autonomy of national monetary policy. It still commands second place as an international currency, held in large sums by private investors and public entities, including its role as a readily usable reserve currency. Willingness by foreigners to add to their D-mark holdings often accentuates the problems confronting a surplus country, but at times reverse flows will also cause problems.

If the Bundesbank's autonomy is not that great after all, why should it not agree to share its key role in the EMS more evenly with other partner's central banks? If other partners assume greater responsibility in the formulation of common objectives and their achievements, existing sources of friction might be eliminated. Here, as elsewhere, confidence seems to be of the essence.

Could one be confident that common decision-making would carry credibility? There are still reasons for doubts. The existing differences on such things as objectives, tradeoffs, and instrument effectiveness remain sizable, and so does the degree of political autonomy of central banks. In the Federal Republic of Germany, common decision-making would still cause unease at this stage—which will be overcome only if price stability is fully accepted as a priority objective of monetary policy, based on a basic consensus with the government and the wider public—and if responsibility for the currency is seen to be in the hands of central banks that enjoy a high degree of autonomy from political instruction. At present, reference to the strong position of Germany and the Bundesbank in the system helps to calm the concerns that still exist in Germany, concerns that the EMS will undermine the stability orientation of the Bundesbank's policy. In other words: the time is not yet ripe for common decision-making in the EMS. This will become *the* crucial point in efforts to develop the EMS into a Monetary Union, envisaged as a final stage of the process, laid out by the Delors Committee. It would, in my view, require adequate safeguards to ensure that common decision-making will not leave room for inflation laxity because individual partners would by definition no longer be able to opt out of the system. Even based on the Delors Report, agreement on such safeguards may still prove difficult enough at the European level. It is an entirely open question—and this I would like to say also in reaction to Cooper's paper—whether they could be agreed on at the global level.

Giavazzi's discussion about the trade-off between inflation and growth leads him to ask: "What incentives does Germany have to belong to such a system?"

My inclination has been to look at the cost-benefit equation this way: If Germany's closest trading partners—which are also its partners in a common effort that extends beyond the monetary and economic field—make greater efforts to achieve overall economic balance and price stability, this is likely to be to Germany's benefit in the long run.

What are these benefits? They derive partly from the belief that price stability will help sustained growth because resource allocation will be favourably affected. This view is supported by the observation that countries with high inflation do not consistently have higher growth and less unemployment, though the causalities may be difficult to establish, given the numerous other factors that may be relevant. Also, less homemade inflation in Germany's partner countries will reduce the potential for imported inflation and should in turn reduce the need for exchange-rate adjustment, since exchange rate changes pose severe political problems, for example, for agricultural policy, as discussed earlier.

Obviously, the benefits for Germany should exceed the costs that may arise in the context of a fixed rate system, such as the EMS. The EMS has prevented real exchange rates between countries participating in the ERM from overshooting reasonable equilibrium or PPP levels. Not all European non-ERM countries have been able to achieve this, as the British example shows. Given the high share of Germany's trade with its European partners, this relative stability of the D-mark real exchange rate within Europe is without doubt a benefit for Germany in a world environment with repeated misalignments vis-a-vis the dollar.

To conclude my remarks on Professor Giavazzi's paper, may I say how much I agree with him when he states that the exchange rate regime of the EMS has worked satisfactorily under very special circumstances. The EMS is part of a much broader integration concept in Europe and is just—to use the words of Giavazzi—"one element of a much richer set of agreements among European countries in the trade, industrial, and agricultural areas." And I may add, all these integration efforts in the economic field must be seen as part of a much wider political framework. Therefore, the EMS could not simply be copied at the global level, although we could draw useful lessons also for the good functioning of the international monetary system.

Comments

Koichi Hamada

I am grateful to the organizers of this conference, particularly because they assigned me to comment on these really excellent papers.

Cooper's paper starts with a concise history of the international monetary regime throughout the century, gives a balanced diagnosis of the problems of various exchange rate regimes, and then presents a proposal... this time not particularly balanced, but motivated by his strong inclination toward a single currency. His paper is written in a lucid style and his main points are crystal clear.

To me, Giavazzi's paper is more difficult to comprehend. This reflects the fact that Professor Cooper was my thesis adviser at one time—our information sets have much in common—and that I am less familiar with the European economic situation. Giavazzi's paper, however, is very exciting. It relates ongoing theoretical debates in open macroeconomics to the actual process of the European Monetary System (EMS) and to careful empirical analysis. Here, even the exceedingly abstract game situation introduced by Barro and Gordon begins to look as if it were a practical policy problem. The effect through credibility of monetary restraint in the future is vividly explained in the context of the EMS. However, because of my comparative advantage, I would like to spend my time more unevenly on Cooper's paper.

In general, if not in detail, I agree with Dick Cooper in respect to the diagnoses of various international monetary regimes. Let me rephrase them in my own terms. The Bretton Woods system collapsed because of the lack of incentive mechanisms to stabilize the world. The appropriate policy assignment—the United States playing the role of paternalistic guard against worldwide inflation and other countries playing the game of watching their balance of payments—did not work, first, because the U.S. could not play this leadership role due to its own domestic problems, and, second, because an asymmetry exists in the balance-of-payments adjustments, and surplus countries were not necessarily motivated to reflate their economies.

Hence, the Bretton Woods system collapsed. Flexible exchange rate regimes looked like an ideal system when experimented with only in Canada. A person at a distance can easily be romanticized. After 15 years of this floating or managed float system or nonsystem, we are beginning to be disillusioned because real exchange rates showed a tremendous degree of volatility that should be no means be required for the smooth allocation of resources. The allocation of resources, in turn, is sluggish and plagued by hysteresis. Thus it is understandable that people are inclined to feel nostaligia for the past fixed exchange rate system or to look for a new idol such as a single-currency world.

Let me comment briefly on some of the more immediate and therefore more practical alternatives.

(1) *Tobin's tax system*: It is customary in Japan not to criticize one's teacher. My question to the Japanese audience today is, however, "Is it worthwhile, or are you willing to repeat again all the ordeals of sales-tax implementation you just experienced in all international financial transactions?"

(2) *Target zone proposal*: A target zone works not only through actual interventions, but also through its effect on people's expectations for potential future interventions. The monetary authorities can earn more time: Paul Krugman calls it a honeymoon effect. The problem with the target zone proposal is that there hardly exist any scientific theoretical or empirical rules to determine the center and the width of the band.

(3) So we want some rules of policy coordination. What is going on at the summit is highly *ad hoc* coordination without scientific principles. Finance ministers decide roughly what the appropriate target zones are or what the exchange rate box is and at most how to contain real or nominal interest rate differentials among countries. There is a wide gap between these practices and rather sophisticated, game-theoretic or not, theoretical discussions of policy coordination. We cannot solely blame government officials: economists are also to blame because they are not yet capable of providing sufficient empirical information on which policymakers can base appropriate rules of coordination or intervention.

It is natural to look for some feedback rule simple enough that even finance ministers can understand it. With Shin-ichi Fukuda, I presented a joint paper at the most recent Bank of Japan conference in which we showed that the optimal simple monetary feedback rule depends on the nature of disturbances to which our economic universe is subject. If worldwide real disturbances are more prevalent than worldwide monetary disturbances, the global monetarism similar to McKinnon's proposal will be desirable. If worldwide monetary disturbances are more prevalent, coordination toward the average interest target will be desirable. If country-specific real disturbances are more prevalent than country-specific monetary disturbances, flexible exchange rates will be desirable. If country-specific monetary disturbances are more prevalent, fixed (or highly managed) exchange rates will be desirable. In another paper I presented jointly with Jai-Won Ryou and Yoshiro Tsutsui, we examined the relative dominance of real and monetary disturbances. We found that there might be a case for a mild form of global monetarism, but for the choice between fixed and flexible exchange rates, our data were not yet decisive.

Let me now comment on Cooper's main proposal, the "common currency proposal." In a classical setting with completely flexible prices and with perfect information, money would not matter. With some imperfection of information in an otherwise classical world, money may not matter in macroeconomic management, but it matters in resource allocation because monetary regime affects the transaction costs and economy of calculation and information processes. There the natural choice is a single currency.

A few remarks are in order. First, the actual world possesses price and wage rigidities. Then can we say for sure that the world is the optimal currency area? This was the basic theme of Mundell's argument in his classical paper on the optimal currency area. With all the diversity of economic, social, and institutional conditions among many countries, and with all the barriers to trade and factor movements that prevent the transmission of price and wage movements across national borders, can we safely assume that the total world passes this test of optimal currency area?

Second, without a unified government and fiscal policy coordination, even currency union may not function properly, as pointed out in Giavazzi's paper. His reference to the advantage of stabilizing effects of coordination is illuminating. The single-currency area without the unified government should be studied more carefully because there may be some instability in the strategic interaction between fiscal authorities if they choose to finance their expenditures by increased public debt.

Third, not in his paper but in his spoken remarks, Cooper implied that the flexible exchange-rate system is responsible if, for example, prices of Japanese exports happen to violate the U.S. anti-dumping law because of a volatile movement in exchange rates. I consider that this argument is upside down. Stringent American trade laws have their own problems. One cannot judge an exchange rate regime by a possibly distorted trade legislation.

Fourth, I wonder what the world central bank would look like when a single-currency proposal is adopted. Central banks gather outstanding human resources by their prestige, but they also can be authoritative, benign, and sometimes bureaucratic. Benefit-cost performances of some international organizations often seem to be dubious. We should watch the integration process of money so that Parkinson's Law is to be suppressed at the world central bank.

Finally, suppose the world would be ideal if we were able to embed a single currency in it. How can we achieve it, however, through actual political processes? I lost the incentive to elaborate on this, my favorite theme of incentive compatibility to adopt a single currency, because Cooper fully admits its political difficulty. No defense is the best defense. Giavazzi describes all the difficulties concerning the process toward, if not a single-currency, a more stable exchange-rate regime in Europe. This is an exciting experimental ground, indeed.

The Imperial Palace that some participants see from their hotel rooms here in Tokyo was originally built by the Tokugawa family. Tokugawa Ieyasu, the founder of the family, gained hegemonic control by his "watch-and-see" attitude. This attitude could often appear too shrewd, and it frustrates foreign government officials in trade and monetary negotiations dealing with Japan. I personally think that Japanese diplomats, bureaucrats, politicians, journalists, and scholars alike should get rid of this "wait-and-see" attitude to communicate more articulately with foreigners and to assume more constructive leadership in the international community. On this occasion, however, why should we not watch the progress in Europe to understand both the difficulty and the merits of the currency reform in the direction of more fixed exchange rates, and possibly of a single currency there?

Comments

Jacob A. Frenkel

Being the last discussant in this morning's session leaves me with the advantage of noting that the first two discussants focused almost exclusively on the excellent paper by Francesco Giavazzi; thus, following Koichi Hamada's example, I will largely confine my oral comments to the paper by Richard Cooper.

Richard Cooper's paper is very rich in terms of methodology, facts, imagination, and challenges. The methodology is indeed fascinating. He starts by saying that we really should not ponder the future without first looking at the past. He then gives us a marvelous review of the evolution of the international monetary system. If there is one lesson to be learned from the past it is that there is *no* single exchange rate regime for all seasons, a remark that was also made in our discussions yesterday. It is, therefore, unlikely that by some brilliant stroke of ingenuity we will find a new "ideal" regime. The very fact that there have been changes in regime, and one might add interregnums, over the years suggests that this experience is likely to be repeated in the future. Thus, even though, as someone once said, "the past is not what it used to be," the lessons from history certainly put us in a better position to meet the challenges ahead. I sincerely hope that this series of conferences will continue to play a part in helping us confront these challenges.

Richard Cooper identifies two subject areas which provide criteria for assessing the international monetary system, namely the problems of adjustment and adequate liquidity. These are indeed key areas or criteria for analysis. But I would add the third leg of Robert Triffin's trio, namely the confidence problem; and I would do so in a somewhat broader context than that envisaged by Triffin. As we assess alternative monetary systems we must ask how much confidence alternative regimes or systems may give us in terms of the following issues: in providing a mechanism for resolving conflicts; in enhancing the credibility of exchange rate commitments; in increasing the flexibility of the policy instruments that are needed to implement a specific system; and in giving recognition to differing national priorities, modes of analysis, constraints, and degrees to which sovereignty is considered to be negotiable. As we look at alternative systems we should want to look at these issues of confidence.

The conclusions drawn by Francesco Giavazzi in his paper are pertinent here. He found that the nature and timing of changes in expectations in the Italian economy had very little to do with exchange rate commitments, but rather with the implementation of credible domestic policies. And that is indeed a key finding. Exchange rate commitments may provide a very useful framework or "anchor" for expectations and decisions, but they will not be credible unless policies consistent with the commitments are in place. I think it is useful to think about the Plaza and Louvre Accords in this light: have they or have they not brought forth consistent domestic economic policies in the countries that were party to them?

Another criterion I would propose is that the comparative advantages of different policy instruments in affecting various target variables over the longer term must be acknowledged and utilized. Monetary policy should always be directed at achieving secular price stability. Fiscal policy should always be considered in a medium-term perspective, with due recognition of the difficulties of attempting to engage in fine-tuning. Structural policies should be aimed at ensuring that the necessary microeconomic signals and incentives are provided, and in addition should be regarded as complementary to the macroeconomic framework.

Let me now turn to the lessons that Richard Cooper draws from the gold standard. First, he points out that despite the fact that the mechanism underlying the gold standard is traditionally called the "price-specie-flow mechanism," gold did not seem to flow very much, prices did not appear to change very much, and I would also add, based on work by Barry Eichengreen and others, that discretionary policies appear to have been the norm. It was, in sum, not a very automatic system. Richard Cooper makes an important point when he asks why we did not see the gold flows and why we did not see the large price changes. My answer would be that market agents do not need to see large specie flows and price changes: incipient changes are all that are needed to stimulate adjustment. Here Cooper in effect takes a position in the debate between Keynes and Ohlin which related to the problems posed by German reparations after World War I: that debate concerned the question of whether changes in income and expenditures provide a sufficient impetus to adjustment, or whether we also need relative prices to change. I think it is well recognized by now that both must play a role in the adjustment process: that relative price changes (which can be brought about by exchange rate changes) and income and expenditure changes are complementary.

Let me digress momentarily to take up the question of the role of the SDR in the international monetary system. Cooper made reference to this in passing. Just for the record I would like to say that we have something of a paradox in our present international monetary system. There was a decision long ago to make the SDR the principal reserve asset of the international monetary system. Yet there has been no continuity in SDR allocations, and use of the SDR as a reserve asset has been minimal: in fact, the SDR may appear to be disappearing from the international monetary system. I think the time has come to confront this difference between commitment and reality: either steps should be taken to make the commitment a reality, or the commitment itself should be re-examined and modified in an appropriate way.

Following his exposition of the gold and gold-exchange standards, Cooper turns to the period from 1973 to the present. He highlights, correctly I believe, the role of international misalignments of fiscal policy in affecting the performance of the system. But there is one broader lesson which emerges, and that is the need to look not just at the exchange rate/current account nexus, but rather to recognize that it is the overall package of macroeconomic policies that influences the performance of the system. This leads Richard Cooper later on to refer to the saving-investment gap as providing the key analytical framework for the consideration of current account imbalances and policies that may be needed to address them. He asks, very provocatively, what's wrong with current account imbalances? After all, some countries may save for a while, while others dis-save for a while. I would make a number of points here. The first is implied in Dick Cooper's emphasis on the phrase "for a while": we cannot forget that there is an inter-temporal budget constraint, and we may need to ask how easy it may be for an imbalance to be reversed. My second point is that when you look at a saving-investment gap it is important to know where it originates: does it originate in the public sector or the private sector? If we have a deficit country where the external deficit is associated with public sector dis-saving, then it may be relatively easy to say that the deficit should be corrected through fiscal policy. If we have an external deficit associated partly with unusually low private-sector savings, as has been the case in the U.S. and the

U.K. in recent years, then we must ask where this originates and what underlying distortions there might be. Dealing with such distortions will tend to entail structural policies. Third, and importantly, in a deficit country the saving-investment gap could always in principle be narrowed by means of a reduction in investment, but this is clearly the worst solution. I mention this particularly because of a recent tendency in some countries for real interest rates to rise. It would be something of a paradox after a decade of emphasis in policy strategies on the supply side, investment, and growth, if investment were to suffer from an overburdening of monetary policy resulting from a paralysis in other policy instruments.

Let me address a couple of points on policies that first come up in Dick Cooper's remarks. First, the transactions tax. I am not inhibited like Koichi Hamada by having had Tobin as my professor, but Koichi was in fact very straightforward, and I wish to do little more than underscore what he said. I must admit that I cannot understand the logic of the transaction tax, either in economic or in political terms. The idea is essentially that a transactions tax would inhibit undesirable capital flows. But how can we be sure that we are going to inhibit bad flows and not good flows? Moreover, unless the tax is implemented globally, regulatory arbitrage will tend to make the tax ineffective, as Dick Cooper recognizes. My third problem with the transactions tax is that it is not clear to me that volatility in markets is necessarily reduced by transaction costs. If we look at the real estate market, there seem to be large transactions costs, yet there appears also to be quite a high degree of volatility. I think theoretical considerations also should lead us to be more agnostic about the effect of transactions costs on volatility. Finally, the imposition of taxes on capital flows would seem to me to go against the welcome global orientation toward outward-looking policies, liberalization, the lowering of protectionism, and debtor countries' access to capital markets. And I think that it is important to bear in mind that it is a lot easier to put "sand in the wheels" than to get it out.

Let me now turn briefly to target zones. Dick Cooper and Alex Swoboda have both already spoken about target zones, and I shall not consider all the questions that need to be addressed: the width of the zones, the frequency of realignments, the policy instruments to be used, the question of whether the margins should be "soft" or "hard," whether the zones are "quiet" or "loud," and so on. But I will emphasize one important issue, which is the role of fiscal policy. As a purely theoretical matter, the Williamson-Miller approach rectified a difficulty in the original plan by giving a prominent role to fiscal policy. That is fine if in practice you can use fiscal policy. But the experience of the last decade shows that fiscal policy is not an instrument that can be called on at short notice. Fiscal policy must focus on the medium term, not the short term. Otherwise you will find that you are using fiscal policy to fight the previous war, because by the time you succeed in adjusting fiscal policy to any shock, you are likely to find that the shock you wanted to deal with has disappeared. This is a major difficulty with the idea of fine-tuning fiscal policy, and also a major difficulty with the idea that fiscal policy may be used to implement target zones.

Finally, let me say a few words about the notion of a common currency. As Dick Cooper said, this is not a proposal, but material for thought. Let me quote something that shows that it was also material for thought in the last century. John Stuart Mill wrote, "So much of barbarism still remains in the transactions of most civilized nations, that almost all independent countries choose to assert their nationality by having, to their own inconvenience and that of their neighbors, a peculiar currency of their own." Political progress and the decline of what Mill saw as barbarism would eventually yield, Mill thought, a common currency. Well, a century has passed, and the question is, where is the common currency? Was Mill wrong on the economics, or was he wrong in his projection of political progress, for example? My personal hunch is that we live in a world in which the time horizons of philosophers differ from the time horizons of politicians, and in which politicians are the more likely to prevail. Therefore a common currency for the industrial countries is unlikely to be created, notwithstanding all the benefits that Dick Cooper emphasized.

Of course he raised an important question in asking why the U.S. can have a common currency, while a common currency seems impracticable in broader contexts. One answer at least is given by the possibility of inter-regional and inter-state fiscal transfers within the U.S. Of course within a monetary union monetary policy is by its nature a global policy: if you have a monetary expansion, it will affect the entire domain. Monetary policy cannot help regional or sectoral adjustment to shocks. But harmonized fiscal policy within a monetary union like the United States does provide a policy instrument that can help regional adjustment. This is one of the reasons why I am a little bit more skeptical than some others about the formation of a European Central Bank in the near future. It is not that I do not see the potential benefits; but I see it as part and parcel of a broader economic unification that will also need to involve fiscal policy.

Finally, on the question of a common currency—when might such a revolution take place? Dick Cooper says, well, of course, it's a program of thought for the next century. But he also makes a very perceptive point. He says that we should not move in the direction of a common currency—and I would generalize this to any fundamental change—as long as we have major disequilibria. We must first tackle the major disequilibria and restore a greater degree of order: it is then that we might consider rectifying the legal framework. But perhaps there is another element of political realism that needs to be taken into account. This is that it is precisely when you do not have a major disequilibrium that you do not have recognition of a crisis and the political support for a fundamental reform. To have a major change or shake-up I am afraid that you may need a perception of crisis; while a crisis or major disequilibrium may make fundamental reform impracticable. This is indeed a "Catch-22" situation, and perhaps it makes the absence of fundamental reform not too surprising.

Program of the Conference

"The Evolution of the International Monetary System:
How Can Efficiency and Stability Be Attained?"

Fourth International Conference
sponsored by
The Institute for Monetary and Economic Studies
Bank of Japan

May 30–June 1, 1989
Tokyo

Background and Aims of the Conference

Since the collapse of the Bretton Woods regime in 1973, the floating exchange rate system has provided the basic framework of the international monetary system. However, the performance of this system has not been as uniformly satisfactory as some people had anticipated in the early 1970's. Among the problems brought about under the current exchange rate system, two merit special attention. First is the uneasiness resulting from extraordinary trade imbalances among the major developed countries. This may, in some instances, threaten the primary objective of free and open trade. Second, since the United States has become a debtor nation, one of the conceivable conditions for confidence in the dollar may have changed. Because the dollar has been the most important international currency, any such change in confidence would have major implications for the stability of the international monetary system.

Along with these problems, we have been seeing rapid technological innovations in data processing and financial transactions. These innovations have been a driving force not only of domestic financial innovation but also of increased international capital mobility, thus leading to the integration or "globalization" of financial markets. This "globalization" has affected the roles of money in international exchange as well as the workings of the international monetary system.

These changes in the world financial system lead us to a fundamental question: How can efficiency and stability best be attained in the international monetary system? This conference will convene to seek answers to this question. Our agenda calls first for a historical analysis and then an examination of the theoretical issues followed by exploration of appropriate policy measures. The points we have raised for discussion are difficult to treat definitively, but we are confident that discussion by economists from academia, central banks and various international organizations will make a significant contribution to our understanding of this very important topic.

Tuesday, May 30

Session I (morning): Opening Addresses and Keynote Speeches

Chairman:
Yoshio Suzuki (Executive Director, Bank of Japan)

Opening Address
Satoshi Sumita (Governor, Bank of Japan)

Keynote Speeches
Allan H. Meltzer (Carnegie-Mellon University), "Efficiency and Stability in World Finance"
Stanley Fischer (World Bank), "Factor Mobility and the International Monetary System"

[Coordinator for Sessions II, III, IV, and V: Junichi Miyake, Director, Institute for Monetary and Economic Studies, Bank of Japan]

Session II (afternoon)
Lessons from the History of the International Monetary System

Chairman:
Allan H. Meltzer (Carnegie-Mellon University)

Papers by:
Barry Eichengreen (University of California, Berkeley), "International Monetary Instability between the Wars: Structural Flaws or Misguided Policies?"
Yoichi Shinkai (Osaka University), "Evaluation of the Bretton Woods Regime and the Floating Exchange Rate System"

Leading Discussants:
Teh Kok Peng (Monetary Authority of Singapore)
Jan Michielson (Banque Nationale de Belgique)
William E. Norton (Reserve Bank of Australia)
Richard Marston (University of Pennsylvania)

General Discussion

Wednesday, May 31

Session III (morning)
Theoretical and Empirical Issues Concerning International Currencies and the International Monetary System

Chairman:
Stanley Fischer (World Bank)

Papers by:
Stanley W. Black (University of North Carolina), "The International Use of Currencies"
Alexander K. Swoboda (International Center for Monetary and Banking Studies, Geneva), "Financial Integration and International Monetary Arrangements"

Leading Discussants:
Michael J. Prell (Board of Governors, Federal Reserve System)
John Murray (Bank of Canada)
Masahiro Kawai (University of Tokyo)

General Discussion

Thursday, June 1

Session IV (morning)
Towards a Better International Monetary System

Chairman:
Hugh Patrick (Columbia University)

Papers by:
Francesco Giavazzi (University of Bologna), "The EMS Experience"
Richard N. Cooper (Harvard University), "What Future for the International Monetary System?"

Leading Discussants:
Philippe Lagayette (Banque de France)
Leonhard Gleske (Deutsche Bundesbank)
Koichi Hamada (Yale University)
Jacob A. Frenkel (International Monetary Fund)

General Discussion

Session V (afternoon)
Summary Presentation and General Discussion

Chairman:
Michael Dealtry (Bank for International Settlements)

Summary Presentations by:
Ralph Bryant (Brookings Institution), "The Evolution of the International Monetary System: Where Next?"

Andrew D. Crockett (Bank of England), "The Evolution of the International Monetary System: Summing Up"

General Discussion

Participants*

Akbar Akhtar
Vice President and Assistant Director of Research
Federal Reserve Bank of New York

Jean-Pierre Beguelin
Director, Head of Economic Studies
Banque Nationale Suisse

Robert P. Black
President
Federal Reserve Bank of Richmond

Stanley W. Black
Professor
University of North Carolina

Eduard J. Bomhoff
Professor
Erasmus University, Rotterdam

Donald T. Brash
Governor
Reserve Bank of New Zealand

Ralph Bryant
Senior Fellow
Brookings Institution

Thomas F. Cargill
Professor
University of Nevada

---

* Affiliations listed are those at the time of the Conference.

PARTICIPANTS

Richard N. Cooper
Professor
Harvard University

Andrew D. Crockett
Executive Director
Bank of England

Michael R. Darby
Under Secretary for Economic Affairs
United States Department of Commerce

Thomas E. Davis
Senior Vice President and Director of Research
Federal Reserve Bank of Kansas City

Michael G. Dealtry
Deputy Head of Monetary and Economic Department
Bank for International Settlements

Barry Eichengreen
Professor
University of California, Berkeley

Stanley Fischer
Vice President and Chief Economist
World Bank

Jacob A. Frenkel
Economic Counsellor and Director of Research Department
International Monetary Fund

Siri Ganjarerndee
Director, Department of Economic Research
Bank of Thailand

Francesco Giavazzi
Professor
University of Bologna

Leonhard Gleske
Mitglieder des Direktoriums
Deutsche Bundesbank

Koichi Hamada
Professor
Yale University

Takatoshi Ito
Associate Professor
Hitotsubashi University

Moon-Soo Kang
Fellow
Korea Development Institute

Masahiro Kawai
Associate Professor
University of Tokyo

Silas Keehn
President
Federal Reserve Bank of Chicago

Philippe Lagayette
Sous-Gouverneur
Banque de France

Kang-Nam Lee
Head, Office of Monetary and Economic Studies
Bank of Korea

Tim J. Lee
Senior Economist
G.T. Management Ltd., Hong Kong

Goran Lind
Acting Head of International Secretariat
Sveriges Riksbank

Richard Marston
Professor
University of Pennsylvania

Rei Masunaga
Director of Foreign Department
Bank of Japan

Allan H. Meltzer
Professor
Carnegie-Mellon University

Jan Michielsen
Head of Foreign Department
Banque Nationale de Belgique

Junichi Miyake
Director of Institute for Monetary and Economic Studies
Bank of Japan

John Murray
Deputy Chief, International Department
Bank of Canada

PARTICIPANTS

William E. Norton
Head of Financial Markets Group
Reserve Bank of Australia

Mitsuaki Okabe
Chief of Research Division I
Institute for Monetary and Economic Studies
Bank of Japan

Francesco Papadia
Manager, Research Department
Banca d'Italia

Hugh Patrick
Professor
Columbia University

Michael Prell
Director, Division of Research and Statistics
Board of Governors of the Federal Reserve System

Juan D. Quintos Jr.
Deputy Governor
Central Bank of the Philippines

André Robert
Directeur Général Adjoint des Services Etrangers
Banque de France

Gary Saxonhouse
Professor
University of Michigan

Yoichi Shinkai
Professor
Osaka University

Satoshi Sumita
Governor
Bank of Japan

Yoshio Suzuki
Executive Director
Bank of Japan

Alexander K. Swoboda
Director
International Center for Monetary and Banking Studies, Geneva

Ryuichiro Tachi
Chief Councillor of Institute for Monetary and Economic Studies
Bank of Japan

Teh Kok Peng
Deputy Managing Director
The Monetary Authority of Singapore

Thomas D. Thomson
Executive Vice President
Federal Reserve Bank of San Francisco

Widharto
Deputy Manager of Monetary Division
Bank Indonesia

J.A.H. de Beaufort Wijnholds
Deputy Executive Director
De Nederlandsche Bank

Index

adjustable peg systems, 65, 67, 118, 157-58
agriculture, 41, 271-73
Argentina, 75
Asia, 42, 192, 231-32, 234
asset settlements, 138, 139-40, 143, 233
asymmetry, 233-34, 311-12
Australia, 74, 75, 163-67
Austria, 73, 75, 101, 102, 107

bank failures, 107-9
Bank for International Settlements (BIS), 35-36
Bank of England, 75, 97, 105, 106
Bank of France, 97, 105, 106, 107
Belgium, 73, 76, 79, 105, 107, 204, 252, 268
bid-ask spreads, 187-89, 230
Bissaro, G., 185-86, 236
Bolivia, 254
Bonn Summit, 126, 136, 142
Brazil, 75
Bretton Woods Agreement, 5, 22, 43, 45, 66, 65, 97, 117, 153, 160, 252, 258, 278, 280-82, 311, 12
Bundesbank, 258, 266-69, 306, 307
business cycles, 89, 90

Canada, 75-76, 240-43, 293-94
capital: controls on movement of, 205-7, 243, 252, 257; long-term, 179-80; mobility of, 65, 165, 195, 201, 203; short-term, 180-81
central banks, 33, 53-54, 74, 75, 76, 93, 94, 98-99, 103-4, 107, 108, 176, 183-84, 239, 254-57, 307, 314
Chrystal, K. A., 187, 189, 190
Clarke, S. V. O., 98
commodity-exporting countries, 163-65
common agricultural policy, 272, 306
common currency, 9, 12, 13, 34, 59-67, 140-42, 196,-219-21, 225-26, 232-33, 238, 240, 250, 277, 295-99, 303, 313-14, 319-20
convertibility, 60, 72, 176
credibility, 11, 51, 73, 111, 197, 215-16, 257, 266, 316
Cuba, 76
current account imbalances, 27, 43, 65, 67, 120, 127, 131, 139, 154, 197, 198, 263, 282, 317
Czechoslovakia, 76

DeGaulle, Charles, 31
deficits, 43, 55, 61-62, 130, 245, 264, 317-18
Delors Report, 11, 60-61, 62-63
Denmark, 258-61
depreciations, 105, 125
Deutsche mark. *See* mark
devaluations, 75-76, 77, 83, 111, 129, 159, 163
diffusion index, 146
dollar, 41, 43, 45-46, 47-48, 74, 76, 90, 101, 122-23, 128, 129, 135, 139, 140-42, 170, 175, 178-79, 182-84, 191, 199, 224, 283. *See also* United States dollarization, 46, 48
Dornbusch, R., 123, 207

economic indicators, 7, 52, 137, 145-46
Einzig, P., 77, 78
equilibrium paths, 28, 32
European Central Bank, 319
European Currency Units (ECU), 42, 210
European Economic Community (EEC), 11, 19, 199, 262, 272-72, 305
European Monetary System (EMS), 11-12, 19, 23, 45, 65, 158, 183, 184 191-92, 204, 240-41, 249-52, 254-55, 258-62, 264, 266-73, 301-2, 305-9
European Monetary Union (EMU), 240-41
exchange controls, 75, 105, 160, 265
Exchange Rate Mechanism (ERM), 11
exchange rate regimes, 4-6, 9-10, 32-33, 50-53, 65-67, 71, 89, 157-59, 253
exchange rate risks, 85-88, 185-86, 236-37
exchange rates: adjustment of, 12-13, 18, 53, 64, 73-74, 278-82; equilibrium of, 28, 32, 66, 67, 109, 122-24, 143, 144-45, 169, 170, 171, 209; predictability 4, 86-88; stability of, 30, 68, 192, 302, 305-6; variability of, 52, 83-86, 245; volatility of, 13, 73, 121-24, 169, 170, 233, 267-68
external debt, 47-48, 66

factor mobility, 13, 62-63, 68
Federal Reserve System, 105, 106, 108, 295
feedback rule, 312-13
financial centers, 8-9, 195, 196-200, 225, 232
fiscal policies, 55, 61-62, 201, 214, 216-19, 264, 319
Fischer, Stanley, 31
fixed exchange rate systems, 4, 5-4, 13, 44, 50, 52-53, 61, 65, 71, 72, 73,-75, 88, 89, 90, 92-93, 96-97, 103, 104-7, 121, 140-41, 151-52, 157-58, 163, 167, 171, 200-1, 202, 208, 212-13, 214-16, 245, 253, 257
flexible exchange rate systems, 4, 6, 9-10, 12-13, 50-51, 65, 71, 73, 76-77, 85, 86-87, 90, 92, 117, 118, 119-21, 124, 154-55, 158-59, 163, 166-67, 176-77, 201, 203, 204, 206-7, 208, 213-14, 220, 238, 243, 245, 278, 279-80, 285-90, 312, 313-14
forecasting, 6, 49
forward market quotations, 77-78
France, 73, 74, 76, 79, 83, 98, 105, 107-8, 252, 258-61, 262
Frankel, J., 6, 138, 139, 171, 244
Frankfurt, 196
free floating exchange rates, 4, 31, 77, 79, 85, 86-87, 89, 90, 92, 152, 278, 279-80
Frenkel, Jacob, 31, 154
Friedman, M., 73
Fukai Index, 23-24

"Gaullicycle," 19
General Agreement on Tariffs and Trade (GATT), 41
Genoa Conference, 101
Germany, 43, 45, 54-55, 73, 75, 78, 83, 101, 102, 104, 107, 119-21, 127-29, 130, 252, 258-61, 262, 266-69
gold standards, 5, 33, 45, 47, 64, 72, 73-74, 75-76, 90, 93, 98, 100, 101, 104-5, 108-9, 110, 127, 139, 140, 151-52, 175, 252, 278-79, 284, 316, 317
"goods mobility," 62, 68, 201-3
government intervention, 72, 73, 76, 134-35, 143, 236
Gramm-Rudman-Hollings Amendment, 136
Great Depression, 71, 77 89, 102-3, 104, 107, 110, 151, 152
Group of Seven (G-7), 30, 35, 153
Guatemala, 76

Hall, T. E., 54
Hamaui, R., 185-86, 236
hegemonies, economic, 21, 96-97,

140, 142-43, 199
Higgins, C. I., 126, 128
Hong Kong, 46
Hungary, 73, 107
hysteresis, 169, 170, 312

industrial production, 89-91, 94, 258-61
inflation, 46-47, 55, 73, 158, 253-57, 259, 301
information, costs of, 44, 46-47, 54
interbank market, 181-83, 187-91
interest rates, 130, 210, 216-17
international cooperation, 24-25, 26-36, 98-99, 126-38
international currencies, 7-10, 44-47, 175, 177-84, 191-92, 198
International Economists' Humble Index, 26-27
International Monetary Fund (IMF), 35, 129, 140, 160, 250
international monetary system, functions of the, 22, 205, 226, 284-85
Iran, 46
Ireland, 252, 258-61, 264
Israel, 48, 254
Italy, 73, 79, 252, 258-61, 262, 264, 265
Ito, Takatoshi, 122

Japan: economic policies of, 51-52, 54-55, 27-29, 130, 224-25; international financial role of, 42, 197-98, 199, 225, 234, 236, 237; macroeconomic performance of, 43, 119-21, 127-29
Jones, R. A., 189, 190

key currency monetary coordination, 294-95
Keynes, John Maynard, 93, 105
Kindleberger, C., 96, 99, 140, 141, 153
Krugman, P., 170, 187

labor markets, 17
labor mobility, 63
Laffer curve, 132
leadership, 96-97, 99-100, 153

London, 9, 182, 196, 200
Louvre agreement, 30, 135-37, 160, 218, 303

macroeconomic interactions, 17-18, 22-25, 27, 32-33
managed floating exchange rates, 4, 71, 76-77, 79, 85, 86-87, 89, 90, 92, 118, 121, 152, 158-59, 278, 282-84
mark, 11, 42, 45, 55, 179, 181, 250, 251-52, 267, 269, 283, 306-7
markets, integration of, 16-17
Masson, P. R., 7
McCallum, B., 54
McKibbin, W. J., 120-21
McKinnon, R. I., 12, 121, 140-41, 208, 210, 211, 249-50, 194
Meltzer, Allan, 31
Milan, 182
misalignments. *See* exchange rates, equilibrium of
models, 7, 30-31, 99, 126, 131-33, 138, 139, 152, 185-86, 201
monetary policies, 96, 161, 200, 201, 214-15, 254-55
monetary unions, 60-76, 319-20. *See also* European Monetary System
money illusion, 201
multicurrency systems, 34, 42-43, 140, 192
multipolarization, 20-21, 199, 233-34
Mundell, R., 240, 241, 253
Mundell-Fleming model, 214

Netherlands, 76, 79, 83, 105, 268
New York, 182, 196, 198
New Zealand, 75
Nixon shock, 125, 126-30
nominal exchange rate regime, 83-92
Nurkse, R., 73, 93

Okun, Arthur, 23
Organization for Economic Cooperation and Development (OECD), 35, 160

INDEX

Panama, 46, 76
Paraguay, 75
pegging, of exchange rates, 65, 125-26, 157-58, 176, 204, 257-58
Peru, 75
Philippines, 76
Phillips curve, 49
Plaza agreement, 50, 126, 134-35, 153, 172
Poland, 76
policy coordination, 5, 6-7, 10, 12, 21-22, 28, 30-33, 49-56, 61-62, 68, 75, 98-100, 103, 105, 111, 118, 128-129, 136, 151-55, 159-60, 171-72, 192, 196, 208-11, 243-44, 294-95, 312
policy instruments, 212-19, 316
political integration, 19-20
prices, 53, 54, 72, 254, 258
property rights, 197, 198, 232
protectionism, 9, 41, 64, 65, 208

Reagan administration, 122-24, 125, 130-34, 142
Reichsbank, 106, 108
research, economic, 27-28
reserve assets, 33-35, 42-43, 55, 66-67, 74, 93, 100-102, 176-77, 317
reserve currencies, 34, 74, 175-7, 192, 197, 224, 231, 233
risk premiums, 83, 88
Rockett, K., 6, 138, 139, 171
rules, for monetary policy, 10, 28, 54-55, 56, 93-94, 219, 227, 262, 312-13

Sachs, J. D., 120-21
savings-investment imbalances, 16, 27, 44, 282-83, 317
SDRs, 33, 34, 35, 140, 159, 281-82, 283, 317
seigniorage, 46, 61, 62
shocks, 17-18, 50, 88, 103, 120, 121, 124-26, 161, 171
Smithsonian agreement, 125, 129, 139
Smoot-Hawley Tariff, 97
Southeast Asia, 231
speculative bubbles, 123, 125, 134

spot rates, 78-83, 85-86, 88
Stackelberg strategy, 99
sterling, 11, 74, 75-76, 90, 101, 122, 170, 175, 182, 200. *See also* United Kingdom
Strong, Benjamin, 98
surveillance, 29-30, 136
Sweden, 74, 105
Swiss franc, 200
Swiss National Bank, 52
Switzerland, 74, 76, 79, 83, 105
symmetallism, 140

target zones, 10, 12, 52-53, 65-67, 120-21, 129, 140, 141, 143-45, 209-11, 233, 250, 292-94, 312, 318-19
tariffs, 64, 272
Taylor, J. B., 120-21
technological change, 3, 236, 297
terms of trade, 163-65
Tiebout hypothesis, 62
Tobin, James R., 12, 24, 207, 250, 312
Tokyo, 182, 196, 198
trade agreements, 41-42, 55-56
trade, currency denomination of, 44-45, 177-79, 185-86, 191-92, 229-30
transaction costs, 44, 47-48, 68, 187 236
transactions taxes, 12, 24-25, 135, 205-6, 207, 243, 250, 291-92, 312, 318

United Kingdom, 43, 67, 74, 75, 104, 258-61. *See also* sterling
United States: current account deficit of the, 55, 130, 216-18; economic policies of the, 6-7, 27, 98, 100, 122-37, 142; international role of the, 20, 43, 75, 97, 137, 141-43, 152, 233; macroeconomic performance of the, 47, 119-21, 127-29. *See also* dollar
Uruguay Round, 67
Uruguay, 75

variance ratios, 90-92

vehicle currencies, 8, 182-83, 187, 189-91, 197, 223-24, 230-31, 233, 236
Venezuela, 75
Vietnam War, 141-42

wages, 254, 258
World Economic Conference, 105
world currency. *See* common currency

yen, 8, 42, 55, 127, 128, 129, 179, 180, 182, 183-84, 192, 198, 199, 224, 230, 231-32, 234, 236, 237, 283

Zurich, 196, 200